D0929657

Treating Panic Disorder and Agoraphobia

A STEP-BY-STEP CLINICAL GUIDE

Elke Zuercher-White, Ph.D.

NEW HARBINGER PUBLICATIONS, INC.

Distributed in the U.S.A. by Publishers Group West; in Canada by Raincoast Books; in Great Britain by Airlift Book Company, Ltd.; in South Africa by Real Books, Ltd.; in Australia by Boobook; and in New Zealand by Tandem Press.

Copyright © 1997 Elke Zuercher-White
New Harbinger Publications, Inc.
5674 Shattuck Avenue
Oakland, CA 94609

Cover design by SHELBY DESIGNS & ILLUSTRATES
Edited by Kayla Sussell
Typeset by Michele Waters

Library of Congress Catalog Card Number: 97-66078
ISBN 1-57224-084-9 Paperback

New Harbinger Publication's Website address: www.newharbinger.com

First Edition

This book is dedicated to my dear husband Robert,
with whom I hope to share many years to come.

Table of Contents

Acknowledgments

First and foremost, I would like to thank Dr. Matthew McKay of New Harbinger Publications for the opportunity to write my second book. It has been a pleasure to work with him and the rest of the New Harbinger staff. They are exceptionally well organized, courteous, innovative, supportive, and open to new ideas. I could not wish to work with a better publishing house.

I wish to thank Randall Solomon, M.D., a colleague and friend, for being willing to co-author the medication chapter. He also provided invaluable input to help me organize my thoughts in a few chapters. My dear friend Gundula Behr edited the entire book, even when her life was filled with numerous other responsibilities. Geraldine Alpert, Ph.D., my long-term friend and colleague, was very supportive throughout the entire process. Special thanks also go to Sara Pimental, the librarian at Kaiser Permanente Medical Center, South San Francisco, who was untiring in securing articles and references for me.

I thank Kayla Sussell for her skillful editing of the manuscript. She edited my first book *An End to Panic: Breakthrough Techniques for Overcoming Panic Disorder*. She has a unique ability to work with and improve on my own style. Michele Waters did the excellent typesetting and Theo Crawford the proofreading.

I first started working with clients with phobias at the University of Louisville, Kentucky, where I learned behavioral techniques for treating these disorders. Hence, it seemed natural for me to treat clients with panic and phobias from the time I joined the Permanente Medical Group in 1981. My in-depth training in panic disorder was provided and shaped by Drs. David Barlow and Michelle Craske, true masters is this field. When preparing this book, I found myself consulting Dr. Barlow's book *Anxiety and Its Disorder: The Nature and Treatment of Anxiety and Panic* again and again. Although the book was written in 1988, it continues to be relevant and exceptionally informative. I have also learned from other researchers and clinicians, some in person, some from their writings, notably Drs. David Clark, Richard McNally, Lloyd Williams, Albert Bandura, Aaron Beck, Gary Emery, and Donald Meichenbaum. My friends and colleagues, Drs. John Peters at Redwood City Kaiser and Jim Boyers at Santa Clara Kaiser have been great sources of collaboration and inspiration.

Last, but not least, I am grateful to all the clients who have shared their struggles with me and who continue to challenge me to do my best for them.

Introduction

This book is intended for clinicians who treat panic disorder in various settings. I offer a cognitive-behavioral program with detailed descriptions of the components, methods, and techniques involved presented in a step-by-step fashion. A good number of my clients receive pharmacotherapy as well; some could not function without it. Approaches for the physician in medical settings are also included; these might be utilized by psychologists and other providers in behavioral medicine programs as well.

Recommended Treatments

The National Institutes of Health (Treatment of Panic Disorder, NIH Consensus Development Conference 1991) stated that two treatments are effective for panic disorder: Cognitive-behavior therapy (CBT) and medications. These two treatments represent very different theoretical views (Gould, Otto, and Pollack 1995). As Gould et al. point out, pharmacotherapy is based on the premise that disturbed biochemical and physiological mechanisms in the brain cause panic disorder. Consequently, the brain chemistry is targeted with medications in an attempt to eliminate panic and anxiety symptoms. Cognitive-behavior theory proposes that some individuals greatly fear anxiety symptoms and thus interpret them catastrophically. Both the pharmacological and psychological approaches have their advocates. As a psychologist, I advocate psychological treatments, specifically, CBT.

The more we learn about this disorder, however, the less tenable it becomes to acknowledge only one approach. A more complete understanding involves examining panic disorder along the diathesis-stress model. According to this model, the disorder develops as a result of a constitutional predisposition (genetic and/or biochemical) and psychological vulnerabilities, within a stressful context that makes the disorder manifest. The triggering stress can be biological (illicit drug or medication effects or illness) or psychosocial (interpersonal, such as a painful divorce or a difficult work environment, and/or a major change that threatens the person's sense of safety and security).

Efficacy of Recommended Treatments

There is proven efficacy of pharmacological treatments with specific disorders, at least in the short term (Barlow 1996). Likewise, as Barlow states, there is irrevocable evidence of the efficacy of psychological interventions for many disorders. Psychological interventions have proven to be as effective, or more so, than pharmacological approaches. This includes the treatment of anxiety disorders and, within this group, panic disorder with agoraphobia. There is also evidence that psychological interventions change brain function.

The superiority of CBT over pharmacotherapy is demonstrated particularly when the following factors are taken into consideration (Gould et al. 1995):

1. CBT produces lower attrition rates, fewer risk factors and side effects, and lower cost, especially with group treatment.

2. Medication treatment often leads to discontinuation symptoms.

3. The long-term outcome after treatment ends is better with CBT, i.e., lower relapse rates.

On the other hand, CBT requires motivation and hard work. A great deal of time and effort is needed for a successful outcome. Clearly, there is no one treatment for everyone. The risk/benefit ratio of using either or both treatment modalities should be assessed with each client.

When assessing various treatments, both effectiveness and cost must be considered (Barlow 1996). Cognitive-behavior therapy is one of the most cost-effective and tolerable treatments available for panic disorder, according to Jacobson and Hollon (1996) and Gould et al. (1995). The latter authors computed the cost based on fifteen sessions, a common length of treatment reported in many studies. Their results showed that the least costly treatments were imipramine and group CBT. Individual CBT was less costly than fluoxetine and high-dose alprazolam at the end of one year and less costly than a lower dose of alprazolam at the end of two years of treatment.

With all of the advantages of CBT, why is pharmacological treatment the more widely used option? Zarate and Agras (1994) point out that there is a gap between the validated treatments and actual practice by mental health professionals. Fewer than 25 percent of individuals with panic disorder seek out psychotherapy (Michelson, Marchione, Greenwald, et al. 1990). Even those individuals who seek medications do not necessarily get the optimum treatment.

When recruiting subjects to volunteer for studies of panic disorder, researchers found that there was an underutilization of behavior therapy and imipramine, two of the most effective treatments for this condition, each used in less than 15 percent of the subjects (Taylor, King, Margraf, et al. 1989). Monoamine oxidase inhibitors were rarely used. In contrast, benzodiazepines were commonly used. Many physicians prescribing medications may have been unfamiliar with the benefits of tricyclic antidepressants. When psychological treatments were offered, many clients received other types of psychotherapy (e.g., general counseling and relaxation). Given the proven effectiveness and safety of in vivo exposure, the authors speculated that psychotherapists often prefer working with less directive types of therapy or are inadequately trained in this specific behavioral intervention. Likewise Gould et al. (1995) speculate that there are relatively few therapists skilled in the cognitive-behavioral treatment of panic disorder.

Why Multimodal Treatment

Anxiety disorders, including panic disorder, are complex and multidimensional. Fear can manifest physiologically, cognitively, behaviorally, or in combination, and is generated by the person's unique biological makeup and psychosocial history. As long as we do not know precisely what a specific client needs, it is best to offer those psychosocial interventions that include different treatment strategies (Michelson 1984). Also, targeting one of the response systems mentioned does not automatically show the same gain in other areas. For instance, cognitive change does not necessarily produce a change in behavior characterized by avoidance of fearful situations. Avoidance may continue in spite of cognitive change.

Does Research Efficacy Translate to Clinical Utility?

Barlow (1996) contends that clinical practice guidelines must be based on the efficacy shown in controlled clinical trials and their applicability to clinical settings, i.e., the clinical utility of these treatments. Similarly, Goldfried and Wolfe (1996) state that therapeutic effectiveness should be based on both research findings and clinical reality. These authors recognize that it can be difficult for the practicing therapist to keep abreast of research findings as these are not always presented in usable form. Research articles are written for other researchers emphasizing research design, methodology, and directions for future research. This information, while important, is less often targeted to the clinician.

While usually unable to do pure research (i.e., randomized, double-blind studies) in a clinical setting, patient-focused research is an excellent alternative (Howard, Moras, Brill et al. 1996). This requires tracking an individual's progress over the course of treatment, which provides excellent learning opportunities for the therapist.

In this book I attempt to provide the clinician with the relevant theoretical background, including sources for further study. I have relied extensively on review articles. Consequently, my account of the research findings does not include a critique of methodology, which would make the book too lengthy.

For more scientific reviews, the reader is referred to David Barlow's *Anxiety and Its Disorders: The Nature and Treatment of Anxiety and Panic* (1988) and Richard McNally's *Panic Disorder: A Critical Analysis* (1994).

Cognitive-Behavior Therapy and Beyond

Anxiety is elusive and fear can take a strong hold on the person. Anxiety cannot be eliminated, and our challenge as therapists is to help our clients harness it, direct it in more adaptive ways, and move beyond gripping, uncontrollable fear. Research has shown that good treatment is not just elimination of panic symptoms. Panic fear, handicapping agoraphobia, residual anxiety, and quality of life issues also must be addressed. Beyond conquering the disorder, can the person be free to pursue goals and interests that have been truncated by it? For some clients, it is difficult to give up familiar fears, as uncomfortable as they are, for fear of facing disturbing life issues buried beneath the panic disorder. This effort to empower the person to face such issues is precisely what many therapists attempt to do, according to Goldfried and Wolfe (1996).

The treatment for panic disorder looks rather simple on the surface, but when working with the myriad difficulties clients present, having more than a mere handful of techniques gives you a better base to pursue solutions. On the one hand, you have established that your client suffers from panic disorder with or without agoraphobia, on the other hand you have a unique individual seeking help for distressing symptoms. What are the psychological mechanisms underlying this person's problems? And how do they interface with the CBT program I offer?

Let me elaborate. You may wish to analyze what lies behind this client's symptoms and offer dynamic therapy to uncover unconscious motives. However, we cannot ignore effective state-of-the-art treatments developed for this condition, and we have a responsibility to offer them as a first line of intervention. Hence we use a *nomothetic* formulation, i.e., a formulation based on principles specific to the disorder and treatment based on proven efficacy. This approach works with many clients.

As treatment progresses, however, it behooves the clinician to be alert to the client's idiosyncrasies. As you delve deeper into a person's core beliefs, or as you observe behavior patterns impeding progress, you need increasingly to take the unique characteristics of the individual into account and move to an *ideographic* formulation, i.e., a formulation or hypothesis based on this client's specific underlying psychological mechanism. Then you ask, "What are the schemas operating in this particular individual? Which core beliefs may be getting in the way of recovery?" Chapter 5 (Treatment Module II) offers many approaches to help you work with the client at this level. I also recommend Jacqueline Persons' book *Cognitive Therapy in Practice: A Case Formulation Approach* (1989) on how the case formulation guides the therapist's cognitive work.

Innovations From My Clinical Experience

I did not set out to specialize in panic disorder to the extent that I have. Originally, I was interested in it because of my behavioral training and work with phobias at the University of Louisville. Although I did some research on evoked potentials with the University of California, San Francisco, I later moved to a clinical setting. Since 1981 I have treated individual clients presenting with agoraphobia and panic attacks at Kaiser Permanente Medical Center. Initially, I treated them mainly with relaxation and exposure methods. As I had the opportunity to work with many clients and to learn from them, I began expanding my treatment approaches.

In 1987, a wonderful opportunity came to me when the conference of the Anxiety Disorders Association of America was held in San Francisco. I received my first training in panic control treatment at the workshop of Drs. Barlow and Craske. Soon thereafter I designed the first version of my Panic/Phobia Group. Over time, as I attended more workshops and seminars, I was increasingly drawn to study the research and theoretical background in the treatment of this disorder. Yet the more I learn, the more there is to learn.

Clients have appreciated my knowledge in this field. Although unable to answer all of their questions, I attempt to present informed, even controversial views. Some typical questions are: "But why did this happen?" "Why do I have panic disorder?" "I was told this is a chemical imbalance, a biological condition. Why should I get psychological treatment?" "My body just gets aroused, sometimes for no reason. This makes me have gag attacks. How can I control it when I am not having anxious thoughts?" There are no easy answers to the question of what caused the disorder in any given individual, or why fearful thoughts cannot always be accessed.

Perhaps because of my research background, I found myself frequently pondering how to improve the treatment, how to combine what I have learned from the research and experience of the great masters with my own clinical experience and intuition, and with the limitations imposed by the many demands in a psychiatric clinic. My internal debates have led me to some innovative paths. Here are a few of the more salient ones:

When to Start Agoraphobia Work

The initial training I received in panic control treatment did not include moderate to severe agoraphobia, yet the clients who came to our clinic had many avoidances. Intuitively I speculated that just because clients could overcome their fear of panics this did not necessarily mean that they would automatically rid themselves of phobias. I had also observed that clients needed time to overcome their phobias, in part, because they did not usually engage in massed exposure. That is why I incorporated plans for home exposure, starting with the very first treatment session.

For many clients it is a great discovery to find themselves able to confront a situation they have avoided for a long time. Without minimizing the very difficult task ahead, they often say in the second session, "It wasn't as bad as I thought it would be." The group seems to provide a tremendous motivator. Clients are exceedingly proud to announce their accomplishments to the group. One of the best deterrents against early dropout is for the client to observe his or her rapid success. However, research has not yet shown unequivocally whether it is best to treat the agoraphobia concomitantly with or after treatment for panic and fear of panics. Although there may be an ideal sequence, many clients have a limited number of sessions available and/or lack the motivation to stay in treatment for a longer period of time.

Combining Panic and Crisis-Oriented Therapy for New Panickers

I learned from the *Anxiety Disorders Interview Schedule for DSM-IV* (*ADIS-IV*, DiNardo, Brown, and Barlow 1994) to ask clients if they had experienced significant stress prior to their first panic, which they usually answered affirmatively. I also read in the literature that end-state functioning had not been as high as the achievement of panic-free status. After many possible scenarios of how to provide the services needed to target these two issues, I came up with the New Panickers Group in 1990. In this group, clients could work on precipitating stresses and chronic worry. I reasoned further that new panickers should not wait for treatment, since their condition was at risk for quick deterioration and the development of agoraphobia. Hence my New Panickers Group offered immediate access to treatment, even if it meant that the treatment components were not introduced in the ideal sequence for each client. Thus, some clients joined the group in the middle of the interoceptive exposure. I observed that although this was the most difficult point at which to join, it *did* work. The advantages outweighed the disadvantages by far.

Group Treatment

Even prior to 1987, many clients suffering from panic disorder with agoraphobia sought services at the South San Francisco Kaiser facility. Group therapy seemed the only viable treatment format. Once I started my first Panic/Phobia Group in 1988, I was "sold" on group therapy. The group was twelve sessions (later fourteen) and closed. However, a closed group became less and less feasible. Clients complained that they had to wait too long, some dropped out in the interim, and it was hard work to contact everyone anew in order to start a group. I came up with a compromise. Because the Panic/Phobia Group was much more structured than the New Panickers Group, I did not wish clients to start and end in the middle of a treatment component, which led me to plan the modularized version. Clients now wait for a maximum of one month to enter this group. The modularized design with its relatively quick access is also much easier on the clinician for the reasons stated above.

Including Assertiveness Work

I had observed that many clients with panic and phobias were very nonassertive. My reasoning was that nonassertiveness could play into fears and avoidances because nonassertive clients did not develop a sense of mastery in their interpersonal relationships. This could even feed lack of control issues. Consequently, from the beginning I included work on assertiveness. I have not yet seen studies on this, although it has been mentioned in the literature.

How to Use This Book

Chapter 1 provides the information needed for the initial assessment. Chapter 2 summarizes etiological issues, and chapter 3 discusses the research that demonstrates the efficacy of CBT and the proven treatment components. Chapter 4, the first Treatment Module, describes the psychoeducational material and breathing retraining. Chapter 5 covers cognitive restructuring, and chapter 6 interoceptive exposure. These are the components deemed necessary to treat uncomplicated panic disorder. In chapter 7, "Adjuncts to Success," chronic worry, stress, nonassertiveness, control issues, perfectionism, and relapse prevention are targeted. Chapter 8 details the agoraphobia work.

The basic plan for individual or group treatment is presented in chapters 4 through 8. Chapter 9 elaborates group treatment specifically. In chapter 9, there are summaries on each group session, including the assignments to be given to clients. These can be adapted and applied to the individual sessions. The treatment lengths, twelve for individual therapy and fourteen to sixteen for modularized group sessions, are given as guidelines. However, even if you learn to deliver the treatment well, that does not guarantee that your client will improve within that time frame. Not every client functions the same way, and very often the clinical profile of the person is complicated by comorbidities, medical problems, and so forth. Even within a brief treatment format, it is ideal to have some flexibility, such as in the New Panickers Group that I conduct at Kaiser. In this group, members stay from six to twenty sessions, depending on *their individual need*. Subsequently, any of my clients can use the Anxiety Support Group if they have a setback that requires attention. I also allow clients who once attended the New Panickers Group or the Panic/Phobia Group, who have had a major relapse, to reenter the Panic/Phobia Group at a later time. (Clients who once attended the New Panickers Group do not reenter this group.)

Chapter 10, coauthored with Dr. Randall Solomon, is about treatment with medications, and chapter 11 provides guidelines to deal with panic disorder in medical settings. In Appendix A you will find all the worksheets duplicated for easy copying, and a list of resources.

My work as a psychologist has involved clients with many varied problems. Yet I have increasingly enjoyed developing an expertise in panic disorder and phobias and being able to help many clients. Although you may not become as engrossed in this field as I have, I hope that this book will give you the knowledge and guidance needed to effectively help the anxious client, as well.

A Note About the Worksheets

Most of the worksheets in this book have been changed since the first edition of *An End to Panic: Breakthrough Techniques for Overcoming Panic Disorder* (Zuercher-White 1995) and will appear in the upcoming second edition. Since the initial publication, I have received a great deal of feedback from clients and colleagues, foremost among them Dr. Jim Boyers at Santa Clara Kaiser Medical Center, that prompted the changes. Most worksheets have been simplified and actually made more user friendly. Worksheet 4: Challenging Automatic Thoughts (which went through several revisions before this final version) continues to pose a challenge. However, once clients learn to use it, they find it an invaluable tool in learning to confront their fears. Of all the worksheets, it is the most important, because by using it clients learn a skill that is always with them. They also can learn to apply the process of testing hypotheses to other areas of their lives, including dealing with other difficult emotions. All worksheets appear in full size in Appendix A for copying. They can be enlarged for easier use.

1

Diagnosing Panic Disorder and Agoraphobia
(The Assessment Session)

This chapter provides information pertaining to the diagnosis of panic disorder and differentiating it from other conditions. This is followed by a number of highly specific questions for assessing panic disorder and phobias. The complete assessment form can be found in Appendix B. The summary at the end of the chapter is a brief review of the main points that will need to be addressed in the assessment session.

Prevalence of Panic Disorder

Panic disorder is a common condition and a major public health concern. The National Comorbidity Survey (Kessler, McGonagle, Zhao, et al. 1994) showed that the lifetime prevalence of panic disorder is 3.5 percent of the population, with a higher rate in females than males. The typical age for onset appears to be in the twenties and early thirties, but it can occur in childhood and in later life (Barlow 1988; Hassan and Pollard 1994; Lelliott, Marks, McNamee, et al. 1989; Wittchen and Essau 1993). Lifetime prevalence estimates for agoraphobia are 6.7 percent with the median age of onset at twenty-nine (Magee, Eaton, Wittchen, et al. 1996). When agoraphobia is compared to panic disorder, the female to male ratio is even higher, with females constituting about 75 percent (Barlow 1988; Clum and Knowles 1991; Wittchen and Essau 1993). Sheikh (1992) found that the onset of panic disorder after the age of fifty-five was associated with less impairment.

It is noteworthy that individuals with panic attacks seek help sooner than those with other types of mental health conditions. Some of them show hypochondriacal behavior, seeking help for their physical complaints from primary care physicians exclusively or in addition to seeking mental health services (Barlow 1988; Siegel, Jones, and Wilson 1990; Stahl and Soefje 1995). This leads to frequent misdiagnoses, which ultimately prolongs the course of the disorder. Only a minority of individuals with phobias (including agoraphobia) seek professional help (Magee et al. 1996).

Panic disorder seriously limits the everyday functioning of many individuals. A fair number report feelings of anxiety and depression (Sherbourne, Wells, and Judd 1996). This has an adverse impact on the patient and his or her family, economically, socially, and emotionally (e.g., in lowered self-esteem), compromising the quality of their lives. Many panickers miss work days and some have stopped working altogether due to their condition (Siegel et al. 1990). In some patients the result is severe disability.

Panic attacks per se are experienced by a large percentage of the population (Michelson et al. 1990). Although most of these panic attacks occur in situations of high stress, such as taking an exam or giving a speech, out-of-the-blue panics occur quite often as well. Yet only a small percentage of these people go on to develop panic disorder.

Diagnosis and Symptomatology

Panic disorder as a distinct category was listed for the first time in the *Diagnostic and Statistical Manual of Mental Disorders, Third Edition* (*DSM-III*, American Psychiatric Association 1980). The diagnosis has been revised in each subsequent edition. Before diagnosing panic disorder, the clinician must first ascertain whether the client is truly describing panic attacks or other anxiety states. Furthermore, does the client describe fears and avoidances consistent with agoraphobia or other phobias? In what context do these symptoms occur? The newest version of the diagnostic manual, *DSM-IV* (American Psychiatric Association 1994), highlights the sequential reasoning involved by listing the criteria for panic attacks and agoraphobia first in the Anxiety Disorders section. Once these criteria have been established, the next decision is to determine which anxiety disorder applies to the individual. This is sometimes difficult, in part, because of the wide incidence of panic attacks, which can occur in depression and also in the context of substance abuse and withdrawal. (The diagnostic categories that follow are from the *DSM-IV*, American Psychiatric Association 1994.)

Panic Attacks

A *panic attack* is a sudden, discrete episode of intense fear or anxiety accompanied by a number of somatic and/or cognitive symptoms. There is often a sense of impending doom with a strong urge to flee the situation. When asked, most patients say that their panic attacks peak within seconds or minutes, usually within five minutes. Clients further report that actual panic attacks last up to thirty minutes, but rarely longer, and often are followed by a high level of anxiety (Agra 1993; Treatment of Panic Disorder 1991).

The *DSM-IV* makes the following distinction between panic attack experiences:

1. Unexpected or uncued panic attacks, i.e., coming "out of the blue."

2. Situationally bound or cued panic attacks occurring when exposed to (or anticipating being exposed to) a particular situation, e.g., someone with the fear of snakes is very likely to have a panic attack when confronted with a snake.

3. Situationally predisposed panic attacks *often* occur in certain situations, e.g., having panics sometimes, but not always, while driving.

The criteria for a panic attack are as follows: The attack is defined as a sudden episode of intense fear or anxiety peaking within ten minutes. At least four of the following thirteen symptoms must be reported (although many clients report far more than four symptoms):

Panic Attack Symptoms*

1. Palpitations, pounding heart, or accelerated heart rate

2. Sweating

---

* Reprinted with permission from the *Diagnostic and Statistical Manual of Mental Disorders,* Fourth Edition. ©1994 American Psychiatric Association.

3. Trembling or shaking

4. Sensations of shortness of breath or smothering

5. Feeling of choking

6. Chest pain or discomfort

7. Nausea or abdominal distress

8. Feeling dizzy, unsteady, lightheaded, or faint

9. Derealization (feelings of unreality) or depersonalization (being detached from oneself)

10. Fear of losing control or going crazy

11. Fear of dying

12. Paresthesias (numbness or tingling sensations)

13. Chills or hot flushes

Agoraphobia

Agoraphobia is the fear of being in places or situations from which escape is difficult or embarrassing, or where help is not readily available in the case of a panic attack. It includes the fear of being in crowds, outside the home alone, using public transportation, driving in streets, tunnels, on freeways, bridges, and so forth. The anxiety leads to avoidance of the situation, or the situation is endured with intense anxiety and discomfort.

Panic Disorder

Panic Disorder is defined by recurrent, unexpected panic attacks. *At least two* panic attacks must have occurred *unexpectedly,* i.e., out of the blue. Further requirements for the diagnosis include either at least one month of persistent *worry about* having another *attack,* worry about the *consequences* of the attacks, or significant *behavioral change* as a result of the attacks (e.g., avoidance, visits to the emergency room, etc.). The attacks are not due to the effects of physical illness, medications, or illegal drugs. Once panic disorder develops, there is often increased general anxiety, apprehension about many ordinary activities, and catastrophic fears. Panic disorder often takes on a chronic and fluctuating course (Acierno, Hersen, and Van Hasselt 1993; Brown and Barlow 1995; *DSM-IV*, American Psychiatric Association 1994), and stress brings on the symptoms again (Acierno et al. 1993).

Further Diagnostic Issues Regarding Panic Attacks and Panic Disorder

The population at large is becoming familiar with the terms "panic attack" and "panic disorder," and it is quite common to label many experiences as "panic attacks." Yet the terms are also applied loosely by physicians and nurses in medical practice, and by some mental health professionals. The most common errors in diagnosis are failing to establish the time it takes for the attack to peak, e.g., peaking in fifteen to thirty minutes or later, instead of the required ten minutes, or having fewer than four symptoms present. The requirement of four vs. fewer symptoms for the *DSM-IV* diagnosis is somewhat arbitrary, as there are individuals who report being equally terrified by one to three symptoms (de Beurs, Garssen, Buik-huisen, et al. 1994).

The *DSM-IV* calls these episodes *limited symptom attacks*. Keep in mind, however, that the distinction is probably not so much qualitative as quantitative (Rapee 1993). The *DSM-IV* acknowledges the arbitrariness of this distinction, as well.

In cases where the peak is not reached within ten minutes, fewer than four symptoms are present, and the frequency criterion and/or the feared consequences are not met, I may use the diagnosis of Anxiety Disorder Not Otherwise Specified (*DSM-IV*, American Psychiatric Association 1994) or Adjustment Disorder With Anxiety (*DSM-IV*, American Psychiatric Association 1994), but I proceed to provide the same treatment as I do for clients with panic disorder, that is, the treatment I give to my New Panickers Group. In these cases, the clients show functional disability similar to those meeting the criteria for panic disorder (Katon, Hollifield, Chapman, et al. 1995). The authors speculate that individuals who have had this experience may be more prone to developing panic disorder in stressful life situations.

Fears in Panic Disorder

In the *DSM-IV* revision vis-à-vis the *DSM-III-R* (American Psychiatric Association 1987), the fearful aspect of panics, i.e., the cognitive component, was emphasized as well as the behavioral repercussions of having the attacks (Ballenger and Fyer 1993). The *DSM-IV* symptoms cluster along three categories (Barlow, Vermilyea, Blanchard, et al. 1985; Cox, Swinson, Endler, et al. 1994):

1. Dizziness (dizziness, faint feelings, vertigo, hot/cold flushes). These symptoms are often interpreted as signs of imminent fainting when in fact they may suggest hyperventilation or vestibular dysregulation.

2. Cardiorespiratory (rapid heartbeat, palpitations, shortness of breath). These are, at times, associated with the fear of dying or of being seriously ill.

3. Cognitive fears (going crazy, losing control, creating a scene, wanting to escape).

The most common *symptoms* are heart pounding, trembling, and sweating (Norton, Harrison, Hauch, et al. 1985). In *unexpected or uncued panics* the *fears* of losing control and dizziness are the most common (Barlow et al. 1985). Cox et al. (1994) emphasized feelings of helplessness and thoughts of escape, and Cox, Swinson, Kuch, et al. (1993a) fear of causing a scene.

The findings seem to emphasize both physical and mental aspects of panic fear. McNally, Hornig, and Donnell (1995) compared clinical (patients with panic disorder) and nonclinical (college students with unexpected panic) samples. The authors noted three cognitive symptoms that best discriminate between clinical and nonclinical panic attacks: fear of dying, fear of having a heart attack, and fear of losing control. These catastrophic misinterpretations discriminate better than physical symptoms per se. The authors found that suffocation sensations are also likely to lead to catastrophic cognitions.

Although we currently are using *DSM-IV* criteria, it is likely that they will change over time. For instance, Cox et al. (1994) question whether the existing *DSM-IV* symptoms (or the *number* of symptoms, as mentioned earlier) may not be the best indicator of panic attacks. They had subjects rate the intensity of their symptoms on a five-point Likert scale and found that the symptoms with the highest mean severity were feelings of helplessness, thoughts of escape, difficulty concentrating, and fear of creating a scene. In contrast, nausea, choking, chest pain, numbness and tingling sensations were reported as being less severe.

The conclusion drawn from these studies appears to be that although the physical symptoms are the precipitants, the inability to control these symptoms leads some people to conclude that they will result in catastrophes of a physical, behavioral, or social nature. Zoellner, Craske, and Rapee (1996) found that the concern about physical threats tends to decrease over time, whereas the concern over mental and social threats remains the same or increases. The authors speculate that physical threats are more readily disconfirmed than mental or social threats.

It is important to remember that some persons who have panic attacks do not report fear as a symptom. These cases are documented primarily in medical (nonpsychiatric) settings (Kushner and Beitman 1990). In my experience, some clients are not fearful, while others complain solely of the physical symptoms and are not aware of fear cognitions. That is, some people have great difficulty accessing their fearful thoughts.

Panic Disorder and Agoraphobia

There is *Panic Disorder With Agoraphobia* and *Panic Disorder Without Agoraphobia.* When panic disorder progresses to include phobic avoidance, i.e., panic disorder with agoraphobia, it is a more serious condition. Phobic avoidance is an attempt to prevent the panic attacks from recurring. The amount of avoidance varies greatly, but in some cases it can be quite extensive. The effective treatment of panic disorder without agoraphobia will then play an important role in the prevention of agoraphobia, as the disorder will be diminished rather than progress to the more treatment-resistant agoraphobia (Michelson et al. 1990).

In addition to showing a clear avoidance pattern, many clients with and without agoraphobia engage in subtle avoidances (e.g., ingesting caffeine, engaging in strenuous activity such as exercising, experiencing heat, etc.). These subtle avoidances are often hidden from the outside observer compared to avoidance of elevators, freeways, and similar obvious places. All types of avoidance perpetuate fear. In this vein, it is difficult to find someone who has panic disorder who does not practice some kind of avoidance. Assume, therefore, when interviewing your client that there is some avoidance, even if it is hard to elicit precisely what that avoidance behavior is. This also demonstrates how fluid the distinction is between panic disorder without and panic disorder with agoraphobia, and why it is useful to think of these two disorders as existing along the same continuum.

The Development of Agoraphobia

It has been found that at least 60 percent of clients with panic disorder also have agoraphobia (Klerman 1992). Agoraphobia may develop in a few days to a few weeks after the first panic attack, or it may also occur after a delay (Faravelli, Pallanti, Biondi, et al. 1992; Lelliott et al. 1989). More often than not, however, the onset of agoraphobia occurs within one year of recurrent panic attacks, and it has the potential to become chronic whether or not the person continues to have panic attacks (*DSM-IV*, American Psychiatric Association 1994). Other studies suggest that the first panic may be preceded by phobias (including agoraphobia) hypochondriasis, and generalized anxiety (Fava, Grandi, Rafanelli, et al. 1992; Lelliott et al. 1989). There is still a debate whether panic disorder often leads to agoraphobia, or agoraphobia just frequently co-occurs with panic. It has also been found that panic disorder may lead to other phobias in addition to agoraphobia, such as social phobia (Cox, Endler, and Swinson 1995).

Agoraphobia Without History of Panic Disorder

According to the *DSM-IV*, in *Agoraphobia Without History of Panic Disorder*, the focus of the fear is being incapacitated or embarrassed by panic-like symptoms or limited symptom attacks. As indicated by the name of this diagnostic category, the person must never have fulfilled all the criteria for panic disorder. This condition may also be associated with considerable impairment (Goisman, Warshaw, Peterson, et al. 1994). Typical fears in this condition are dizziness, vomiting, headaches, and losing bladder or bowel control (Pollard, Tait, Meldrum, et al. 1996). These symptoms have essentially the same function as full-blown panic attacks have in panic disorder with agoraphobia, i.e., incapacitating or embarrassing the person.

Although epidemiological studies have identified a high percentage of people with this condition, Horwath, Lish, Johnson, et al. (1993), when reinterviewing a number of the original subjects, found that many actually had specific phobias. In another study, the subjects with agoraphobia—*not* fulfilling the requirements for panic disorder—had situationally bound or cued panic attacks or limited symptom attacks (Goisman, Warshaw, Steketee, et al. 1995). Catastrophic fears were common in this group, as with panic disorder. Goisman et al. (1995) as well as Marks (1987), drew the conclusion that this type of agoraphobia should be viewed on a continuum with panic disorder (with and without agoraphobia) rather than as a separate entity. Here, as in panic disorder, there is a sudden rise of intense anxiety combined with a chronic avoidance pattern.

There is a condition labeled "space phobia" that looks very similar to agoraphobia without history of panic disorder (Brandt 1996; McCaffrey, Rapee, Gansler, et al. 1990). In contrast to the latter, individuals with space phobia exhibit a fear of falling exclusively. They fear open spaces where they do not have the benefit of visuo-spatial support. Usually this condition develops late in life with the average age of onset at fifty-five. It seems linked either to neurological impairment involving difficulty integrating visual and spatial cues, or to a fall. In some people, the fear is so extreme that they become housebound. The cognitive component is an exaggeration of the potential risk of falling.

Why Agoraphobia Occurs

As stated earlier, agoraphobia, in a nutshell, develops when the person fears having panic attacks in various situations and, as a consequence, avoids them. Notice, however, in the following sections that research points to a complex interplay between panic and agoraphobia and other factors that maintain agoraphobia.

How Does Avoidance Occur?

Some possibilities of how avoidances occur according to Lelliott et al. (1989) and Marks (1987) are as follows:

1. Conditioning. Fear becomes associated with places in which panics occur. Because the avoidance reduces fear, it breeds further avoidance.

2. Avoidance occurs because of fear of panicking when help is not available and escape is difficult or embarrassing.

3. The sites that evoke fear are not random. The authors found that fear, panics, and avoidance occur mostly outside the home, in public places such as streets, stores, work, school, public transportation, auditoriums, and crowds. Public places may be perceived as dangerous because of being outside the "safer"

home range. This may be linked to territorial issues found in various species, according to the researchers.

Factors Leading To and Maintaining Avoidance

When the question, *"Why do some people avoid?"* is examined more closely, it has been determined that neither frequency, intensity of panic attacks, nor duration since the first panic predict the development of agoraphobia (Clum and Knowles 1991; Cox et al. 1995; Craske and Barlow 1988). Craske and Barlow report as possible factors contributing to avoidance the following (although further research is needed to substantiate these observations):

1. Anticipatory anxiety about panic taking place in a *specific* situation.

2. Lack of mastery in dealing with stress and anxiety.

3. Social demand, i.e., cultural roles, where it is more acceptable for women to stay home and not venture out much, and there is more demand on men to go out and work. The role assumed appears to be the crucial factor here, rather than gender per se.

Hence, rather than being a function of panic severity and frequency, agoraphobia may be a strategy for coping with fear, albeit a nonadaptive strategy. The use of this strategy is determined primarily by cultural and psychosocial factors, though biological factors may be involved (Barlow 1997).

The authors above list the following factors as contributing to the *maintenance of avoidance:*

- Use of escape and safety signals.

- Overestimation of the likelihood of panic.

- Occurrence of unexpected panic attacks (because these individuals find ways to avoid panics, unexpected panics may lead to more avoidance in their attempts to control the attacks).

- When avoidance leads to a reduction of fear, it increases the likelihood of future avoidance.

- Possible secondary gain (e.g., having a support network as a result of avoidance).

Many individuals engage in safety behaviors such as resting, leaning against objects, controlling their thoughts, etc., which also helps to maintain avoidance (Clark and Ehlers 1993). These are examples of the subtle avoidances described earlier.

Why Panic and Agoraphobia Improve Independently of Each Other

It is important to note that people with panic disorder with agoraphobia do not automatically overcome their avoidances by overcoming the fear of panic attacks. Agoraphobia must be addressed directly as well (Craske, Brown, and Barlow 1991; van den Hout, Arntz, and Hoekstra 1994). In addition to the factors mentioned above, Başoğlu, Marks, Kiliç, et al. (1994b) speculate as to why panic manifests independent of avoidance. Their speculations follow:

1. In those with severe agoraphobia, extensive avoidance often prevents them from having panics.

2. Avoidance becomes an entrenched habit separate from panics and occurs often without the client ever having panicked in a given situation. This suggests a complex set of factors beyond simple secondary conditioning.

Williams (1992) believes that although panic seems to play a significant role in the historical etiology of agoraphobia, agoraphobia is later maintained by the person's judgment of being unable to cope with situations that are perceived as potentially dangerous. That judgment is termed "low self-efficacy," and because it is a major cause of phobic disability, it needs to be targeted and dealt with in treatment.

To summarize this section, there appear to be an increasing number of empirical findings that question whether agoraphobia is indeed secondary to panic disorder. It is possible that panic and phobias are highly interactive and the end result of "panic disorder with agoraphobia" occurs along various routes, as so well-phrased by Bach, Nutzinger, and Hartl (1996).

Interoceptive and Exteroceptive Sources of Fear

I hope I have conveyed that these disorders, with their myriad variations and nuances, are far more complex than they appear to be at first glance. Now, to further intrigue your curiosity, there is another dimension that must be discussed: exteroceptive and interoceptive sources of fear. Although these concepts had appeared in the literature, Dr. Michelle Craske elucidated them most clearly in a conversation I had with her in 1994.

Exteroceptive refers to an externalized fear of objects or situations, as is often the case in the fear of snakes and flying. In these cases, the fear may be that the snake will hurt the person or the airplane will crash: the threat comes from the feared object/situation. *Interoceptive* refers to the fear of internal sensations, which may be elicited either randomly (out-of-the-blue panics) or in a given situation (riding in the backseat of a two-door car on a hot day, with the windows closed and no air-conditioning).

An agoraphobic person may fear airplanes because he or she fears having a panic attack in them and, consequently, being unable to breathe or causing a scene. Although panic is defined as the fear of internal sensations, essentially a phobia of these sensations, and snake phobia is a fear of an external object, many fears exhibit aspects of both. Indeed, Thorpe and Salkovskis (1995) found that even in specific phobias (e.g., spider phobia), there is a combined belief that harm will come from the phobic object ("the spider will bite me") as well as from within one's self ("I'll lose control of myself," or "I'll be paralyzed"), which are typical fears in panic disorder).

A further example of the fascinating interplay between interoceptive and exteroceptive sources of fear was illustrated in an interview I had recently with a person with social phobia. Unlike the average social phobic, he was not concerned about being judged negatively, doing or saying something embarrassing or humiliating, or showing outward signs of anxiety. He was fearful of his panic attack symptoms (shortness of breath, palpitations, light-headedness, numbness and tingling, and sweating), which occurred exclusively in social situations. Even the discomfort of sweating did not include the fear that others might see his perspiration. Thus, his fears were interoceptive, because he did not fear being judged externally for his noticeable symptoms, but the attacks occurred in specific, i.e., social situations.

Phobias can acquire exteroceptive fear qualities, even if they were not there initially. That is, what may start as fear of panicking on the freeway often becomes blurred with the thought that freeways are dangerous places where accidents happen easily. The more you learn about the exact nature of your clients' fears, the more apparent it becomes that most fears contain a combination of both interoceptive and exteroceptive qualities. Cox et al. (1995) have suggested that a classification system be developed, where different phobias, including social phobia, and the avoidance of interoceptive cues be subsumed under panic disorder.

This is why the protocol for the treatment of panic disorder with or without agoraphobia, which I set forth in this book, can be applied very well to clients who have agoraphobia without history of panic disorder or many specific phobias, such as claustrophobia, fear of heights (acrophobia), etc. For instance, many clients with claustrophobia are afraid of suffocating in enclosed places. Similarly, I have treated a few clients with social phobia in my Panic/Phobia groups. This has proved advantageous when they also had some panic or agoraphobic fears. Pervasive social fears, however, are best treated in Social Phobia groups.

Differential Diagnoses and Comorbidities

Comorbidity means that the person has two or more disorders. It has been reported that at least 50 percent of all clients with panic disorder have an additional disorder (Pollack, Otto, Rosenbaum, et al. 1990). Research shows that the most common additional diagnoses (to panic disorder with or without agoraphobia) are specific phobia, social phobia, generalized anxiety disorder, obsessive-compulsive disorder, major depression, substance abuse, minor tranquilizer addiction, and somatization (Acierno et al. 1993; Hoffart, Thornes, Hedley, et al. 1994; Kessler et al. 1994; Starcevic, Uhlenhuth, Kellner, et al. 1993b; Wittchen and Essau 1993). Anxiety Disorder Not Otherwise Specified (*DSM-IV*, American Psychiatric Association 1994) frequently does occur with panic disorder, i.e., anxiety symptoms that do not fully reach the criteria for the other diagnostic categories.

Understandably, these complications tend to render the client more resistant to treatment (Otto and Whittal 1995; Pollack and Smoller 1995). Additional treatment as needed for the comorbid condition improves the overall outcome over the long term (Otto and Whittal 1995). When should you assign a client another Axis I diagnosis? Clearly, it is not always a simple matter, as the discussions below demonstrate.

Other Anxiety Disorders

Agoraphobia frequently contains a number of social fears, e.g., embarrassment about panicking in front of others such as in a restaurant or at a party. Some clinicians more easily give an *additional* diagnosis of social phobia. The same is true for specific phobia. For example, for years a client of mine was afraid of flying before she developed panic disorder with agoraphobia. She held the view that it is unnatural for humans to be up in the air, and she feared the plane would crash. This would have warranted the diagnosis of specific phobia if she had been distressed by it or if her life had been circumscribed and limited by that fear. After developing panic disorder, however, she also feared not being able to breathe in the plane (or in a number of other situations), in addition to her original fear of plane crashes. (This also illustrates how interoceptive and exteroceptive fears can mix together and reinforce each other.)

Generalized anxiety disorder presents another difficult differential diagnosis. When questioning the client during the interview for other worries, general tension, and anxiety, I have always asked *when* these became a problem. The interviewees often responded, "When my panics first started." It was my observation that for many clients the first panic precipitated a host of other worries, and this seemed part of the panic disorder. Consequently, I did not assign to them an additional diagnosis of generalized anxiety. Later, I found these discussions and conclusions substantiated in the literature, as well. Indeed the *DSM-IV* (American Psychiatric Association 1994) now states that an associated feature of panic disorder is experiencing constant or intermittent general anxiety, as well as worries about health and separation from loved ones. Although generalized anxiety disorder is one of the prominent comorbid diagnoses, it often improves as a result of cognitive-behavior therapy for panic disorder (Otto and Whittal 1995).

Sometimes, creative solutions are required in the presence of comorbidities. I had a client with severe social phobia and mild panic disorder with agoraphobia. She was almost housebound by her social fears. However, in this state, a Social Phobia Group would have been impossible for her to attend. Instead, I treated her in my Panic/Phobia Group, where her main task was to practice leaving her house. She was able tolerate this group, because the focus was not primarily on how to interact with others. Her progress was slow but good. At the end of treatment, she felt exhilarated by a new sense of freedom. Once she feels ready for the next challenge, she can obtain further treatment in a Social Phobia Group.

Hypochondriasis

Panic disorder is often associated with hypochondriacal complaints, and it may be difficult to distinguish between the two. Several studies have looked at this diagnostic differentiation, and Bach et al. (1996) drew the conclusion that the two disorders are phenomenologically separate. Panic patients fear sudden autonomic nervous system symptoms, while those with hypochondriasis misinterpret bodily anomalies such as lumps and spots (McNally 1994). Successful treatment of panic disorder *may* reduce concurrent hypochondriacal concerns (Bach et al. 1996). The latter authors also state that while hypochondriasis is strongly associated with panic disorder, it does not generally lead to it.

Depression

Panic disorder is the subtype of anxiety most highly comorbid with depression (Merikangas, Angst, Eaton, et al. 1996). Recognition and treatment of depression is important because long-term panic disorder with depression increases the risk of cardiovascular complications and/or death from suicide. After determining that a client has a depressive comorbidity, your next question should be, "Which diagnosis is primary and which secondary?" For instance, is the depressive symptomatology due to the panic and phobias, somewhat attributable to the panic disorder and somewhat independent, or is it primary? Clients who are severely depressed, whatever the reason, may not be able to benefit from panic-specific treatment for three reasons (Laberge, Gauthier, Coté, et al. 1992):

1. Habituation to feared stimuli may not occur as it does in normal people because of impaired psychophysiological processing. The latter may interfere with interoceptive and in vivo exposures.

2. There may be poor homework compliance because of poor motivation while the client is in a depressed state.

3. Being in a depressed state may interfere with the person's positive evaluation of his or her accomplishments, and thus interfere with an increase in self-efficacy.

While many depressed clients may improve with panic treatment, others may not. Even when depression shows improvement, it often re-emerges some time after the end of treatment (Otto and Whittal 1995). Therefore, these authors recommend that the clinician monitor ongoing or emergent difficulties with depression or other comorbid diagnoses and, if warranted, provide additional treatment. Some depressed clients benefit from medications to accompany panic treatment; others need to have the depression addressed first, with psychotherapy, medications, or both.

In my practice, I sometimes see clients who are depressed. In my opinion, some of them are so absorbed by their sadness that they cannot attend to the group tasks. In such cases, I help the client see that the rigors of panic treatment may be too much for him or her to handle at that time, and they need to treat the depression first. I offer to call the person at a specific future date to jointly assess her/his readiness for group. Thus, we collaborate on the treatment course.

Substance Abuse

A number of studies (Keyl and Eaton 1990) and reviews (Brown and Barlow 1992; Cowley 1992) show that there is a significant comorbidity of panic disorder and substance abuse. Besides alcohol, other substances used by people with panic disorder are cocaine, amphetamines, and marijuana, as well as benzodiazepines (Cohen 1995). Drugs and alcohol can precipitate states of anxiety and panic. While some abusers develop anxiety and panic disorder later, many begin their use of controlled substances to "medicate" their condition. In a panic-challenge study with carbon dioxide (inhaling oxygen and 35 percent carbon dioxide to elicit anxiety), subjects who had ingested alcohol did indeed show decreased anxiety and panic (Kushner, Mackenzie, Fiszdon, et al. 1996).

Although controlled substances can reduce anxiety momentarily, the individual may experience rebound arousal (increased anxiety and/or withdrawal symptoms) following heavy drinking or the use of benzodiazepines. A vicious cycle of continued use and anxiety symptoms can be established and reinforced in this manner. In the long run, the condition worsens as the person continues to resort to the substance when experiencing high levels of anxiety. In sum, it doesn't matter whether panic disorder or substance abuse occurs first— they reinforce each other.

If the person is abusing controlled substances, this must be confronted before the anxiety is addressed for two reasons. First, the person cannot learn new material effectively under the influence. Second, it is difficult to assess other pathologies in the presence of substance abuse. Sometimes, after abstinence is achieved, panic and anxiety are lowered. On the other hand, if the anxiety problem continues, treatment can then be offered.

While I recommend the latter course as a matter of principle, sometimes a fine balance must be struck in the treatment sequence. If the substance use masks an underlying panic disorder and phobias, the client is at a risk for relapse when the anxiety problem is not addressed. My colleagues in the Alcohol and Drug Abuse Program at Kaiser and I collaborate closely in such instances. Some clients have been clean and sober for only one month when I start treating them, but naturally they continue simultaneously with the other program. (The substance-abuse treatment is not restricted as other psychiatric treatment is.) Two recent clients come to mind, albeit not two suffering from panic disorder. These were men whose alcoholism masked a social phobia, whom I treated in the Senior Anxiety Group. Their social distress when not under the influence was so high that they needed anxiety-targeted treatment immediately.

I have observed cases where short-acting benzodiazepines appeared to exacerbate general anxiety. A client whom I interviewed for panic disorder initially chose only to take medications (and not to undergo CBT). She was prescribed a high-potency benzodiazepine by the psychiatrist. She was a new panicker and all her symptoms subsided with medication;

she was too comfortable on it to quit. A few years later, however, she wanted to become pregnant and chose to seek cognitive-behavior therapy while she tapered off the medication. In the early phase of treatment she complained of her persistent high anxiety in addition to the panic attacks themselves. To her surprise, her anxiety greatly diminished as she got off the medication.

Although more women than men develop agoraphobia, more men tend to use alcohol as a coping mechanism for dealing with anxiety (Barlow 1988; Cox, Swinson, Shulman, et al. 1993b). It is used both to cope with social fears and to allay physical symptoms. I have found that many women are less willing to admit openly to having used controlled substances to calm themselves in the context of panic disorder. The clinician should be particularly alert to this possibility during the assessment.

Personality Disorders

A high percentage of clients with panic disorder have a coexisting personality disorder (Brown and Barlow 1992; Mavissakalian 1990). Among the more common are avoidant, dependent, and histrionic personality disorders. When looking at personality characteristics (vis-à-vis diagnoses), clients with agoraphobia seem overanxious, avoidant, dependent, un-assertive, and have low self-confidence (Mavissakalian 1990). On the positive side, improvement in panic disorder is often accompanied by decrease in dependent and avoidant measures of personality pathology. In my experience, personality disorders can complicate the treatment of panic disorder, but some clients with personality disorders are able to focus well on the panic work.

Rule Out Physical Illness

Some medical conditions must be differentiated from panic disorder because they exhibit similar symptoms. If your client has had a recent onset of panic attacks and has not had a physical checkup within a year, it is advisable to refer him or her to a physician. If the client is over forty when the panics start, a medical checkup is even more important. Some of the more common physical conditions to differentiate from panic disorder are as follows (Barlow 1988; Brown, Rakel, Wells, et al. 1991; Goldberg 1988 [this article is the most complete]; Raj and Sheehan 1987):

1. **Syndromes related to medications and illegal drugs**
   Use of and intoxication from caffeine, amphetamine, bronchodilators, steroids, marijuana, hallucinogens, cocaine, etc., or withdrawal from alcohol, tranquilizers, barbiturates, or narcotics. Caffeine can trigger symptoms identical to anxiety episodes with doses as low as 200 mg, which is less than two cups of coffee. Cocaine can induce anxiety and panic states after the initial euphoria. Withdrawal from alcohol often precipitates panic symptoms, and the benzodiazepines most likely to do so are those with shorter half-lives. Other drugs that sometimes produce anxiety are decongestants, antihistamines, calcium channel blockers, and theophylline.

2. **Cardiovascular**
   Mitral valve prolapse is a relatively common valvular abnormality. Although generally a harmless condition, it can produce cardiac complications. The palpitations experienced in mitral valve prolapse have been linked to panic attacks; however, it has been concluded that mitral valve prolapse does not cause panic disorder. Cardiac arrhythmias may produce palpitations, dyspnea, and light-headedness. If cardiac arrhythmias are suspected, Holter monitoring

can help to confirm the diagnosis. Angina pectoris can be experienced as dyspnea, palpitations, and chest discomfort. Though easily confounded with anxiety, episodes of angina are often precipitated by exercise and emotional stress. Patients with myocardial infarction usually complain of a crushing sensation seldom experienced by panic patients.

3. **Respiratory**
   Hyperventilation syndrome is common in general medical practice, yet it often goes unrecognized. Physical symptoms are feeling faint, dizziness, palpitations, paresthesias, blurred vision, nausea, and headaches. These result from overbreathing, which leads to excessive elimination of carbon dioxide. One way to diagnose hyperventilation is to have the patient overbreathe for up to three minutes to determine whether the same symptoms are then exacerbated. Note that asthma attacks can mimic the shortness of breath experienced by a number of panic patients.

4. **Endocrine**
   Hypoglycemia can be brought on by large fluctuations in plasma insulin levels and cause anxiety and panic symptoms. It can be suspected if panic attacks are associated with hunger; some symptoms are similar, but the fears, such as a sense of impending doom, are absent. Hypoglycemia also can be precipitated by a number of drugs, e.g., antihistamines, monoamine oxidase inhibitors, propranolol, estrogen, and alcohol. Individuals suffering from hyperthyroidism can look "neurotic" with a number of anxiety- and panic-type symptoms, which will subside with successful treatment. Pheochromocytoma is a rare condition; it involves catecholamine secretion by a tumor of the renal medulla. The symptoms produced are intense headaches, palpitations, flushing, and sweating on the torso. Cushing's syndrome and menopause also can present symptoms similar to panic.

5. **Neurologic**
   Complex partial seizures may result in symptoms similar to panic, including feelings of fear and unreality; one must consider head injury, hallucinations, seizures, altered consciousness, and neurologic deficits. Vestibular dysfunctions also can mimic panic symptoms.

A physical illness does not preclude the possibility of panic disorder as a coexisting condition. In fact, it usually complicates the picture the client presents. For instance, a person may develop an illness-specific panic fear, as in asthma, often with dyspnea as the most common symptom (Carr, Lehrer, and Hochron 1995) or vestibular dysfunction, with complaints of dizziness and feelings of unsteadiness (Jacob, Furman, Durrant, et al. 1996; Margraf, Ehlers, and Roth 1986). The illnesses or dysfunctions do not in and of themselves cause panic disorder, but they can interact with fear and manifest in complex ways.

Consider a Medication Referral

When do you refer a client for pharmacotherapy? That depends on several factors that must be taken into consideration.

1. **Time Since Onset of Panic Disorder**
   The more recent the onset, the more beneficial it may be for your client to try CBT without medications. This circumvents the complications of side ef-

fects involved in the use of medications and difficulties with drug discontinuation.

2. **Client Tolerance of Symptoms**
Does your client tolerate the symptoms? That is, is she/he willing to go through a period of discomfort while learning coping strategies and overcoming fear? The more frequent and intense the panic attacks are, the more likely that the client will want medications, but this is not necessarily the case. Tolerance to intense, uncomfortable symptoms varies.

3. **Level of Functional Impairment**
If the client has difficulty going to work, going out, or performing daily activities, i.e., shows behavioral impairment in functioning, medications should be seriously considered. I take the stance that it is better for a client to function with medications than not to function at all. Occasionally, *I urge* the client to take medications, if distress is very high and impairment is extensive.

4. **Client Is in Turmoil and/or Has Comorbidities**
Consider a medication referral if the client cannot concentrate on the task at hand due to crises or other disturbing emotional problems. This is particularly relevant if they interfere with the client's progress.

5. **Client Requests Medications**
If the client requests medications, even in the case of recent and mild panic attacks, a referral cannot be denied. You may, however, try to influence your client by stating the pros and cons of pharmacotherapy, so the client is able to make an informed decision. If you persuade your client to try doing without medications, he or she should know that the decision can be changed at any time.

6. **Lack of Progress**
Consider a medication referral if no progress is observed after six to eight weeks of CBT, or if the client's distress level remains high or increases.

7. **CBT Fails to Help Your Client**
If your client has gone through CBT, and has chosen not to combine it with pharmacotherapy, but no significant improvement has been made, seriously consider a medication referral.

Preparing Your Client for the Work Ahead

At the end of the assessment session I describe the treatment program to the client, including the work that will be covered in each treatment module, and answer the client's questions. If the client wants to commit to treatment, I tell him or her that I expect regular attendance, especially at the group therapy sessions, and that the likelihood of a successful outcome is greatly increased the better their attendance and follow-through with assignments.

Furthermore, for treatment to be successful, he or she must be willing and able to invest time and hard work on confronting the fears. This includes reading assignments in *An End to Panic: Breakthrough Techniques for Overcoming Panic Disorder* (Zuercher-White 1995), using the worksheets, and practicing in vivo assignments. It has been shown that clients who comply with home assignments demonstrate a more pronounced decrement in fear and avoidance behavior than those who do not comply (Edelman and Chambless 1993). For a client without agoraphobia, a minimum of one to two hours per week is needed, and if agoraphobia is present, an additional four to eight hours a week is necessary for the in vivo exposures. The client who is willing to set aside a significant amount of time for exposures, preferably daily, has a tremendous advantage. In my experience, clients who experience quick and steady results usually do better than those who show slow improvement. I have speculated that the more drawn out the accomplished changes are, the more the client loses motivation and faith in recovery. If the time is not available, I encourage clients to wait for a time when they can make a serious commitment. Otherwise, clients cannot do justice either to themselves or the treatment.

Monitoring Panic Attacks

Panickers tend to consistently overreport both frequency and severity of panic attacks (Dijkman-Caes, Kraan, and deVries 1993; Craske 1991a). Furthermore, during the onset of their panic disorder, they were very aware of every panic attack, but after a while, the anxious apprehension that many experience between panic attacks overlaps with the panic Başoğlu, Marks and Şengün 1992). Worksheet 1: Panic Frequency and Intensity allows the client to record how many panic attacks he/she had on each day of the month and to rate SUDS level (Subjective Units of [Anxiety-] Distress Scale). For them to notice improvement, it is important to distinguish between high anxiety and panic. If every experience of high anxiety is labeled panic, the frequency is inflated and panickers tend to feel worse about their condition. Because of these findings, several researchers emphasize the need for clients to monitor their panic attacks as they occur (Craske and Barlow 1993). By getting used to monitoring the panics, the client becomes a *participant-observer,* which is the first step toward healing. However, since noncompliance is a frequently observed problem, I have prepared a simple monitoring form that allows the client to easily watch his or her progress over time.

Assignment

At the end of the assessment session, I ask the client to start recording his or her panic attacks on Worksheet 1: Panic Frequency and Intensity, and to bring it to the first treatment session. I also ask the client to read Chapters 1 through 6 in *An End to Panic.* These assignments get my client started on their homework.

In the case of a client who essentially does not go out alone (although not totally housebound) or does not drive alone, I ask that he or she immediately begin to walk or drive daily, seven days a week, starting with one city block or less and extending the distance farther and farther. Because of the short distance involved, I ask that he or she repeat the same exposure two to three times in succession. This, I explain, allows the client to move ahead even before the first treatment session. If this is not done, progress will be too slow (especially compared to that of the other members in a group). (If the treatment involves a group, I may set up another individual appointment with this client to assess progress before he or she begins the group treatment.)

Worksheet 1: **Panic Frequency and Intensity**

Name: _____   Month & Year: _____

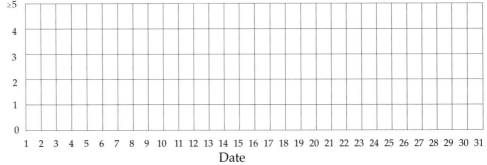

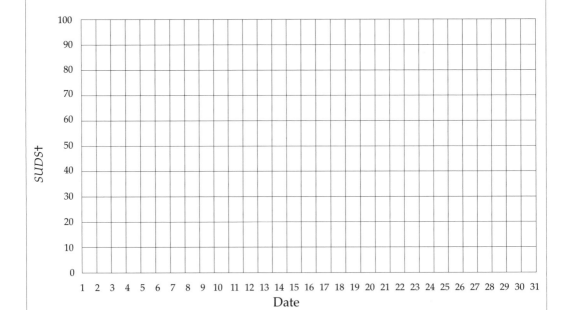

---

*   Panic is defined here as a very sudden, intense surge of fear.

†   If one or more panics, rate highest SUDS. SUDS: Subjective Units of Anxiety-Distress Scale. 0 = Totally
     calm, no anxiety or fear. 50 = Moderate level of anxiety/fear. 100 = Intolerable level of anxiety/fear.

ASSESSMENT QUESTIONS*

PANIC DISORDER

Panic Attacks

1a. Have you *ever* had an anxiety episode that was very intense and came on suddenly, like a sudden, intense rush?

 b. How long does it take from the beginning of the symptoms until they reach a peak? (Must be within ten minutes.)

 2. What symptoms do you have with these sudden and intense anxiety episodes? (Ask about the specific symptoms from the *DSM-IV* panic attack symptom list.)

First Panic

3a. When did you have your *very first* panic attack, the first one in your life, and what happened?

 b. Were you going through any unusual stress just prior to that event?

Panic Disorder

 4. In what situations have you had these sudden, intense panic attacks?

 5. Have they ever come unexpectedly, totally out of the blue?
    If Yes: How often have they occurred unexpectedly?

    Have you ever awakened in panic from sleep, other than from a nightmare?

 6. Have you gone to an Emergency Room or sought other medical help because of these attacks? _____ If Yes: What did the physician tell you?

 7. Are the panics worse now or were they worse in the past?

    At their worst, how frequent are/were the attacks?

Fear Cognitions, Safety Signals/Behaviors

8a. Do you fear these attacks a lot?
    What is your worst fear during these attacks? (Usually one, sometimes two or three are given.)   b. On a scale from 0 to 100% (0% = You don't believe at all it will happen, 100% = You believe absolutely it will happen, and any number in between), how strongly do you believe _____ will happen?[†]

---

* These are useful questions for the assessment. They are adapted from Anxiety Disorders Interview Schedule for DSM-IV (ADIS-IV, DiNardo, Brown, and Barlow 1994). Copyright ©1987 by Graywind Publications, Inc. Reproduced by Permission of publisher, The Psychological Corporation. All rights reserved.

† The idea to elicit Belief Ratings of central (focal) fears during assessment for later comparison is from Cox (1996).

   c. This fear (*repeat the above-stated fear*, e.g., "of heart attack"), what leads you to believe it will happen _____ ?

9a. What do you do then to help yourself? For example, do you sit, stand, walk, talk in a certain way?

   b. Do you carry with you things that can save you, or do you bring another person along? (Medications, water?)

   c. Do these things work, i.e., do they stop the worst in panic from happening?

PHOBIAS

10a. Do you have *any* phobias? That is, are there situations you *avoid* because of fear or do you do them anyway, *with fear*? (E.g., driving, being a passenger in a car or bus, going to grocery stores or malls, crowds, airplanes, elevators, being at home alone, movies, tunnels, bridges, restaraunts, parties.) Check also for social and specific phobias.

   b. How long back does your very first phobia date?

11. Do you worry *a great deal* about saying or doing something embarrassing or humiliating, or that others may think badly of you?

Fear Cognitions, Safety Signals/Behaviors in Phobic Situations

12. What are you afraid will happen in (list a few of the phobic situations mentioned)?

13. How do you attempt to cope? (What actions do you engage in to help you deal with the fearful situation/activity?)

14. Have the panic attacks and phobias actually prevented you from working, traveling, or engaging in other activities (other than the avoided situations you mentioned above)?

OTHER ASSESSMENT QUESTIONS

Further issues to be assessed are

- Symptoms of generalized anxiety disorder, obsessive-compulsive disorder, and depression
- Presence of suicidal ideation
- Medical conditions
- Prescribed medications and over-the-counter drugs
- Use of substances (alcohol, illegal drugs, caffeine, nicotine)
- Family history and past treatments
- Living conditions (family life, job)
- Current stresses
- Assertiveness level
- Support system, physical exercise, coping skills
- Events during childhood or adult life related to fears and worries

Summary

The diagnostic criteria are summarized here, along with other considerations required for a thorough assessment.

Panic Attack

- Sudden rise of intense fear or anxiety, peaking within ten minutes.
- At least four of the 13 *DSM-IV* symptoms must be reported. (Fewer than four are called limited symptom attacks.)

Panic Disorder

- At least two recurrent, unexpected panic attacks.
- At least one attack has been followed by at least one month of:
    - Worry about another attack.
    - Worry about its consequences.
- Behavioral change (avoidance, visits to the emergency room, etc.)

Panic Disorder With or Without Agoraphobia

- Fear of being in places or situations from which escape is difficult or embarrassing or help is not available. It includes fear of crowds, being outside the home alone, being at home alone, driving, using public transportation, going to movies, restaurants, etc.
- Look for subtle avoidances/activities, e.g., exercise, heat, caffeine, etc.

Agoraphobia Without History of Panic Disorder

- Avoidances as above with fear of limited symptom attacks or other symptoms.

Factors That Maintain Avoidance

- Escape, safety signals, safety behaviors.

Sources of Fear

- Exteroceptive (Fears attributed to outside objects/situations).
- Interoceptive (Fears attributed to internal sensations). Treatment must address these sources of fear.

Differential Diagnoses and Comorbidities

- Other anxiety disorders.
- Depression.
- Substance abuse.
- Personality disorders.

Ruling Out Physical Illness

- A number of physical conditions present with symptomatology similar to that in panic disorder and should be considered: Syndromes related to medications and illegal drugs; cardiovascular, respiratory, endocrine, and neurologic dysfunctions and illnesses.
- Consider referring your client for a physical exam.

Considerations in Referral for Pharmacotherapy

- Time since onset of panic disorder.
- Client tolerance of symptoms.
- Level of functional impairment.
- Client is in crisis or has comorbidities.
- Client requests medications.
- Lack of progress.

(For further information on medications, see chapter 10.)

Prepare Your Client for Treatment

- Give assignments, including having your client start monitoring panic attacks.

2

The Etiology of Panic Disorder

A large percentage of the population experiences occasional panic attacks (Norton et al. 1985), although very few go on to develop panic disorder. Why and how? The following text presents some theoretical models and empirical findings. My account is brief and incomplete, but it is an attempt to document some of the most important findings, which you may wish to study further.

Models Based on Biological Findings

Many researchers and clinicians believe that panic attacks are indicative of biological dysfunctions. The evidence is based on findings from different types of studies. I have relied on reviews by McNally (1994), Barlow (1988), and Fyer, Mannuzza, and Coplan (1995). I refer you to them and to other sources published elsewhere for a more complete account of these studies.

Methods of Study

Several different methods and approaches have been used to study whether biological factors cause or contribute to panic disorder.

Genetic Studies

Panic disorder is observed across generations. A number of family studies suggest a genetic basis for anxiety (Silove, Manicavasagar, O'Connell, et al. 1995). However, just because panic disorder has been observed in families does not prove that it is, in fact, inherited. The ideal study of genetics, barring a test to prove a dysfunction, involves a comparison of identical (monozygotic) twins reared in separate environments; these comparisons are, however, difficult to do on a large scale. Torgersen (1983) did study monozygotic and dizygotic twins, who had been reared together. He found a higher rate of anxiety disorders in the monozygotic group compared to the dizygotic group. Although he did not find such a relationship when studying panic disorder alone, the results were positive when he combined panic disorder with the category agoraphobia without panic attacks. Krystal, Niehoff Deutsch, et al. (1996) reviewed studies on the biological basis of panic disorder and quoted other avenues measuring heritability. Patients with panic disorder and their first-degree relatives, even those not experiencing naturally occurring panic attacks, showed greater sensitivity to the effects of carbon dioxide compared to healthy controls. Similar findings have been reported with lactate infusion.

In their reviews, McNally (1994) and Fyer et al. (1995) conclude that genetic studies have provided inconsistent estimates of the degree of heritability in panic disorder, yet it is possible that future studies will reveal a more definite genetic component. At this time, it appears that a *general vulnerability to anxiety* is inherited rather than a single biological dysfunction causing panic (Barlow 1988; Margraf et al. 1986).

Although our knowledge of genetic inheritance in anxiety disorders is incomplete, we do know that particular environmental influences, such as prolonged stress, adversity, or trauma can trigger certain genetic vulnerabilities (Barlow 1988; Rosenbaum 1992). In some studies, women with anxiety disorders in adulthood have reported experiencing higher than normal separation anxiety during childhood; this may have predisposed these women to adult anxiety disorders (Silove et al. 1995; Silove, Manicavasagar, Curtis, et al. 1996; Silove, Manicavasagar, O'Connell, et al. 1993). Even in these cases, a hereditary component may not be specific to the separation anxiety but may involve a general vulnerability to anxiety.

Pharmacotherapy

A genetic contribution may take the form of a vulnerability to a lower threshold of limbic arousal or sympathetic arousal. Thus, pharmacological interventions are targeted at the limbic or central noradrenergic systems (Rosenbaum 1992). Pharmacotherapy is based on the view that dysfunctional biochemical and pathophysiological mechanisms cause or maintain panic disorder.

Biological Challenge or Provocation Tests

These are experiments designed to induce panic in the laboratory. Subjects have been challenged with infusions of sodium lactate, sodium bicarbonate, norepinephrine, or isoproterenol; with oral and intravenous administration of other agents to influence the serotonin function and the benzodiazepine system. They have also been challenged with oral ingestion of yohimbine and caffeine; and inhalation of carbon dioxide with oxygen (Barlow 1988; McNally 1990, 1994). When comparing subjects with and without panic disorder, panic disorder subjects are much more likely to panic when subjected to these challenges (Tesar and Rosenbaum 1993).

A sodium lactate infusion is one of the best known pharmacological means of inducing panic. It has been found that lactate infusions increase subjective anxiety and physiological arousal in both normal subjects and panic patients, according to a review by Margraf et al. (1986). Yet only panic patients respond to the physical changes with panic attacks.

Brain-Imaging Studies

Positron emission tomography (PET) and single photon emission computed tomography (SPECT) techniques allow three-dimensional functioning to be studied (Fyer et al. 1995). They aim at finding the regions of the brain that are active during panic. Findings to date involving cerebral blood flow in lactate-induced panic have shown inconclusive results.

Overactivity in the region of study may reflect compensation for dysfunction elsewhere in the brain, and some studies have not distinguished unique metabolic activity from artifact.

Physiological Processes

Based on the methods described above and other findings, theories have been formulated to explain various physiological processes involved in panic disorder. Some of the more prominent theories involve breathing irregularities and audiovestibular abnormalities.

Hyperventilation Model

It has been suggested that some people hyperventilate when stressed and that this is linked to panic disorder (Ley 1985, 1988; Smoller, Pollack, Otto, et al. 1996). They engage in rapid, shallow, thoracic breathing. Acute hyperventilation results in hypocapnic alkalosis. The symptoms produced are light-headedness, dizziness, and feelings of unreality (a result of cerebral vasoconstriction), palpitations and chest discomfort (a result of coronary vasoconstriction), and tingling in the extremities (a result of peripheral vasoconstriction). These symptoms are then misinterpreted as life-threatening. Fear activates the fight/flight response but when no physical action takes place, the increased respiration leads to excess dissipation of carbon dioxide, bringing on hypocapnea, which escalates into a panic. Chronic hyperventilators are especially at risk for hyperventilation-induced panic attacks. Ley (1988) has proposed that nocturnal panic results from chronic hyperventilation.

Dyspnea-Fear Theory

The dyspnea-fear theory was a further development of the hyperventilation model. Espoused by Ley (1989), it hypothesizes that when panic patients experience severe dyspnea (the sense of having difficulty in breathing and of impending suffocation), they respond with intense fear and panic. Ley theorizes further that catastrophic cognitions are a consequence of dyspnea, and may result from cognitive deficits resulting from hypoxia. Asmundson and Stein (1994) speculate that a subpathologic pulmonary obstruction causes the experience of "air hunger" and the greater effort in breathing, and that the resulting dyspnea causes panic.

In actual pulmonary diseases, such as asthma or pulmonary hypertension, the dyspnea experienced may be related to carbon dioxide sensitivity and can trigger panic (Smoller et al. 1996). Carr et al. (1995) suggest that, when the central nervous system centers that control respiratory drive become hyperreactive, they may trigger hyperventilation, which, in turn, can induce a full-fledged asthma attack in patients suffering from asthma.

Carbon Dioxide Sensitivity and Klein's Suffocation Alarm Theory

Carbon dioxide inhalation triggers panic in patients with panic disorder. The panicogenic effects may indicate abnormally sensitive carbon dioxide chemoreceptors in the brain stem. Panic patients seem to respond to increases in carbon dioxide with an exaggerated ventilatory response accompanied by dyspnea. This mimics the experience of suffocation, triggering fear and panic.

Klein's suffocation alarm theory (Klein 1993; Papp, Klein, and Gorman 1993; Papp, Martinez, Klein, et al. 1995a) proposes that a rise in carbon dioxide levels in the brain, in light of the above-mentioned chemoreceptor hypersensitivity, signals lack of air, triggering the suffocation alarm system. In panic patients, there is an abnormally low suffocation alarm threshold, leading easily to "false" suffocation alarms. This results in spontaneous panic attacks often accompanied by the urge to flee. Some clients chronically hyperventilate to reduce arterial carbon dioxide below the levels that would trigger the suffocation alarm.

Audiovestibular Dysfunctions

Researchers have found visuo-spatial, vestibulo-ocular reflex and other vestibular abnormalities (Clark, Hirsch, Smith, et al. 1994; Hoffman, O'Leary, and Munjack 1994; McCaffrey et al. 1990). In these instances, a patient may, fear veering to one side and falling down. Sometimes avoidance behavior results from deficits in perceptual-motor skill rather than from an abnormal balance system (Yardley, Britton, Lear, et al. 1995). When physical reactions, deficits, or abnormalities make a person susceptible to disequilibrium, panic disorder ensues only if the person is unduly fearful of the symptoms and their consequences. This is especially clear when the physical condition per se does not lead to catastrophic outcomes. For instance, a client may have fallen down only once but become very fearful and react as if falling were always an imminent possibility.

Neurophysiological Theories

The following theories purport to explain panic disorder as caused by dysfunctions in the central nervous system.

Noradrenergic System Dysregulation

Pharmacological and animal studies have involved specific neurotransmitter systems such as the noradrenergic system. It has been proposed that dysregulation in this system produces panic. The locus ceruleus is a major nucleus in the noradrenergic system. Stimulation of these neurons has been shown to produce intense fear in animals. Hence, the locus ceruleus is believed to mediate fear, alarm, and anxiety. This theory has been further studied by infusion of yohimbe (an alpha-2-adrenergic receptor antagonist), which increases locus ceruleus activity. Panic patients are indeed more likely to experience panic attacks in this provocation test. However, since panic patients are also hypersensitive to alpha-2-adrenergic receptor agonists (e.g., clonidine) that diminish locus ceruleus firing, it is speculated that a noradrenergic dysregulation may arise from dysfunctions in other neuronal systems (e.g., gamma-aminobutyric acid or GABA, benzodiazepine receptors, or dysfunctional respiratory control neurons). Any of these can lead to surges in arousal, resulting in panic.

It is believed that tricyclic antidepressants stabilize noradrenergic dysregulation. Although noradrenergic dysregulation may be involved in some panic attacks, it does not explain all occurrences of panic disorder. For instance, selective serotonin reuptake inhibitors do not affect central noradrenergic receptors but do decrease panic attacks. Hence, the evidence for this model is mixed.

The Benzodiazepine System

It has been suggested that the benzodiazepine receptor system is involved in generalized anxiety and panic disorder. Benzodiazepines block panic attacks and control anxiety. They exert their anxiolytic effects by enhancing GABA-ergic inhibition of the postsynaptic neuron. Although the GABA system may be anxiolytic, benzodiazepines have other effects through the suppression of general arousal (sedation, muscle relaxant, and anticonvulsant effects), which reduce emotions in general.

Serotonin System Dysregulation

Serotonin dysregulation has been studied with biological challenge tests. Test results show normal presynaptic serotonin functioning, but hypersensitive postsynaptic serotonin receptors in some panic patients. These findings are consistent with the effects of serotonin reuptake inhibitors, such as fluvoxamine. However, some studies show a lower serotonin level, while others show a normal one. It is possible that these medications dampen fluctuations in the serotonin system rather than specifically augmenting or diminishing overall serotonin levels.

Interesting Challenges to Some Findings

Cox, Swinson, and Endler (1991a) are concerned that some biological studies may be confusing etiology with symptomatology. As much as the findings discussed above have been taken as "proof" that panic attacks are directly caused by a central nervous system anomaly, other equally convincing studies have been conducted suggesting that the induced panic attacks in challenge tests can be mediated by the "cognitive set" that results from the instructions given in the test (Barlow 1988; Clark 1993; Margraf et al. 1986; Salkovskis and Clark 1990). (Note, however, that in a recent study by Papp, Welkowitz, Martinez, et al. 1995b, the instructional set did not alter the outcome in a respiratory challenge test.) The presence of a "safe" person in biological challenge tests reduces physiological arousal and anxiety (Carter, Hollon, Carson, et al. 1995). Thus, a person's sense of control, expectations, etc., are important factors in determining the response to challenge tests.

According to Barlow (1988) sudden physiological changes experienced as loss of control, which the client has learned to fear, can provoke panic in the laboratory. The perception of control (real or imagined) has indeed been shown to determine whether the person panics or not (Sanderson, Rapee, and Barlow 1989). High anxiety sensitivity (i.e., fear of anxiety sensations) may also explain a number of these findings. For instance, carbon dioxide challenges provoke intense cardiorespiratory sensations that people with high anxiety sensitivity scores greatly fear. It has also been found that subjects with high, compared to low, anxiety sensitivity show a greater tendency to panic in a hyperventilation challenge test, even when the heart rate remains unchanged (Asmundson, Norton, Wilson, et al. 1994).

The mechanisms underlying the provocation procedures are too diverse to be explained by one theory. Panic clients generally exhibit high baseline anxiety on various measures. A panic attack is likely to occur when these anxious clients sense a loss of control over a sudden and intense somatic event. Other innocuous situations that tend to provoke panic attacks in individuals with panic disorder are aerobic exercise, sauna, heat, sexual relations, relaxation, and even false heart rate feedback. In the case of false heart rate feedback, researchers (Ehlers, Margraf, Roth, et al. 1988) gave patients false auditory feedback indicating a sudden rise in heart rate. Panic patients responded with more fear than the normal controls. In their review Ehlers and Breuer (1996) concluded that patients with panic disorder become anxious when they believe that their heart rate is accelerated.

The fact that medications work is not proof that a dysregulation in the system believed to be impacted by the drug has caused the panic disorder. Furthermore, many of the medications that seem to ameliorate panic disorder have a broad spectrum of effects, which affect the functioning of different neurotransmitter systems.

Conclusion of Biological Findings

After reviewing all of the findings to date, I find it impossible to believe that biological factors do not play a rather significant role in panic disorder. However, as you probably have concluded from reading the brief rendition above, there are many thories, and none is capable of explaining *all* panics. As McNally (1994) states, biological research has not shown one system or dysfunction consistently responsible for all panic attacks. The research points rather to a multiplicity of different neurobiological pathways to panic disorder (Barlow 1988;

Cox et al. 1991a; Krystal et al. 1996; Lelliott and Bass 1990; Margraf et al. 1986; McNally 1994). If provoking the feared symptoms—by any means—can precipitate panic, it opens the door to the influence of psychological factors. Keep in mind that regardless of the relative contribution of biological and psychological factors in any given individual, the treatment options can be pharmacological and/or psychological.

Models Based on Psychological Findings

Based on empirical findings and speculation there are several psychological theories that attempt to explain panic disorder.

Fear Theories

Different "fear" theories have been proposed. They are summarized by Barlow (1988) and Williams (1987).

- The two-factor theory is based on classical conditioning and operant learning procedures.

- The physiological fear theory is based on the proposition that autonomic arousal is a clear indicator of fear.

- The phenomenological fear theory defines fear in terms of the subjective experience.

- The three-response system model of anxiety suggests that fear can be analyzed along physiological, cognitive, and behavioral components. Note that, although this model is very useful for working with clients (see chapter 4), there are strong doubts also about its validity, especially in regard to phobic avoidance. The three systems are rather general and often weakly intercorrelated. For instance, avoidance behavior often persists without any autonomic arousal.

- The bioinformational theory of anxiety proposes that anxiety is based on informational structures consisting of stimulus, response, and meaning propositions represented in a network of memory nodes. This cognitive structure represents a prototype for overt behavior, i.e., a tendency to act, for instance, to flee a feared situation.

None of these theories is fully explanatory and they have all been refuted by empirical findings. The conceptions of fear and anxiety are likely to continue to change. Kagan (1996) criticizes the simplified views on the one hand and the high abstractions resorted to, on the other hand, to explain fear. He reminds us that the data indicate there are many forms of fear reactions. A fearful state produced by separation from an attachment figure is different from the anticipation of an undesirable future event and both are different fear states than that aroused when faced with life-threatening danger. Just as responses vary, the brain circuitry and psychological experiences are likely to be different, too. The notion of a single fear state must thus be replaced with distinct, albeit related, states with their own incentives, neurophysiologies, and behavioral reactions.

Cognitive Models

The model put forth by Beck and Emery, with Greenberg (1985), Clark (1986), and Clark and Ehlers (1993) suggests that individuals with panic disorder interpret these attacks, either initially or subsequently, as threatening. They misinterpret their bodily sensations in a catastrophic way, fearing that the sensations signal an impending physical or mental disaster. For instance, a panicker perceives an increase in heart rate and thinks he or she is having a heart attack or that the heart will explode. It is the panicker's *conception* of these sensations as dangerous that precipitates the attack. While there might indeed be some biological anomalies, they do not directly cause the panic. Out-of-the-blue panic attacks can occur as a response to a clear precipitant, such as caffeine ingestion, standing up suddenly after sitting, and experiencing a different emotional state, but the panicker is unaware of the precipitant.

Clark and Ehlers (1993) present a summary of studies testing the cognitive theory of panic disorder. In a sentence completion test (panic-related, fear-provoking concepts were compared with neutral words) subjects with panic disorder processed the panic-related words faster than the neutral words. In another study reviewed by the same authors, subjects were asked to read aloud pairs of words that coupled bodily sensations with catastrophic outcomes and neutral words. Just reading the cards with the catastrophic outcomes induced panic in the panic disorder patients. Patients and normal controls were given false auditory heart rate feedback that suggested a sudden heart rate increase. Panic clients showed significantly more anxiety, and their physiological measures rose. In a panic challenge test of carbon dioxide inhalation (the Sanderson et al. study of 1989), subjects were given the illusion of control over the quantity of carbon dioxide they were breathing. Subjects were told that they could reduce the carbon dioxide flow by turning a dial if a light was illuminated; half the group had the light illuminated, half did not. Although the illusion-of-control group (light illuminated) did not actually exercise the control they believed they had (the dial did not work), they were less likely to panic. From this Clark and Ehlers drew the conclusion that two processes maintain distorted beliefs:

1. Because they are frightened, hypervigilant, and are scanning their bodies for signs of danger, panickers notice sensations more readily, and

2. Subtle avoidance mechanisms serve to maintain distorted beliefs. For example, clients who fear heart attack will rest and slow down their breathing during panics; those who fear fainting will lean against solid objects; and those who fear going insane try very hard to control their thoughts.

Further cognitive mechanisms may predispose individuals with panic disorder to develop avoidances (Agras 1993; Starcevic, Kellner, Uhlenhuth, et al. 1993a). Both fear of loss of control and fear of the social and physical consequences of panic attacks seem to initiate and then to maintain agoraphobia.

Self-Efficacy Theory

This theory is based on social learning theory and has been set forth by Bandura (1977, 1988) and Williams (1992) and has been applied particularly to phobias. Avoidance behaviors are the result of people's judgments of their inability to cope with threatening activities. Much of the support for this theory comes from findings that perceptions of self-efficacy predict phobic behavior more accurately than other measures based on fear of harm. Feelings of fear and avoidance behavior are related but do not cause each other. Once avoidance is established, it is difficult to eliminate even though the original threat is no longer present. (See chapters 5 and 8.) A recent study by Hoffart (1995) showed that self-efficacy contributed to performance accomplishments in agoraphobic situations more than catastrophic beliefs did.

Anxiety Sensitivity

Why are some people more prone to catastrophizing than others? Reiss and colleagues (Reiss 1987; Reiss, Peterson, Gursky, et al. 1986; McNally 1990, 1994) posit "anxiety sensitivity." Anxiety sensitivity is the belief that symptoms of anxiety have harmful consequences; and this belief leads to the tendency to respond fearfully to anxiety symptoms. Some clients with panic disorder believe that specific bodily sensations, which result from physiological arousal, can cause heart attacks, strokes, and other calamities. Anxiety sensitivity may either precede or result from panic. It is believed to enhance the acquisition of fears. When anxiety sensitivity precedes panic, the experience of frightening attacks may further increase the sensitivity. And yet, why do some people tend to interpret minor physical symptoms as more dangerous to begin with?

Two possibilities are vicarious learning (having observed others cope poorly with such symptoms), and verbal transmission of misinformation from significant others about the physical and mental dangers resulting from anxiety and certain bodily symptoms (Craske and Rodriguez 1994; McNally and Lorenz 1987). Ehlers (1993) reported a study on how panickers learned to fear anxiety symptoms. The author found that when some panic patients were children and they experienced anxiety symptoms, there was greater encouragement of illness behavior (allowed to skip school, homework, and chores, given special foods, etc.) than normal controls received. There was also more chronic disease in panickers' families. The author speculates that these are some of the ways for anxiety sensitivity to develop.

Schmidt, Lerew, and Jackson (1997) measured the anxiety sensitivity of a large number of Air Force Cadets by means of the Anxiety Sensitivity Index (ASI), (Reiss et al. 1986) prior to their basic training. The reasoning was that in basic training, the cadets experience an extreme lack of personal control. He found that those with high ASI scores were significantly more likely to panic than those with low scores and that this was true independent of past panic attacks. Lack of control seems to trigger panics in those who are psychologically vulnerable (i.e., high anxiety sensitivity). The ASI may be one way to identify these people.

Other Cognitive Mechanisms

McNally (1994) states that cognitive therapeutic approaches have not been based on cognitive experimental inquiry. However, more recent efforts in testing cognitive theory have revealed cognitive styles, that is, perceptual and/or memory processes involved in panic disorder. McNally summarizes these studies. Panic patients with and without agoraphobia tend to interpret internal cues as threatening. Interestingly, those with agoraphobia also apply these interpretive biases to external cues. Although these biases are automatic and to some extent persist upon recovery, treated patients apply coping strategies to counteract these anxiety-related biases. Patients with anxiety disorders, including those with panic disorder, show an attentional bias for processing threat, i.e., they attend selectively to cues related to threat. There seems to be a memory bias, suggesting that the person is primed to recall anxious thoughts. Panic patients show an enhanced acuity to perceiving interoceptive cues.

Foa and Kozak (1986) and McNally (1994) describe another phenomenon, "overvalued ideation," where the client does not respond to behavioral experiments designed to test whether a catastrophic consequence will occur. Here, there may be an impairment in inductive reasoning. Although it is true that having never had a heart attack in a panic does not prove that it cannot happen, most people, unlike those with overvalued ideation, learn to accept the irrationality of assuming that it is a highly probable event. (Note that in chapter 5 when the person resorts to the cognitive trap, Exaggerating or Overestimating Risk, he or she is greatly exaggerating the odds that a dangerous event will happen. In treatment, I always emphasize there is risk in everything, nothing is absolutely certain. To recover, the client must learn to accept this premise in the area of fear as in other areas of his or her life.) Other reasons for this overvalued ideation in clients are very robust beliefs about harm and elaborate scenarios involving long-term consequence of harm, which cannot be tested in the short-term. Some of these clients resort to another cognitive trap I call Disaster Expectation (see chapter 5), which in this context, according to McNally, takes the form of the belief that after many uneventful panic attacks, their luck will run out and the next one will surely be catastrophic.

In a recent study on overvalued ideation in panickers, Zoellner et al. (1996) found that about 16 percent of panickers retained strong convictions of their fears even when not panicking. Their concerns were primarily over mental and social threats rather than physical threats. These findings were obtained in assessment, not after cognitive-behavior therapy. It is therefore unknown how these clients would fare in treatment, and whether this overvalued ideation always is inflexible.

In sum, all these ways of processing information tend to exacerbate anxiety. What is not known at this time, according to McNally (1994), is whether these cognitive biases precede or follow the development of panic disorder. There are some findings suggesting that they precede the manifestation of anxiety disorders. There are further debates and studies in the literature attempting to answer the question whether a cognitive style characterized by catastrophic thinking exists prior to or subsequent to the manifestation of panic disorder, i.e., are we observing trait or state anxiety. Cox (1996) points to the fact that there has been virtually no investigation into the possibility of a general *fear of death* in relationship to the development of panic disorder.

Psychodynamic Theories

Unconscious conflicts may surface when psychological defenses can no longer contain the anxiety. Very briefly, repressed sexual or other unacceptable wishes may emerge into consciousness. If the ego's defense mechanisms no longer shield the person from the danger that these unacceptable desires imply, symptoms of anxiety emerge. Panic results from feeling totally overwhelmed. Agoraphobia arises from the symbolic substitution of suppressed desires (Fyer et al. 1995). These theories have proven difficult to study and verify, nonetheless they remain popular in psychological practice.

In a small study delving into the past histories of clients with panic disorder (Shear, Cooper, Klerman, et al. 1993), clients reported having at least one parent who was critical and controlling, or angry and frightening. These clients grew up feeling frightened and guilty about aggressive feelings. This led to low self-esteem, shyness, and anxiety. In another study (Moisan and Engels 1995), high rates of sexual and/or physical abuse, the witnessing of family violence, and parental alcohol abuse were found in the histories of women with panic disorder. These experiences were likely to lead to the development of personality disorders. Furthermore, as Shear et al. (1993) speculate, the sense of emotional vulnerability and loss of control can result in neurophysiological changes, which, in turn, render the person vulnerable to panic. It is possible, according to Pollack, Otto, Rosenbaum, et al. (1992), that personality disorders are merely another manifestation of an underlying anxiety disorder.

Conclusion of Psychological Findings

As mentioned earlier in the studies of Silove et al. (1993, 1995, 1996), a number of clients have been shown to have had early separation anxiety, but it may also be that this is the result of biological factors, such as a temperament characterized by behavioral inhibition in response to the unfamiliar (Pollack et al. 1990). As with the biological studies, just because cognitive-behavior therapy has proven successful does not in itself prove that psychological vulnerability caused the panic disorder. Biological and psychological factors clearly interact, and we cannot completely separate one from the other.

Triggering Stress Factors

Many clients, but not all, recall stressful life experiences prior to their first panic. These include marital or other interpersonal conflicts, e.g., frustration due to entrapment in relationships and unfair treatment by others, illness, the death of a loved one, moving, a major change in occupation, and frustration or dissatisfaction with work (Barlow 1988; Lelliott et al. 1989; Rapee 1991; Shear et al. 1993; Shulman, Cox, Swinson, et al. 1994). The stress often seems to involve a threat to the person's sense of safety and security (Rosenbaum 1992; Rosenbaum, Pollock, Otto, et al. 1995). Craske and Barlow (1993) found stress from interpersonal issues, illness, and medication or illegal substances a common occurrence. Bandura (1988) defines stress as being deprived of all means of control while being subjected to a stressor. The relinquishing of control leaves the person totally vulnerable.

I have found that stressors that led to the first panic attack often involved not being able to accept feelings from within, minimizing feelings, hoping that a problem will go away, hiding feelings from others, or not being able to stand up to others. The following are some examples from my practice. They reflect typical precipitants to panic. In the intake interview the clients were asked to describe the circumstances leading to their first panic.

- Jeannie, age 45: "I was in the process of a divorce. We were going to court, and I got a letter that day (the day of the first panic) from the credit union saying that my husband had withdrawn all the money in our joint account. I was very angry and felt helpless."

- Delores, age 37: "I had lost my baby to crib death. It happened two months after the death. I was talking to a friend and suddenly I felt the panic attack."

- Laurie, age 42: "I was separating from my husband of twelve years, and had moved to Marin County from which I was commuting to San Francisco. I was working in the same place as my husband. My first panic was crossing the Golden Gate Bridge while I was going to work."

- George, age 30: "I had just taken LSD. I had gotten out of school and was looking for a job, but I felt confused. A career did not seem attainable, and I had to settle for a lot less. My family was pressuring me. I was having difficulty making decisions."

- Gloria, age 35: "I was overwhelmed at work and felt like I was losing my mind. I was in Los Angeles visiting my mother, experiencing a lot of anger toward her and the family for their lifestyle, but I also felt a lot of guilt. While there, I had my first panic."

Integrating Theories

Panic disorder will certainly not be explained by a single biological or psychological abnormality or dysfunction. Some people are biologically vulnerable; currently, however, there is no compelling evidence for a specific central nervous system dysregulation (Otto and Pollack 1994). Even when biological dysfunction produces certain physical reactions, these do not account for all panic attacks. Panic disorder is thus a multidimensional phenomenon involving disturbances in neurobiological, autonomic nervous system function, cognitive, and behavioral domains.

Barlow (1988) summarized studies with monkeys that suggest that negative, stressful experiences early in life produced long-term, heightened anxiety. When these monkeys were later exposed to new stressful events, the anxious behavior reemerged. Both genetic and experiential factors exhibit their effects. High biological (perhaps genetic) reactivity predisposed the monkeys to more extreme anxiety reactions. When the early experiences were characterized by control and mastery, later under stress, their behavior showed more adaptive coping and less anxiety. Barlow drew the conclusion that in biologically vulnerable humans lack of control during early development may be implicated in the origins of anxiety.

A Biopsychosocial Conception of Panic

Barlow (1986, 1988, 1997) presents his biopsychosocial model in this way: A biological vulnerability to stress exists, which may involve an overreactive autonomic nervous system and/or labile neurotransmitter systems. A psychological vulnerability may involve an enhanced fear of illness or physical injury and a past learned inability to cope with life events that are unpredictable and uncontrollable. Individuals with a biological and/or psychological vulnerability to panic often have their initial panic attack in the context of a real stressor. Although there is no impending physical threat to the person's life, the fight/flight reaction is as great as if there were one, constituting a "false alarm." The perceived unpredictability and uncontrollability of the false alarm, and thus the fear that it will occur again are particularly frightening to the individual. A negative affective state is produced. The person's attention becomes narrowed and results in hypervigilance to somatic events. When the person perceives even slight physiological sensations again, fear activates the autonomic nervous system, which increases the somatic sensations, which increases fear until the point of panic is reached.

It has been hypothesized that the fear of bodily sensations is a conditioned response to internal sensations (called interoceptive conditioning) and this creates an actual phobia of physical cues. The interoceptive conditioning operates outside of the person's awareness, and the panics are perceived as uncued. This conditioning has been further shown to be relatively resistant to extinction. As the person's fear of these unpredictable and uncontrollable attacks continues, a state of anxious expectancy develops, increasing the probability of further panics. The panic attacks become "learned alarms."

Barlow uses the term "anxious apprehension" to denote the heightened fearful state, which results from combined biological, psychological, and environmental events. The end result is that the triad of panic attacks, anxious apprehension about panicking, and catastrophic misinterpretation of the symptoms is mutually reinforced and creates a cycle of increased fear and further panic attacks. As the person becomes more hypervigilant and avoidant, the tendency to interpret interoceptive and exteroceptive information as threatening increases.

For further elaboration on the psychological and integrating theories, consult the following sources: Acierno et al. (1993), Barlow (1986, 1988, 1990), Clark (1986), Clark and Ehlers (1993), Craske and Rodriguez (1994), McNally (1994), and Zarate and Agras (1994).

Behavioral Impact on Brain Functioning

Taylor and Gorman (1992) speculate that both pharmacological and cognitive-behavioral treatments affect brain sites. Positron emission tomography scanning (PET scan) studies were done with clients with obsessive-compulsive disorder (Baxter, Schwartz, Bergman, et al. 1992; Schwartz, Stoessel, Baxter, et al. 1996). This highly technical method allows the study of cerebral glucose metabolism, which is a sensitive indicator of brain function. Successful responders to both cognitive-behavioral and fluoxetine (Prozac™) treatments showed decreased caudate glucose metabolic rates compared to treatment nonresponders.

We expect that the use of these advanced technologies will continue to reveal mind/body interactions, particularly the effects of cognitive-behavior therapy on the brain function of clients with panic disorder.

Conclusion of Integrating Theories

Most researchers today agree that there is a biological contribution to panic disorder. Panic attacks may arise via a number of different neuroanatomical and neurochemical pathways, but no dysfunction is catastrophically dangerous (Barlow 1988; Gorman, Liebowitz, Fyer, et al. 1989; McNally 1994). Just as with biological models, a variety of psychological models attempt to explain panic disorder. Similar to the varied hypotheses as to the causes of panic, different treatments are available. We now know that both psychologically- and pharmacologically-based treatments potentially affect neurochemical and psychological aspects of the disorder (Gorman et al. 1989; Rosenbaum et al. 1995).

Summary

Biological theories and findings suggest that panic disorder is caused by genetic, neurochemical, suffocation-alarm, vestibular, and other abnormalities. The effects of pharmacological agents and biological challenge tests have been taken as further proof for such a biological basis. Psychological models propose that uncomfortable, albeit innocuous, symptoms are catastrophically misinterpreted, and that fear can be a conditioned response to internal sensations. People with high anxiety sensitivity, and those who have issues with control, are psychologically vulnerable. Stress frequently triggers the first panic attack, particularly when interpersonal conflict, threats to the person's sense of safety and security, illness, and/or substances (legal or illegal) are present. Integrating theories propose a biological predisposition with physiological arousal, an experience of loss of control, and the tendency to fear interoceptive cues and interpret them as threatening.

The mind and the body are inexorably connected and constantly influence each other (Barlow 1988). Hence, the etiology of panic is necessarily a complex biopsychosocial process.

3

Cognitive-Behavior Therapy for Panic Disorder

In 1986, Judd and Burrows stated that psychoanalysis, paradoxical intention, relaxation therapy, and teaching patients how to stop hyperventilating were among the approaches used to treat panic disorder, but no firm conclusions regarding their efficacy could be drawn from the existing studies. Only five years later the National Institutes of Health Consensus Statement (Treatment of Panic Disorder 1991) reported that psychodynamic psychotherapy had not proven effective for panic disorder whereas cognitive-behavior therapy (CBT) and medications had. Nonetheless, in 1994 Goisman et al. found that psychodynamic therapy continued to be the most commonly used treatment for this disorder. Zarate and Agras (1994) also commented on the enormous gap between validated treatments and the actual practice of mental health workers.

There have been a few attempts to determine whether psychodynamic psychotherapy is effective for treating panic disorder. Milrod and Shear (1991) reviewed many studies describing psychoanalytic and psychodynamic therapies for this condition. In those studies where the length of treatment was published, it was found that the majority of patients received "brief" treatment. While "brief" was not really defined, it was stated that most were seen more often than once a week. In these psychodynamic treatments, central conflicts were explored and a link sought between precipitating events, fantasies, and the symptomology. The clients' sense of loss of control over their feelings was a common denominator. Currently, until there are controlled studies on the efficacy of psychoanalytic and psychodynamic therapies, no firm conclusions can be drawn.

Research Findings on Cognitive-Behavior Therapy (CBT)

Chambless and Gillis (1993) suggest that for panic disorder treatments to be effective, cognitive change must take place such that the client no longer catastrophizes about his or her physical symptoms. The treatment does not need to be specifically cognitive to achieve this goal. It is conceivable that behavioral methods and psychopharmacotherapy also may result in cognitive change. Nevertheless, the elimination of fear is of central importance—it remains the final common pathway that must be achieved regardless of the therapeutic approach. The studies described below reflect a variety of treatments, whether cognitive, behavioral, or cognitive/behavioral. Occasionally, the distinctions blur, but I attempt to specify the type of treatment each study employed.

Panic Disorder With Mild or No Agoraphobia

A series of controlled studies demonstrated that the panic control treatment protocol (PCT), which includes interoceptive exposure and cognitive therapy, i.e., CBT, was significantly superior to placebo and wait list conditions (Barlow 1990; Barlow, Craske, Cerny, et al. 1989; Craske 1991b; Craske et al. 1991; Klosko, Barlow, Tassinari, et al. 1990). Although results from the PCT group were better than those of the (Xanax^{TM}) group, and the results of the alprazolam group were better than the placebo control group, these comparisons were not significant. Most of the alprazolam subjects were still on medication at the end of the study, in that only one out of sixteen subjects was able to withdraw from medications. When comparing PCT, PCT plus applied relaxation, applied relaxation, and wait list, about 85 percent of those who completed the PCT and PCT plus relaxation groups were panic-free. In contrast, approximately 60 percent of the relaxation group, 50 percent of the alprazolam group, 36 percent of the placebo group, and 30 percent of the wait list group were panic-free. At two years' follow-up, 81.3 percent of the PCT group, 42.9 percent of the PCT plus relaxation group, and 35.7 percent of the relaxation group were panic-free. The PCT group was significantly better than the others. Adding relaxation to the PCT protocol diminished the results. The authors concluded that although relaxation techniques are generally anxiolytic, they do not target panic specifically. At the two-year follow-up, only about 50 percent of the PCT group reached high end-state functioning; hence, many of the subjects were left with some residual anxiety and impairment in daily functioning.

In another study, cognitive therapy with behavioral techniques was compared to applied relaxation and imipramine (Clark, Salkovskis, Hackmann, et al. 1994). Clients had no, mild, or moderate agoraphobia. The number of sessions varied slightly. There were up to twelve treatment sessions and up to three booster sessions. The imipramine group was kept at the maximum dose for six months, after which medication was gradually withdrawn (with provision for maintenance sessions). Effective results were found in all three treatment groups; they fared better than clients on the wait list. Measures were also taken 15 months later, at which time 80 percent of the cognitive therapy group, 47 percent of the applied relaxation group, and 50 percent of the imipramine subjects were panic-free and did not need additional treatment. Those who had been on imipramine were significantly more likely to relapse within the fifteen-month period compared with those receiving cognitive therapy. Clients from any group who continued to misinterpret physical symptoms in a catastrophic manner at the end of treatment fared less well at follow-up. The cognitive therapy group was significantly more effective on several panic and anxiety measures.

Panic Disorder With Agoraphobia

Treatment of specific phobias began with Wolpe's systematic desensitization work, but it proved less efficacious in ameliorating agoraphobia. In vivo exposure proved to be a more effective treatment and, furthermore, it had more lasting effects. There are several hypotheses regarding the psychological mechanisms underlying the effects of exposure on agoraphobia. Zarate and Agras (1994) summarize the main hypotheses as follows:

1. Extinction or habituation of fear responses

2. Increase in personal self-efficacy upon successful confrontation

3. Alterations in cognitive fear representations in memory

A cross-national study compared the following treatment conditions: Alprazolam and exposure, alprazolam and relaxation (considered a psychological placebo), placebo and exposure, and placebo and relaxation (Marks, Swinson, Başoğlu, et al. 1993). The 154 patients had eight weeks of treatment and were followed up to forty-three weeks. All groups improved on panic measures. On the nonpanic measures (phobias, mood, and general disability) both exposure and alprazolam were effective, however, exposure was twice as effective as alprazolam. Only the subjects in the exposure group maintained their gains at follow-up, however. It is noteworthy that although the combined therapies of alprazolam and exposure showed good results during treatment, the improvement diminished over time.

In a meta-analysis, assessing the effect of behavior therapies on agoraphobia, Trull, Nietzel, and Main (1988) determined that in vivo exposure in particular produces significant outcomes, as measured by self-reports, and the results are maintained at follow-up. However, exposure alone is problematic (Craske and Rodriguez 1994; Hoffart 1993; Michelson and Marchione 1991). The authors report that the dropout rate from in vivo exposure tends to be approximately 12 percent. Furthermore, although 50 percent of clients show significant improvement, only about 25 percent recover fully, i.e., show no avoidance behavior. From about 30 to 40 percent fail to improve (Barlow 1988). Therefore, in vivo exposure is best integrated with other cognitive-behavioral methods.

Another study compared twelve sessions (the full treatment) of cognitive therapy (CT) with eight sessions of supportive psychotherapy (Beck, Sokol, Clark, et al. 1992). After eight weeks of either treatment, those receiving CT showed a significant reduction in panic symptoms and general anxiety compared to the supportive therapy group. Seventy-one percent of subjects in the CT group were panic-free versus 25 percent in the psychotherapy group. Afterwards, most clients from the psychotherapy group elected to receive CT. There were further improvements in this CT group at the end of twelve weeks, again, in panic and general anxiety, as well as in avoidance measures. Most clients maintained their improvement after one year.

Applied relaxation was compared with in vivo exposure and with cognitive therapy (Öst, Westling, and Hellström 1993). Each participant received twelve individual therapy sessions and self-exposure instructions. Clients in all three treatment modes showed significant improvement when compared to their pretreatment status, and the improvements were maintained one year posttreatment. In this study, it is possible that the self-exposure component accounted for the improvement seen in all the groups.

One study compared pre- and posttreatment status without employing a comparison group (Fava, Zielezny, Savron, et al. 1995). The authors wanted to study the long-term effect of exposure treatment. Treatment consisted of twelve sessions of thirty minutes each. Patients were given close guidance in doing exposure work and subsequently showed their exposure diaries to the therapist. Almost 88 percent had been taking benzodiazepines regularly before behavior therapy; however, the drugs were tapered off and discontinued during treatment when at all possible. By the end of behavior therapy, 24.7 percent were still taking benzodiazepines, but in lesser quantities. Of the ninety-three patients who completed treatment, eighty-one were found to be panic-free and judged much improved in agoraphobic avoidance. They were followed two to nine years later. Many had maintained the gains. When there was a relapse, another course of behavior therapy was given, but of shorter duration. No patient relapsed more than once. The authors found that status at the end of treatment strongly predicted long-term outcome. The results were worse in patients with personality disorder and residual agoraphobia at the completion of treatment. The authors concluded that these findings, along with those of other studies, challenge the view that long-term drug treatment is the most appropriate therapy for patients with panic disorder and agoraphobia.

A more individually tailored program was attempted, where clients received between eight and twenty-four individual sessions (Shear, Ball, Fitzpatrick, et al. 1991). The components were psychoeducation, diaphragmatic breathing, progressive muscle relaxation, cognitive restructuring, and interoceptive and in vivo exposures. Some assertiveness work was included. After treatment, 83 percent no longer had full-blown panics. There was improvement on all phobia measures (these clients were only mildly phobic), general anxiety, and overall level of functioning.

Other Versions of CBT

Few studies have been done to measure the outcome of group therapy. However, the few that have been done show it to be a very effective mode of treatment (Evans, Holt, and Oei 1991; Marchione, Michelson, Greenwald et al. 1987; Margraf, Barlow, Clark, et al. 1993; Telch, Schmidt, Jaimez, et al. 1995). Some researchers have concluded that group therapy is equally or more effective than individual treatment (Michelson and Marchione 1991). It is both time-efficient and cost-effective (Gould et al. 1995).

In the study by Marchione et al. (1987), there were sixteen group therapy sessions with four to six subjects per group. The patients' significant others were invited to the first two sessions to foster social support and facilitate in vivo practice. Sessions three to sixteen differed according to one of three treatment conditions: In the therapist-directed graduated exposure (GE), patients were told to remain in situations until they felt comfortable; the second condition entailed GE plus cognitive restructuring; and the third involved GE plus progressive relaxation. The combined treatments were most potent when compared to GE alone, providing further support for an integrated treatment package.

Other, less traditional, approaches have been tried. Some researchers found that therapy delivered in eight sessions of one-hour duration over the phone was very effective in reducing phobic avoidance, fear, and anticipatory anxiety (Swinson, Fergus, Cox, et al. 1995). One of the latest developments is computer-generated virtual reality graded exposure. This was tried successfully with individuals with fear of heights (acrophobia) (Rothbaum, Hodges, Kooper, et al. 1995). The authors predict that it will be used widely in exposure-based treatments of anxiety disorders. It allows for therapist guidance without requiring the time needed for doing in vivo exposures. In refractory cases of agoraphobia, i.e., those not benefiting from outpatient treatment, inpatient treatment has been tried, but it is very expensive (Pollard, Obermeier, and Cox 1987).

A study was conducted to assess the efficacy of cognitive-behavior therapy applied by clinicians, who had not been previously trained in behavioral techniques (Welkowitz, Papp, Cloitre, et al. 1991). They provided a twelve-session treatment course to clients with panic disorder who preferred nonpharmacological treatment or had failed medication treatment. The successful outcomes were somewhat lower than those in behavioral centers. The clinicians found that the lack of prior, formal CBT training made it difficult to stay focused on the cognitive and behavioral aspects, especially when they ran into difficulties. They concluded that it is not enough to learn techniques without also acquiring a thorough understanding of the underlying theory.

One study compared CBT with "nonprescriptive" treatment (NPT) (Shear, Pilkonis, Cloitre, et al. 1994). The first three sessions of both treatment conditions identified the anxiety components (physical sensations, thoughts, and behaviors) and stressed that anxiety and panic are not dangerous. The physiology of panic and hyperventilation was also covered. In the CBT condition, the remaining twelve sessions focused on breathing retraining, cognitive restructuring, interoceptive exposure, and in vivo homework exposure. The intervention in the twelve sessions of the NPT group focused on life problems and identifying the triggering stressors. The message was that if these problems and stressors were dealt with, anxiety and panic would diminish. Both treatments showed similar outcomes.

Craske, Maidenberg, and Bystritsky (1995) compared four sessions of nondirective, supportive therapy similar to that described above with four sessions of CBT. The first session was the same for both therapeutic conditions. Sessions two to four in nondirective therapy focused on the relationship of anxiety and panic to daily life stressors. The results showed that CBT provides significantly superior results for panic disorder, worry about panic, and phobic fear, but not for general distress. Although the clients had signed up for medication treatment, 38 percent declined pharmacotherapy after the short intervention with CBT. These findings suggest that CBT is even more effective in the more common format of twelve to sixteen sessions. The authors conclude that CBT should be the first treatment option. Thereafter, additional CBT and/or pharmacotherapy can be offered. In real life, however, medications are usually given first.

Conclusion on CBT Findings

To conclude, excellent studies from various countries show over 80 percent of clients with panic disorder becoming panic-free after short-term, cognitive-behavior therapy, and these outcomes are maintained one to two years later (Clark and Ehlers 1993; Margraf et al. 1993; Michelson and Marchione 1991). Improvement has been seen in general anxiety, phobic avoidance, anticipatory anxiety, and depression.

There is consensus among a number of researchers that integrated, multimodal treatments are most effective at this time, i.e., those that encompass the major therapeutic components to be discussed below (Gould et al. 1995; van den Hout et al. 1994; Lidren, Watkins, Gould, et al. 1994; Marchione et al. 1987; Margraf et al. 1993; Telch et al. 1995). Multimodal treatments help prevent drop-out from treatment (Margraf et al. 1993). Also, it is generally agreed that panic attacks require panic-focused treatment, while agoraphobia must be treated with exposure, preferably performance-based exposure.

Components of Effective CBT

Psychoeducation, breathing retraining, cognitive restructuring, interoceptive exposure, in vivo exposure in agoraphobia, and relapse prevention are deemed the necessary components of a multimodal cognitive-behavioral treatment package. A brief rendition of each follows.

Psychoeducation

This component provides the information and rationale for the treatment. Panic disorder is seen as arising from a combination of biological, psychological, and stress factors. When clients ask why they developed this disorder, I respond that it is impossible to know the precise contribution of each factor for any given person. Clients are taught the physiology of fear, anxiety, and panic, and anxiety is demystified and normalized. A panic attack is a response with physiological, cognitive, and behavioral components. The goal of treatment is to change the catastrophic view of panics and phobias via cognitive and behavioral methods. The client learns coping techniques for dealing with panics directly and for confronting fearful situations. These techniques are aimed at raising the client's self-efficacy (confidence in his or her ability to cope).

Breathing Retraining and Relaxation

Breathing retraining involves teaching the client slow, diaphragmatic breathing. When doing an overbreathing test, 50 to 60 percent of panickers describe the symptoms produced by the acute hyperventilation as being very similar to panic attack symptoms (Craske and

Rodriguez 1994; Salkovskis and Clark 1991). If the person is a chronic hyperventilator or experiences panic-induced, acute hyperventilation, diaphragmatic breathing offers somatic management of physiological symptoms. It is a helpful coping skill even for those who do not hyperventilate.

As Barlow (1997) points out, breathing retraining constitutes the weakest contribution to the cognitive-behavioral treatment of panic disorder, but clients like it and attribute great gains to it. I have also observed that many clients find diaphragmatic breathing exceedingly valuable. It appears, among other things, to give them a great sense of control.

Relaxation also may be useful in reducing fear and anxiety when it is taught as an active coping strategy. When used in the initial stages of anxiety, it can break the escalating panic cycle. It helps to provide a sense of control and mastery (Michelson et al. 1990). If a relaxation procedure is to be taught, Öst's Applied Relaxation (cue-controlled relaxation) is more effective than more passive methods (Öst 1987, 1988). However, although Öst found that applied relaxation has a positive outcome on panic disorder, other researchers have concluded it does not appear to be as potent for addressing panic disorder as other targeted, cognitive-behavioral interventions (Barlow et al. 1989; Margraf et al. 1993; Marks, Gray, Cohen, et al. 1983; Michelson and Marchione 1991). One recent study (Stanley, Beck, Averill, et al. 1996) compared the efficacy of cognitive therapy and relaxation over ten weeks without exposure and found that, although cognitive therapy skills took longer to acquire than relaxation skills, they were more effective at the end of treatment. (Note that relaxation is often used as a psychological placebo in research, i.e., it is the equivalent to pill placebo usage in drug studies.)

In any case, if you teach relaxation techniques to clients with panic disorder, you must be prepared to deal with clients whose anxieties will *increase*, sometimes to the point of panic, when they attempt to relax. This was observed by Waddell, Barlow, and O'Brien (1984). They also found that diaphragmatic breathing was less likely to increase panic. If you become aware of a client's fear of relaxation, you can use relaxation as an interoceptive exposure, thus helping the client to decondition from that fear.

Cognitive Restructuring

Clients with panic disorder feel that they cannot think clearly or realistically while they are in the throes of a panic attack. This cognitive difficulty has to do with the compelling pull of danger-related thoughts when feeling anxious.

Thoughts and beliefs concerning the perceived dangerousness, unpredictability, and uncontrollability of panic need to be challenged with the use of cognitive restructuring techniques. Theories and techniques for such cognitive restructuring have been developed by a number of prominent researchers and clinicians (Beck and Emery, with Greenberg 1985; Clark 1989; Clark and Ehlers 1993; Salkovskis and Clark 1991; Sokol, Beck, Greenberg, et al. 1989). The goal of cognitive restructuring is to modify the client's catastrophic misinterpretations of the bodily sensations produced by anxiety and panic. Over the course of treatment, by learning how to access corrective and helpful information, clients increasingly substitute logic for catastrophic misinterpretation of bodily sensations and thereby decrease rather than increase anxiety and panic symptoms. These cognitive changes are achieved via verbal challenges and behavioral experiments.

Verbal Challenges Purport to:

- Identify the sequence of symptoms and thoughts in a panic.

- Monitor and record automatic thoughts related to panic and phobias.

- Recognize which cognitive errors the automatic thoughts represent.

- Challenge the automatic thoughts by providing new information contradicting the misinterpretation.

- Generate alternative, accurate, and credible explanations regarding the physical sensations.

- Demonstrate via belief ratings that the automatic thoughts do not withstand empirical scrutiny.

Much of this work is accomplished by means of Socratic dialogue (see chapter 5), which has a decidedly larger impact on the client than if the therapist attempts to provide quick explanations, and is more likely to produce lasting change.

Behavioral Experiments Purport to:

- Demonstrate the true cause of the symptoms by means of interoceptive exercises.

- Test the catastrophic interpretations and predictions concerning the consequences of symptoms during panic and phobic situations.

It has been argued and demonstrated in studies that cognitive techniques are effective without the behavioral experiments. However, in regard to the interoceptive component, some authors have recommended including it (Salkovskis, Clark, and Hackmann 1991), some others consider it essential (Barlow 1986, 1988; Hoffart 1993).

Reduction of negative cognitions seems to be significant for the maintenance of improvement (Chambless and Gillis 1993; Clark 1986; Clark et al. 1994; Hoffart 1993; Rachman 1993). Cognitive changes (correction of the misinterpretations and misappraisals of danger) must take place—by whatever avenue—and sometimes this is achieved through exposure alone (Chambless and Gillis 1993; Margraf et al. 1993; Rachman 1993).

Cognitive Restructuring Vis-à-Vis Superficial Changes in Self-Talk

A number of researchers believe that if the cognitive work is aimed solely at changing the content of thoughts (or self-statements) compared to focusing on core beliefs (the processes and structures of cognition), they are then targeting only the most superficial level (Chambless and Gillis 1993; Hoffart 1993; Michelson and Marchione 1991; Rachman 1993; Salkovskis and Clark 1991). Hence, the cognitive interventions must target the panic-specific fear structure and impact on the core beliefs. Often, these kinds of cognitive shifts are slow to develop and may take weeks. Otto and Whittal (1995) contend that although pharmacotherapy may be effective for reducing panic and anxiety, the core fears are not necessarily impacted by the medications.

Interoceptive Exposure

As discussed above, cognitive therapists often use behavioral experiments to test clients' assumptions and beliefs. The difference between them and cognitive-behavior therapists may be very small indeed. If there is a difference, it is in the emphasis on the behavioral strategies used and in the therapist's theoretical background, but, as a rule, cognitive and behavioral techniques cannot be fully separated (Hoffart 1993). Sometimes, it is confusing to ascertain what different researchers mean by "cognitive-behavior approaches," especially if they also use the term "behavioral interventions" in the same context, without clarifying whether they are talking about the same or different strategies.

Barlow's group places a great deal of emphasis on behavioral interventions in their own right and not simply to test the validity of an hypothesis. They contend that the deeply entrenched, automatic associations between bodily cues and the learned alarm reaction (panic) are, in part, conditioned and are best altered via exposure to the feared interoceptive cues (Barlow 1986, 1988; Craske and Rodriguez 1994; Rapee and Barlow 1988).

Interoceptive exposure is usually introduced after cognitive restructuring has begun (Barlow and Craske 1994; Craske, Meadows, and Barlow 1994). It is practiced hand-in-hand with the cognitive work in that the client is instructed to challenge the negative cognitions arising during the exposures. Usually interoceptive exercises are first practiced in the office, followed by the same exposures at home and in other places to allow for generalization. By repeating the interoceptive exposures, extinction of fear is accomplished (not unlike exposure to fearful outside situations, e.g., driving); and cognitive modification is achieved through the disconfirmation of catastrophic outcomes.

Michelson (1984), in studying individual differences and treatment consonance, distinguishes between fears that are acquired via conditioning (involving psychophysiological and behavioral channels) and those acquired cognitively (based on expectations of danger, cognitive appraisal, or misinformation). He recommends that treatment should be based accordingly. However, it is not possible at this time to make these distinctions of how the fear was acquired or to be able predict the outcome of a specific intervention.

In Vivo Exposure in Agoraphobia

Agoraphobic avoidance is persistent and unremitting if not treated (Barlow 1988; Pecknold 1993). One cannot assume that cognitive shifts automatically result in reduction of avoidance behavior. This is because the relationship between panic attacks and avoidance is quite complex. It involves, among other things, the predictability of panic, the use of safety signals, and the appraisal of danger (Michelson et al. 1990). In vivo exposure means repeated confrontation with or approach to an object or situation that is avoided. This type of exposure can be considered the essence of the behavioral treatment of agoraphobia (Barlow 1988; Craske and Rodriguez 1994; Sholomskas and Woods 1992). It has been shown that heart rate habituates rather rapidly when exposed to fearful stimuli, even to stimuli that provoke intense fear (Sartory, Rachman, and Grey 1977). Although it has been postulated that for habituation to occur, the levels of anxiety must be sufficiently high and long-lasting to activate the fear structure (Foa and Kozak 1986), other researchers have found that this does not have to be the case (Williams and Zane 1989; Williams 1990). Both Williams and Zane have found that guiding the client in the exposures in order to increase his or her sense of mastery (guided mastery treatment) was more effective than simple exposure. Guided mastery treatment includes identifying and eliminating self-protective rituals as well as achieving a realistic cognitive appraisal of successful exposures. (See chapters 5 and 8.)

Agoraphobia has cognitive features, i.e., thoughts and images that are anxiety-producing (Marchione et al. 1987). They often include issues regarding control and the ability to deal with the perceived danger associated with the object or situation. In their study, van Hout, Emmelkamp, and Scholing (1994) found that habituation alone did not explain the positive effects of exposure. Clients who improved exhibited substantially less negative self-talk during exposures than those with limited improvement. The authors speculated that the latter group could have benefited from cognitive therapy. These findings show again that cognitive change does not occur in everyone as a consequence of exposure alone.

Van den Hout et al. (1994) studied the impact of exposure and cognitive therapy on agoraphobia and panic. They found that cognitive therapy reduced panic but not agoraphobia, while in vivo exposure reduced agoraphobia but not panic. They concluded that in vivo exposure is crucial in the treatment of agoraphobia. The authors reported findings from other studies in which agoraphobics have benefited from cognitive therapy aimed at social fears (being laughed at, thought of as weird, and/or embarrassing others) and fears regarding loss of control (fear of screaming, becoming hysterical, going crazy). Indeed, Poulton and Andrews (1996) found that treatment combining cognitive and behavioral methods significantly reduced irrational cognitions pertaining to physical illness and loss of control (including the fear of going insane) in agoraphobic patients. A pilot study was done to determine if interoceptive exposure (without cognitive restructuring) adds to the effect of in vivo exposure on agoraphobic avoidance (Ito, Noshirvani, Başoğlu, et al. 1996). Although the results were nonsignificant, they support such a conclusion, but as the authors state, this must be studied on a larger scale.

Interpersonal issues may play a role in the development, maintenance, and treatment of agoraphobia. Although no firm conclusions as to their effects can be drawn at this time, it appears that there is some benefit in including spouses (or significant others) in every aspect of the treatment (Craske and Barlow 1994).

Relapse Prevention

Strategic planning for relapse is deemed an important, even indispensable, part of treatment. Provisions need to be made for setbacks, recurrence, and relapse. If clients have been well prepared for a recurrence of symptoms, they may be able to ward off a relapse of the syndrome. It is the emphasis on skill development in CBT that helps clients retain benefits after treatment termination (Otto and Whittal 1995). On the other hand, the authors contend that when clients are withdrawn from medications, the untreated fear of anxiety symptoms and the loss of the pill as a safety signal lead to high rates of relapse upon discontinuation of medications, especially from benzodiazepines.

Craske and Rodriguez (1994) consider the following a key factor in relapse prevention: practicing in vivo exposures long enough for the client to become habituated to the fearful situation. In addition, it is helpful for the client to expose himself/herself to the situation where the fear first started. As long as there is residual avoidance, the likelihood of relapse is greater. It also strengthens treatment gains to do interoceptive exposures in the field, especially in situations where panics are likely to occur.

Information Processing and Learning: Application to Cognitive-Behavioral Treatment of Panic Disorder

According to Epstein (1994) people perceive reality and adapt to the world by two main systems: Rational and Experiential. They have constructs about the self and the world in both systems, and all behavior is seen as a product of the joint operation of the two systems.

1. The Intuitive-Experiential information-processing system is natural, nonverbal, automatic, and narrative. It is generally adaptive in concrete, natural situations, and in some situations it is smarter than the rational system. The implicit beliefs or schemata found here are mainly generalizations derived from emotionally significant past experience. Hence, it is often associated with affect.

2. The Analytical-Rational information-processing system requires effort and is verbal and deliberative. This abstract system operates in the medium of language and is more affect-free. Epstein labels the constructs here "beliefs." Although capable of high levels of abstraction, it responds rather inefficiently to everyday events.

How These Systems of Information Processing Relate to Fears

According to Epstein, irrational fears are examples of nonrational information processing. Yet people hold onto unrealistic, distressing beliefs at great personal cost, even while recognizing that they do not make sense. How does this happen? When highly emotional, e.g., frightened by certain stimuli, the natural tendency is to think in categorical, personal, and concrete ways. Because the automatic processing of the experiential system requires less effort and is more efficient, it may dominate the rational system, and thus the fear-driven information processing will seem valid. People then believe that the nonrational, experientially derived judgment is rational. Only when they place this automatic thinking under the scrutiny of the rational mind, do they come to realize that their fear does not make sense.

The objective of therapy is to produce changes in the experiential system, changing the maladaptive schemata. Although affect plays an important role in the acquisition of information in the experiential system, as behavior is practiced, it becomes increasingly proceduralized and affect-free. There are three ways to influence and change the maladaptive schemata in the experiential system:

1. Using the rational system to influence the experiential system (disputing irrational thoughts, as in cognitive therapy).

2. Learning directly from experience, i.e., working through the experience in real life.

3. Communicating with the experiential system in imagery and fantasy.

If you keep this conceptualization in mind, you will see how well it applies to the treatment of panic disorder with cognitive-behavior therapy. Cognitive restructuring is a way of influencing the experiential system using the power of the rational mind. It is, however, not fully effective with all clients. Many clients will say, "Yes, it all makes sense, but how do I change my emotional reaction?" They often convey the belief that their reactions cannot be changed simply via reasoning. This is consistent with Epstein's theory: Intellectual understanding, even when profound, is never enough.

Indeed, many, if not most, clients need the additional interoceptive and in vivo exposures in order to have new, first-hand experiences that disconfirm the catastrophic outcome they expect. This is best seen in the work with agoraphobia, where cognitive restructuring usually will not change the avoidance pattern, and in vivo exposure is required. Furthermore, exposures must be repeated over and over for the fear to subside. Changes in the experiential mind do not take place easily. (According to Craske and Rodriguez (1994), individuals with agoraphobia overestimate the degree of panic and fear they expect to feel and only through repeated disconfirmation of these overpredictions is the therapeutic effect achieved.) As mentioned previously, some researchers emphasize the need for the client to experience high levels of anxiety arousal during exposure, while others do not find that to be necessary. These findings are consistent with the information processing of the experiential system, which is slower to change, but does change with repetitive or intense experience.

Treatment Outcome

Using outcome measures to track your client's progress over time allows you to conduct patient-focused research, from which you can learn about the effectiveness of the treatment you are providing. These measures are far better than therapists' global impressions.

Outcome Predictors

Factors that influence posttreatment outcome are as follows: Continued fear of anxiety sensations, the severity of agoraphobia, a longer duration of the illness, older age, past history of depression, drug dose, duration of drug treatment, withdrawal symptoms during taper, and how strongly the client attributes improvement to medications (Başoğlu, Marks, Swinson, et al. 1994c; Craske and Rodriguez 1994).

Improvement in Panic Disorder Versus Agoraphobia

Increasingly, researchers question measures of panic as the primary criterion for treatment outcome, especially when panic disorder is accompanied by agoraphobia. Panic and avoidance behavior seem to improve independently during treatment, so global improvement may be more a function of a decrease in avoidance behavior than frequency of panic attacks. Therefore, avoidance must be assessed (Başoğlu 1992; Başoğlu et al. 1994b).

Assessing/Measuring Treatment Outcome

Treatment success is a relative phenomenon. Clients welcome any relief from symptoms that allows them to function better and to experience less anxiety, and this is especially true in severe cases. Ideally, we would like the client to be able to lead a life free from excessive anxiety, to function at a level equivalent to the premorbid level, and not to require ongoing treatment, whether psychotherapy or pharmacotherapy.

It is very helpful to monitor our clients' progress objectively. Some of Shear and Maser's (1994) published recommendations for outcome measurement in research apply to clinical settings. I have found the following particularly helpful.

1. **Diagnosis**

   Structured interviews. I find these to be exceedingly helpful. When a client says that he or she has panic disorder, or even panic attacks, the statements do not always correspond with an accurate clinical diagnosis. Yet even when a client has made a correct diagnosis, the structured interview gives the therapist a more precise profile on the particular fears experienced, and helps indicate where to target the treatment. You will also want to determine the presence of any comorbid diagnoses (see chapter 1). For these purposes, the *Anxiety Disorders Interview Schedule-IV* (*ADIS-IV*, DiNardo et al. 1994) and the *Structured Clinical Interview for DSM-IV, Axis I, Clinical Version* (First, Gibbon, Spitzer, et al. 1996) are excellent instruments. (Both are too lengthy for regular clinical use and shorter versions would be welcome.)

2. **Occurrence of Panic, Fear About Panic Symptoms, and Avoidance Behavior**

   (a) Occurrence of panic: A record of panic attacks two to four weeks prior to treatment serves as an excellent baseline measure. This can then be compared to the records taken during and at the end of treatment, and preferably at a later follow-up date.

   (b) Fear about panic symptoms: (This includes confidence in the ability to cope with panic and anxiety sensitivity.) The Anxiety Sensitivity Index (ASI) is a good questionnaire that measures concerns regarding the consequences of experiencing anxiety symptoms (Reiss et al. 1986; Bruce, Spiegel, Gregg, et al. 1995). In other studies, the ASI has demonstrated significant decrease in scores as a result of cognitive-behavior therapy and is a sensitive measure (Hazen, Walker, and Eldridge 1996; McNally and

Lorenz 1987). It has been suggested that the continued presence of fear of anxiety symptoms at posttreatment signals a higher probability of relapse.

(c) Avoidance behavior: The Fear Questionnaire assesses agoraphobia, social phobia, and blood-injury phobia (Marks and Mathews 1979; Cox, Swinson, and Shaw 1991b, Mizes and Crawford 1986), and the Mobility Inventory for Agoraphobia distinguishes between situations avoided when accompanied and alone (Chambless, Caputo, Jasin, et al. 1985; Cox, Swinson, Kuch, et al. 1993a). Both are used extensively.

The Self-Efficacy Scales for Agoraphobia (Kinney and Williams 1988) are more accurate reflectors of avoidance behavior. The battery consists of hierarchies of specific behavioral tasks in different areas of functioning, listed in order of difficulty. The client rates his or her confidence in performing the task. These scales are rather lengthy. However, the authors suggest that the therapist prepare ad hoc self-efficacy measures according to need. You can ask your client to describe how confident he or she feels about engaging in any given task, and this measure can be taken at various points during treatment.

3. **Anxiety and Depression**
   (a) Two excellent and well-tested measures of anxiety and depression are the Beck Anxiety Inventory (Beck, Epstein, Brown, et al. 1988) and the Beck Depression Inventory (Beck, Ward, Mendelson, et al. 1961).

   (b) The Burns Depression Checklist and Burns Anxiety Inventory have been validated as well (Burns 1997). The Brief-Mood Survey, a shorter version, can be used easily by the clinician in various settings to assess depression, anxiety, panic, and anger. I have started to use the latter weekly with some of my groups, and I have found it exceedingly helpful.

4. **Level of Disability**
   It is imperative to assess disability in the following areas: Work, family and home life, and social and recreational activities. It has been shown that the best prediction of disability after treatment is disability at baseline, and 20 percent of patients may remain disabled (Katschnig, Amering, Stolk, et al. 1996). Note that symptom severity per se does not predict disability.

Summary

Research shows that over 80 percent of clients with panic disorder become panic-free after short-term, cognitive-behavior therapy. Improvement is also seen in general anxiety, phobic avoidance, anticipatory anxiety, and depression. The results are maintained one to two years posttreatment. Integrated, multimodal treatments work best. The effective components are psychoeducation, breathing retraining, cognitive restructuring, interoceptive exposure, and in vivo exposure in agoraphobia. Relapse prevention strategies must be incorporated. Outcome measures allow the clinician to assess the efficacy of treatment.

Irrational fears in panic disorder convey nonrational information processing in the experiential system. The main strategies to bring about change in this system are the use of cognitive methods to dispute irrational thoughts, learning from direct experience, i.e., behavioral methods, and accessing the experiential system in imagery.

4

Treatment Module I: Psychoeducation and Breathing Retraining *(Sessions 1–3)*

Overview of Module I

The goal of Module I is to educate your client about the nature of fear, anxiety, and panic, and more specifically, the physiological and emotional connection between true alarms (fear reaction to life-threatening events) and panic. It is often a relief for clients to know that there are innocuous explanations for the symptoms that are experienced during a panic.

Next, you want to demonstrate how closely linked hyperventilation and panic symptoms are, although as you will recall, hyperventilation does not *cause* panic. Finally, your client will learn how to do diaphragmatic breathing and will understand its application to high-anxiety and panic situations.

Session 1

I start this session by stating what the expectations of treatment are, as I did at the end of the assessment interview (see chapter 1). I then ask the client to show me Worksheet 1: Panic Frequency and Intensity and I give assistance as needed. I also ask whether there are any questions about chapters 1 through 6 in *An End to Panic: Breakthrough Techniques for Overcoming Panic Disorder* (Zuercher-White 1995). Then, I familiarize the client briefly with Worksheet 2: My Personal Coping Affirmations. In this worksheet, clients record useful phrases and other reminders of helpful techniques they will learn. I introduce the client to the worksheet during the session by asking if there was anything in chapters 1 through 6 that seemed worthwhile to record in the worksheet. Clients are then instructed to bring Worksheets 1 and 2 to every session.

In this first treatment session, I cover information about anxiety and the physiology of fear and panic (in a more condensed form than presented here), and the three components of anxiety and panic. Thus, this session is more didactic than all later ones. Even though I usually stay with the task at hand and do not digress, I do invite pertinent questions and use a flow chart to illustrate the material. I also ask clients to fill out Worksheet 3: The Components of a Panic Attack and to bring it to all sessions of Modules I and II. This worksheet is used to break down the specific details of panic attacks and highly anxious situations (e.g., phobic encounters). Hence, I expect clients to fill out Worksheet 3 whether or not they have had panic attacks.

Worksheet 2: **My Personal Coping Affirmations**

1. *Don't bolt! I will stay put and continue doing what I was doing, even if it is hard.*

2. _____

3. _____

4. _____

5. _____

6. _____

7. _____

8. _____

9. _____

10. _____

At the end of this and each subsequent session, I give the client the task of reading the equivalent section in *An End to Panic* and of making a brief report at the beginning of the following session. This report consists primarily of questions the client may have, or the recounting of items that he or she found helpful or interesting. Consequently, I start each session by asking for a brief report on the reading material. This greatly increases client compliance with the reading assignments. In a group I often divide the material to be covered among the group's participants. At the end of this session I also help with setting up the first exposure assignments with the client (see chapter 8).

Session 2

I ask clients to share Worksheets 1 through 3. The information on nocturnal panics, fainting, and biological "toughening up" is conveyed in Sessions 2 and 3 of this module, often in response to questions. The information on fainting is presented here in a factual manner, without attempting to convince the client that he or she will not faint. This fear is usually worked on extensively in the cognitive restructuring phase (Treatment Module II).

After the brief review on the physiology of panic, I quickly move in this session to the breathing retraining. I do little preparation for the overbreathing test. I simply say that I will go over the physiology of breathing but that I first want to take an overbreathing test with the client to assess how much breathing is an issue. I go over the exclusionary criteria and then I overbreathe with the client. This is followed by a brief report on the sensations produced, which allows me to introduce the physiology of breathing and hyperventilation. Next, I have the client take a deep breath in and out, on which I comment. I go over the various ways to stop hyperventilation. Finally, I teach diaphragmatic breathing, demonstrating the steps involved.

Session 3

In this session, I again ask the client to share Worksheets 1 through 3. I have the client stand up and show me the progress he or she has made on the diaphragmatic breathing. I ask how much the diaphragmatic breathing was practiced and I often encourage the client to practice even more. I describe how to extend this type of breathing to everyday life and subsequently to high-anxiety situations and panic. In the next session (Module II), I ask the client to again demonstrate the diaphragmatic breathing, and I make comments and plans for further follow-up, as needed.

Section 1: The Physiology of Fear and Panic Attacks

To introduce the subject of the physiology of fear and panic, I like to begin by asking the client, "Is anxiety a good thing or a bad thing?" Many clients will say that it is "bad," while others have recognized the tremendous value of anxiety. Building on their responses, I point out that anxiety is a naturally occurring emotion. It is a genetically programmed alarm or alerting mechanism that arouses us, thereby activating our defenses when we are confronted with life-threatening danger. Hence, it is important for self-preservation. The alarm also goes off when we perceive a threat to another significant person, such as a child or a spouse. Another benefit of anxiety is that it motivates us to undertake challenges, and to make plans for the future. Anxiety also helps alert us to an unresolved problem, especially when we are attempting to ignore or otherwise deny the problem exists. On the other hand, when anxiety becomes excessive, it can debilitate and inhibit our functioning. The goal of therapy is not to eliminate anxiety but learn how to manage and channel it so it does not interfere with our lives.

Fear: The Fight/Flight Response to Threat

In order to understand panic, we need to first look at and understand the mechanisms of fear. The information on fear and panic in this chapter is based on the following sources: Barlow and Craske (1994); Craske and Barlow (1993), Goldstein (1987), Guyton (1991), and Selye (1976).

Stress can be positive or negative. In principle, the most important negative stressor is a threat to one's life. The physiological response to this threat has evolved over eons through natural selection. It allows us to react rapidly to threats, thereby ensuring the organism's (and the species') survival. This reaction is variously called the fight/flight response, the alarm response, or the stress response. The "fight/flight" response asserts that the reaction involves either fighting the danger or fleeing from it.

The fight/flight response involves activation of the autonomic nervous system. This system controls the visceral (internal organs) functions of the body, such as gastrointestinal functions, body temperature, sweating, arterial pressure, as well as many others. It is capable of producing intense internal changes very rapidly, even within seconds. The autonomic nervous system has two main branches, the sympathetic nervous system (SNS) and the parasympathetic nervous system (PNS). Both the SNS and PNS excite some organs and inhibit others. The SNS mobilizes the body for the fight/flight response, while the PNS is responsible for restoring the body to a more normal and relaxed state, hence the two maintain balance in the body. The hypothalamus is the main subcortical center that regulates sympathetic nervous system activity.

When a person perceives threat, fear, or severe pain, the hypothalamus is activated, sending a signal to the SNS. The SNS then discharges (i.e., is fired off) as a unit, called a mass discharge, resulting in a widespread reaction, the so-called stress, alarm, or fight/flight response. (Note that at other times, e.g., in heat regulation, only isolated parts of the SNS are activated.) The mass discharge allows the body to engage in strenuous physical activity very quickly, which is usually not possible. The main SNS effects on the body are as follows:

- Cardiovascular: The heart muscle increases its pulse rate and the force of contraction. If the heart is seen as a pump, it increases its effectiveness. It allows blood flow to be redistributed, so that more flows to the skeletal muscles. The increased output of the heart and resulting greater blood flow allow more oxygen and glucose to be delivered to the muscles (glucose is released into the blood by the liver) facilitating the greater muscular strength needed in the fight/flight response. There is decreased blood flow to the skin, hands, and feet; and, as a result, the extremities may be perceived as numb, tingling, and cold. The digestive processes are suspended.

- Pulmonary: Breathing becomes deeper and faster to maximize oxygen intake.

- Skin and Sweat Glands: There is decreased blood flow to the skin through vascular constriction. The sweat glands are activated. Sweating prevents body temperature from reaching dangerous levels.

- Other Physical Effects: Pupils dilate to increase the visual field. The rate of blood coagulation increases to protect against hemorrhage, blood pressure rises to improve circulation, and basal metabolic rate increases.

- Mental and Behavioral Changes: The attention narrows and focuses on the threat. Mental alertness and the ability to concentrate increase, which may have an energizing effect. The behavior and the emotions go hand in hand with the physical changes, i.e., anger and fear are summoned if fighting, and fear is mustered up if fleeing from the danger.

When the SNS becomes active, stimulating the organs directly, the sympathetic nerves going to the adrenal medulla are also stimulated. The adrenal medulla, in turn, releases large quantities of adrenaline and noradrenaline (also termed epinephrine and norepinephrine) into the blood. When these hormones reach the tissues, they have almost the same effect as the SNS, further increasing the metabolic rate, so that the arousal of the body lasts longer. Although the organs can be stimulated either by the SNS or by the hormones, they (the SNS and the hormones) can substitute for each other, especially if one mechanism has been damaged. Hence, there is a built-in safety factor that permits the vital fight/flight response to operate when needed.

You may wonder if this so-called SNS-adrenal-medullary arousal could escalate to the point of producing harm. This is, in fact, a common fear among panickers. They believe that their panic symptoms will continue to rise indefinitely. This does not happen. The PNS automatically stops the activity of the SNS (remember, the two maintain balance in the body), and the two hormones, adrenaline and noradrenaline, are eventually dissipated and destroyed by other chemicals in the blood. Nature is too "smart" to build a system that would harm the organism in the process of protecting it. However, as Barlow and Craske (1994) pointed out in their excellent description of the process, adrenaline and noradrenaline are not destroyed right away, i.e., the person remains keyed up for a while. This is adaptive because the danger might not have dissipated. If the danger lies in wait unperceived, or returns, the body must be aroused again immediately.

Panic: A Fear Reaction in the Absence of Imminent Danger

The SNS-adrenal-medullary arousal described above can be activated by different stressors than fear of imminent threat to the person's life. Physical stressors can be drug responses, injury, and surgery. Yet our nervous system responds to internal as well as external cues. Genetic abnormalities may cause inappropriate elicitation of the stress response, but how a given situation is perceived, and the individual's conditioning, can do so as well. For example, although the hypothalamus is a major center for programmed patterns of responses, these patterns can be modified from higher cortical centers by learning, memory, attention, and motivation. We can look at stress as a mismatch between our expectations and our perception of the internal or external environment, i.e., stress is defined by how we react to a given situation. To illustrate, think of the tremendous disappointment and stress experienced by a couple who are absolutely set to have a baby of one sex, and the baby born is of the opposite sex. This mismatch or disparity brings about some very specific compensatory responses. Thus, even thinking about aversive and unpleasant events can activate autonomic responses that determine the release of specific hormones (Maier, Watkins, and Fleshner 1994). This explains how strong emotions such as rage, and even emotional responses to symbolic threats (e.g., to self-esteem or success) can activate the SNS arousal. The SNS-adrenal-medullary stimulation, in turn, may activate specific emotions or behavioral effects. Thus, the interactions between the mind and the body go both ways.

In light of the above, we can better understand Barlow's (1988) terms, "true alarm," "false alarm," and "learned alarm." When one is confronted with imminent threat to one's life, the fear response (fight or flee) is a true alarm. A panic attack is a false alarm in the sense that there is no threat to one's life; the fear system simply misfired. As we saw earlier, a person with biological and psychological vulnerabilities often has a first panic attack while under significant stress. In addition to stress, or in conjunction with it, the false alarm could have been triggered by hyperventilation, a general central nervous system arousal, or the release of various hormones or neurotransmitters (Rapee and Barlow 1988). However, the client perceives the panic attack as coming out of the blue, i.e., without a trigger. Then, after the first attacks, the panics occur increasingly when the person responds with anxiety to unexpected somatic sensations. If the person feels a lack of control, over time his or her increased attention to even normal sensations may elicit anxiety. Anxiety results in even stronger sensations, and the cycle spirals upward. As the person learns to fear the alarm reactions, and the fear helps elicit more of them, they become learned alarms.

Differences Between Panic and Fear

In fear, one's attention narrows because of the need to prepare for danger. For instance, if you were walking in a neighborhood with a reputation for being dangerous, you would hardly notice any "normal" or pleasant cues, sounds, smells, etc. Your attention would be focused on looking for possible signs of danger. While this is very adaptive behavior in a real-life situation, in panic and phobic situations, looking for possible danger signals is not adaptive.

There is a major difference between the fear one feels when one's life is threatened and a panic attack. In the former case, the body will put its energy build-up into action by fighting or fleeing the danger. In a panic attack there is no such release, even though the body prepared itself for vigorous action. The panic response will therefore involve some symptoms not usually found in a true threat situation. Remember, in the fight/flight mode, the lungs work hard to bring more oxygen to the tissues. In a panic attack, with its lower metabolism, this increased oxygen is excessive. The paradox is that even while too much oxygen has been brought in, less oxygen is available to the tissues, including the brain. (For more on this particular physiology, see section 2 in this chapter.) This leads to symptoms of dizziness, light-headedness, blurred vision, feelings of unreality, and tingling in the extremities. Then, because of the perceived lack of air, people in a panic may try to breathe harder, unwittingly causing the symptoms to become even more severe.

Basic fear, anxiety, panic, and phobic fear do differ to some extent, but pointing out to clients the overwhelming similarities between fear and panic can be particularly helpful.

The Unpredictability of Panic

I like to have the following conversation with my clients. "All of us who drive have probably at one time or another had a close call, i.e., almost getting into an accident. Think of those situations. What did you notice?" Then, I elicit the symptoms they experienced. "Right after, what went through your mind?" They were probably relieved by the fact that a terrible accident did not happen. "Did you worry about your rapid heart rate, sweating, etc., then?" They probably answer that they did not. "So, what is the difference between that episode and a panic attack?" Clients most likely will say, "But a panic attack is different; there is no trigger. It came unexpectedly." This often becomes a good lead-in to exploring the cognitive component of panic attacks.

A major difference between the individual who has an occasional panic attack and the one who develops panic disorder is primarily in the interpretation of the event. The average person may say, "I haven't had much sleep lately with the deadline of the project at work and all. I've got to calm down." The person who will develop panic disorder may say, "What is happening? I'm not in control. What if I go crazy?" Furthermore, while many panickers do seek reassurance by going to an emergency room or to their primary care physician, when they are told that they are in no danger and in good health, a number of them will not believe it.

The Uncontrollability of Panic

Panic attacks can be so overwhelming that it is understandable why some people believe that a physical ailment must be the cause. You may have observed that many panic clients become obsessed with catastrophic thoughts of impending doom. They try in vain to control the panic attacks. Frequently, they begin to avoid situations or activities, or, at least, to show the tendency to want to escape in case of a panic. Sometimes, this is the only means the client has of exercising control. The need to escape is also very understandable, inasmuch as fleeing is a natural tendency in the fight/flight response. This, in turn, explains why it is easy for clients to feel trapped and subsequently to fear entrapment, which adds greatly to the experience of uncontrollability.

The Three Components of Fear/Panic/Anxiety

Clients with panic disorder tend to describe their panic attacks almost as an "entity" that engulfs them unexpectedly and over which they have no control. This experience elicits a strong emotional response. One therapeutic goal is to help them examine this more objectively, which is partly achieved by having them record their panic attacks, as described in chapter 1, and partly by having them look at the different components thereof.

The three components are as follows:

- Physiological (physical sensations, e.g., dizziness, palpitations, suffocation symptoms)

- Cognitive (thoughts associated with the symptoms, e.g., "There isn't enough air here, I can't breathe," "What if I lose control, or worse yet, go crazy?")

- Behavioral (actions observable by the client; obvious or subtle, e.g., looking for an exit sign in the department store, tensing the muscles and leaning forward when driving on the freeway, or avoiding fearful situations)

Looking at these components helps the client realize that the panic attack is a *reaction*, a *response*. The method involves very precise questioning. "What was the very first thing you noticed in that panic episode? And then what happened? And then what did you notice?" When your client describes symptoms, ask about the thoughts involved; when a thought is conveyed, ask what happened then to the symptom; and so on. Also, ask at intervals, "When you noticed that symptom/had that thought, what did you do?" It is helpful to ask this question as if you assume that the person did do something behaviorally, no matter how subtle it might have been. (People engage in numerous subtle safety behaviors, which do not help them disconfirm their belief. See chapter 8 for more on safety behaviors.)

By becoming increasingly aware of each component, the person can learn to intervene at different points along the panic sequence. Writing down each and every step of the panic sequence helps the client identify the sensations, misinterpretations, and behaviors involved, and see how closely and intimately intertwined they are. Such writing, with the consequent increased awareness, can be applied in phobic and high-anxiety situations as well, particularly if the client has not had a recent panic attack.

An example follows: (To make it very explicit, the therapist can use a flip chart or a blackboard to write down the sentences and the client's responses.)

C -I panicked on the freeway.
T -What exactly happened?
C -I had just gotten on the freeway when I panicked. I got so scared.
T -Okay, let's see if we can take this event apart and look at each small component. You got on the freeway. What was the *very first thing* you noticed?
C -My heart started beating fast and I panicked.
T -Wait, let's backtrack. Your heart started beating fast. Did you have a thought about it?
C -I thought I'd lose control of the car.
T -And then what did you notice?
C -My breathing changed, I guess. And my heart was racing.
T -When you noticed your breathing change and your heart racing, what was the very next thing that happened?
C -I thought I would have a heart attack while driving and cause an accident.
T -Then what happened?
C -I got off the freeway.
T -What happened next?
C -I calmed down.
T -Good, this is an excellent way of describing your panic response, in every detail. Now, when I repeat each part back to you, please tell me if that part reflects a physical

symptom, P (for physiological), a thought, C (for cognitive), or a behavior, that is, an action, B (for behavioral), as I described earlier.

1. My heart started beating fast. (P)

2. I thought I'd lose control of the car. (C)

3. My breathing changed. My heart was racing. (P)

4. I thought I would have a heart attack while driving and cause an accident. (C)

5. I got off the freeway. (B)

Your client can break down a panic attack into its components and record these in Worksheet 3: The Components of a Panic Attack. This helps to objectify the experience. Also, it lays the groundwork for recognizing thoughts, which will be worked with in the next module. If your client does not have panic attacks, have him or her apply the worksheet to high-anxiety situations, e.g., encountering a phobic situation. The worksheet appears twice to allow for the recording of two separate events. Your client can copy the worksheet to break down other panics into their component parts.

Nocturnal Panics

About 20 percent of clients who have panics report the frequent occurrence of nocturnal panics. Many describe them as more severe than daytime attacks (de Beurs et al. 1994). Nocturnal panics do not arise from REM (rapid eye movement = dreaming) sleep, but from late stage-2 or early stage-3 sleep (Mellman and Uhde 1990). There are different theories about the causation of night panics. It has been reported that benzodiazepines and tricyclic antidepressants have a diminishing effect on nocturnal panics (de Beurs et al. 1994; Mellman and Uhde 1990), which would support a biological etiology of panics. Ley (1988) proposed that some people start breathing shallowly from the thorax as they reach the deeper stages of sleep, resulting in a rise in arterial carbon dioxide. To achieve a drop in arterial carbon dioxide, the person begins to hyperventilate. The accompanying increase in heart rate combined with the hyperventilation-caused dyspnea results in panic. This theory has not been supported by other studies (Craske and Barlow 1990; McNally 1994).

Craske and Barlow (1990) proposed that nocturnal panics do not distinguish themselves in any significant way from diurnal panics. During sleep, the body goes through many changes with fluctuations in heart rate, breathing, etc. If a particular physiological symptom during sleep is reminiscent of feared symptoms during the day, the person may respond to it with alarm. Remember, the brain continues to function during sleep, and we often respond to important stimuli by awakening. Thus, cognitive-behavior theorists believe that physiological changes, whatever causes them, do not lead to night panics without there also being fear attached to the symptoms. Craske and Freed (1995) found some support for this theory in a study showing that fearful misappraisals about physical symptoms occurring during sleep do indeed contribute to night panics. It is then expected that night panics would respond to successful cognitive-behavior treatment in a manner similar to the way that day panics are affected.

Fainting

The fear of fainting is a very common fear expressed by panickers. When I asked, seldom had any of them ever fainted in a panic. Only rarely, while taking the initial history,

Worksheet 3: The Components of a Panic Attack

Event/Situation: _____ Date: _____ Put each component of the specific panic attack or fearful event on a separate line.	State if P, C, B: Physiological, Cognitive, or Behavioral
1. _____	
2. _____	
3. _____	
4. _____	
5. _____	
6. _____	
7. _____	

Event/Situation: _____ Date: _____ Put each component of the specific panic attack or fearful event on a separate line.	State if P, C, B: Physiological, Cognitive, or Behavioral
1. _____	
2. _____	
3. _____	
4. _____	
5. _____	
6. _____	
7. _____	

has an occasional client reported having fainted during a panic in the past. If you hear a similar response, the next question to ask is "What actually took place?" Many people define fainting as becoming extremely weak in the legs and feeling as if they were barely "there."

The very few people who told me that they actually had fallen unconscious to the floor had other mitigating circumstances. One had been severely anemic at the time and fainted several times (only once in a panic), another had been pregnant, a third fainted in a hospital upon leaving the room where a relative had been taken after an accident. In the latter case, we ascertained that she actually had a blood-injection-injury phobia. More recently, a client with very low blood pressure reported having fainted about ten times as an adult. These situations involved witnessing a dental procedure performed on her small son and intense interpersonal interactions in a hospital. Even in her case, she never fainted in a life-threatening situation.

In the case of a panic attack, the SNS arousal does anything but lead to fainting. The blood pressure goes up a bit, and the system is tremendously activated. In contrast to people who have panic disorder and all other phobias, those with blood-injection-injury phobia do faint at times. Their first physiological reaction may be SNS arousal, but it gives way to a sudden drop in physiological arousal, caused by the PNS. It is believed that this phobia is unlike others, in that it involves the vasovagal reaction, which sometimes results in fainting (Barlow 1988). The vasovagal reaction can also be elicited by acute pain. (This condition can be treated by behavioral means, even though it may be genetically inherited in some people. I have treated a few of these people successfully in my Panic/Phobia Groups. They suffered from panic disorder and agoraphobia.)

In sum, actual fainting is reported to occur in persons with very low blood pressure, in illness, in the context of medical and dental procedures, while standing for a prolonged time, especially in a warm, crowded area, or while receiving tragic news in public. Sympathetic nervous system activity plummets, the blood pressure goes down, and the person usually experiences it as "fading away." I teach those very few clients who do faint (i.e., have a tendency to faint, including during a panic attack), to tense up their entire body when feeling faint. This usually raises the blood pressure enough to prevent fainting. Clearly, this is not a strategy to be used by nonfainters, or it will become a "safety behavior."

Although panickers persist in interpreting sensations of dizziness, light-headedness, and weakness as signs of imminent fainting, they do not faint. They use their sensations as evidence of fainting, which is a misinterpretation, because these panic sensations do not lead to fainting. To the best of my knowledge, none of my clients ever fainted from a panic after we started sessions. Furthermore, I have never heard of anyone fainting from a panic while driving or in another life-threatening situation. The few faintings reported to me took place in very safe situations. I tell my clients that I believe their survival instincts take over, preventing them from endangering their lives.

Biological "Toughening Up"

The stress response tends to be nonspecific, and it is not always harmful, but may be prophylactic, as well (Selye 1976). A great deal depends on how the stressor is perceived. In cases of potential for harm or loss, stress tends to be perceived in a negative light. On the other hand, if stress has the potential for gain and growth, i.e., is challenging, it can be perceived as positive. Developing some tolerance for stress can help the body confront a new stress by mobilizing the body's general adaptive system (Selye 1976).

Dienstbier (1989, 1991) has expanded on these views. He draws the conclusion from a number of animal and human studies that two factors often help determine whether stress is perceived as positive or negative. They are (1) the degree of predictability and (2) control over the situation. If stress is perceived negatively there is a greater likelihood that excessive cortisol is released. This may also occur when a stressful situation lasts too long. High cortisol base rates are often found in depression, anxiety, and neuroticism in general. When people are taught coping skills to deal more successfully with stressful situations, their cortisol levels tend to drop.

According to Dienstbier, exercise is one proven way to increase one's ability to deal with stress. It has been shown consistently that those who exercise regularly are less emotionally labile, and exhibit less anxiety and depression. Furthermore, once people who exercise regularly confront a stressful challenge, they show an increase in catecholamine, which is associated with a positive response to stress.

How does this relate to panic and agoraphobia? Clients often perceive intense, negative stress around their symptoms and, as stated earlier, many develop chronic, anxious apprehension pertaining to those symptoms. The studies mentioned above suggest that there is a threefold advantage to cognitive-behavior treatments for panic disorder. If panickers learn to become less afraid of internal sensations and external situations, and if they can learn to view those sensations and situations as challenges, the stress can be perceived as more positive. Learning coping skills to deal with difficult situations, be they breathing retraining or mental coping strategies, allows for a different perception of the stressful situation. Finally, if clients (who are not already doing so) can be persuaded to exercise on a regular basis, they may become better equipped to deal with stress, psychologically as well as physically. It is also speculated (as cited in Dienstbier's articles) that relaxation-based therapies (if the person continues to avoid challenging exposures) and tranquilizers may provide short-term relief but actually *interfere* with the toughening up process. Tranquilizers may also interfere with learning during cognitive-behavior therapy. (Note, however, that this does not appear to be the case with antidepressants.)

One of my clients in the Panic/Phobia Group consciously worked on reversing her perception of her avoidances from negative to positive. It had been difficult for her to leave her house on foot and take a walk alone in her own neighborhood. (She had no problem leaving the house alone in a car.) At the beginning of treatment, she was as fearful as the other group members. But from about the fifth session, instead of thinking about her outings with dread, she would say to herself, "Cool, I am going out there and facing this fear! Let me see what actually happens. It's an adventure." Needless to say she was an unusual person as evidenced by her ability to change her attitude to such a positive one, and by combining it with humor.

Summary

The goals of the psychoeducational component of the module are to convey the following information:

- Fear and anxiety are natural emotions. Because they are there for self-protection, they are adaptive. Anxiety is also a tremendous motivator.

- Physical panic sensations are connected to physiological changes in the fight/flight response that are designed to *protect* the person, hence they are not harmful.

- Physiological symptoms of anxiety are harmless.

- Panic is not an entity. It is a response to a perception of threat, comprised of physical, cognitive, and behavioral components.

- Nocturnal panics are governed by the same fear as diurnal panics.

- Panickers seldom ever faint.
- Regular exercise is excellent preparation for dealing with future stress.

Section 2: Diaphragmatic Breathing

Munjack, Brown, and McDowell (1993) found in their study that 30 percent of clients with panic disorder chronically hyperventilate. As discussed in chapter 2, hyperventilation has been speculated to be a major causative factor in panic disorder. This may have come about in part because the symptoms of hyperventilation and panic are so similar. Hyperventilation may produce light-headedness, dizziness, breathlessness, blurred vision, chest pain, cold hands, numbness and tingling sensations (in the arms, hands, and legs, and may affect one side of the body), palpitations, hot and cold sensations, nausea, weakness, and fatigue. Dyspnea, or the sensation of not being able to breathe in enough air, is often described as a sensation of suffocation, "air hunger," or choking.

In addition to the similarity of symptoms between panic and hyperventilation, the latter can mimic a number of organic diseases, e.g., neurocirculatory asthenia and mitral valve prolapse. Hyperventilation can also interact with diseases, at times making them worse, e.g., asthma. That is why a medical exam is recommended for your client—to rule out possible organic illness.

In their review of the literature, Garssen, de Ruiter, and van Dyck (1992) concluded that hyperventilation does not cause panic attacks. Rather, as I stated earlier, panickers frequently become overly vigilant to any somatic cues. Since many of them hyperventilate chronically, and the symptoms are so similar to those of panic, hyperventilation can indeed trigger panics because of the fear associated with its symptoms. In other words, if there was no fear, hyperventilation would not trigger a panic attack.

More frequently, clients with panic disorder acutely overbreathe during a panic attack. In my experience, this is particularly the case when the person is obsessively fearful of suffocating or of being too hot and therefore being unable to breathe. Clients who hold the belief they cannot take in enough air in a panic or phobic situation are more likely to breathe hard to make sure that they do not suffocate. Unfortunately, this makes the situation worse. Garssen et al. (1992) reported that no difference has been distinguished between the symptoms of panic attacks with and without hyperventilation. It is possible that overbreathing can cause some symptoms to appear even *before* a state of hypocapnea takes place physiologically. Moreover, the authors concluded that breathing retraining is a helpful treatment component, whether or not panickers hyperventilate. It helps them relax and thus reduces their anxiety; they have a structured task to attend to which promotes a sense of mastery, i.e., breathing retraining promotes a sense of self-efficacy.

I have found that diaphragmatic breathing, if done properly during a panic, is the fastest way to help slow down the physical arousal. As I tell my clients, if they sustain slow, deep breathing for a few minutes, it will affect their physiology; that is, the heart rate will eventually slow down, other symptoms will abate, and they will be able to think more clearly. This seems natural if we see the SNS working as a whole and not in isolated segments. Therefore, even if the client is not hyperventilating, diaphragmatic breathing is a useful tool to gain control over bodily symptoms and to help the anxious mind slow down.

I no longer teach relaxation techniques to my panic clients. Diaphragmatic breathing can be learned relatively quickly and it targets the panic symptoms more directly. In the past, most clients were unwilling to practice relaxation as extensively as is required for it to be helpful. I have found that time is better spent on panic-targeted treatment approaches. If a client needs and wants to learn relaxation techniques, he or she can take classes from a colleague. However, I encourage the client to concentrate on the panic work when the number of sessions is limited.

Hyperventilation

The information in this section derives from the following sources: Barlow and Craske (1994), Craske and Barlow (1993), Ley (1985), Lum (1987), Magarian (1982), and Schoene and Pierson (1992).

Overbreathing Test

Before describing hyperventilation, its symptoms or causes, it is useful to have your clients take an acute hyperventilation test. I label it an "Overbreathing Test" in order to decrease any fears associated with the word "hyperventilation." (An added advantage to doing this exercise early in treatment is that by the time you start work on the other interoceptive exercises, you will have already done one of the most challenging ones—under the guise of breathing retraining. Having already done it helps clients feel less anxious when embarking on the interoceptive work.)

What You Need: A timer or a watch or clock with a second hand.
Instructions

"Today we are going to work on diaphragmatic breathing, but before we start, let's do an overbreathing test. While this test is in itself harmless, some people should be excluded from doing it, in case a physical condition is in any way exacerbated by this exercise. If you have had epileptic or other seizures, chronic arrythmia, heart or lung problems, moderate to serious asthma, a history of fainting, extremely low blood pressure, or if you are pregnant, let me know. Do you fall into any of these categories?"

"Please stand up. First, let's practice a bit. I would like you to breathe as I'm showing you a few times to make sure you know how to do it."

I demonstrate a breathing pattern like panting but a bit slower, breathing deeply—in and out through the mouth.

"Try to make a sound like I did, when you exhale. Make it strong enough so that I can hear it."

Have the client take three to five breaths this way. Demonstrate again if it is not done correctly.

"Good! Now we will do it for one and a half minutes. I'll do it with you. Pay attention to any sensations that you may feel while doing this, or right after. If you can't stand the sensations, you may stop earlier, but try to feel the sensations and stay with them for the full time, if you can."

After the test, I ask the client to describe any sensations that were felt and whether or not they were similar to the sensations in a panic. If no sensations were experienced, the client either did not do it correctly or needs to do it longer. (Sometimes, up to three minutes are needed for the full experience of the sensations, according to Hornsveld, Garssen, and van Spiegel 1995.)

After the client does the overbreathing test, I go over the physiology of breathing and hyperventilation. (You can condense the material below.)

The Physiology of Breathing and Hyperventilation

Our lungs breathe in air and the hemoglobin in the blood carries the oxygen via the arteries to the tissues, where the cells use the oxygen in their metabolism. As a by-product of this metabolism, carbon dioxide is produced and carried back by the blood to the lungs, where it is exhaled. When the breathing exceeds metabolic need, the person is overbreathing. This may lead to hyperventilation. The time at which symptoms are produced and their severity depends on the rate and volume of air per breath. Intense symptoms can become present within seconds.

When a person is overbreathing, oxygen levels increase, and there is excess expiration of carbon dioxide from the arteries. Loss of carbon dioxide results in hypocapnic alkalosis, a condition where the blood becomes more alkaline and less acidic (scientifically, a rise in the blood pH level). This manifests in a unique constellation of autonomic changes identified as the "hyperventilation syndrome." In this syndrome, there is vascular constriction (tightening of the blood vessels), which results in less blood reaching the tissues, and oxygen binds more tightly to the hemoglobin, which results in less oxygen being released to the tissues. The resulting diminished oxygen in the brain produces sensations of dizziness, light-headedness, faint feelings, blurred vision, and feelings of unreality. Diminished oxygen to the extremities produces symptoms of tingling, numbness, and cold. Furthermore, overexertion of the thoracic muscles can result in chest pain, sharp or dull. Even slight increases in the pH can intensify all of these symptoms rapidly. After some time, renal compensation (involving the kidneys) takes place to lower the pH. This suppresses the symptoms, but minimal changes in breathing or exertion may set them off at full intensity again. In sum, the paradox is that while too much oxygen is inhaled, less is available for use by the tissues.

According to Ley (1988) mild, episodic hyperventilation is a normal response to stress, the emotional reactivity of day-to-day living. Furthermore, he says it takes place when laughing, excited, or involved in animated discussion in addition to manifesting when anxious and in the fight/flight response.

Identifying Overbreathing

When anxious, many of us will breathe more rapidly and shallowly. However, some people are chronic overbreathers most of the time. This may result from general stress and anxiety (even from repressing strong emotions such as anger), faulty breathing habits, and sometimes organic causes (use or withdrawal from substances such as drugs and alcohol, being in high altitudes, etc.). Hyperventilation can occur subtly, which is why it often goes unrecognized. You can look for the following signs: Shallow breathing with the upper chest expanding, irregular breaths, mouth breathing, a rate of 18 breaths or more per minute while relaxed, sighing, gasping for air, yawning, frequent clearing of the throat, and outwardly apparent, heavy breathing. Although hyperventilation is harmless, it does produce feelings of breathlessness and smothering, i.e., perceptions of lack of air. As mentioned earlier, the paradox is that while the person is taking in too much air, it is perceived as too little. Attempts to breathe more, while a natural reaction, only aggravate the condition further.

Many women clients have told me that they were taught to hold the stomach in and the chest up, which led them to hyperventilate from a young age. Two of these clients also reported chronic chest pain, which was never diagnosed as indicative of a disease, and this pain began to dissipate after they learned to do diaphragmatic breathing.

How to Stop Hyperventilation

What You Need: A timer or a watch with a second hand
Instructions for the Client
There are four ways to stop hyperventilation:

1. **Hold your breath**
   Let's assume you have a panic tomorrow and you have not learned diaphragmatic breathing. What can you do to stop possible hyperventilation and slow down your symptoms? You can hold your breath a few times in a row for as long as you feel comfortable, maybe from ten to fifteen seconds. Why do you think this may work? (Elicit answers.) It is because it temporarily prevents the dissipation of carbon dioxide.

2. **Breathe in and out of a paper bag**
   If you have gone to an emergency room for panics, you may have been told to do this. Why do you think this works? (Elicit answers.) The carbon dioxide is in the bag and is breathed back in. Now, you cannot do this everywhere. For instance, you cannot drive safely at the same time you try holding a bag to your mouth and nose. You would probably not want to sit in a meeting at work or in a classroom breathing into a bag.

3. **Vigorous exercise**
   You could run up and down stairs, do aerobics in place, run or walk briskly, etc. Why does this work? (Elicit answers.) The person will breathe in (and out) rapidly but, in this case, the metabolism increases quickly to produce more energy; the inhaled oxygen will be used up and a larger quantity of carbon dioxide will be produced. Again, you cannot do this while driving, or in many other places. Vigorous exercise and breathing into a bag can be done at home.

4. **Deep diaphragmatic breathing**
   This is the best way to stop hyperventilation. It allows you to use the full capacity of your lungs. Even if you are not a hyperventilator, this is the best means I know to help your body slow down and to diminish the symptoms while in a panic. Therefore, it is a very useful coping skill for most people.

   (The instructions for diaphragmatic breathing follow.)

Breathing Retraining

Ask your client to stand up again and take a deep breath in and out. Watch for signs of the rib cage and shoulders lifting, breathing quickly, and the mouth opening. Then demonstrate how to do diaphragmatic breathing while standing; and when you finish your demonstration, have your client try it. Note that most people find it hard to do, the first few times they try it.

Subsequently, I demonstrate diaphragmatic breathing by leaning back in my armchair so that I can get as close as possible to lying down. I place a pillow (or a folded jacket) on my diaphragm/stomach and demonstrate the following steps:

Instructions for the client

1. Lie on your back on a bed or carpeted floor and, if you can, do this without a pillow. Instead of placing the pillow under your head, place two pillows

on your stomach/diaphragm. Watch the top of the pillows. When you breathe *in,* your diaphragm/stomach should expand (to allow for the extra air), thus *raising the pillows.* When you breathe *out,* the pillows should move down again. It helps to exaggerate the movement of your diaphragm, especially while learning the technique. Breathe slowly in and out through your *nose,* not through your mouth. (The only exceptions are if you have a bad cold, asthma, or something impeding the air flow through your nostrils, in which case, keep your mouth open only a little and allow the same amount of air to flow in and out.)

2. Lying on your back as described above, discard the pillows and place your hand over your waist and navel. Look at the ceiling or close your eyes. Proceed as above. This time feel your stomach rising up and falling down with your hand.

3. Lying on your back as above, place your arms at your sides. Look at the ceiling or close your eyes. Proceed as in step 1. Focus on your diaphragm/stomach, and *feel* it move up and down. I like to think of it as, "becoming one with your breathing."

4. Sit on a sofa, leaning back, so that you can watch your stomach area. Watch your diaphragm/stomach move up as you breathe in, down as you breathe out.

5. Sit straight up and breathe in and out while your stomach moves out and in (that is, your breathing and your stomach move in opposite directions). As in steps 1 through 4, make sure that your upper chest and shoulders are perfectly still.

6. Stand up and do the same as in step 5.

7. Remember to breathe through your nose. At rest, nasal breathing is more efficient. Practice breathing this way as slowly as possible, ideally between eight and twelve breaths per minute, generally, the slower the breathing the better.

8. Breathe in slowly and then out slowly. Either breathe out a bit slower than breathing in or breathe out at the same pace and hold a little while before taking your next breath. Hold at the end of the breathing-out cycle only for as long as you feel comfortable. The more you practice, the more you will feel comfortable in slowing down your breathing. (Do *not* take in a breath and then hold it unnaturally before breathing out.)

9. Practice twice a day for five minutes. Do this daily.

I emphasize the need to start practicing by lying down, since it is very difficult to learn this type of breathing while standing. If a client does very poorly when I follow-up on the breathing technique at the third session, I specifically inquire whether he or she practiced lying down. More often than not, the client tried to skip this step.

As Ley (1988) has pointed out, severe chronic hyperventilators find it very difficult to breathe slowly, even at rest. For them it can be exceedingly difficult to learn diaphragmatic breathing, because they may perceive the hyperventilation symptoms (especially light-headedness) from the mere fact that they are changing their breathing pattern. The renal compensation to restore the acidic blood chemistry mentioned earlier is so precarious that any change in breathing, such as slowed diaphragmatic breathing, can bring the uncomfortable symptoms back in full force again. For these clients, Ley recommends that breathing retraining should progress slowly and gradually to reduce hypercapnea. You may instruct your client to concentrate on only one aspect of the breathing at a time, e.g., doing diaphragmatic breathing first, breathing through the nose later, and slowing down the breathing still later. I encourage my clients not to become discouraged. Practice and patience are the answers.

Follow-Up on Breathing

In the third session, I have the client stand up again with me and show me his or her progress with diaphragmatic breathing. I will get a good idea of whether the client has practiced, and I may need to make some corrections. As is my practice, you might want to tell your client to pay attention to his/her breathing during the day; while at work, watching TV, etc., by asking himself/herself, "How was my breathing?" Then, the client takes a few minutes to do diaphragmatic breathing. Once he or she can do that, have the client apply diaphragmatic breathing when feeling anxious, feeling a panic attack coming on, or when in the middle of a panic. The client needs to know that the only way this procedure will work is if he or she practices. It can be applied to high anxiety and panic situations only if it was learned very well. The level of necessary skill cannot be reached without practice.

The follow-up on the breathing techniques may continue over two or three more sessions. Most clients learn it in two to four weeks and find it quite useful. I have had only one client who was angered by this part of the treatment. She said that she had never been able to do this type of breathing and had gotten angry in the past when people tried to teach her how to do it.

Using Diaphragmatic Breathing to Fall Asleep

Some clients may become proficient enough to use this technique to fall asleep. I tell my clients how I do it. Essentially, I make a commitment to myself that I will stay with the breathing and everything else can wait for the next day. Lying on my side, I concentrate fully on my breathing. I exaggerate the movements of my stomach/diaphragm and make sure that I breathe as slowly as I can. The way I conceptualize it is that I become one with my breathing, i.e., all my attention is focused on my diaphragm area, and I feel my breathing as if it were all of me at that moment. After a minute or two, if my thoughts wander, I immediately return to concentrating on my breathing. I need to make a firm commitment to stay with my breathing, so that I do not pursue other thoughts beckoning to me. Invariably, within five to ten minutes I am fast asleep.

Breathing as a Coping Mechanism

Panickers want quick relief from their symptoms and are often impatient. In this module I emphasize that breathing retraining is their best initial coping mechanism. When a panic attack comes in the early stage of treatment, the breathing can be used to ride through the panic, surfing with it as on an ocean wave. Just as one cannot stop a wave, if the panic is already there, a smart tactic is to go along with it. Trying to fight an attack most likely will exacerbate the symptoms.

Summary

The sequence of the breathing retraining requires that these steps be followed:

1. Have the client take the overbreathing test.

2. Educate the client about the physiology of hyperventilation and the ways to stop it.

3. Ask the client to take a deep breath in and out.

4. Teach diaphragmatic breathing.

5. Follow up client progress in subsequent sessions.

6. Emphasize that the first step in teaching control in the treatment of panic is to learn diaphragmatic breathing and how to apply the technique to learn to ride through, rather than fight, panic attacks.

5

Treatment Module II: Cognitive Restructuring *(Sessions 4–6)*

Overview of Module II

The beginning of this chapter, the theoretical background, is for you, the therapist. It is intended to help you understand the cognitive theories and what the treatment protocol is targeting. This information is not very useful for the client. Section 1: Challenging Automatic Thoughts includes most of the techniques to achieve cognitive restructuring with the client. Section 2: Changing Core Beliefs may be applied with some clients, not with others, depending on the time available, the interest, and the openness of the person you are treating.

If you read this section prior to completing the previous module, and if time permits, you could give your client Worksheet 4: Challenging Automatic Thoughts, 1st Step at the end of Session 3 (in Treatment Module I) to start preparing for the work ahead. If you give this short worksheet as an assignment without much background, your client probably will write rather general thoughts. This then becomes a nice lead-in to the beginning of Session 4, where you can help elicit specific thoughts from the general thoughts the client has provided.

Session 4

1. Explain what automatic thoughts are, and how to identify *specific* automatic thoughts.

2. Show how to use Worksheet 4: Challenging Automatic Thoughts, 1st Step.

3. Go over the cognitive traps the automatic thoughts represent. (In subsequent sessions, you can challenge these traps, using the cognitive techniques presented.)

4. Assign homework from *An End to Panic: Breakthrough Techniques for Overcoming Panic Disorder,* using the equivalent topics and worksheets from chapter 9.

Session 5

1. Follow up on Worksheet 4: Challenging Automatic Thoughts, 1st Step, and expand it to the full worksheet.

2. Identify the person's focal fears.

3. Use any of the methods described to challenge your client's automatic thoughts.

4. Home assignments from *An End to Panic*, Worksheet 4 pertaining to focal fears.

Session 6

1. Go over Worksheet 4 as pertaining to focal fears.

2. Continue working on fearful automatic thoughts.

3. Work on core beliefs.

Cognitions in Panic

People with panic disorder and phobias have specific thoughts related to their fears. Sometimes these thoughts are implicit or not well articulated. Some people are aware of images or vague emotions, such as a sense of impending doom. Therapeutic success depends on the client's ability to become aware of specific thoughts and images, to recognize the cognitive traps they represent, and then to challenge and change them. The reduction of fear is of central importance. No matter which coping skills are learned, as long as fear persists, even if masked, the problem is still there or is likely to return.

Clients with panic disorder are perfectly capable of rational thought. It is in the domain of their fears that they are not able to think rationally. You must remember, however, that they have their own logic, even if this logic seems unrealistic or is not shared by others. You may wonder why it is so hard for clients to give up their irrational fears. Part of the answer may be that fearful thoughts are elicited more easily in panickers than in the average person, especially when anxious. Furthermore, even if the person can see the irrationality of fear in a calm state, experientially, there is always the possibility that next time the attack might be different, more intense, etc., an endless possibility of "what . . . ifs." These fear thoughts, in turn, may be fed by underlying beliefs and assumptions (e.g., negative beliefs about the self), as well as by the many uncertainties in life. That is why cognitive processes are critical in the development and maintenance of panic disorder.

The following list names some of the most common fears expressed by my clients in panic and phobic situations. Some of these clients have had panic disorder for a long time. As you can see, fears experienced in agoraphobic situations often involve losing control and embarrassing oneself, i.e., they are fears of social consequences. Many people have fears focusing on the physical consequences of panic attacks, such as dying of a heart attack.

- What if I faint in a room full of strangers?

- I've got to get out of this grocery store before someone sees how dizzy I am. Thank God for the shopping cart to hold onto!

- Something awful is going to happen. I don't know what. I just know something awful is going to happen.

- I may panic while driving on the freeway and crash.

- I may get choked up on the phone (if I panic). I will feel exposed and embarrassed about sounding like a loony, crazy person.

- I'll run away from an important meeting and then I'll be fired for being crazy.

- This warm, stuffy, blowing air could make me gasp for air, and I may not make it down the hall to the elevator. My legs will get wobbly, and I'll walk crookedly. Someone may think I'm drunk!

- I just see myself in an insane asylum.

- If I get light-headed or dizzy in a store, I may physically collapse. The panic could make me faint, and I could hurt myself badly as I slump to the ground.

- I'll stand in a checkout line with my cart filled with groceries, panic, and then I'll run away. They'll think I'm insane.

- What if I'm on the beach walking and get dizzy? Who will help me find my way back to my car?

Some excellent references for cognitive theory and the practical application of cognitive techniques in panic disorder are: Bandura (1988), Barlow (1988), Barlow and Craske (1994), Beck (1995), Beck and Emery, with Greenberg (1985), Burns, (1989), Clark (1989), Clark and Ehlers (1993), Fennell (1989), Foa and Kozak (1986), Hoffart (1993), Ingram and Kendall (1987), Lang (1979), Salkovskis and Clark (1991).

The Perception of Threat

We humans have a need to understand ourselves and the world. Therefore, we appraise and categorize our experiences. However, before we even become *aware* of a stimulus, it has already passed through a selection and interpretation process (Beck and Emery, with Greenberg 1985). Most of this occurs outside of awareness. It allows the more relevant information from our environment to pass through to higher brain centers. What information is attended to by any one individual depends on the person's interests, concerns, and expectations. These constitute the person's "cognitive set." (You may recall from chapter 2 that biological challenge-test findings can be explained by the instructions that are given to the subject, i.e., what the cognitive set of the experiment is.)

The following discussion pertains to the cognitive processes related to anxiety (Arntz, Rauner, and van den Hout 1995; Barlow 1988; Beck and Emery, with Greenberg 1985; Foa and Kozak 1986). When threat is perceived, certain cognitive fear *structures* (also called *schemas*) become activated. These structures contain a number of core beliefs and assumptions. They are based on past experiences and help the person label and interpret the threatening event. The fear structures convey information about the fear stimulus (object, situation, event), the response (physiological reactions, verbal expressions, and behaviors), and their meaning. The meaning could be that anxiety may increase and last indefinitely, and that the stimuli and responses are likely to produce harm.

At the level of automatic thoughts, the "meaning" can take the following concrete forms (examples from my clinical practice):

- These feelings that I experience could get worse each time until I have no control over them. (Anxiety will increase indefinitely.)

- What if I'm traveling, and the car breaks down, or there is an accident? (Stimulus produces harm.)

- What if I get trapped in the elevator for hours and can't get out? I couldn't stand it. (Stimulus produces harm.) I'll panic the whole time. I'll be yelling, and screaming, and kicking the walls, and I'll be so embarrassed. (Response produces harm.)

- In a panic I may have a heart attack and die. (Response produces harm.)

The stimulus, response, and meaning constitute nodes of anxiety information that are linked. Hence a single concept, or node, can prompt a whole network of information. The goal of cognitive restructuring is to change the content of the nodes and develop a new associative network (Craske, Workshop on Panic Control Treatment, Los Angeles 1994).

As mentioned in chapter 4, the fight/flight response becomes activated when confronting true, imminent danger, a *true alarm*. Barlow (1988) has expanded on true, false, and learned alarms. The response can be activated in other situations that are not life threatening, which constitutes a *false alarm*. Further, these false alarms can become *learned alarms*. When there is a false alarm, the "normal" person *reappraises the situation* and acknowledges that there was no real danger. The appraisal may take the form of an innocuous explanation of the panic attack, e.g., "This deadline at work is putting too much pressure on me. I better slow down!" or "I had a fight with my husband this morning." Whether these explanations are accurate or not, they explain the event in nonthreatening ways. The false alarm becomes a one-time experience that may or may not recur.

In contrast, another person based on his/her past experience will show a bias in the selection and processing of data toward seeing danger, while ignoring other information. This person infers danger not only from the outside event but from the anxiety response itself. He or she has a more salient fear structure, i.e., the fear structure is more readily accessed. Why is the fear structure more salient? Some individuals have high autonomic reactivity, others have had major life stresses (e.g., early separation) that were perceived as unpredictable and/or uncontrollable (Barlow 1988). These factors may facilitate the processing of danger cues in many situations judged to be of vital interest to the person (from threat to life to socially embarrassing situations) (Beck and Emery, with Greenberg 1985). When experiencing stress later, a false alarm (panic attack) can be triggered. This uncontrollable event threatens the person's vital interest. It sets off a chain of responses characterized by distorted information processing such as misinterpretation and overgeneralization. Examples are, "Unfamiliar surroundings are dangerous." "Inexplicable physical symptoms are a sign of disease." "I need to be in control at all times." Once the sequence of events is set in motion, more anxiety is generated. The person does not check out the reality of the false alarm: *A reappraisal does not take place.*

Other structures that become activated at the same time have to do with the assessment of one's capacity to deal with the threat (Bandura 1988; Beck and Emery, with Greenberg 1985; Williams 1995). The potential damage gets weighed against one's coping resources. The entire process is very rapid and largely automatic, in part because the fear and coping structures, which are based in long-term memory, are already in place. The outcome of this weighing determines the emotional response and the behavior. If the threatened person perceives that the internal or external dangers are beyond his or her control and mastery (i.e., unable to cope), the person becomes preoccupied with his or her deficiencies and ruminates about these dangers. The person feels vulnerable, "weak," and experiences high levels of anxiety arousal.

Against this background, when the person experiences an out-of-the-blue panic, it can feel overwhelming, as the person tries in vain to control the physical symptoms and his/her mind. The experience of not being in control is paramount, especially in individuals who have a schema containing the core belief "I must be in control at all times." The sense of vulnerability is thus not necessarily a temporary experience. In other words, it is not just that they do not have temporary control over one small aspect of their being. The fear is now that of *losing all control*. Furthermore, the vulnerable person holds onto beliefs about his or her vulnerability in spite of information that contradicts it. "I held myself together this time, but next time I may really lose it." This person also will selectively recall the times when he or she felt more vulnerable. This results in feeling compelled to take action to decrease the anxiety, which often means escaping from the threat.

The individual with an anxiety disorder has lost perspective in the sense that only fear and vulnerability structures are operating—at the expense of more adaptive structures. The pathological structures are very resistant to modification. On the other hand, if the person perceives being able to mitigate, prevent, or terminate the aversive event, i.e., having control, he or she will feel "self-confident" with little reason to fear or to avoid situations. That person is more likely to buffer the anxiety with coping responses, if early-in-life-coping behaviors that impart a sense of mastery and control were developed.

One final comment: Remember, the mind and body continuously influence each other. Naturally, all of the above-mentioned cognitive mechanisms and processes are bound to have neurochemical effects. They do not operate in a vacuum separate from our bodies.

Decreasing Fear: Accomplishing Change in the Fear Structure

The person with panic disorder very often reacts either by avoiding activities and/or situations, or by using various safety signals or safety behaviors. Hence the avoidance may be obvious or infinitely subtle (covert, cognitive avoidance is one of the most subtle ways of avoidance). Foa and Kozak (1986) propose that to decrease fear response (excessive physiological reactivity, emotional experience of fear, and escape and avoidance behavior), the fear structure must first be activated. For instance, if an agoraphobic person can go to the mall comfortably with a companion, as opposed to going alone, the fear structure may not be activated. Second, information that is incompatible with the biases in the fear structure must be incorporated. For example, if the person remains in the anxiety-producing situation, he or she may learn that anxiety will not last forever, and that the symptoms of weakness and numbness in the limbs will not lead to a stroke. In panic disorder, the numerous safety signals (companion, medication, paper bag to breathe into), and safety behaviors (sitting down to prevent fainting, keeping close to exits in a department store) used preclude the person from fully activating the fear structure and thus modifying it. This partly explains why many people say, "I always expose myself to this situation, but my fear does not go away."

For treatment to be successful, there must be full exposure to fearful situations (without safety signals or safety behaviors), the person must remain in the situation long enough (at least one and one-half hours), and the exposures must be done often enough (usually at least three times a week). When those conditions are met, habituation occurs. Habituation means that physiological fear responses, such as elevated heart rate, and the emotional feeling of fear decrease over time. Fear arousal must be sufficiently high, and exposure to the phobic situation must be prolonged and frequent enough, for habituation and emotional fear reduction to occur. This theory has the support of many researchers.

However, not all researchers agree with the above-stated view. Bandura (1988) and Williams (1988) have criticized the "exposure principle," although, as seen above, Foa and Kozak (1986) never argue that exposure alone changes the fear structure. Yet many studies do not show a relationship between anxiety arousal and phobic behavior. Although anticipated anxiety and panic strongly predict actual anxiety, they are less accurate in predicting phobic behavior. Arousal is neither required to initiate avoidance nor to eliminate it.

Bandura and Williams are proponents of the self-efficacy theory, which states that the main cause of phobic avoidance is low self-efficacy, which is the perception of being unable to cope with certain activities that are potentially threatening (Bandura 1988; Williams 1988,

1990, 1995; Williams, Dooseman, and Kleifield 1984). The relationship between self-efficacy level and subsequent coping behavior in agoraphobic situations has been shown again and again to be high, about .80 (Williams 1995). Further, the relationship between thoughts of danger and phobic behavior is about .30, and the relationship between anticipated anxiety and panic on one hand and behavior on the other is .70. Although there are gaps in our understanding of the relationship between self-efficacy, behavior, and anxiety arousal, it is speculated that cognitive processes are involved (Bandura 1977; Williams 1995).

According to self-efficacy theory, to reduce fearful reaction and avoidance, a sense of control over the situation must be attained. Bandura (1988) reports studies demonstrating that plasma catecholamine (epinephrine, norepinephrine, and dopac) levels change as a direct result of the perception of control over phobic threats. When no control is perceived, the levels rise; conversely, when a sense of control is high, the levels are lowered. (This shows a direct link between mind and body.) Self-efficacy theory emphasizes performance accomplishments. By successfully accomplishing increasingly more challenging tasks, a sense of control and mastery is gained. The therapist helps clients to actively apply cognitive and behavioral methods in order to accomplish the difficult tasks. Williams' guided mastery approach for confronting fearful situations is successful even when little anxiety is experienced.

Core Beliefs, Assumptions, and Automatic Thoughts

The following theories are based primarily on Beck and Emery, with Greenberg (1985) and Padesky (1994).

Core Beliefs

Cognitive structures or schemas were described in the section above. If a schema is a structure for information processing and behavior, then it includes (in my conceptualization) core beliefs and associated memories, perceptions, assumptions, automatic thoughts, feelings, and behaviors. Core beliefs are the most fundamental beliefs that we hold about ourselves (e.g., self-worth), about others, and life itself. They are absolutes, expressed in *blanket statements* that are sweeping, generalized, and rigid. They are usually learned in childhood from significant others. Children develop these beliefs because they see their adult models as all powerful and "right." They do not have the cognitive capacity to question the beliefs or to apply them in flexible ways. As we grow, however, we naturally challenge and change many beliefs.

Core beliefs seem to fall into a few large categories, foremost among them are lovability, competence, and power. We are often not aware of the core beliefs that underlie our more superficial thoughts. Nonetheless, they have a powerful impact on our thoughts, attitudes, moods, and behaviors. Each of us holds positive and negative beliefs. When we feel good, positive beliefs are often operating. However, difficult events in life, such as the loss of a loved one, illness, traumatic experiences, unreasonable demands, life's misfortunes, i.e., when feeling low and vulnerable, bring out our negative beliefs. This may help to explain why prior to a first panic someone might not have exhibited high anxiety sensitivity or a vulnerable structure. Many panickers assure me that they had no problems with anxiety prior to their first panic.

Some negative core beliefs are based on strong, negative experiences, and, as such, they tend to be harsh and unforgiving. They are especially resistant to change because we become adept at distorting, denying, and discounting contradictory evidence, thus they may remain unchanged into adulthood. Core beliefs themselves do not cause panic, but they serve as powerful maintenance factors. They help maintain the panic disorder.

The following are some negative core beliefs, which may underlie a panicker's thinking:

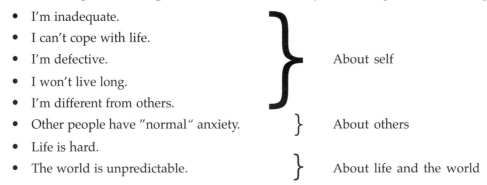

- I'm inadequate.
- I can't cope with life.
- I'm defective.   } About self
- I won't live long.
- I'm different from others.
- Other people have "normal" anxiety.   } About others
- Life is hard.
- The world is unpredictable.   } About life and the world

Assumptions

Assumptions lie between core beliefs and automatic thoughts. They are the rules that we live by. They are often expressed in conditional "if . . . then," and "should" statements. They can also be expressed in statements that contain the words "never," "always," "must," and "everyone." Assumptions are often ways to try to cope with the core belief or a way of testing the validity of the belief. In the latter case, assumptions tend to place unreasonable and unattainable demands on the person, thus the test often fails, and the core belief remains true. ("If I do my job perfectly, people will not know that I'm incompetent.") This leaves little room for human error.

Although we may not be aware of our general assumptions, we become more conscious of them as they become more specific and concrete. In a healthy individual, the rules tend to be flexible and adaptive; in a person with a psychiatric disorder, they are more rigid. In anxiety disorders, the assumptions are about danger and vulnerability and the ability to cope with danger. The rules are often conditional, e.g., "If someone is with me, that person can save me." "I was able to control my thoughts (in the panic) this time, but next time I might go crazy." "If I get too confident, bad things will happen/a panic is sure to strike."

Some assumptions related to the core belief "I'm defective" could be:

- If I don't stick my neck out, people won't know about me.
- I never can do things right.
- I should not make mistakes.
- If the panics don't go away, I'll never be normal.

Some assumptions related to the core belief "I can't cope with life" could be:

- If I weren't so sensitive, I could cope with anxiety.
- If something bad unexpectedly happens, I won't be able to cope.
- I shouldn't get upset over small things.
- It's best to always expect the worst.

Automatic Thoughts

Automatic thoughts lie at a more superficial level than core beliefs and assumptions. They arise spontaneously and may take the form of brief statements, images, and memories.

They emanate from and are closely related to everyday experiences and comprise many of our moment-to-moment thoughts. Automatic thoughts can be so well rehearsed that they occur easily, without much effort, and can operate outside of conscious thinking. While people cannot always easily identify their automatic thoughts, they tend to be more accessible than assumptions and core beliefs. They too can be either positive or negative.

Here, we are mainly concerned with negative automatic thoughts related to panic and phobias, which are linked to physical symptoms, emotional fear reactions, and avoidance behaviors. One reason why such thoughts are so resistant to change is that they are usually associated with very strong emotions (e.g., dread of unexplained physical sensations). When people are in distress, they tend not to examine their thinking too closely. They are more concerned with their emotional state, and often assume that their thoughts are the result of their emotions. They believe that if only their emotions would change, their thoughts would return to "normal." Many do not realize that their automatic thoughts influence their physical arousal, emotions, and behaviors. It is much easier to be aware of the emotion than of the brief, automatic thought that preceded or accompanied the emotion. In sum, these thoughts are often not challenged because people lack awareness of their presence, keep them vague, avoid confronting them, think they cannot be altered, or take them for granted, even when they are irrational. The critical aspect of the automatic thought is that it is believed to be the truth.

Your clients come to you with "here-and-now" problems. Therefore, in treatment, the cognitive restructuring begins with work on their automatic thoughts. These represent the level of cognitive processing most closely linked to the symptomatology. Your client wants to get rid of his or her panics and phobias. As the therapist, you may want him/her to do more extensive work, but it may not be what the client wants. Once the client is comfortable with working on automatic thoughts, you may find opportunities to delve deeper. Therapy time is limited, however, and you would not do your client a service to work on his/her deeper core beliefs if the panic and phobic symptoms have not been addressed and improved. Although the preferred sequence might be to first identify and modify automatic thoughts so the client gains some relief from his/her symptoms, some clinicians work with core beliefs early on in therapy.

In my practice, the work on core beliefs is sometimes limited. It depends largely on the time factor and the interest of the current clients in a given group. As the topic is in my self-help book *An End to Panic*, my clients are at least introduced to it. Only once did one of my clients become angry when I probed into her core belief. Since then, I usually ask the client, "And what would it mean to you if you went crazy? Is it okay for us to proceed and look deeper?" None of my clients has said "No," but by consenting, resistance may have been lowered. When I can work on a client's core beliefs, it almost always seems to produce more extensive and deeper change. Further research remains to be done to prove whether or not it contributes to higher end-state functioning in panic disorder.

In the next two sections I describe many cognitive techniques. You will not use all of them with every client. My colleagues and I at Kaiser have found that although several of the main methods (for the most part those listed under numbers I through VII) work with many clients, some of the additional techniques listed are necessary for others.

Section 1: Challenging Automatic Thoughts

The bulk of the cognitive restructuring work will focus on automatic thoughts and challenging them. These are the closest related to the panic symptomology. First, I will briefly review the common confusion between feelings and thoughts and then how emotions and thoughts influence each other.

Distinguishing Between Feelings and Thoughts

Many people have a hard time making a distinction between feelings and thoughts. One of the best ways to help the client make this distinction is by having him/her express the feeling in *one* word, e.g., "I feel loving, sad, disappointed, angry, scared, guilty, ashamed, lonely, happy, unhappy, mad, furious, jealous, hurt, frustrated, insecure, irritated, tense, suspicious, content, jittery, excited, afraid, etc." If the client starts a sentence with "I feel that . . . ," the word "that" is usually a lead-in to a thought, e.g., "I feel that everyone has a right to express their opinion." "I feel that he doesn't listen to me." "I feel that you never take me into account." These are thoughts although they are often accompanied by emotions. Hence, the two tell-tale signs to thoughts are the use of "I feel" followed by "that," and the greater number of words used, the more likely a thought is being expressed.

Emotions Affect Thoughts and Thoughts Affect Emotions

Teach your clients to understand how feelings and thoughts interact. Although thoughts may be difficult to change, they are often a good avenue to take toward changing feelings. Usually, we cannot make a strong emotion just go away. If, instead, a more positive view (i.e., helpful automatic thoughts) can be established and sustained, it will have a positive effect on emotions. Therefore, the client must become aware of and repeatedly challenge his or her negative automatic thoughts.

I have found that, just as the person with a deep depression translates all negative emotions into sadness, the highly anxious client frequently interprets all undesirable physical discomfort and negative emotions as anxiety. This person does not differentiate well between emotions but is locked into one: the experience of anxiety. Hence that person experiences anxiety instead of anger, frustration, or sadness. It is the one familiar and "accepted" emotion. By learning to challenge anxiety-related automatic thoughts, that person can disengage from the fear mode and begin paying attention to and accepting other emotions.

Identifying *Specific* Automatic Thoughts During Panic and Phobic Encounters

Some of my clients have described experiencing the following fears while in a panic:

1. What's happening to me? I'm not in control.
2. Oh, my God, I can't breathe. I have to leave. I need to get fresh air or I'll suffocate.
3. I'm losing it.
4. I need to get off the freeway so I can stop it (the panic), or I can't control my car.
5. I may have a heart attack and die.
6. I want to run. I feel trapped and caged. Something will happen to me and no one will be there to help me.

7. I'm going crazy.

8. This feeling will never go away. I can't handle it.

When you read the phrases, did you find them specific or general? In other words, did you learn what the person's *exact* fear is? In fact, numbers 2 and 5 reflect quite specific fears. In number 2 the person fears being unable to breathe and suffocating as a consequence, and in number 5 the person believes that he or she will have a heart attack and die. In all other instances, you must help the client elicit a more specific thought or image.

"I'm not in control," "I'm losing it," "I won't control my car in a panic," "Something will happen to me," "I'm going crazy," and "I can't handle it" reflect various degrees of vagueness. Examine these two extremely vague statements, "I'm afraid" and "I'm anxious." As a therapist, would you know how to help your client get rid of the fear or anxiety? I would not—and I tell my clients so. The same goes for any of the statements above, e.g., "I'm not in control." However, if I know *exactly* what it is that my client fears or worries about, I am in a much better position to help him or her. One of your tasks as a therapist is to train your client to become aware of *specific* automatic thoughts.

The following questions and strategies help to elicit *specific* automatic thoughts in panic and phobic situations. The first four questions may be sufficient for some clients, and the last four strategies are likely to help clients whose specific thoughts are less accessible. Also, teach your client to translate questions into *specific statements/predictions*, e.g., "I will die from a heart attack" instead of questions like "What if I die?"

1. What exactly do you mean by _____ (going crazy, losing control, being unable to control the car)?

2. How would _____ (you die, stop breathing)?

3. What exactly are you afraid will happen if _____ (your heart skips a beat, you become light-headed)? Do you have an image?

4. What is the *worst* that you think could happen if _____ (you couldn't leave the meeting, the feeling didn't go away)? Ask for thoughts or images.

5. Have your client close his or her eyes and imagine being in the middle of a "bad" panic. Ask, "Why is it bad? What do you think will happen right now?"

6. Have your client imagine approaching a fearful situation or doing a feared activity. Ask, "Why don't you want to proceed? Something is holding you back. Remember, right now it does not matter if it is rational or not. We need to understand what exactly is holding you back."

7. Give your client the instructions to approach a real phobic situation (if your client is phobic) and then ask himself/herself, "Why exactly don't I want to do this right now?"

8. Tell your clients to pay attention when and if they suddenly become anxious. Tell them to ask themselves what were they thinking right before they noticed the anxiety. Have them try to re-create any thoughts or images.

One way or another, my clients have always succeeded in becoming aware of very specific automatic thoughts. You can use Worksheet 3: The Components of a Panic Attack in chapter 4 to look at thoughts that have been recorded and to demonstrate how to generate specific from general thoughts.

As preparation for using a thought record to challenge specific automatic thoughts, clients can be asked to fill out half of a record first, a technique that I learned about from

Greenberger and Padesky (1995), hence Worksheet 4: Challenging Automatic Thoughts, 1st Step. The instructions for Worksheet 4, 1st Step follow the actual worksheet. Worksheet 4, 1st Step can be practiced briefly in Session 4 and then assigned as homework. Hence, when you ask your client to recall a recent panic or another fearful event to use for practice on the worksheet, you will be able to demonstrate again how to become aware of the specific automatic thought. If you were able to introduce these earlier, you can proceed to work on the entire Worksheet 4.

Methods and Techniques to Challenge Automatic Thoughts

To produce a change in thinking, your clients must be able to reflect on their thoughts with full awareness. This involves being open to recognizing that their thoughts are subjective and possibly erroneous. Note that using "positive self-statements," taught by a number of therapists as a primary "cognitive" technique, produces only superficial change.

Some Basic Rules for Cognitive Restructuring

Socratic dialogue is the essence of the way to carry out the cognitive work. Other helpful approaches are summarizing frequently, encouraging doubt, directing your client's attention to real data from his/her life, being supportive, and using humor.

Collaborative Empiricism and Socratic Dialogue

The general approach is called collaborative empiricism in that you guide your client to view his or her negative automatic thoughts as hypotheses, and *together* you employ verbal and behavioral methods to test out these hypotheses (Clark 1989). Are these hypotheses accurate? Are they helpful? Instead of trying to give your client all the answers based on your authority as a therapist, you want to employ Socratic questioning. This involves asking a series of questions designed to help *your clients evaluate their own thinking* processes and arrive at new answers themselves. You help direct your client's attention to pertinent issues. You may start with your client's hypothesis and pursue it to its logical conclusion, at which time it will become evident that the initial hypothesis is in need of revision. The strength of Socratic questioning is in the logical argument. Additionally, you collaborate with your client to design behavioral tests to check out empirically the client's original hypothesis and to support alternative views. The clients thus take responsibility for their own thoughts and assumptions and for changing them. You will want to frequently help summarize and synthesize the information (Padesky, Workshop on Depression, San Francisco Bay Area 1996). Padesky emphasizes the importance of having clients summarize their work at the end of small therapeutic segments, preferably by writing in their therapy notebooks. Summarizing helps to focus and move forward. You can also help the client synthesize the information by asking, "What do you make of this?" "How do you put this together with that?" When more effort is put into learning, the learning is more profound and long-lasting. Recall here Epstein's (1994) view of information processing and learning, stated in chapter 3.

In a workshop with Dr. Craske, I learned that in a group, clients can pair up and be given the task to challenge each other. One client asks questions and the other responds. The same pairing can be done when the challenge involves a phobic situation, e.g., if one client is afraid of elevators, this client can be paired with someone who is not afraid of elevators to work on the elevator fear.

Worksheet 4: **Challenging Automatic Thoughts, 1st Step**

1. Date.

2. Specific Trigger: **Situation and/or physical symptom.**

3. Automatic Thought (Negative Thought). **The *exact* bad thing that will happen if you feel or do** (write #2 here): _____
   is:

   How strongly do you believe your Automatic Thought will happen, 0–100%? _____

Instructions to Worksheet 4: **Challenging Automatic Thoughts, 1st Step**

1. Date. By always recording the date, you will be able to monitor your progress over time.

2. Specific Trigger: **Situation** (driving over the bridge, going to the mall) **and/or physical symptom** (dizziness, tightness in chest, numbness in arms). What brought on your fear thought (Automatic Thought)? (Don't write "panic" or "anxiety," but what *specifically* in the panic or anxiety made you afraid.)

3. Automatic Thought (Negative Thought). **The *exact* bad thing that will happen if you feel or do** (write #2 here): _____ **is:** The thought should be stated in the form of a *specific theory/prediction* (not as a question, e.g., "I will have a heart attack and die," not "Will I have a heart attack and die?"). Questions to guide you: What are you afraid might happen with these symptoms? What's the worst thing that you think will happen in this situation?

   How strongly do you believe your Automatic Thought will happen, 0–100%? _____

0 = You do not believe the Automatic Thought will happen (in which case there should be no Automatic Thought).
50 = You're 50% sure that the Automatic Thought will happen.
100 = You're 100% sure the Automatic Thought will happen.
Use any number between 0 and 100%.

Encourage the Expression of Doubts

It is important to encourage the expression of doubt. After listening actively to the doubt, say, "You may well be right. Let's also look at other possible alternatives. Is that okay?" By listening, you give support to your client and thus bring him/her on board your territory, i.e., your way of looking at the dilemma.

Always Come Back to the Data

Craske (Workshop on Panic Disorder, San Francisco Bay Area 1996) emphasizes that when someone keeps returning to the fear, it is necessary to go back to the actual data, repeatedly if needed, e.g., "In spite of your trembling, you must be incredibly good at your job." (The client in this case discounted all of his successes because of his having trembled on one occasion.)

Validate Your Client, Be Supportive, and Add Humor

At Padesky's Workshop on Depression in the San Francisco Bay Area in 1996, I learned something very helpful; that is, to *interpret negative behaviors of clients as coping strategies.* For example, you can say, "When you lash out at others with sarcasm, I get the sense that you may be trying to cope with your fear of rejection. Unfortunately, it may lead people to reject you, confirming your fear." It also helps to use humor in this type of work, whenever possible, but, of course, in a sensitive way. In my groups, we use humor and have fun, but clients also leave feeling supported and optimistic.

Methods and Techniques

A number of cognitive-behavioral methods and techniques are available to the clinician. By "methods" I mean major procedures, including identifying, labeling, and challenging negative, danger-laden automatic thoughts and related behaviors. (These are identified by Roman numerals.) By "techniques" I mean the very specific and detailed challenges employed. (These techniques are in boldface type.) You will notice that some of them overlap. In fact, you will want to learn how to overlap the methods and techniques, as needed, in your work. I will illustrate with numerous examples from my clinical work.

Negative Automatic Thoughts Reflect Cognitive Traps—I

Often clients do not realize that their erroneous cognitions are very common. In fact, they are so common, that categories to classify them have been identified. For clients, recognizing which cognitive traps they employ, how the traps lead to the wrong conclusions, and challenging them, can be very helpful.

The negative automatic thoughts are categorized as irrational thoughts (also called cognitive distortions) or unhelpful thoughts (also called maladaptive thoughts). An example of an irrational thought is "Things never go right for me." An example of an unhelpful thought is "I feel so down, it's no use even trying."

These traps, or errors in the rules of inference, are important to recognize, because they *invariably arrive at a negative conclusion.* One consequence is a negative affective state. If I say to myself "I'm a rotten person," "I can't count on others," I am not likely to feel good about myself or other people.

Irrational Thoughts or Cognitive Distortions

Irrational thoughts constitute errors in logic. In therapy, the faulty logic is analyzed in great detail and challenged. Various clinicians have identified a number of cognitive distortions. Here, I will list a few that I find particularly relevant in panic and phobia disorders. The first two are emphasized by Barlow and Craske in *Mastery of Your Anxiety and Panic II* (1994). For a more extensive list, refer to *The Feeling Good Handbook* (Burns 1989).

1. **Exaggerating or Overestimating Risk**

   This means that the person greatly exaggerates the odds that a dangerous or bad event will happen. In other words, the event possibly could happen someday, but the probability of its happening is infinitesimal. Yet the predicted event is taken as established fact. The italicized words are the exaggerated events. Examples:

   - I could *faint* in a panic.
   - In a traffic jam, I will *lose control and leave the car and run.*
   - When I cross a busy street, I *won't concentrate*, and *I'll get hit by a car.*
   - If I panic, my breathing may slow down to the point of *suffocating to death.*
   - If I'm on a bus with no windows open and panic, my knees will get so *wobbly that I'll collapse.*
   - I was just lucky this time that it (*the feared event*) did not occur.

To challenge, use the **cognitive technique: Establishing the Facts or Probability vs. Possibility.**

When clients say "It could happen" about highly unlikely events, they are confusing possibilities with certainties. Response: "Yes, you are right. Anything can happen. An airplane may fall on us right now, but how likely is it? Can you live with the realization that you cannot control everything, and that occasionally bad things happen to people? (Or do you believe that by worrying you prevent the bad thing from happening? Are you resorting to the trap called Disaster Expectation?)"

Questions and challenges (establishing the facts and examining the evidence):

- Is this an established fact or is it a hypothesis?
- Do you know for certain that _____ will happen, or is it a remote possibility?
- What evidence do you have that this symptom is dangerous?
- Are your conclusions based on facts, or are you greatly inflating the danger?
- Is it helpful to take your thoughts as facts? For instance, the thought of going insane, does it prove or in any way increase the probability of you going insane? If yes, then let's check it out. (Here you can design a behavioral experiment. You and your client can try very hard to go insane and see what happens.)
- What are the *real* odds of _____ happening?
- Has it happened before?
- If it happened once, can you see why it did, and does that mean it will always happen?
- Is it just *possible* that _____ will happen some day, or is it highly likely? Let's look at the realistic probability here. How likely do you think it is that _____ will actually happen, on a scale from 0–100 percent? What probability *can you live with*? Let's see what happens to this number over time.

If the fear persists that certain symptoms will lead to fainting, dying, etc., review the physiology of fear with the client, i.e., present a detailed account of why these particular symptoms occur (see chapter 4, Section 1). Have the client review this material, and repeat it back to you in the next session.

Conclusion:

Your client needs to recognize that there is not necessarily a logical connection between X and Y; it is an error in processing. *Just because X occurs, does not mean that Y will, too.* "Just because my heart skipped a beat, doesn't mean I'll have a heart attack." "Just because I feel light-headed and unreal, doesn't mean I'm going to faint."

2. Catastrophizing

Catastrophizing, which is closely related to Overestimating Risk, involves one of two situations:

(a) Not only will the bad event happen, but extreme and *horrible consequences* will follow. It involves the worst-case scenario and is often expressed in "What if . . . ?" terms. Note that some people express the worst-case scenario in images rather than thoughts. Examples:

- In a panic I could lose control. Then I'll *lose my job, husband,* and *apartment* due to this "thing." What if I become *homeless*?

- If I panic and hit another car, there will be *agony, surgery, scars,* and *physical impairment.*

- If I drive on a bridge, traffic will stop and I'll *be there forever. I'll die there.*

(b) The person *underestimates his* or *her ability to cope* with the event. A negative emotion is often embedded. Examples:

- I will *go wild* with anxiety and be fired for *being crazy.*

- If I panic in a city far from home, I'll have a *terrible time* because of my anxiety. I'm *afraid of my fear.*

- If I get stuck in the elevator, I'll *look silly, cry,* and *faint.* People *will think I'm crazy.*

- If I leave the reception prematurely, everyone will *think of me as an idiot. I couldn't bear it.*

- If I'm trapped in the elevator, I'll yell, scream, and kick the walls. *I will embarrass myself.*

Example of both (a) and (b):

- I will get *emotional* and *hysterical.* When my family and friends realize how incompetent I am, they will *disown me. I'll be totally alone.*

To challenge, use the **cognitive technique: Decatastrophizing.**

Decatastrophizing involves *talking the person through the event.* In fears involving social consequences, e.g., loss of control and embarrassment, the person may be overestimating risk, or, if the risk is likely to happen (e.g., blushing, sweating), coping strategies can be used. If the person fears serious consequences, e.g., permanent impairment and/or death, decatastrophizing involves *replaying the event over and over* in its entirety until the fear response diminishes. Decatastrophizing lends itself very well to work on core beliefs. "What would it mean to you if _____? And then what? And what would that say about you?" (See later section on core beliefs.)

Questions and challenges for (a) and (b) above, respectively (it often helps to use the worst-case scenario):

(a) Will one bad event (e.g., a panic attack) really have these extreme consequences? How exactly would that occur?

Work *with images* and *follow them to completion*. Do not stop the image at the worst point (fainted, dead). Rather, find out what is the special meaning of the catastrophe. It may lead to a new problem or a core belief.

- Let's assume for now that you would faint (client had said that she would find it awful). What's so awful about it? Okay, now, how exactly would you faint? What would happen next? How long would you be unconscious? When you came to consciousness, what would you do? What would you do the rest of the day and the next day and the next? The aim here is to show that life continues—even after fainting.

- Let's assume for now that the worst-case scenario would happen. You would end up with scars and a physical impairment. Describe your life then. How would you cope? How do you think others in that situation cope? Have you ever seen or heard of anyone who coped quite well under those circumstances? If the person coped well, do you think it was because he or she felt ready for the accident that led to the impairment? If the person was not ready, how do you imagine he or she arrived at that point? Now, imagine yourself in that situation. God forbid that you would ever become seriously impaired for any reason. But if it happened, what might the impairment be? How would you try to cope? What would you do about your scars? How would you want to spend your time? What are the things you *could* do?

- Let's assume the worst, you would die. How would it happen? How would you feel? And what would happen then? And how would your family and friends then react? And would their lives somehow go on?

  (While none of us can predict how we would cope with a catastrophe, for the panicker it is imminently present, which is why decatastrophizing works.)

(b) Did you ever in your life react poorly to a situation and manage to cope with it?

- Does it matter terribly what others think? (From here, you may want to go to core beliefs.)

- Is there life after embarrassment?

- Is embarrassment a fatal condition?

- If you saw someone _____ (faint, cry, yell), what would you think and how would you respond?

- Do people really even notice and care? If your client says that others saw him or her react poorly, ask, How many times have you panicked and not acted in that way? What does that tell you?

Conclusion:

So what if _____ ? Can I somehow handle _____ ?

3. Control at All Costs

People with panic disorder seem to be obsessed with two kinds of control:

(a) *Control over outside events.* Examples:

- I can't fly in an airplane. What if the *pilot* is on a *suicide mission*? *I wouldn't have any control.*

- I don't want to be around people. What if I panic, and they try to hold or calm me down? Then I'll come unglued! *I'd feel controlled.*

- I can't stand situations where *I'm not in control*: Stuck in traffic, waiting in line, flying, being a passenger in a car, sitting in the middle of the row in a movie theater, sitting in a meeting at work, being at the dentist.

(b) Full *control over one's emotions* at all times. Examples:
- I *should* be able to *control my anxiety* like everyone else does.

- When an anxiety attack occurs, I'll *lose control completely.*

- These feelings could get worse each time, until I have *no control in my life.*

To challenge, present your client with questions about **Uncertainty and Human Nature, and Distinguishing Between What Can and What Cannot Be Controlled.**

Questions and challenges:

- Do you think that there is anyone who does not want control? Are you willing to accept the reality that some things are under your control and other things are not?

- If you are able to accept that not everything is under your control, it follows that life is uncertain. How do you generally cope with uncertainty?

- Can you learn to distinguish between what you can and what you can't control and put your energy into things that are under your control? This means that although you cannot necessarily prevent a panic attack from coming on (not having ultimate control over the occurrence of panics), you can control your response to a large extent. Could you learn to accept such a balance of control?

- Can you allow yourself to be a human being with feelings as opposed to a robot without any?

- Do you feel drawn to people who never show their feelings?

4. Perfectionism or All-or-Nothing Thinking

Perfectionism and all-or-nothing thinking are related. Perfectionists and extremists tend to think in "either/or" terms. They set unobtainable standards for themselves, hence they often fall short. They are a success or a failure. If something is not 100 percent, it is no good. Things are seen in black and white. Words such as *always, never, should, must, ought,* and *need to,* are often involved. Things are "either/or," there's nothing in between. Examples:

- I must keep it together and *be perfect. I can't allow others to evaluate* my actions or behavior. (This example also illustrates issues of control.)

- If my hands *shake*, I won't be able to perform. My clients will think *I don't know my job* and I'll lose them. My previous successes won't count. I don't want my hands to shake! (This is also an example of catastrophizing.)

- I don't want to live this way, with this panic disorder. *I want to be perfect.* I can't allow myself to *appear anxious* or *cry* in front of people. I have to be perfect or people won't respect me. (This is also an example of control at all costs.)

To challenge, use the **cognitive technique: Unobtainable Standards vs. Evidence Continuum.**

Questions and challenges:
- Can you allow yourself to be human, sometimes imperfect and vulnerable?

- What is the worst that could happen if you are not perfect?

- Can you learn to think in percentages, e.g., I did this work project at 70 percent of my capacity. Considering the limited time I had/my flu, I did quite well.

- Draw a line (see Clark 1989). At one end of the line write "Always perfect job performance," and at the other end write "Never perfect job performance." Have the client write the names of family members, friends, and acquaintances and where they would fit on the line in terms of the particular descriptor. Then have the client place his or her own name on the line. It may help the client to see what the norm is, and then ask why the same rules should not apply to him or her. The same procedure could be done with other areas where the client's expectations are unreasonable.

5. Emotions as Evidence

The person interprets his or her emotions as evidence of reality to the exclusion of more objective evidence. The stronger something is felt, the more it is believed to be a sign of truth. Examples:

- If I feel *anxious*, it *is dangerous*!

- This *scared feeling* of panic and avoidance *means* I can't do it.

- When I *feel* these symptoms, I *know* there is something seriously wrong.

- *Pain* in my arm *means* a heart attack.

- I have this *feeling* of impending doom. I *know* something bad will happen.

To challenge, use the **cognitive technique: Establishing the Facts.**

Questions and challenges:
- Are feelings good evidence of facts?

- Have your feelings ever been wrong?

- Have you ever made a decision based on your feelings that turned out to be a big mistake or disappointment? (This should be easy to elicit.) If the answer is yes, what does that tell you about relying on feelings?

Unhelpful or Maladaptive Thoughts

Unlike irrational thoughts, unhelpful thoughts may seem logical and reality-based. They are difficult to dispute with logical reasoning. However, they do not promote well-being. People engage in maladaptive thought patterns when they constantly criticize themselves (e.g., as a way of self-punishment), worry in excess, berate themselves over past mistakes, give up trying, or have unfulfilled expectations. Although unhelpful thoughts may not come up directly in the context of panic attacks, they may be in the background and impede progress in overcoming the disorder.

You can test whether a thought is maladaptive by asking your client:

- Does this thought make you feel good about yourself?

- Do these thoughts promote your well-being?

1. Disaster Expectation

This is often found in people who worry chronically, which involves a number of panickers. There are three versions of this:

(a) The person worries because he or she cannot possibly cope if bad things happen unexpectedly. Therefore, the person takes the stance of always preparing for the worst. Example:

- I can't stand the idea of being *relaxed without worrying* and *then* hearing of a *disaster*.

(b) Magical Thinking (this is actually an irrational thought). Many average people engage in this. Usually it means that if the person worries intensely enough, the bad event will not happen. Worrying somehow "saves" them. Few people will admit holding this belief openly, yet I have found it to be extremely common (even among therapists). Example:

- If I *really worry* about having a heart attack when I panic, it *won't happen*.

- God will spare me. I *paid my dues worrying*.

(c) Another version of magical thinking is that after many uneventful episodes, the client's luck will run out and the bad event will happen. Example:

- I haven't had a heart attack in a panic so far. I have been really lucky. But I'm *bound to run out of luck* anytime.

To challenge, have your client try on the **Rose Colored Glasses** (Sobel and Ornstein (1996)) and do **Behavioral Experiments.**

Questions and challenges:

- Are you willing to take the risk of not worrying and see what happens?

- Are you willing to try out the *Rose Colored Glasses*, i.e., expect positive things and see what happens? Are you willing to take that challenge to grow beyond your prison of worry? If yes, that involves selectively paying attention to good memories from your past, but most of all it means focusing on the present, and if you must look ahead, that means that you'll expect things to turn out well.

- A *behavioral experiment* involves making positive predictions about upcoming worrisome events and later comparing those predictions with what actually took place. See Behavioral Experiments (The Experimental Method) VI, later in this chapter.

2. Giving Up

This state of mind occurs in a person whose thinking is dominated by the expectation of a negative outcome and who no longer wants to exert any effort to change it. Examples:

- I'll never get over these fears, so *why try? It's of no use.*

- Driving on the freeway is too hard. I'm just *going to forget it.* I can drive on surface streets.

To challenge, **Look at Past Evidence, Ask about Pros and Cons.**

- Was there ever a time when you felt hopeless about something and it turned around for you? Was there ever some joy in your life afterwards?

- Does this stance make you feel good about yourself?
- What are the pros and cons of trying again?

3. The Unanswerable Question: Why? Why? Why?

Everyone would like to know why something happens, including why he or she developed panic disorder. The best you can do is provide an educated guess based on your knowledge about panic disorder and the client's history and current profile. But some people get "stuck" in this questioning mode, plaguing themselves with a question that cannot be answered. Rather than really trying to find an answer, the question becomes a vehicle for self-torture and condemnation. Examples:

- *Why* do I have panic attacks, why?
- *Why* am I always anxious?
- *Why* don't these panics go away?

To challenge, help your client switch to a **Problem-Solving Mode: How or What Questions.**

- Does this way of thinking help me solve a problem?
- What can I do to help decrease my anxiety?
- How can I best learn to cope with panics?

Challenging Automatic Thoughts—II

Worksheet 4: Challenging Automatic Thoughts is another example of a verbal method (vis-à-vis behavioral methods) for your client's use. As mentioned earlier, there is quite a bit of overlap between the verbal approaches. The worksheet is best used with specific instances, not with general feelings in panic and other anxious situations. The worksheet is followed by the instructions on its use and three examples. Learning to use this kind of thought record to challenge negative automatic thoughts leads to lower rates of relapse following treatment (Padesky, Workshop on Depression, San Francisco Bay Area 1996). Note that initially the client is asked to do this in writing, but the ultimate purpose is to learn to do it mentally.

The main difficulty clients have with this worksheet is that they make it too complicated by including too much material. When you examine the examples, you will notice that very few words are used. The fewer words used, the easier it is to stay focused. You may want to help your client be brief. This includes working on one automatic thought at a time. If a panic generates more than one (e.g., "I will have a heart attack and go crazy"), have the client use a separate worksheet for *each* automatic thought (one for the fear of heart attack, the other for the fear of going crazy). If several *related* fearful thoughts are identified, work with the worst fear, e.g., when a client says that he or she fears collapsing and fainting, the fear of collapse is often related to the fear of fainting. Fainting is then the automatic thought with which to work.

Working On and Challenging Focal Fears—III

The central fear that most terrifies a person in a panic attack is called the focal fear. As a rule, clients' fears during panics can be condensed into one major fear, but sometimes they have two or even three focal fears. A number of other fears may lie on the surface. Clients often say, "What if I fall down, cry, or something else terrible happens?" thus listing several

Worksheet 4: **Challenging Automatic Thoughts**

1. Date.

2. Specific Trigger: **Situation and/or physical symptom.**

3. Automatic Thought (Negative Thought). **The *exact* bad thing that will happen if you feel or do** (write #2 here): _____
   is:

   How strongly do you believe your Automatic Thought will happen, 0–100%? _____

4. My Evidence. **Why do you think #3, your Automatic Thought, will happen?**

   Then Refute!

5. Alternative Thought(s) (Positive Thought). **Can the trigger** (#2 above) **have an explanation/lead to something** (other than #3) **with a harmless result?** List 1–3 with the probability of each, from 0–100%.

6. Face Up to Automatic Thought (#3). **"Just because** _____ **does not mean** _____**"** or **"So what if** _____ **!"**

   How strongly do you believe in your Automatic Thought (#3) NOW, 0–100%? _____

Instructions to Worksheet 4: **Challenging Automatic Thoughts**

---

1. Date. By always recording the date, you will be able to monitor your progress over time.

2. Specific Trigger: **Situation** (driving over the bridge, going to the mall) **and/or physical symptom** (dizziness, tightness in chest, numbness in arms). What brought on your fear thought (Automatic Thought)? (Don't write "panic" or "anxiety," but what *specifically* in the panic or anxiety made you afraid.)

3. Automatic Thought (Negative Thought). **The *exact* bad thing that will happen if you feel or do** (write #2 here): _____
   is: The thought should be stated in the form of a *specific theory/prediction* (not as a question, e.g., "I will have a heart attack and die," not "Will I have a heart attack and die?").
   Questions to guide you: What are you afraid might happen with these symptoms? What's the worst thing that you think will happen in this situation?

   How strongly do you believe your Automatic Thought will happen, 0–100%? _____

4. My Evidence. **Why do you think #3, your Automatic Thought, will happen?** It is the evidence (proof) used for your Automatic Thought.

   Then Refute! You can refute your evidence based on past experience, logic, and other evidence (e.g., do your emotions really dictate your behavior?).

5. Alternative Thought(s) (Positive Thought). **Can the trigger (#2 above) have an explanation/lead to something** (other than #3) **with a harmless result?** List 1–3 with probability of each, 0–100%.
   Questions to guide you: Were you resorting to a cognitive distortion? What else makes these sensations happen? Does it really matter what others think?

6. Face Up to Automatic Thought (#3). **"Just because (#2) occurs, does not mean (#3) will too."** or **"So what if (#2) happens!** It's not the end of the world!" (Apply "So what if _____ " to social fears.)

   How strongly do you believe in your Automatic Thought (#3) NOW, 0–100%? ____

Example 1: Challenging Automatic Thoughts

Worksheet 4: **Challenging Automatic Thoughts**

1. Date. 9-30-97.

2. Specific Trigger: **Situation and/or physical symptom.**
   I'm having a panic and I feel unreal and dizzy.

3. Automatic Thought (Negative Thought). **The *exact* bad thing that will happen if you feel or do** (write #2 here): *feel unreal and dizzy*
   is: *I will go crazy.*

   How strongly do you believe your Automatic Thought will happen, 0–100%? <u>40%</u>

4. My Evidence. **Why do you think #3, your Automatic Thought, will happen?**
   I can't control my thoughts. I never felt this way before. If it lasts any longer, I'll lose it forever.

   Then Refute!
   Well, I have had many panic attacks and I never have gone crazy yet.

5. Alternative Thought(s) (Positive Thought). **Can the trigger** (#2 above) **have an explanation/lead to something** (other than #3) **with a harmless result?** List 1–3 with probability of each, 0–100%.
   Maybe the symptoms are caused by anxiety. The anxiety will subside. 60%.
   What are the real odds of my going crazy? People just don't go insane because of anxiety. 70 %.

6. Face Up to Automatic Thought (#3). **"Just because _____ does not mean _____" or "So what if ____!"**
   Just because I feel unreal and dizzy, does not mean I will go crazy. Even though it's a strange feeling, going crazy is at the other end of the scale!

   How strongly do you believe in your Automatic Thought (#3) NOW, 0–100%? <u>10%</u>

Example 2: Challenging Automatic Thoughts

Worksheet 4: **Challenging Automatic Thoughts**

1. Date. 12-15-97.

2. Specific Trigger: **Situation and/or physical symptom.**
   Getting light-headed and dizzy while driving.

3. Automatic Thought (Negative Thought). **The *exact* bad thing that will happen if you feel or do** (write #2 here): *getting light-headed and dizzy while driving*
   is: *I will faint.*

   How strongly do you believe your Automatic Thought will happen, 0–100%? <u>55%</u>

4. My Evidence. **Why do you think #3, your Automatic Thought, will happen?**
   I have trouble seeing, I can't focus, I can't keep my balance. I'm losing consciousness.

   Then Refute!
   I have not fainted in a panic yet, so I probably won't faint now.

5. Alternative Thought(s) (Positive Thought). **Can the trigger** (#2 above) **have an explanation/lead to something** (other than #3) **with a harmless result?** List 1–3 with probability of each, 0–100%.
   My anxiety can bring on the sensations. Maybe I'm hyperventilating. 75%.
   I may be overestimating, drawing the wrong conclusion, even if it's hard to believe. The real odds may be insignificant. 65%.
   Because of my fear, I may be monitoring my dizziness level all the time. 80%.

6. Face Up to Automatic Thought (#3). **"Just because _____ does not mean _____"** or **"So what if _____!"**
   Just because I feel light-headed and dizzy, does not mean I will faint.

   How strongly do you believe in your Automatic Thought (#3) NOW, 0–100%? <u>5%</u>

Example 3: Challenging Automatic Thoughts

Worksheet 4: **Challenging Automatic Thoughts**

---

1. Date. 6-1-98.

---

2. Specific Trigger: **Situation and/or physical symptom.**
   At work I got a panic and started to shake.

---

3. Automatic Thought (Negative Thought). **The *exact* bad thing that will happen if you feel or do** (write #2 here): *shaking in a panic at work*
   is: *If my coworkers notice my shaking, my anxiety will be exposed . . . I'll be so embarrassed!*

   How strongly do you believe your Automatic Thought will happen, 0–100%? 90%

---

4. My Evidence. **Why do you think #3, your Automatic Thought, will happen?**
   When I panic, my shaking is obvious. When others become anxious at work, they can keep their act together and don't tremble. People at work gossip a lot, and they'll talk about me!

   Then Refute!
   I'm not sure people really notice if I am shaking.
   People may notice and may not even care.

---

5. Alternative Thought(s) (Positive Thought). **Can the trigger** (#2 above) **have an explanation/lead to something** (other than #3) **with a harmless result?** List 1–3 with probability of each, 0–100%.
   People may have opinions, but I may never find out, unless they tell me. It's okay for people to think what they want to think. 80%.
   If they do comment, it would just be curiosity or concern, not maliciousness. 70%.

---

6. Face Up to Automatic Thought (#3). **"Just because _____ does not mean _____"** or **"So what if _____!"**
   So what if they gossip? Who cares? I'll survive that!

   How strongly do you believe in your Automatic Thought (#3) NOW, 0–100%? 20%.

fears. Yet, if you question them about what they *primarily* fear, you will find that each client's fears are actually very focused. This is one reason why it is so important to have clients describe automatic thoughts in very specific ways. If you work on the more superficial thoughts and miss your clients' focal fears, they will not overcome their panic disorder. Typically, focal fears center on disasters in one of the following areas:

- Physical (having a heart attack or stroke, suffocating to death, fainting while driving).

- Mental (going mad, totally losing judgment, hurting someone else).

- Social (being humiliated, laughed at, criticized, embarrassed, judged).

- Behavioral (losing control of the car, running back and forth uncontrollably, yelling and screaming).

Behavioral and social fears are closely related. That is, some people may not mind their own yelling and screaming if no one is around to hear and observe them, while others may become frightened about having "lost control," even if they are alone and there is no one to witness their loss of control.

When doing therapeutic panic work, the basic approach is first to become aware of the focal fear and learn how the client arrived at that fearful conclusion. Usually, this is accomplished by very detailed questioning. You explore the logic behind the fear. You could say to the client that, if the theory presented were true, you, too, would be frightened. Yet theirs is a *hypothesis*, which cannot withstand close scrutiny. Use Worksheet 4: Challenging Automatic Thoughts to confront focal fears, but use the other methods, as well.

The Focal Fear of Dying From a Heart Attack

Feared symptoms in a panic are usually palpitations, heart racing, heart fluttering, skipped heart beats, and chest pain. Some clients have the habit of frequently checking their pulse.

Medical Fact: Panic attacks do not lead to heart attacks. On an electrocardiogram (EKG) the panic shows up as a slightly increased heart rate. Your client can ask his or her physician about what the actual symptoms of a heart attack are. These usually involve very strong pressure in the chest, intense chest pain, and, only occasionally, palpitations. The symptoms often diminish with rest. In contrast, when the anxious or panicked person lies down, the symptoms frequently persist.

Challenges:

- The client is probably using an Overestimation error. Use the questions in that section.

- Review the fight/flight response again, and specifically explain why the heart beats faster during that response.

- Has the client been checked out medically? What did the physician say?

The Focal Fear of Dying From Suffocation

The feared symptoms are usually the sensation of not getting enough air, i.e., breathlessness, the throat closing up, choking sensations, or chest pressure. Just being in an enclosed, hot, and/or crowded place often causes the client to believe that he or she will not get enough air.

Medical Fact: People do not die from suffocation during a panic. Although it is extremely common for people to *feel as if* they were *not breathing*, they actually are breathing all along. In fact, the harder they try to breathe, the more likely it is they might hyperventilate. The perception is paradoxical, because when hyperventilating, the person breathes in too much air, all the while having the sensation of not getting enough air.

Challenges:

- The client is probably using an Overestimation error. Use the questions in that section.

- Review the physiology of breathing again; point out what happens when the body is saturated with oxygen and releases too much carbon dioxide.

- If clients think that they were holding their breath or breathing too little during panics, tell them to hold their breath for as long they possibly can and see what happens. You should demonstrate first. Invariably, of course, the client will be forced to breathe after holding for a while. This behavioral experiment should demonstrate that it is not so easy to stop breathing, and that the need to breathe is governed by a very strong autonomic function.

- If there is enough air in a tight, crowded place for everybody else, how could there not be enough air for you?

The Focal Fear of Having a Stroke

Symptoms interpreted by clients as those leading to a stroke are numbness, tingling, weak sensations (especially if perceived on one side of the body), and/or a heat wave moving up the spine to the head. At times, the client checks his or her pulse or blood pressure.

Medical Fact: Panic attacks do not lead to strokes. When blood pressure rises during a panic attack, it does so only slightly, not enough to trigger a stroke.

Challenges:

- Your client is probably using an Overestimation error. Use the questions in that section.

- I do not encounter this fear as frequently as some others. However, when I do, I explore what having a stroke means to the client. Usually, there is a special reason. One client's father and grandfather had both suffered from high blood pressure and strokes when they had been the same age he was. He feared the same fate. It was helpful to counter his fear with the fact that his lifestyle was very different: he did not smoke, exercised diligently, and ate only healthy food. Ultimately, he had to accept the existential truth of not being able to control whether or not he would have a stroke. Putting an end to his habit of checking his pulse and blood pressure helped him let go of his fear. Another client I treated was a physical therapist who often worked with stroke victims. She was in her forties and she kept saying, "But there are so many young people who have strokes!" In group, when we explored the meaning of her fear, she revealed a long history of guilt feelings, for which she believed she would be punished with a stroke. Because she worked with stroke patients, she knew what strokes often lead to and found them particularly frightening. She believed that God was going to punish her in that way. Revealing her guilt from past wrongdoings and her fear of punishment were the first steps in her recovery.

The Focal Fear of Fainting

Sensations leading to this fear are light-headedness, dizziness, feelings of faintness, numbness, blurred or tunnel vision, inability to concentrate, feeling hot, and being unable to breathe. This fear goes hand in hand with the fear of collapse. Often, when the client says that he or she is afraid of collapsing, fear of fainting is behind the fear of collapse. Hence always ask your client what is meant by "collapse." If your client claims to have fainted, ask for a detailed account. Many clients use the term "fainting" to indicate feeling very close to fainting. This is a very different physiological state than lying on the ground unconscious, even if only for a few seconds.

Medical Fact: People do not faint from panics, except in very rare circumstances. This is because blood pressure rises slightly during the physiological arousal in panic. For someone to faint, the blood pressure must plummet, involving the parasympathetic nervous system. Fading away is the most typical sensation prior to fainting. To help reassure clients who have this fear, I state that I have *never* heard of anyone fainting in a life-threatening situation; i.e., there must be a survival instinct, which prevents this from happening. (People with blood-injection-injury phobias constitute the exception; they sometimes do faint. There is a sudden drop in their blood pressure. See the section on Fainting in chapter 4.)

Challenges:

- The client is probably using an Overestimation error. Use the questions in that section. Since this event is seldom life threatening, when you ask, "What is so awful about fainting?" you usually get Catastrophizing errors as well. Use the questions in that section also.

- Review the fight/flight response again, and specifically the symptoms associated with a slight decrease of oxygen to the brain.

- Review the conditions required for fainting: Decreases in blood pressure and heart rate. In panics these rise.

- Here it is extremely useful to do voluntary hyperventilation (see chapter 4, Section 2) to demonstrate its effects and the fact that it does not lead to fainting. In addition, the client can subsequently stop the symptoms with diaphragmatic breathing.

- If there is a risk of fainting during panic attacks based on past history, the client can use a coping mode of tensing the muscles, and/or coughing (Craske, Workshop on Panic Disorder, San Francisco Bay Area 1996). These techniques seem to help by slightly raising the blood pressure and/or stopping hyperventilation.

The Focal Fear of Going Crazy or Having a Nervous Breakdown

The feared symptoms are often feelings of unreality or depersonalization, losing the ability to focus and concentrate, racing thoughts, feeling dominated by fear with the belief that the fear will damage the person's nerves forever, unusual thoughts and bizarre images, and the mind going blank. When these clients feel that they cannot "control" their thinking, they interpret that as a sign of beginning madness.

Medical Fact: Panic attacks do not lead to insanity. A schizophrenic may have panic attacks in addition to the psychosis, but panic disorder does not lead to schizophrenia. If someone does have a "nervous breakdown," it is never due solely to panic disorder. There are probably a *number* of other psychological and maybe physiological factors involved. It is normal at times for people to have strange, bizarre thoughts and images. It is also common for people to feel so stressed at times that it is hard to cope, concentrate, and focus. This does not lead to insanity. Rather it demonstrates that some people fear such experiences, and that they may have high anxiety sensitivity.

Challenges:

- The person may be Overestimating Risk, Catastrophizing, or using Emotions as Evidence, in which case, use the questions in those sections. These can be closely associated with the cognitive traps Control at All Costs and Perfectionism, thinking that one must be in control of one's emotions and thoughts at all times, and that one is defective if anything out of the ordinary is experienced.

- The Self-Administered Brief Mental Status Exam is a technique described by Williams and Laberge (1994) to be used by persons who believe they are on the verge of going insane. They are told that this self-administered test is similar to a mental health professional's method of assessing for thought disorder. The person answers the following questions: His or her name, the current date, the person's address, where the person is currently, who is the president, and who is the governor of the state. If all of these can be answered properly, that demonstrates the client is not losing his/her sanity.

The Focal Fear of Losing Control

"Losing control" tends to be an emotionally loaded expression, often involving Catastrophizing errors. The term is vague, and it needs to be broken down into the *specific* fear involved. For instance, the strong impulse to run during the fight/flight response is thought of by many people as losing control. Others fear crying, running and screaming, becoming paralyzed with fear, frightening others, having a sensation described as "crawling out of their skin," and so forth.

Fact: The fight/flight response actually *increases* the ability to think faster and more clearly. However, the thoughts are focused on the threat. Some people label crying as losing control. Here, it is helpful to show the person how to accept crying as a normal human emotion, even though there are some situations where we prefer not to cry. The most "uncontrolled" behavior I have ever heard of was one client who bolted out of a room, and another who once screamed out of fear on one airplane flight.

Challenges:

- Most of these fears reflect Catastrophizing errors, hence use the questions pertaining to decatastrophizing. Reassure clients that even if they did act strangely, that does not brand them forever.

The Focal Fear of Embarrassment or Humiliation

The fears here are closely associated with those of losing control. Feared symptoms are shaking, trembling, crying, blushing, unsteady or cracking voice. There is a common fear of being thought of as "anxious," as if anxiety were a crime. Many clients view anxiety as weakness, which they disdain. Some of my clients fear running, leaving a meeting, a queue, a store, or collapsing, or any of the other fears listed above under the focal fear of losing control. They are mostly afraid that others will think of them as "crazy," "weird," or "strange."

Fact: It is a reality for everyone to sometimes do or say something that feels embarrassing or humiliating. Although no one looks forward to it, we all can learn to survive it.

Challenges:

- This often reflects Catastrophizing, Control at All Costs, and Emotions as Evidence errors. Use the questions in those sections. Emotions as Evidence is applied also when a person feels shaky internally. Even though many people do not manifest shakiness outwardly in any way, they believe that because it is felt internally, it must nonetheless be observable to others.

The Focal Fear of Becoming Too Weak to Move or Falling Down

The feared sensations are numbness, tingling, extreme weakness, feeling "wobbly." The weakness is felt especially in the knees and legs, sometimes in the arms.

Medical Fact: Even when people feel weak, numb, and stiff when anxious, that does not mean that their muscles are too weak to support them. It is a *perception*, and the person assumes that it is not possible to move, stand, or drive under those circumstances. The fight/flight response actually *increases* physical strength, as it prepares the body for vigorous action.

Challenges:

- These fears often reflect Overestimating errors. Use the questions in that section.

- This fear lends itself well to behavioral experiments. The next time the client feels that way, ask him/her to scratch their head, move an arm, or walk. This experiment can be done beautifully in the office if the client claims to be having a panic or otherwise having those feelings.

Belief Ratings—IV

Belief ratings pertain to how strongly a thought (the feared disaster) is believed (Clark 1989; Salkovskis and Clark 1991). They can be used both for challenging and for assessing progress during treatment. Belief ratings allow you to monitor what is happening to your client's fear over time, especially fears pertaining to focal fears. Have your client rate the belief in the disaster on a 0–100 percent scale.

0 percent = You don't believe at all _____ (the feared disaster) will happen.

50 percent = You believe halfway _____ (the feared disaster) will happen.

100 percent = You believe absolutely _____ (the feared disaster) will happen.

Further, the belief ratings are used with two time frames: (1) while here with the therapist right NOW, and (2) THEN, i.e., in the middle of a bad panic attack. Say, "Sitting here right NOW, using the scale from 0 to 100, how strongly do you believe that in a panic your fluttering heart will result in a heart attack?" "And in the middle of a bad panic, when you feel the same sensations, how strongly do you believe it will happen THEN?" Since your client is most likely to respond with a higher rating for the thought during the panic, the next line of questioning involves, "Why it is different?", that is, "Can you tell me how the probability changes?"

Challenging the Belief Rating: Putting It to a Logical Test

This involves aspects of Playing Columbo (see section V below). Drs. Michelle Craske and Jim Boyers taught me about this approach.

Example:

T -You said that you believe the probability of collapsing, which for you means falling down in a panic, is 25 percent. Are you willing to look at this?

C -Yes.

T -How many panics have you had in all? Give me a very rough estimate.

C -Oh, maybe a hundred.

T -You have had a bad time, having collapsed twenty-five times already. How did you deal with these?

C -Oh, no. I haven't actually collapsed.

T -You are kidding? (Said in an incredulous tone.)

C -No.

T -But I don't understand. You said that the probability of collapse is 25 percent. If the probability were 25 percent, you would already have had twenty-five episodes of collapsing. But you said that hasn't happened. What I don't understand is how you manage to hold onto this belief without any evidence. How do you accomplish this?

C -But it *could* happen.

T -Okay, let's assume for a moment that some day it *possibly could* happen. What would be a more realistic probability? What would be the number?

C -Oh, maybe 1 percent.

T -It is good that you realize that you were greatly exaggerating the probability. (As a therapist, you know that one percent is still a very high figure; it means that your client would already have had one episode of collapsing in a panic. You can choose to pursue this matter right then or in the next session.)

Assessing Treatment Progress With Belief Ratings

The belief ratings can be used within sessions as well as across sessions. They can help you observe in a concrete way whether the cognitive restructuring is having an impact, i.e., did the focal fear really change as a result of the cognitive technique you used with the client? I have found it extremely helpful to use the method across sessions in the following way. When I have finished challenging the client's thought (in group or individually), I write down the belief ratings I obtained in full view of the client. During the next session, as soon as possible, I turn my attention to the client and ask, "Remember the work we did with you in the last session? We looked at how strongly you believed that you would have a heart attack in a panic. How strongly do you believe it now? Rate your belief from 0 to 100 percent." If the person gives a higher number than at the end of the last session, I inquire about what happened during the week to change the number. I find it is very useful to demonstrate to clients that this is not simply a game I was employing during the previous session, but rather that they need to assume responsibility for their thoughts and beliefs, and own up to them all of the time.

Example:

T -Sarah, remember last week when we were working on your fear that you will go crazy in a panic? At the end of the session, your belief that you would actually become insane during a panic was 5 percent. How about right now, what number would express your fear?

C -Fifteen percent.

T -So, it is higher than the last time. What happened this week to change it?

C -Well, I did not think much about it because I didn't have a panic.

T -Let's stay with this. How did the rating change?

C -I guess I'm just so used to fearing it.

T -So, it is almost as if the habit of thinking that way returned, and this is not uncommon. How can you work on this thought?

C -I have to challenge it whenever I become aware that I'm thinking that way.

T -Great! That way you won't keep reinforcing your old fear.

Playing Columbo—V

If you have seen the TV series "Columbo," you have noticed the police detective Columbo's style of questioning. (Dr. Donald Meichenbaum demonstrated this method at a workshop in 1996.) Essentially, Columbo comes across as very naïve and asks the following types of questions:

-I'm a little confused, could you help me out here?

-How did you come to that conclusion?

-That's fascinating. You have a way of putting things together . . .

-I don't quite follow you there. . . .

-Can you tell me more about it?

-I just want to get things straight in my mind. How are X and Y related?

-Yes, you may be right, but . . .

At times, the therapist can play the devil's advocate, but these questions must be asked in a sensitive way; clients should never feel they are being mocked.

Examples:

-I'm a little confused. How can your migraine symptoms, which you have had before, lead to a stroke? I want to understand how you arrive at that conclusion.

-I want to get this straight in my mind. How is it that when you worry about your son, that will prevent him from getting into a car accident?

-Yes, you think that you will do well at the party, but what if your worst fear comes true and you make a total fool of yourself?

Another aspect of applying this approach to challenging your clients is to ask questions indicating total surprise and naiveté when the client has taken a positive step. This is especially useful in response to early signs of changed thinking, and particularly with clients who are very resistant or those who had a very hard time challenging their negative automatic thoughts.

Examples:

-You mean that *in spite of the bad panic*, you did not let the fear overwhelm you, and you were able to challenge your automatic thought?

-You mean to tell the group that you are now questioning your fear *even* while you are in the *middle* of a panic attack?

-Are you telling us that now you can start to challenge your fears? That's quite an accomplishment!

-In spite of how hard it is for you to drive on the freeway, you mean that you did it and actually felt *good* about doing it?

-So, in spite of feeling terrified in the hot, closed room, you *stayed* there?

-How, how, *how* did you accomplish getting on the train?

-Let me see if I understand what you said. You mean to say that you *can cope* with your fears? What coping techniques did you use that were helpful?

Behavioral Experiments (The Experimental Method)—VI

This involves designing a behavioral experiment to test the validity of negative automatic thoughts, putting the ideas to the test. By observing what happens, new information is obtained behaviorally. That information is then used to question the credibility of the original automatic thought. Some clients respond readily to verbal challenges, others need to "see it to believe it." These experiments are closely associated with the client's use of safety signals and safety behaviors. (For a more comprehensive list of these, see chapter 8.) In other words, what is the client doing that currently prevents him or her from disconfirming the erroneous automatic thought? To design convincing tests, these factors must be identified.

Doing Without Safety Signals and Safety Behaviors

Typical safety signals are going to places accompanied by another person and carrying medications, water, a paper bag to breathe into, a telephone, phone numbers of hospitals, etc. Common safety behaviors are: tensing up, sitting down, and holding onto a shopping cart (when feeling faint); staying close to exits in department stores (to prevent losing control); making a strong effort to control one's thoughts (to prevent insanity). The use of these safety devices results in what Foa and Kozak (1986) describe as not accessing or disconfirming the fear structure. This is what makes it possible to do many exposures and still continue to feel fear. These safety devices can be accessed, e.g., by asking the person why the feared catastrophe did not occur: "Did you do anything that prevented you from having a heart attack, fainting, going crazy?"

Sometimes a verbal challenge can set the stage: "If someone was going to have a heart attack, do you really believe that using distraction would stop it from happening?" Your client is likely to admit that this is an illogical conclusion. Next, the behavioral experiment consists of the person refraining from engaging in the safety behavior, or not carrying the safety signal. "Would you be willing to engage in an experiment? Next time you are in the grocery store and feel dizzy, instead of holding onto the shopping cart, would you be willing to stand or walk without it? Let's see what happens. Do the experiment and tell the group next week how it went." "What would happen if you didn't get out of the movie theater right then? Would you be willing to wait for ten minutes and see what happens?" If the thought is too frightening, have the person try the experiment for a briefer time span, e.g., five minutes, and then lengthen the time in short increments. Another client may be too terrified to go anywhere without a bottle of medication. Have him or her begin with tiny excursions without carrying the medications, e.g., to the corner store. In sum, if a safety signal or safety behavior has been identified, the behavioral experiment consists of doing without it; if needed, starting with small steps. It is helpful if the client writes a prediction of what he or she thinks will happen beforehand. This can be done during the session. Then, at the next session ask the client what actually happened, and compare the response to the prediction. As many of these examples illustrate, it is often a good idea to start with small steps.

Empirical Hypothesis Testing

Once you know the client's irrational fear, you can have the client test the hypothesis behaviorally by making a prediction and comparing its validity to the actual outcome. The experiments should be set up to be efficient and to maximize a positive outcome. When properly set up, they can be powerful agents of cognitive change. Frequently, you as the therapist may invent some good experiments. You should also enlist the client in the planning. His or her input is critical to pinpointing more precisely what contributes to disconfirmation of the fear. "What could you do to convince yourself that you will not faint, have a heart attack, a stroke, go crazy?"

Fennell (1989) suggests taking the following steps:

1. Make a prediction.

2. Review evidence for and against the prediction.

3. Set up an experiment to test the validity of the prediction.

4. Make a note of the results.

5. Draw conclusions.

You may want the client to set up a written prediction to be compared later with the actual occurrence. Be sure to always compare the prediction with the actual outcome. It is particularly helpful to finish by asking the client to state a rule about the finding. Some rules might be, e.g., "My heart can safely beat very fast under a variety of conditions, even when I am not exerting myself physically." "People are tolerant about observing anxiety in others." Hypothesis testing can thus be used in phobic situations and in combination with interoceptive exercises. Example of a behavioral experiment:

(The first part helps the client to identify each step in the panic response.)

C -I was at the deli with my co-worker last Friday and I had a panic. I can't handle these panics.

T -Can you describe exactly what happened?

C -I felt dizzy, and I left the deli.

T -You are still describing the event vaguely. I'd like to look at each step of your panic response. Can we take one tiny step at a time?

C -I was with my co-worker at the deli picking up a sandwich for lunch.

T -What was the very first thing you noticed?

C -I felt hot and dizzy.

T -And then what do you remember was the very next thing?

C -I thought I was going to have a panic and faint.

T -What happened next?

C -I grabbed the counter for stability. But my heart rate increased and I felt sweaty. I couldn't stop focusing on my symptoms.

T -Then what happened?

C -I told my co-worker that I was not feeling well and clung to her until we left.

T -And then?

C -As soon as we left, I felt better.

T -What does this episode teach us?

C -I escaped.

T -That's right. By escaping you did not put to the test whether or not you would really have fainted. The same goes for grabbing the counter for stability and clinging to your co-worker. These actions *reinforced* your belief that the symptoms lead to fainting. What would allow you to test whether or not you would faint?

C -Not to escape or not to use the safety devices.

T -Let's set up a behavioral experiment to test out your hypothesis.

(Here is the planning of the behavioral experiment).

T -How could you test your belief that feeling hot and dizzy will result in fainting? Where else do you usually have those symptoms?

C -At the mall, driving over a bridge, and in the sauna.

T -Okay. Which of these can you envision using for an experiment?

C -I guess the sauna.

T -You are willing to try the sauna? That'd be great! You think you may faint there. Is there a possibility you won't?

C -Yeah, it's possible. (Said in an incredulous tone.)

T -Let's set it up so it won't be too difficult for you. Do you have a friend who also goes to the spa?

C -Yeah.

T -If you can arrange for your friend to go to the spa with you, plan on entering the sauna alone, but have her check on you every five minutes to see if you have fainted. How long do you envision staying in the sauna?

C -Maybe ten minutes.

T -Let's see if you can stretch the time. I'd like you to really test out your hypothesis of whether being hot and dizzy leads to fainting. Do you think you can stay for 20 minutes? Your friend will check on you four times. *If* after a while you don't need your friend to check on you so often, you may want to tell her to come back in ten minutes.

C -Okay.

T -When this week can you do it?

C -Saturday or Sunday. I'll check with my friend.

T -Great, so we are testing whether being hot and dizzy leads to fainting. One last thing, how strongly do you NOW believe it will happen, from 0–100 percent?

C -Sixty percent.

T -Great! You'll test the hypothesis by staying in the sauna for 20 minutes this Saturday or Sunday. Afterwards, write down briefly what happened. Note how strongly you believed in the hypothesis of fainting THEN, from 0–100 percent, and bring it into our next session. Is this agreeable to you?

C -Yes, I'll do it, but I'm very nervous.

T -True, you will probably continue to feel very anxious, but if you are still willing to engage in this experiment, you'll have accomplished a great step.

Assuming that she reports a lower belief rating at the next session, I would ask her for her conclusion in her own words. Then, I might ask her to do the same test without her friend. It is quite likely that her friend constitutes a safety signal, even if she does not state so.

Imagery Reconstruction—VII

Often, the negative cognitions take the form of images rather than words and sentences. By their nature, images are not articulated and are often very brief. However, you can pursue the images just as you do thoughts. Following are examples of images that two clients shared when I asked for detailed descriptions:

Example 1: "I can just picture myself panicking in a long line. Everyone is noticing that there is something wrong with me. They just stare at me as if saying, Get a grip on yourself!"

Example 2: "I can just see myself on the subway. It stops at a tunnel, and there is a delay of an hour. I panic the whole time. I'm yelling, screaming, trying to get off the train. Everyone is staring at me. They think I'm nuts!"

As you have seen, in treatment, you want thoughts and images to be processed in detail. The greater the detail, the more likely it is that the steps are manageable. If, when eliciting automatic thoughts, your client cannot articulate them, ask him or her, "Did you have an image or a picture in that very situation?"

Use the Question "What Happens Next?"

Typically, images are cut off at the very worst point. This also happens with "What if?" questions: "What if the elevator gets stuck?" "What if I lose it and start screaming on the airplane?" The catastrophe remains imprinted, often in the form of an image. Identify the image, recreate it, and draw it to its logical conclusion, and/or change the ending.

T -Okay, let's imagine you are taking the elevator and it gets stuck. What would you do then?

C -I'd panic, and I would feel so embarrassed.

T -You think you would panic. What exactly would happen?

C -I won't get enough air and will faint.

T -Even though you said you have never fainted before, let's assume for a moment you did actually faint. What happens next?

C -I'd lie there on the elevator floor helpless.
T -And then what would happen?
C -I'd wake up eventually. But it would be awful.
T -Okay, you would wake up. And what would you do then?
C -I'd straighten myself out, stand up, and figure out what to do then.
T -Good, and after you got out of the elevator, what would you do the rest of the day? And the next day? And the day after?

The key is *not to allow the image* to stop at the worst point. What happens next? is the question to use a great deal here. The goal is to see that there is life after the catastrophe. If the catastrophe involves death, then you may wish to explore what it would mean to die, i.e., to get to the meaning of the feared event. Often, it is not the event itself that is feared as much as the circumstances surrounding it or the feared impact on others, e.g., small children. One client was terrified of panicking at home alone. She feared dying from a heart attack. However, the possibility of her dying was less of an issue than the thought of her lying near death all alone. In my group treatment with her, we touched on existential issues and the reality that most people would like to have a loved one nearby at the hour of their death. Yet there is no way of ensuring that will happen. The alternative would be to have someone with us all the time, which would be a very high price to pay. Furthermore, as I say to my clients, even if someone were with you all the time, is that a guarantee that you would not die alone? What if that person just went to the bathroom or went out for a few minutes, and you died then? Is there ever absolute certainty and control?

The Survey Method—VIII

The survey method is particularly helpful when clients worry about what others think of their overt symptoms or behaviors. Other peoples' views can be learned by asking them about various scenarios in regard to themselves, a third person, or the inquirer. For example, "When you leave a meeting unexpectedly, what do you believe others are thinking of you?" "What do you think of someone who starts trembling at the checkout line?" What would you think of me, if it happened to me?" This method can be helpful, because the distorted thinking is often in the domain of the self, not of others. Once the person sees and accepts the rules the other person lives by, you can challenge why he/she must live by these other "harsh" rules. It is useful in situations pertaining to the cognitive traps Control at All Costs, Perfectionism, Disaster Expectation, and Giving Up. This work may lead the way to core beliefs.

Externalizing Fears—IX

Dr. Jim Boyers, my colleague at Santa Clara Kaiser, has used the following approaches specifically in groups. They are particularly useful early in the cognitive work. They also help to foster camaraderie among group members and bring some humor into the session.

Normalizing

As soon as a client states a particular fear during a panic attack, ask the other members of the group to raise their hands if they have also experienced that particular fear. For instance, ask: "How many of you have felt shortness of breath? How many of you have felt feelings of unreality? How many of you have feared going crazy?" The likelihood is that a number of people in the group will have had the same fear, which will help normalize the experience.

De-escalating

Ask clients to share their fears (automatic thoughts) from Worksheet 4: Challenging Automatic Thoughts, 1st Step and write them down on a blackboard. Ask the first client to repeat his or her fear many times, louder each time, until you tell the client to stop. Right after the client has started, ask the next client to do the same with his or her fear. Then you repeat the same procedure with each additional client. Soon there will be a crescendo of voices. You can have them all stop at the same time or one by one. Invariably, clients wind up laughing, which helps to blow off steam and lower their apprehension.

Taking the Panic Apart

See Chapter 4, Worksheet 3: The Components of a Panic Attack. This involves asking the client to break down the panic attack into a detailed account of each component. Anytime the client glosses over part of the event, slow him or her down and ask the person to tell you exactly what happened. (You try to elicit physiological, cognitive, and behavioral components.) When thoughts are described, you ask for symptoms. When symptoms are described, you ask for thoughts and behaviors, etc. At the end you ask the client, "What is your conclusion about what happened?" Do not draw the conclusion for the client, let him or her do it. This is particularly effective in groups, because you can ask the other members for feedback. With this technique, you hope to make evident the influence that cognitions have on the panic process.

Role Play—X

Role play may be helpful with resistant clients. You can have the client play your role and you play him or her. Use your client's irrational automatic thoughts and arguments, and have the client take on the role of challenging you. You can play your role tenaciously for a while. Afterwards you may ask, "How did that feel? What did you think of my reasoning?"

Paradoxical Intention—XI

This can be a very powerful behavioral method. Craske (Workshop on Panic Disorder in the San Francisco Bay Area, 1995) suggests that prescribing the feared symptoms can be used particularly well with highly resistant clients. This can be done with any feared symptom, be it rapid heart beat, dizziness, trembling, etc. It is especially helpful when the client believes that if the symptoms were just a bit more intense or lasted a bit longer, the feared catastrophe would occur. One client, who feared appearing tense in a one-to-one meeting, took on the task of purposefully tensing up (but not visibly) for a few minutes while talking to a co-worker. He alternately tensed and relaxed. This client was willing to take the risk that the listener would notice and make a comment or withdraw. The listener neither noticed nor withdrew. Another client, prior to learning about the upcoming interoceptive exercises, felt dizzy at work for the umpteenth time. This time she felt angry and spun in her office chair to challenge the symptom. The dizziness increased as expected but it subsided shortly after she stopped spinning!

Live paradoxical simulations can be performed in the office. You try to purposefully create the feared symptom and/or outcome. This is done best in a group. For instance, the entire group can be asked to try very hard to faint, e.g., via hyperventilation (Craske, personal communication).

Behavioral Coping Strategies—XII

A few strategies will be described here that are not mentioned elsewhere in this section.

Coping Mechanisms

It is important to emphasize coping mechanisms. These should ameliorate the panic experience and facilitate exposures, but not in "magical" ways as safety signals and safety behaviors do. They should allow the client to test automatic thoughts and ride through the anxiety and make it manageable. You might rehearse coping mechanisms and the antici-pated symptoms and fears with the client. Diaphragmatic breathing is one of the most useful of the coping mechanisms.

Doing diaphragmatic breathing has a direct impact on the breathing pattern, and if sustained, will affect the other autonomic functions such as heart rate, tingling sensations, etc. By concentrating on the breathing for a few minutes, the autonomic arousal is lowered, and the client's thoughts get a brief respite. This may allow for a more objective assessment of the situation.

Other behavioral coping tools available to the client are as follows:

- Looking at Worksheet 2: My Personal Coping Affirmations and applying them. The client may need periodic reminders to write down helpful hints.

- Doing the opposite of what fear prompts the person to do. For instance, when wanting to stand still or lie down, walking instead; when wanting to tense the body, relaxing instead.

- Talking to others about what is happening right now.

- Using imagery, envisioning riding on a wave. The panic is like the wave, which comes and goes. Riding with it rather than fighting it, makes the ride smoother. My colleague, Dr. Peters at Redwood City Kaiser, uses the following analogy to convey the principle of going with rather than fighting the panic: Clients view anxiety as a friend (anxiety is a lifesaver and a great motivator) to whom they open their arms. Friends sometimes pay unexpected visits. What is one to do? Slam the door? Hardly. Rather, invite the friend in and handle the situation as best as one can.

- If the person fears observable anxiety symptoms, such as blushing or sweating, telling another person, even a stranger in a supermarket line: "Is it hot in here, or is it just me? Boy I'm sweating."

- Rewarding oneself for any progress made.

Stress Inoculation

This behavioral approach is emphasized by Craske (Workshop on Panic Disorder, San Francisco Bay Area, 1996). It is particularly useful for fears of social consequences and when the person has actually fainted, thrown up, or had diarrhea in a social or work setting. Two approaches can be used: Decatastrophizing and desensitizing in live enactments. Decatastro-phizing has been described earlier. In your office, enact a real situation, and help the person to use verbal and cognitive coping strategies. "What could you actually do if X happened?" For example, "Let's assume the worst, you throw up in front of others and they run from you? How could you cope?" "You go to a party and actually faint. When you regain con-sciousness in a few seconds, everyone is gathered around you staring at you. How would you deal with it?" "You make a blunder in public, and everyone is laughing. How do you deal with the experience?" You can enact these scenarios especially well in group therapy with two to three different outcomes, the negative one the client fears (or that actually took place) and more adaptive ones. The goal to achieve in these types of scenarios is to learn to respond to them as the average person would, i.e., the experiences may be very uncomfortable but they do not have to devastate the person. Life goes on.

Summary

The goal of therapy is to accomplish a change in the client's fear structure. This is done via cognitive restructuring at the level of automatic thoughts, assumptions, and/or core beliefs.

There are numerous cognitive techniques and methods to facilitate your work in helping your client overcome his or her automatic thoughts. The style is collaborative, using Socratic dialogue, rather than confrontational.

Rather than summarizing the treatment strategies in a brief, general way, I will restate the methods and techniques employed.

Identifying Automatic Thoughts

The automatic thoughts must be specific. Use Worksheet 4: Challenging Automatic Thoughts, 1st Step.

Meth ods for Challenging Automatic Thoughts

Main Methods:

I. *Cognitive Traps*

Challenging Techniques:

Irrational Thoughts or Cognitive Distortions

Main Methods	Challenging Techniques
1. Exaggerating or Overestimating Risk	Establishing the Facts, Probability vs. Possibility
2. Catastrophizing	Decatastrophizing
3. Control at all Costs	Uncertainty and Humanness Distinguishing Between What Can and What Cannot Be Controlled
4. Perfectionism or All-or-Nothing Thinking	Unobtainable Standards vs. Evidence Continuum
5. Emotions as Evidence	Establishing the Facts

Unhelpful or Maladaptive Thoughts

1. Disaster Expectation	Rose-Colored Glasses, Behavioral Experiments
2. Giving Up	Look for Past Evidence, Ask About Pros and Cons
3. The Unanswerable Question: Why? Why? Why?	Problem-Solving Mode: How or What Questions

II. *Challenging Automatic Thoughts* and	Worksheet 4: Challenging Automatic Thoughts
III. *Working on and Challenging Focal Fears* IV. *Belief Ratings* (0–100 percent)	Challenging the Belief Rating: Putting It to a Logical Test Assessing Treatment Progress With the Belief Ratings
V. *Playing Columbo*	Naïveté and Incredulousness
VI. *Behavioral Experiments*	Doing Without Safety Signals and Safety Behaviors Empirical Hypothesis Testing
VII. *Imagery Reconstruction*	Use the Question "What Happens Next?"
VIII. *The Survey Method*	Ask Others
IX. *Externalizing Fears*	Normalizing, De-escalating, Taking the Panic Apart
X. *Role Play*	Switch Roles
XI. *Paradoxical Intention*	Prescribing the Feared Symptoms Live Paradoxical Simulations
XII. *Behavioral Coping Strategies*	Coping Mechanisms Stress Inoculation

Section 2: Changing Core Beliefs

When you work on your client's automatic thoughts, pay continual attention to how malleable these thoughts are. Are they being challenged and changed? Sometimes you get absolutely nowhere. No matter how much you try to help your client challenge negative automatic thoughts, the client may say, "But I still believe it." The person's belief makes it hard to take in the data that disconfirms the automatic thought. Another person may think that he or she is more vulnerable than others, possibly based on some very idiosyncratic learning. There can be specific underlying assumptions maintaining irrational thought. In such situations it is also likely that powerful core beliefs lie underneath the automatic thoughts that do not allow for their modification. In such a case, the core belief must be identified first. Sometimes, assumptions give a good clue as to the core belief. Once aware of it, you can work on changing it. In this regard, the reader is referred to Beck (1995), Burns (1989), and Greenberger and Padesky (1995).

Identifying Assumptions and Core Beliefs

Although I describe here how to identify only assumptions and core beliefs related to the *self*, Padesky (1994) suggests that beliefs about others and life itself should be identified and worked on, as well. They are closely interconnected.

When using the following approaches, you want to help the client keep the answers brief and to the point. To that end, use the client's language as much as possible. If your client becomes emotional doing this work, you are probably on target. No affect may indicate that you are not quite on the right track.

Ask Your Client Directly About His or Her Core Belief—I

You can ask direct questions, especially when you suspect that the core belief is closely linked to the automatic thought. This is especially likely when the client uses labels that get repeated.

Example:

"That was stupid of me." "I don't quite get it. I must be stupid." These statements suggest that the person has the core belief "I am stupid."

T -Don't you believe that you are as smart as others?

C -No.

T -Do you have any idea where that belief comes from?

C -When growing up, nothing was expected of me. I was seen as a cute kid, but not smart. Since then I have never trusted my intelligence.

T -What does that mean to you?

C -(In a whisper) I'm stupid.

Look for Common Themes Across the Automatic Thoughts—II

Observe what automatic thoughts and other expressions the person uses. Sometimes themes are repeated, providing good clues as to the core belief.

Example 1:

T -John, do you see a red thread running through your automatic thoughts?

C -Yeah, I keep worrying about what others think of me.

T -You may be on target there. What does it say about you?

C -I don't measure up.

T -And what is underneath not measuring up?

C -I'm a bad person

Example 2:

T -You seem to have a very hard time challenging your automatic thoughts. You say things like "I don't think this is my problem." or "Working with my thoughts helps me cope, but won't make the problem go away." Also at times you seem resigned to having to always struggle with panic, almost like you have given up on the idea that full recovery is possible for you. Do you have any idea what is behind all this?

C -Well, you see, when I was in my early twenties, about twenty years ago, I smoked marijuana daily for over a year. Then I quit. I think it really did something to me.

T -You mean it had an effect that lasts till now?

C -Yes.

T -Do you mean to say that you have a belief that somehow the marijuana damaged you, that it made you defective?

C -Yes, somehow it did.

This man's core belief was "I am defective." It was confirmed again and again. He made a great deal of progress in overcoming his panics, but in spite of the work that I and the group did with him, he left the group with his core belief still rather intact. It was very well ingrained. He attributed all his negative qualities (he described himself as lazy, never very happy, never had much initiative, and very dependent on his wife for his well-being) to the belief that his marijuana use twenty years ago had damaged him and made him defective. Giving up his core belief that he was defective would remove his justification for his negative qualities. If the marijuana use was *not* the reason, what would that say about him? The price of giving up his core belief was too high for him. He was not interested in further therapy to explore the true origin of his core belief "I am defective" and other psychological issues.

Example 3:

In an exercise on challenging automatic thoughts, a client wrote the following catastrophic thoughts: "If I faint, I'll cause a scene and be embarrassed. EVERYONE WILL THINK I'M INSECURE." "If people notice I'm shaking, I'll be embarrassed. INSECURITY." "I'll feel humiliated if I cry in front of people. INSECURITY." She had capitalized the words as I have written them here. On the bottom of the page she wrote that people will treat her with a lack of respect. I thought that her basic assumption was "If you are seen as insecure, people will not respect you." My guess was that the idea of insecurity reflected something "bad" about her, something that was related to why people might not respect her.

T -What is your belief about being insecure?

C -I am not like others. I'm not as adequate.

T -You mean that you think you are inadequate?

C -Yes.

Sentence Completion Method—III

The types of sentences used with this method are: "I am _____," "Other people are _____," "Life is _____." Look for a brief answer, preferably stated in one word (Padesky 1994).

Example 1:

T -You always want to be in control. What's the thought behind this? *Not having control of myself at all times would mean . . . .*

C -I'm powerless.

Example 2:

T -You are afraid of having a panic when alone, because you fear dying alone. We hope that that won't happen, but let's assume for the moment that for whatever reason you were close to death and alone. *Dying alone would mean . . . .*

C -In my hour of need I would be alone again, as always. No one cares.

Let Assumptions Lead You to Core Beliefs—IV

Assumptions are very closely linked to core beliefs, and sometimes they can lead the way to them. One way is to help the client change *should* to *If . . . it means . . .* statements.

Example 1:

C -I shouldn't ask for help.

T -Can you change it to an "If . . . it means" statement? *If I ask for help, it means* (what it says about you) _____.

C -If I ask for help, it means I'm incompetent.

Example 2:

C -I should be able to deal with anxiety.

T -Can you change it to an "If . . . it means" statement? *If I can't deal with anxiety, it means* (what it says about you) _____.

C -If I can't deal with anxiety, it means I have a weak mind.

Unfolding the Belief—V

David Burns (1989) has best described the "vertical arrow or the top down technique," which I call "unfolding the belief." It involves asking a series of questions in succession, which should lead to a deeper level of thought, and hopefully to the underlying core belief. You go as far as you can with it until there is a clear shift in affect (often a deep sadness emerges), or until the client expresses a very basic belief about the self, others, or life itself. When the thought or belief is repeated in the same or similar words, you have reached an impasse. Sometimes this means that you are not moving toward uncovering a negative core belief. It also could mean that there is a positive belief, or that the particular negative belief is flexible. (Some core beliefs are in the process of change, i.e., they are flexible.)

Questions and Statements to Unfold the Belief

1. State the belief as a *theory*.

2. Be as *specific* as possible.

3. If _____ happened, *why* would it be *so upsetting* to you?

4. If this thought were true, what would it *mean* to you?

5. What does that *say about* you? (about others/about life)

6. Why would that be *upsetting*?

7. And what would that *mean* to you?

8. What's *the worst* thing that could happen?

9. And then what?

At the very end of the unfolding process, if you have arrived at a possible reason for the belief, you can remark:

10. So *because* _____ , you *believe* _____ .

And follow up with:

11. *How long* have you held that belief?

Methods to Challenge Assumptions

If the opportunity arises to work on an assumption, you may choose to do it. If successful, it may facilitate work on the related core belief.

Behavioral Experiments—I

Look under the listed methods for challenging automatic thoughts, number VI. The same principles apply to testing assumptions behaviorally.

The Feared Fantasy Technique—II

This is a method described by Burns (1989). It can be used to confront an assumption, during role play. It is especially useful when the assumption is somehow linked to other people's reactions. Initially, you take on the role of the client and have your client badger you for the perceived "unforgivable" quality, e.g., making mistakes. Afterwards, you reverse the roles, and have the client be himself or herself, while you are the badgerer. It has a more profound effect if taken to *extremes.* I always ask the client for permission to use this method.

Example:

Assumption: If I make mistakes, people will think I'm incompetent. (The core belief is probably "I am incompetent.") This example involves a work situation.

C -(as badgerer): You made this mistake. Now my work is affected. Can't you do things right? What's wrong with you?

T -(as client): Yes, I made a mistake. I apologize that it is affecting your work. Yes, I sometimes make mistakes.

C -(as badgerer): You just don't get it. You should not have made such a mistake. You are incompetent, you know.

T -(as client): I made a mistake; I don't think that makes me incompetent.

C -(as badgerer): Incompetent people are no good. They should be fired. You should be fired.

T -(as client): A mistake does not make a person incompetent. If you think so, you are free to your opinion, but I don't agree with you.

This can be done more elaborately, depending on the issue. Afterwards the therapist becomes the badgerer and the client plays himself.

Methods to Change Core Beliefs

People with negative core beliefs do not *always* feel badly about themselves. This is in part because often there are corresponding positive core beliefs, i.e., paired core beliefs (Padesky, Workshop on Depression, San Francisco Bay Area 1996). The positive core belief may be inaccessible, very weak, or, at times, absent. Developing and strengthening new, positive core beliefs takes time.

Once you have identified the original negative core belief, it is useful to identify the modified or new core belief. This can be accomplished by asking the client *which new rule the client would like to live by* if he or she did not operate under the old belief. "It must be tough to live by your rule/belief. Do you want to make it more user-friendly?" An alternative new belief may not necessarily be the exact opposite of the old belief, e.g., if the old one is, "I'm stupid," the alternative to strive for may not be "I'm brilliant," but perhaps "My intelligence is normal," or "I am as smart as the next person." If the old core belief is "I am weak," the modified, new belief may not be "I am totally strong," but could be "I am strong most of the time." Padesky (1994) suggests that a new belief should be identified and articulated as soon as possible.

There are two ways of working on changing core beliefs, using an evidence continuum and a core belief log: and they can be combined (Padesky 1994). Although both methods are logistically simpler to use than challenging automatic thoughts, they require tenacity over a longer period of time. According to Padesky, six to twelve months is required. Note that a great deal of affect is usually associated with this work.

Evidence Continuum— I

Work with Evidence Continua should be done in writing, preferably with a blackboard, so that you and your client can conceptualize the task and absorb its meaning. Padesky suggests that *continua* be done specifically *with the new, positive belief* instead of the old core belief, which you are trying to weaken. You, the therapist, draw a horizontal line, an Evidence Continuum, and write the extreme positions at the ends, 0 percent to 100 percent. The end points *must* reflect extreme points if it is to work. Other points of the continuum can also be numbered with 25 percent, 50 percent, and 75 percent.

Worksheet 5: **Unfolding the Belief**

Automatic Thought

**Unfolding the Belief
(top down)**

Example 1: Unfolding the Belief

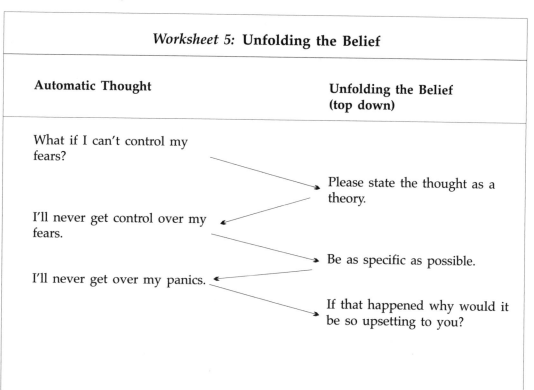

Worksheet 5: **Unfolding the Belief**

Automatic Thought

**Unfolding the Belief
(top down)**

What if I can't control my
fears?

Please state the thought as a
theory.

I'll never get control over my
fears.

Be as specific as possible.

I'll never get over my panics.

If that happened why would it
be so upsetting to you?

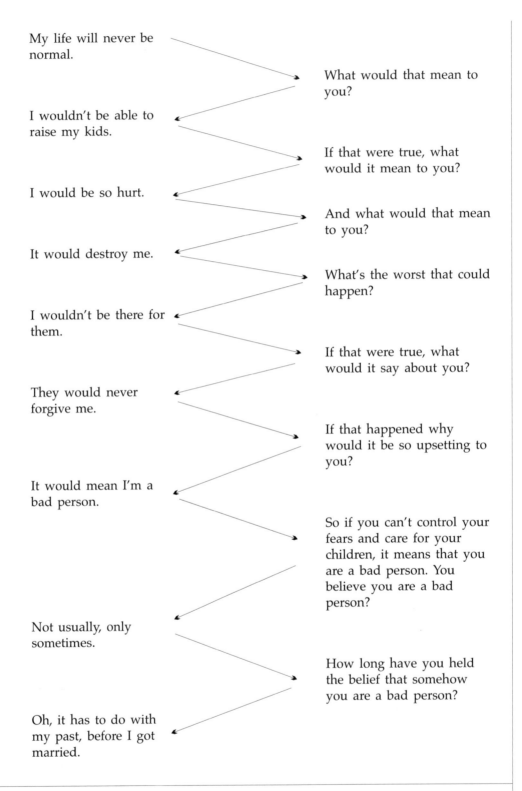

My life will never be normal.

What would that mean to you?

I wouldn't be able to raise my kids.

If that were true, what would it mean to you?

I would be so hurt.

And what would that mean to you?

It would destroy me.

What's the worst that could happen?

I wouldn't be there for them.

If that were true, what would it say about you?

They would never forgive me.

If that happened why would it be so upsetting to you?

It would mean I'm a bad person.

So if you can't control your fears and care for your children, it means that you are a bad person. You believe you are a bad person?

Not usually, only sometimes.

How long have you held the belief that somehow you are a bad person?

Oh, it has to do with my past, before I got married.

In this case, it is possible that she believes that the panic disorder is a punishment for past wrongs that she has done.

Example 2: Unfolding the Belief

Worksheet 5: Unfolding the Belief	
Automatic Thought	**Unfolding the Belief (top down)**
I could go crazy in a panic.	Can you be more specific?
I will go insane.	If you went insane, what would it mean to you?
Having panics shows that you have a mental problem, a mental illness.	What would it say about you to have a mental illness?
No one would care about me. I would be rejected.	Who would reject you and not care about you?
My family.	And what would that mean to you?
I'm an outcast and don't fit into society.	So because you have panics, your family would reject you, and you believe that you are an outcast. How long have you held that belief?
Since we came to America many years ago my family has been very concerned about fitting into the American culture, and any deviation is seen as really crazy. You have to fit the norm.	

I asked this client whether she had ever acted contrary to the family norms. She said that she had. "I've spoken up to my elders, and I'm not supposed to." This was the opening for working on changing her core belief that she does not fit into society because she is an outcast.

Example:
In this example the client's old core belief is "I'm weak." As stated above, the modified, new belief should not be "I'm totally strong." Instead the client chooses "I'm strong most of the time."

New Core Belief: I'm strong most of the time.

0 percent	Strength Continuum	100 percent
Never strong		Always totally strong

Now ask your client for the names of people he or she knows and place them along the line of the continuum. Have your client identify whom he or she likes a lot, a little, or not at all. Last, have the client place himself/herself there. People usually do not rate themselves at 0 in these behavioral scales. The aim is to show that people have different degrees of strength, and that strength is not the only quality that makes them likable or unlikable. It shows that a person can operate very well while being more or less strong. The client is then asked to evaluate on a weekly basis where he or she falls along this new core belief continuum.

Criteria Continua

Work on criteria continua helps to bring some flexibility into the belief system. This is subsumed under the evidence continuum work. Padesky (1994) states that people's negative beliefs are usually global, judgmental, and rigid. (Just as with vague and general automatic thoughts, little can be done to change them in this form.) The picture changes when the beliefs are translated into specific behavioral criteria. To illustrate, the client in the example above, when asked what constitutes "strength," said: "Standing up for oneself," "Going after what you want," "Not letting hardships knock you down." Then, a new criteria continuum from 0 to 100 is drawn up for each of the stated attributes. The client is asked, as above, to rate others and himself or herself along these continua. You will observe, as I did, that usually the client rates himself or herself higher along these criteria than along the original New Core Belief continuum. Using Socratic questioning, you can ask what can be observed from the contrast between the New Core Belief continuum and the criteria continua. This helps the client achieve insight. These continua can be used to plan for behavioral changes along the new core belief, as applicable. (For more information, consult Padesky's 1994 article.)

Core Belief Log—II

When people are in distress, their core beliefs are activated more easily. It is a good time to make changes. Worksheet 6: Core Belief Log allows the client to organize his or her thinking about the new core belief and to begin working on it. The log should be worked with for months. The process of learning to believe in a new, modified belief may take as little as three months or as long as a year. Even if the change seems slow, the value lies in helping the client see that these beliefs are learned and therefore can be revised. The old belief probably brought a great deal of distress to the client's life. The person discounted or minimized evidence that contradicted that belief. Likewise, events that did not prove the old belief were nonetheless interpreted as evidence for it. This log will help the client to gather relevant information more objectively and to catch information processing errors. The worksheet appears first, followed by an example.

Summary

There are methods to identify and change assumptions and core beliefs. When able to do this work, your client is likely to achieve more profound change.

Identifying Assumptions and Core Beliefs

  I. *Ask Your Client Directly About His or Her Core Belief*
 II. *Look for Common Themes Across the Automatic Thoughts*
III. *Sentence Completion Method*
 IV. *Let Assumptions Lead You to Core Beliefs*
  V. *Unfolding the Belief* (Worksheet 5: Unfolding the Belief)

Methods to Challenge Assumptions

 I. *Behavioral Experiments*
II. *The Feared Fantasy Technique*

Methods to Change Core Beliefs

 I. *Evidence Continuum* (with Criteria Continua)
II. *Core Belief Log* (Worksheet 6: Core Belief Log)

Worksheet 6: Core Belief Log

1. Old Core Belief.

2. Why I want to change my old Core Belief.

3. New Core Belief (State a core belief that is more user-friendly).

4. List Current and Future Experiences (however small) that Support the New Core Belief.

Date	Experiences

This list is to be continued for a number of months to really affect change.

Example: Core Belief Log

Worksheet 6: **Core Belief Log**

1. Old Core Belief.
   I'm too sensitive to cope with stress and anxiety.

2. Why I want to change my old Core Belief.
   I have panic disorder; I always worry about everything.
   I am too sensitive, but I am tired of feeling that I just can't cope.

3. New Core Belief (State a core belief that is more user-friendly).
   Often I handle anxiety well; sometimes it is rather overwhelming.

4. List Current and Future Experiences (however small) that Support the New Core Belief.

Date	Experiences
10-97	*In treatment I'm learning to cope better with my panic disorder.*
10-15-97	*When I was waiting for the results of the biopsy, I really had a hard time; I felt overwhelmed. But this would be hard for anyone!*
10-20-97	*I was very anxious having to tell my sister that I can't watch her kids any more, except in emergencies, but I did it!*
11-5-97	*I was afraid to go to the restaurant by myself, but I went for the first time in ages. I coped quite well.*
11-27-97	*I invited the family for Thanksgiving, even if it always gets chaotic with all of us, but I wanted to prove to myself that I could do it.*

(And so forth.)

This list is to be continued for a number of months to really affect change.

6

Treatment Module III: Interoceptive Exposure
(Sessions 7–9)

Overview of Treatment Module III

This module constitutes a major component in treating panic disorder. You will guide your client to elicit feared sensations, using a behavioral method. This is then combined with the cognitive techniques used previously to produce effects in the experiential and rational minds. Because of the complex nature of panic disorder, approaching it from various avenues seems to produce maximum beneficial outcomes for the greatest number of clients.

Session 7

During this session I go through the twelve exercises listed in Table 6.1 (see page 126), or at least most of them. The objective is to find at least a few exercises that elicit sensations producing fear, expressed in SUDS (Subjective Units of Anxiety-Distress Scale). These are recorded in Worksheet 7: Interoceptive Exposure Record. At the end of the session, I collect the worksheet and rank-order the exercises that are checked (SUDS 20 or higher) from the least to the most fearful.

Session 8

I bring Worksheet 7 to the next session and work with my client's relevant exercises, those ranked from the least to the most feared. The client repeats the exercise up to three times, but stops when the SUDS level is lower than 20. In this way the client progresses to the more difficult exercises. These are recorded on Worksheet 8: Repeating Interoceptive Exercises.

In a group, clients work in pairs, spread out through the room. Member A the "coach," holds member B's copy of Worksheet 8 and instructs B to do his or her first ranked exercise. The instructions are on the bottom of the worksheet. Each exercise is done once, twice, or three times, as instructed. Then member B becomes the coach for A and follows the same procedure. A does his or her first ranked exercise once, twice, or three times. Next, B works on his or her second ranked exercise, again one to three times. In this manner, members alternate (work back and forth with each other). I work with the odd person if the numbers are uneven, or more commonly, I go through the initial list (Worksheet 7) with any member who was absent for Session 7.

At the end of Session 8, clients take home Worksheets 7 and 8. For the homework assignment they are to repeat the exercises *daily* during the week. Note that if your client is very fearful of a particular exercise at the end of this session, it can be saved for Session 9. Clients are instructed to bring the worksheets to the next session without fail to show the progress that has been achieved. Clients can start to do naturalistic interoceptives, i.e., engage in more natural activities that bring on the feared sensations.

Session 9

I examine the client's worksheets and assess the progress made. I have the client repeat difficult exercises. Then, I model the expansion of the exercises outside of the office. What this means is that I go with the client to an elevator, a small, enclosed room, and an empty hallway to do some of these exercises. The assignment at the end of the session consists of repeating the interoceptives *daily* in more challenging, even phobic, situations. In a parked car the client can hold his or her breath, breathe through a straw, and hyperventilate. In someone else's home the same exercises can be done in a separate room or bathroom. When standing in line the client can hold his or her breath. If clients have phobias, I encourage them to do the exercises in phobic situations. For example, one client did hyperventilation and straw breathing at work in an empty conference room to prepare himself for his meetings.

The Conditioned Aspect of Fear of Panic Sensations

In chapter 5, a number of methods for challenging feared cognitions in panic were presented. Barlow (1986, 1988) and Argyle (1988) emphasize another aspect of fear acquisition: *conditioning*. Barlow (1988) believes that in panic there is a conditioned association between fear and physical symptoms, just as there is between fear and phobic situations. A panic attack, or false alarm, can occur in a variety of situations. The alarm response becomes strongly associated with the cues where it first occurred, in this case with physical sensations. The more intense the alarm, the more likely that conditioned learning occurs, which takes the form of "learned alarms."

Fear has been shown to condition easily to internal, "interoceptive" (stimuli arising from the body) cues; furthermore, interoceptive conditioning is unconscious and very resistant to extinction (Barlow 1988). In such conditioning, a biological vulnerability can be assumed that may explain why some people condition easily while others do not. For many people, a panic attack, i.e., the "false alarm," is a significant emotional event, even traumatic. According to Epstein's (1994) views on information processing and learning, the learning in the experiential system is often based on emotionally important experiences. The response becomes automatic and resistant to scrutiny by the rational system. When frightened, the person tries to make sense of the emotional reaction, but the content of the cognitions is forced into a narrow domain.

Panic is viewed as a phobia of internal sensations, according to Craske and Barlow (1993). Someone with specific or social phobias or agoraphobia often tries to avoid certain situations and places associated with the fear. Likewise, someone with panic disorder attempts to avoid the feared internal sensations. However, avoidance is more difficult to achieve, because unlike other phobias the person cannot run away from his or her body. Nonetheless, some avoidance is commonly attempted, e.g., many panickers stop exercising, avoid heat, caffeine, and so forth.

Researchers have devoted thought to how interoceptive fears play such a crucial role in panic disorder. The following possibilities have been proposed: Panickers may be physiologically more *reactive, perceive* physiological states more *easily, focus* more attention on their *bodies,* and/or *fear* bodily *sensations* more than normal controls (Ehlers 1993). The research quoted by Ehlers suggests that the interoceptive factors associated with the development and maintenance of panic disorder are that people with the disorder have an increased ability to perceive their heart rate; their attention shifts more readily toward bodily cues; and they view the symptoms of anxiety and panic as more dangerous than others do. In contrast, panickers were *not* found to be physiologically more reactive or to experience more bodily fluctuations compared to controls.

The interoceptive exposure work (including the exercise) described herein was developed by Drs. David Barlow and Michelle Craske. I was introduced to it at a workshop they led in 1987 at the conference of the Anxiety Disorders Association of America. I have also observed that cognitive restructuring alone does not work as well as combining it with interoceptive work. Behavioral exposure is a crucial and very potent way of demonstrating to the client that the feared catastrophic consequences do not take place (Barlow 1990; Craske and Rodriguez 1994; Margraf et al. 1993).

A strict cognitive therapist may use interoceptive exposures primarily in the service of the cognitive restructuring, i.e., as behavioral experiments designed to show that the sensations are harmless. Cognitive-behavior therapists, the group with whom I identify, employ interoceptive exercises repeatedly to decondition the client's fear from the physical sensations. This is analogous to the treatment of phobias, which usually are not cured by cognitively challenging the fears, but by in vivo exposure. The ultimate goal in all aspects of the treatment is to bring about a cognitive change at the deepest level, and the best way to achieve that is by combining cognitive and behavioral methods.

Many therapists find it difficult to do the interoceptive work, in particular, because of the very active role they must take. Yet the treatment component requiring the greatest technical proficiency is the cognitive therapy (Barlow 1997). This is reflected in the relative sizes of chapters 5 and 6. While this does not imply that the cognitive is more important than the interoceptive work, the former requires a more elaborate account to be comprehensive.

How Interoceptive Exposure Works

As stated above, an excellent way to effect a change in the conditioned fear of panic attacks is through interoceptive exposure. This component of the treatment is best introduced after some cognitive restructuring work has been done. Interoceptive exposure is most powerful if it achieves a twofold purpose. First, fear of sensations is deconditioned. Second, the exercises serve as behavioral experiments to test the catastrophic hypotheses the client holds.

Deconditioning Fear

To decondition fear, clients must expose themselves repeatedly to the feared internal sensations. Repeated interoceptive exposure leads to habituation, i.e., the fear diminishes. The client learns experientially that the symptoms are harmless, albeit uncomfortable, and that he or she can predict such experiences by bringing on the sensations on purpose. Thus the client can test his or her beliefs about the uncontrollability and catastrophic nature of panic. By applying breathing and cognitive coping skills, a sense of control is brought into the experience. Clients learn that they can handle formerly terrifying sensations, thus furthering their self-efficacy. The behavioral tests and applied coping skills should strengthen the new, more adaptive thoughts that were learned in the cognitive restructuring phase. Cognitive and behavioral challenges are integrated to strengthen the learning at all levels.

A number of the interoceptive exercises I used were later listed by Barlow and Craske in the 1989 edition of their *Mastery of Your Anxiety and Panic*. (The reader is referred to their new edition [MAP II] 1994; see also Craske, Meadows, and Barlow's *Therapist's Guide for the Mastery of Your Anxiety and Panic II and Agoraphobia Supplement* 1994). Although other researchers developed procedures along similar lines, Barlow and Craske were instrumental in spearheading the interoceptive work I present here.

Feared Symptom Clusters and Avoided Activities

Clusters of symptoms seem to give rise to specific fears, correlated with certain domains of threat and vulnerability (Argyle 1988; Craske, personal communication; Kenardy, Evans, and Oei 1992). The typical clusters of symptoms and related fears are as follows:

- Vestibular (Fear of collapse and fainting):
  Dizziness, light-headedness, faint feelings

- Cardiac (Fear of dying):
  Palpitations, chest pain, tingling

- Respiratory (Fear of dying):
  Shortness of breath (dyspnea), choking sensations, suffocation, smothering, tingling

- Externally observable autonomic arousal (Fear of being scrutinized by others and looking foolish):
  Trembling, shaking, blushing, sweating, "losing control" over behavior

- Psychologically threatening concepts (Fear of losing control or going crazy):
  Depersonalization, dizziness, the mind going blank, thoughts racing uncontrollably, feeling a lack of emotional control and disintegration.

In several workshops I attended, Dr. Craske stated that typical activities avoided by panickers for fear of the sensations produced are as follow. (Note again why it is important to identify the more subtle avoidances during the assessment and subsequent sessions.)

- Physical exercise, running up stairs, dancing
- Emotional discussions producing intense emotions, e.g., anger
- Suspenseful movies and sports events
- Sexual relations
- Ingesting caffeine (coffee, tea, caffeinated sodas, chocolate), wine
- Steamy rooms (shower stalls, saunas)

Common Symptoms Elicited by Interoceptive Exercises

The following interoceptive exercises commonly produce the symptoms indicated in the parentheses. However, not every person experiences the symptoms listed here, and some exercises produced a different set of symptoms. The exercises are also listed in Tables 6.1 and 6.2.

- Shake head side to side (Dizziness)
- Place head between legs (Dizziness)
- Run in place (Heart palpitations)

- Tense body completely (Chest tension)
- Hold breath (Tight chest, suffocation)
- Spin (Dizziness)
- Breathe through a small straw (Suffocation, shortness of breath)
- Hyperventilate (Light-headedness, faint feeling)
- Place external pressure on throat (Suffocation, lump in throat)
- Stare at a spot: wall, mirror, or hand (Depersonalization, derealization)
- Swallow quickly (Lump in throat)
- Focus on worst sensation in imagery: throat closing (Lack of air), heart pumping (Pain and discomfort), etc.
- Use a tongue depressor (Choking)
- Apply pressure to upper arm (Numbness, tingling)
- Press upper arm against torso (Numbness, tingling)
- Stand up suddenly from a lying down position (Dizziness)

Table 6.1: Interoceptive Exercises for the Office

Exercise	Length of Time*	Instructions
1. Shake head side to side	30 sec.	Lower your head a *bit* and shake it loosely from side to side, with your eyes open. When the timer goes off, *suddenly* lift your head and stare straight ahead for a little while.
2. Head between legs	1.5 min.	Sit in a straight chair. Bend your head down between your legs, trying to keep it lower than your heart level. When the timer goes off, *suddenly* lift your head and stare straight ahead for a little while.
3. Run in place	1 min.	Jog in place lifting your legs to hip level, if possible. (Or run up stairs.)
4. Complete body tension	1 min.	While sitting, make fists with your hands, tense your feet, bring your shoulders forward and tense your chest and entire body. If possible, stretch out your legs while holding the tension. Breathe deeply throughout.
5. Hold breath	30 sec.	Just as you begin timing, take a deep breath, cover your nose and mouth with your hand, and try to hold it for 30 sec. *If you cannot hold for that length of time, stop earlier.*

Table 6.1: **Interoceptive Exercises for the Office (Cont.)**

Exercise	Length of Time	Instructions
6. Spin*	(a) 1 min. (b) 1 min. and walk	Spin around at a good pace. Give yourself room and have a wall nearby to put your hand against if you lose your balance. Or use an office chair that spins and push against the floor as you spin.
7. Straw breathing	2 min.	Place a thin straw in your mouth and breathe in and out through it. Pinch your nose *slightly* with your other hand. If there is too much pressure, after a while, let go of your nose before stopping altogether.
8. Hyperventilate	1.5 min.	While *standing*, breathe deeply in and out through your *mouth* (like panting, but slower, and breathing *out* more than breathing *in*). Make it audible, i.e., make a sound that can be heard across the room.
9. External pressure on throat	1 min.	Using either your thumb or two fingers, apply pressure to the middle of your throat. Apply pressure until it feels uncomfortable, but not extremely so.
10. Stare at a spot	2 min.	Pick a spot on an empty wall and stare at it *without deviating your gaze* at all.
11. Quick swallowing	4 times	Swallow as quickly as you can four times in a row.
12. Focus on your worst sensation in imagery	2 min.	Remember your worst panic sensation. Now close your eyes, imagine a very bad panic, and totally focus on that feared symptom. Or think of a feared thought or image, such as your "losing control" or "going insane," (imagining yourself in an insane asylum), etc. Do not allow yourself to be distracted.

* Do (a) first and keep repeating it until your SUDS level is less than 20. Then do (b), and keep repeating until your SUDS level is less than 20

Table 6.2: **Naturalistic Interoceptive Exercises***

Exercise	Length of Time	Instructions
13. Ingest caffeine[†]	(a) Coffee (b) Coffee & chocolate	Drink a cup of caffeinated coffee or tea (rather strong). For part (b) either drink two cups or combine one cup with a piece of chocolate. Here you want to work on sensations brought on by caffeine. One advantage is that the maximum effect of the caffeine is not immediate, allowing you to practice with greater unpredictability.
14. Relax and daydream	(a) 5 min. (b) 10 min.	Sit and try to relax. Allow yourself just to daydream without focusing on anything planned or anything that needs your attention.
15. Create heat	(a) 15 min. (b) 30 min.	Turn up the heat at home and sit with your warmest clothing on. In the car, close the window and turn up the heat, especially on a hot day (if too fear-provoking, start with 5 min.). This is a very powerful exercise for those fearing heat and suffocation.
16. Stare at your mirror image and/or at the palm of your hand	(a) 2 min. (b) 3 min.	Stare at one spot on your person in the mirror or at a spot on your palm 6–8 inches from your face *without deviating your gaze* at all.
17. Tight clothing around neck	(a) 30 min. (b) 1 hr.	Wear something tight around your neck, i.e., a scarf or collar.
18. Vertigo	(a) 30 sec. (b) 1 min.	Stand by a *tall* building and look up at its exterior wall.
19. Crawl under the bed	5–15 min.	Try to create an experience of being closed in.
20. Pressure to upper arm*	1 min.	Raise one arm at the elbow. With your other hand apply pressure to your upper arm, so the circulation is restricted.

---

*   Many of the exercises are from Drs. Barlow and Craske, as mentioned. Numbers 20 and 21 were demonstrated by Dr. Alec Pollard in a workshop at the 1995 conference of the Anxiety Disorders Association of America.

†   Many panickers stop drinking coffee or tea for fear of the sensations produced. The idea here is not to get your client back to ingesting caffeine on a regular basis, but it is good to learn not to be afraid of it.

Table 6.2: **Naturalistic Interoceptive Exercises (Cont.)**

Exercise	Length of Time	Instructions
21. Upper arm against torso	1 min.	With one arm hanging loosely at your side, grasp your upper arm with the opposite hand. Grip the upper arm tightly, and press and turn it firmly against your torso.
22. Hyperventilate and hold breath	1 min.	Do the hyperventilation exercise for one min. and immediately hold your breath briefly.
23. Stand up suddenly		Stand up suddenly from a lying down position.
24. Run up stairs	Up to 5 min.	Run up a few flights of stairs.
25. Vigorous exercise	15 to 30 min.	Do aerobics or other vigorous exercise for 15 to 30 min., depending on your stamina. (If you exercise regularly, this may not be an interoceptive challenge.)
26. Sauna	5–20 min.	Sit in a sauna for varying lengths of time.
27. Intense emotions	1–2 hrs.	Watch something suspenseful (mystery movie, sports event).
28. Intense excitement		Go on an amusement park ride.
29. Pillow over face	1 to 5 min.	Excellent exercise for someone who fears suffocation.
30. Sit in dark closet with door(s) closed	1 to 15 min.	As above.

Choosing Exposure Exercises for Clients

Some clinicians and researchers have their clients practice on exercises specifically related to their fears, e.g., someone who fears dizziness sensations may be asked to spin (Hecker and Thorpe 1992). Furthermore, only those exercises are practiced that bring on sensations similar to those that the particular individual experiences during a panic. I have tried various approaches and have arrived at a slightly different conclusion. I prefer to have everyone do all the basic exercises and subsequently to work on all those that rate high for anxiety, whether or not similar to the individual's panic sensations. My justification is as follows: First, as stated above, even when an exercise is expected to bring on certain sensations, it is surprising how many different sensations clients will report from any given exercise. Second, any sensation that produces anxiety (even if not during panics) may keep anxiety sensitivity high and possibly elicit fear in future panics. All too often I have heard clients say, "I thought I was over my panics, but then I had this one and the sensations were so different from anything I ever felt before. I got really scared."

A client might protest when beginning the interoceptive phase of the treatment, by saying that he or she does not want to feel anything like the panic sensations. In response, you might use the analogy with in vivo exposure in phobia work. It is understandable that the panicker wants to avoid the sensations (sometimes minimizing them through distraction or other subtle ways). But these exercises provide a unique opportunity to learn that the sensations do not produce harm and need not be feared.

Exclusions

Although the listed exercises are not dangerous and, in fact, are quite harmless, clients with certain conditions should be excluded. The primary reason for exclusion is to prevent a medical condition from becoming aggravated. Clients may be excluded who have any of the following medical problems:

- Epilepsy or other history of seizures
- Moderate to severe asthma
- Chronic arrythmia or fibrillations
- Moderate to severe lung or heart problems
- History of fainting and/or *very low* blood pressure
- Pregnancy

If there is any question regarding a client's medical condition, the client should consult a physician. If you have a signed release of information, you can ask the physician whether the person's medical condition precludes him/her from doing the exercise by describing exactly what the exercise entails. Other situations will arise requiring good judgment calls, e.g., if a client has a very bad neck or back, it may be unrealistic for him or her to do certain exercises, such as sitting with the head between the legs or spinning while standing up. (Note that sometimes such clients can spin in a spinning chair.)

If a client does have a medical condition, you can still try to find exercises that he or she can do (see Exercises Nearly Everyone Can Do below). I find that clients want to try to do the work, if their medical condition allows for it at all. I may work with them doing some of the exercises for shorter time periods. Although I do not expect my asthmatic clients to hyperventilate, most of them want to try it, often for shorter periods; naturally, they are free to stop at any time.

Exercises Nearly Everyone Can Do

As stated above, you can always find an exercise that a client can do. The list below consists of those I have found not to interfere with almost any medical condition. (Occasionally there are exceptions, for instance, a rare client has been told to abstain from caffeine due to ulcers or another medical condition.)

In the Office:

- Hold breath
- Apply external pressure on throat
- Stare at a spot
- Use a tongue depressor
- Swallow quickly
- Focus on your worst sensation using imagery

- Apply pressure to upper arm
- Press upper arm against torso

Outside the Office (Some of these exercises can also be done in the office):

- Ingest caffeine: Coffee, black tea, sodas with caffeine, chocolate
- Relax and daydream
- Create heat. Turn up heat in house or car and sit wearing very hot clothing with the windows closed
- Wear tight clothing around the neck
- Go into a small, dark closet, close the door, and stay inside

Instructions for Interoceptive Exposures

The exercises to be done in the office are listed in Table 6.1. Additional exercises and those to be done in naturalistic situations are listed in Table 6.2. "Naturalistic interoceptives" are exercises that mimic more natural situations in life, e.g., daydreaming, being hot, wearing tight clothing around the neck. Included in Table 6.2: Naturalistic Interoceptive Exercises are items that cannot be performed in the office, such as standing by a tall building and looking up its exterior wall to create vertigo and a few additional exercises (so as not to make the list of office exposures too lengthy). This list can also be consulted when clients do not find relevant (fear-provoking) exercises in Table 6.1. (To avoid confusion because of the similarity between the two tables, if referring to an exercise by number, Table 6.2 starts with exercise No. 13.)

General Sequence

The first step is to go through all or most of the exercises listed in Worksheet 7: Interoceptive Exposure Record. This takes most of a session, leaving time only for home assignments. I keep the worksheet and rank-order those exercises that have scores of 20 or higher from the least to the most fearful on the SUDS. The next step, to be done in the next session (Session 8), is to work specifically on the rank-ordered exercises. These are then recorded on Worksheet 8: Repeating Interoceptive Exercises. After the second interoceptive session, I give clients the assignment to *repeat all feared interoceptives daily, three times in a row*. I tell them they should spend at least fifteen minutes daily doing the exercises. Clients are also encouraged to seek out naturalistic activities and situations that bring on sensations. Many such activities are listed in Table 6.2.

There is no limit to the creative possibilities for expanding the exercises. For instance, some of my clients who have terrible suffocation fears have been given the home assignment of placing a pillow on top of their face. Initially, this can be done for one minute or less. Later it can be done for a longer time. The task is totally predictable and under the client's control. Yet each client I gave this task to do was at first very fearful. Other possibilities of expansion are, e.g., wearing a sweater in a warm restaurant, tensing up the arms while driving, doing a few spinning turns in a restroom, and so forth.

It may be necessary to extend the interoceptive work to Module IV, especially if the fears continue. From this point on during treatment, if the client expresses fear of a symptom at anytime, I ask him or her to repeat the relevant exercise anew. I also encourage clients to expose themselves regularly to naturalistic situations after terminating treatment. This helps with relapse prevention.

Worksheet 7: **Interoceptive Exposure Record**

Name: _____ Date _____

SUDS: Subjective Units of Anxiety-
Distress Scale

0 = Totally calm, no anxiety/fear
50 = Moderate level of anxiety/fear
100 = Intolerable level of anxiety/fear

Exercise	Describe Any Sensations Felt	SUDS	Check if SUDS≥20
Shake head, 30 sec.			
Head down, 1.5 min.			
Run in place, 1 min.			
Body tension, 1 min.			
Hold breath, 30 sec.			
Spin, 1 min.			
Straw breathing, 2 min.			
Hyperventilation, 1.5 min.			
Throat pressure, 1 min.			
Stare at spot, 2 min.			
Quick swallowing, 4 times			
Sensation in imagery, 2 min.			

Worksheet 8: Repeating Interoceptive Exercises

Name of person doing the exercises: _____

Use this column first   Then use this column

Date	Exercise being worked on	SUDS	Date	Exercise being worked on	SUDS

COACH: Guide the person doing the exercises.

Before exercise:
- Allow yourself to feel the sensations fully; pay attention to them.

After exercise:
- What was your SUDS level?
- What was going on in your mind, your thoughts/images?

Challenge any negative Automatic Thoughts/Images!
- What is your evidence that _____ would happen?
- What are alternative thoughts (positive thoughts)?

If lower SUDS than previously:
- What do you think you are learning?

Repeat exercise till SUDS is less than 20. Stop any given exercise after three trials. Repeat exercise on other days, in other places.

Supplies Needed

1. *A timer.* You want a timer that sounds an alarm when the time is up. If you attempt to use a watch or a clock, it is distracting during most exercises, e.g., when spinning (you almost have to stop in order to look at a clock). Also, I prefer my clients not to focus on the time as an escape. It is better for both you and your clients to pay full attention to the exercises and the sensations. For subsequent *group* sessions I bring along my five timers, so that when clients are paired up monitoring each other, each pair has its own timer.

2. *Worksheet 7:* Interoceptive Exposure Record, *Worksheet 8:* Repeating Interoceptive Exercises, pad and pen.

3. *Coffee stirrers or cocktail straws.* These are thin straws, often striped red and white, with a tiny hole. A regular straw would defeat the purpose of the test because the opening is too large. There is, however, a large variation among coffee stirrers. Those that have a division in the middle, two tiny holes, are usually too small. Many have slightly larger holes, which makes the breathing much easier. I had to buy several different brands until I found the right type. (The size I use is three millimeters inside diameter. Some of my colleagues start with a straw of about three and one-half to four millimeters in diameter and work with clients toward using the smaller size. I have not done so.)

Specific Instructions

1. *Do Not Tell Your Client What Sensations to Expect.* Some exercises produce sensations while the person is in the process of doing them; others are felt right after stopping. Therefore, right after finishing the exercises, have the client sit (or stand) for a few seconds while paying attention to any sensations and any anxiety associated with those sensations.

2. I encourage clients to stay with the full time allotted for each exercise. Some clinicians instruct their clients to do the exercises for 30 seconds after they start to feel the sensations (except, of course, holding the breath) and then stop. I prefer clients to do them for the specified amount of time. I have found that otherwise some clients do the exercises for as short a time as possible, hence using subtle avoidance. Furthermore, doing them for the full time usually allows for a stronger experience. For instance, if they start to feel a slight sensation from hyperventilating after 15 seconds and then continue hyperventilating for another 30 seconds, the experience is likely to be much less powerful than if they hyperventilate for 1.5 minutes. I do emphasize several times, however, that there is nothing magical about the length of time, that it is not a "test" they have to pass and that, if it is too uncomfortable, they can stop before the allotted time. Nonetheless, if other members in the group and I do the exercises for the full time, the client will try as well. Occasionally a longer exposure is needed. For instance, Hornsveld et al. (1995) recommend at least three minutes of hyperventilation for some clients to achieve the full effect.

3. I have my clients use the Subjective Units of Distress Scale (SUDS) from 0 to 100. However, although SUDS pertains to discomfort and distress, here you are interested in the level of anxiety and fear. Therefore, I describe SUDS as Subjective Units of Anxiety-Distress Scale (i.e., anxiety-related distress). In

fact, I emphasize repeatedly the need to distinguish between *physical discomfort* and *anxiety/fear*. The sensations produced can be very intense, creating a great deal of discomfort, but your client must assess the presence of any anxiety/fear associated with doing the exercises or the sensations produced. The intensity of the sensations may decline in strength as the exercise is repeated and loses its novelty. Others exercises, however, may bring on the same intensity and discomfort.

When using SUDS, the client is asked to use the number between 0 and 100 that best describes his or her anxiety/fear level. 0 = Totally calm, no anxiety/fear. 50 = Moderate level of anxiety/fear. 100 = Intolerable level of anxiety/fear. It is important to work with the client on an exercise until the SUDS is less than 20.

4. There is a great advantage to doing the hyperventilation exercise early on while learning diaphragmatic breathing. It is one of the more challenging exercises, and since clients have already done it once, it helps to decrease their anxiety about this part of the work.

5. Clients often ask whether the exercises will bring on panic. I tell them that they are not designed to bring on an attack per se, and that most clients do not panic. If panic does occur because of their fear of the sensations, then it provides a good opportunity to practice the breathing and cognitive skills already learned. I remind them that confidence comes with the other side of the panic, when the person has had an attack and sees how well he/she has coped.

6. Some clients say with dismay that the sensations produced were exactly like those experienced in a panic. Their SUDS levels may be as high as 80 or higher. At this point, a very positive attitude from you, the therapist, can be helpful. I tell such clients, "This is actually very good, not that I wish you discomfort, but now we have at least one exercise that we know is particularly relevant for you; now we have something concrete to work with. As you keep practicing the exercise and watch your fear diminish, it will provide you with some very powerful learning."

7. If your client is practicing on an exercise that you believe is relevant for him or her, e.g., straw breathing by a person who fears suffocation but denies any anxiety, ask your client to do it again while you observe how he or she does it. In straw breathing, it is easy to subtly breathe out through the mouth (not through the straw), making it quite comfortable. To such a client I emphasize that it is better to do the exercise as indicated for a shorter period of time than to avoid it, to allow the full sensation to appear. Clients should do the exercises without using distractions or any other means to diminish the effects. The aim is to feel the sensations to the fullest, and the more similar to panic sensations they are, the better it is.

8. When I go through the exercises for the first time with a client or a group, *I always do the exercises with them.* This helps them feel less awkward since I am not sitting idly by, and it is much more likely that they will do the exercises up to the time limit. Finally, my participation shows them that I am not afraid of the sensations. Thus I have done these exercises many times. (I encourage you to practice doing them before you see your first client so that you will know what to expect.)

9. Therapists often recommend that clients apply diaphragmatic breathing after completing the exercise to slow down the sensations. However, you want your client first to pay full attention to the sensations. By the time they have written down the sensations and/or SUDS levels on the worksheet, their symptoms have usually subsided. I explicitly suggest the use of diaphragmatic breathing when a client is particularly distressed, feels nausea, or as a means to test how quickly the client can stop the sensations as a means to gain control.

The Therapist's Comfort Level

If you as a therapist are precluded from doing some of the exercises for medical reasons, try nonetheless to use them in your work. In a group, you might consider asking your clients whether anyone would like to demonstrate an exercise to the other members. A client who volunteers may have less fear of this particular exercise. However, if the client does it in spite of fear, he/she will probably progress well. I am basing this guess on the observation that when I pair up clients in group, the coach seems to benefit as much as the person doing the exercise.

Some of my colleagues are very uncomfortable and sometimes fearful of some exercises, e.g., spinning and the dizziness it produces. Unless you cannot do the exercise for medical reasons, remember that you build up tolerance by repeating it. The first time I spun in group, upon ending, I almost flew across the room (which no client has done). After many repetitions, I now can easily keep my balance.

To conclude, the more comfortable you are with the interoceptive exercises, the more effectively you will employ this treatment component. Experience will help you, as it did me. I seldom have clients who refuse to do a given exercise. Rather, even those with medical conditions try eagerly to participate in anyway they can.

Summary

Fear is often a conditioned response to internal sensations produced by anxiety and panic, not unlike the conditioned fear of phobic situations. Deconditioning is achieved through repeated exposure to the fear sensations. In this vein, the client engages in exercises designed to bring on a variety of symptoms, first in the office, and then in more natural environments. These allow the client to test his or her beliefs about the uncontrollability and catastrophic nature of panic.

While the ultimate goal is to effect a change in the client's fear structure, this is best accomplished by a combination of cognitive and behavioral means.

7

Treatment Module IV: Adjuncts to Success *(Sessions 10–12)*

Overview of Treatment Module IV

When providing treatment by module, there is often some overlap. It helps a great deal to follow a specific plan, and I have found that the treatment succeeds better the more I follow the basic structure. This is done more easily in a group than individually. Clients in individual therapy often want to bring up and elaborate on issues that came up during the week that are unrelated to panic. It is also more awkward to do so much "teaching" individually. I do, however, encourage them to work diligently with my self-help book *An End to Panic,* which permits more individualized attention on other issues. I also remind clients that the panic work cannot be completed in a shorter time span, and they will need additional sessions if they also want to work on other problems.

When arriving at this module, I remind clients that termination is approaching and elicit their feelings. This is a good time to review the gains that have been made and to pinpoint areas where there is still a need for intervention. I encourage them to prepare for life after treatment and to try and foresee upcoming difficulties.

Session 10

In this session I introduce and explore some techniques that clients can use to deal with chronic worry. I also emphasize their need to become aware of self-imposed stress, how to limit stress in general, and how to work on assertiveness issues. I ask them to think about difficulties they may have in asserting themselves (at work or at home, with strangers, relatives, or friends) and to bring up such examples in this and the next session. Sometimes a situation involving a difficult interpersonal interaction is described when working on assertiveness. The original and alternate scenarios can then be rehearsed, e.g., via role play.

Session 11

I ask for examples pertaining to worry patterns and assertiveness issues. Again, when applicable, we role play interactions. I describe the difficulties created by an excessive need for control and perfectionism but, as a rule, these topics have been covered in earlier treatment sessions. Unless I have already done so, I also ask them briefly during this session about their exercise and entertainment habits and their goals. In that context, I describe the benefits of meditation.

We discuss setbacks in a more formal way than previously. For the twelfth session I ask clients to prepare a list of circumstances that can bring on a panic attack and the fear of panic. I also ask for a list of strategies for coping with setbacks. Finally, those clients with agoraphobia are asked to bring a written, realistic plan for future exposures. I encourage them to set up monthly goals and describe the steps they need to take weekly to attain their monthly goals.

Session 12

This session is used to wrap up loose ends, to review and further discuss relapse prevention issues and the agoraphobia exposure plans. Finally, we deal with termination issues.

Section 1: Exploring Disruptive Cognitive and Behavior Patterns

Panic disorder and agoraphobia do not occur in a vacuum. They develop within the context of the person's life and his or her personality. This section is devoted to examining personality and lifestyle characteristics that can aggravate panic disorder. These characteristics have to do with chronic worry and anxiety, lack of assertiveness, and dealing with stress. I believe that the treatment of panic disorder is more comprehensive when all of these issues are addressed, although little research has focused on them.

Chronic Worry and Anxiety

A number of panickers report having a long history of worries and the experience of generalized, pervasive anxiety. Some clients say that they have been worriers for as long as they can remember. Others report not having worried excessively prior to their panics but, as a consequence of panic disorder, they became worriers. The *DSM-IV* (American Psychiatric Association 1994) states that an associated feature of panic disorder is intermittent or constant anxiety. This anxiety can be either nonfocused or focused on specific areas, especially those related to health or separation from loved ones. Many panickers are very distressed by their worries, and there are often physical symptoms associated with worry and anxiety, e.g., tenseness, fatigue, and poor concentration.

Cognitions

Disaster Expectation is a maladaptive thought described in chapter 5. This kind of thinking is very easily observed in panickers and other chronic worriers but it is also found in the average population (including therapists). Many people do not admit this easily, because they know that it doesn't make sense. People who consistently expect disaster worry as a way of being prepared for the impending disaster. They think that they will *not be able to cope* if something bad happens *unexpectedly*, and/or they think that if they worry enough, the *disaster will not occur.* (The latter is, of course, an example of magical thinking, which is actually a cognitive distortion.)

A few of my clients have shared with the group very unfortunate events that had happened in their lives, sometimes on a day they did not worry, e.g., a teenage son or daughter having had a car accident. They said that they, too, had been chronic worriers expecting a disaster to happen at any time. Since these events had taken place prior to their current treatment for panic disorder, I asked what effect the event had had on their tendency to constantly expect disaster. To my surprise, they said that it had helped them to worry *less.* They had realized that bad things do happen, and that there had been no connection between the accident and their general worry. Most importantly they learned that life continues after an accident. Somehow they managed to cope with the situation. This gave them confidence that they could cope with difficult life events in the future. For some people it seems that a bad experience jolts them out of their endless worry pattern. They learn to appreciate the precariousness of life.

Strategies for Dealing with Worry and Anxiety

1. **Moving From Fear and Worry to Action**
   One of the best ways to deal with worry is to take action that counteracts the feared event. The wisdom of this strategy is that the action will help absorb the anxiety, e.g., if the worry pertains to fear of a disease, the person's energy and time can be devoted to eating only healthy food, exercising regularly, and stopping smoking. If the worry pertains to finances, making a budget and sticking to it can help solve the problem and provide a sense of control. Unfortunately, many people go right on eating junk food and smoking, not exercising, and spending money unnecessarily while spending countless hours worrying, which, in turn, feeds the worry cycle.

   A more specific example follows: A woman in my New Panickers Group and her husband had separated before she entered the group treatment. She had not heard from her mother-in-law and worried continuously that her mother-in-law would blame and reject her. One and a half months after the separation, her mother-in-law phoned her and told her that she had not been in touch because her sister was dying of cancer. When my client brought this up in group, another group member asked her, "Why didn't *you* call her? I would have!" (The latter is an excellent example of moving from worry to action.) Even in the event that her mother-in-law were to reject her, she would then have had a concrete situation to adjust to rather than dwelling on imaginary adversities.

2. **Challenging Worrisome Automatic Thoughts**
   Taking action, the strategy described above, is a *behavioral* way of dealing with worry. The best *cognitive* strategy is to challenge the worrisome thoughts just as you taught your client to do earlier with automatic thoughts pertaining to specific fears in panic, i.e., using Worksheet 4: Challenging Automatic Thoughts. In order for your client to change his or her thoughts, it is essential first to capture the automatic thoughts and recognize them for what they are.

   There are a few avenues that your client can use to become aware of the automatic thoughts associated not only with worry but with other negative affective states. These are:

   • The person asks himself or herself several times during the day, "What am I saying to myself right now?" and writes down the thoughts.

- When the person becomes aware of uncomfortable emotions such as anxiety or depression, he or she asks, "What was I saying to myself right before this feeling came on?" or, "What have I been telling myself all along while I have been feeling like this?"

- When the person "catches" negative thoughts, it is helpful to ask "What was the circumstance (event, situation, or encounter) that preceded my negative thoughts?"

- At times of major life transitions, or when anticipating a difficult situation or a very stressful event, it is helpful for the person to pay attention to his or her thoughts, "What do I expect from this new situation?" "How do I believe I'll cope with this change/event?"

- One of the best questions to ask is, *"What's the worst thing that could happen?"*

These thoughts are best written down as they occur. They can then be looked upon as hypotheses to be challenged and compared with alternative ways of looking at the situation.

The challenging can involve several steps (for a complete list, see chapter 5):

- Asking what the evidence is.

- Looking at past outcomes, "What was the outcome when I thought that way in the past?"

- Looking for alternative hypotheses, "How can I refute the evidence, and what are alternative hypotheses?" A behavioral test might entail making (and writing down) a specific prediction and comparing it with the actual outcome after the event takes place.

Every opportunity should be taken to challenge the unhelpful automatic thoughts and to replace them with more helpful thoughts. With time the positive thoughts become easier to believe.

3. **Confronting "What Ifs"**
   "What if . . . ?" is probably the most commonly articulated anxious question. The worst response is to leave it unanswered. I teach my clients to say, "Okay, let's assume X will happen. What will I do then?" And then answer that question in terms of coping strategies. The feared event is almost never as disastrous as the question "What if?" implies, and even if it is, it is better to confront it. Some common examples of this question among panickers are: "What if the elevator breaks down?" "What if I get stuck here in traffic?" "What if I don't pass the driver's test?" "What if I get a low evaluation?" If the fear is truly extreme, something involving death or other horrendous fears, it is worthwhile to go over the worst-case scenario repeatedly, preferably in writing, with the inclusion of many details. This approach helps to decatastrophize the feared event and allows the person to rehearse coping responses.

4. **Scheduling Worry Time**
   Worry time should be scheduled when the imaginary fears (or real losses) consume a great deal of the person's day, challenging cannot be done often enough, or the worry keeps repeating itself. Worry time should be a part of the daily schedule, preferably done at the same time every day, or at a certain time for weekdays and another for weekends. The amount of time can vary

from fifteen minutes to one hour per day, depending on how much time the person has been worrying. (Thus, one hour of worry time is appropriate for a person who normally worries three or more hours a day.) Anytime a worrisome thought arises during the day, the person jots it down so as not to forget it and tells himself or herself, "I'll worry about it during my worry time (or, as a child I treated called it, "the time capsule"). Then, during the worry time, the person *does nothing but worry* about the event(s). It is helpful to write down both the worry and the possible solutions. During the worry time, if the mind becomes distracted, every effort should be made to return to the worries. If time is spent on other activities or thoughts, the worry time will not be effective. Any worrisome thought that comes to mind after the worry time should be jotted down and postponed for the next worry time. Worry time should not be scheduled for bedtime but for another part of the day or evening. This strategy also works well for people who keep busy all day but then at bedtime, as a consequence of worrying, cannot fall asleep.

Clients have remarked, "I try not to worry. This will make me worry more!" What they do not realize until they try it is that this is an excellent way to gain control over the worry. Let us look at this. When great *effort* is expended *in not* worrying, the worry is thereby brought to the forefront. Through the paradox of inviting the worry, control is brought into the situation. Control is also exerted by encapsulating it (into the time frame). If your client truly follows this plan, he/she invariably becomes saturated and bored after a number of days or weeks, at which time the scheduled worry time can be shortened.

This approach can be used for other emotions, for example, mourning the loss of a loved one. In such misfortunes, this is not the first strategy to be used because, of course, it is important to grieve. However, I have known parents who had lost a child whose lives were still paralyzed two to three years later. A feeling of betrayal toward the lost person can exist underneath the grieving. Scheduling mourning time allows the person to still grieve but helps dedicate the rest of the day to other activities. In this case, the time is used to allow all the emotions to be fully experienced. It may help to write down all of the thoughts and feelings, as well.

5. **Putting on Rose-Colored Glasses**
Rose-colored glasses is a term used by Sobel and Ornstein in their book *The Healthy Mind, Healthy Body Handbook* (1996). The authors say that since we cannot see reality exactly as it is, we might as well try to view it in a positive rather than a negative light, i.e., through rose-colored glasses. Optimism and pessimism are learned habits, and optimistic thinking has a positive impact on our emotional and physical health. To practice acquiring an optimistic outlook, it is important to stay in the present, to reflect on good rather than bad past experiences, and to celebrate one's accomplishments. For my pessimistic clients I recommend Seligman's book *Learned Optimism* (1990).

6. **Thought Stopping**
Thought stopping alone does not combat chronic worry. It should be the last strategy used, when all else has failed, or used in conjunction with any of the strategies listed above. Thought stopping is useful when the same negative thought pops up again and again, there is no solution to the problem, and/or the worrisome thought is overly persistent. Once aware of the thought, the person says, "Stop!" emphatically. It can be said loudly at home

or in the car, otherwise subliminally, and/or the client may envision a STOP sign in front of himself or herself. Then the client must change the thought to something else. But soon the unwanted thought returns. The thought-stopping technique works only if it is repeated over and over, as soon as the person becomes aware of the unwanted thought. After many repetitions the negative thought should subside.

Excessive Stress

Stress can be positive or negative. It is perceived as negative when a bad event happens that exceeds our coping resources, e.g., serious illness in the self or family. Serious stress can also occur as a result of many small stressors accumulating. This can have an adverse effect both physically and mentally. Borkovec, Grayson, and Cooper (1978) identified most tension as arising from social situations, school and exams, and work. Sometimes clients put themselves under an inordinate amount of stress, and expect that they should be able to deal with it without it having an effect on their bodies or minds.

Panic disorder can provide people with a unique opportunity to reflect on whether they are ignoring signs that have a negative impact on their lives, as the following example demonstrates. One client in my New Panickers Group was experiencing extreme stress on her job. Her stress seemed to have precipitated her panic disorder. Her focal fear of suffocating while in a panic was more intense than I had observed in other clients with that particular fear. She felt that she could barely cope and was trying to figure out what to do. Although she had completed too many years with the company to want to quit, the other available positions were not very appealing. When she had overcome her fears and was close to graduating from the group, she casually mentioned that she was going to buy a fancy truck, which would entail a monthly payment of $700. The other group members and I were astonished because she was about to add even more stress to her life by putting herself in debt with high monthly payments for years to come, even though she had not yet resolved her job situation. I pointed out that she would be better off deciding what to do about her job first, even if that meant making a deliberate decision to stay and to achieve an attitudinal shift to better cope with the stress. Once she accomplished that, then buying the truck might be a sensible option.

Cognitions

Cognitions play a significant role in stress. Research has shown that it is not so much what happens to us that determines how an event affects us, but rather how the event is perceived. If it is perceived as a positive challenge, certain beneficial hormones are released. If perceived as negative, e.g., as a threat, certain harmful hormones are released. The positive stress may lead to biological "toughening up," which means that the person will be able to deal with future stressful events more easily (Dienstbier 1989).

Strategies for Dealing with Stress

1. **Limiting Stress That Is Under One's Control**
   The example above of the woman who wanted to add more pressure to her already stressful life illustrates how people tend to create undue stress in their lives. This kind of behavior can result from viewing the world in terms of how things ought to be rather than how they are. Help your clients to increase their

awareness of their true resources and to limit the stress they subject themselves to accordingly.

2. **Relaxation**
Learning how to do progressive relaxation can significantly reduce tension. It serves as a positive coping skill. Borkovec et al. (1978) demonstrated that gains derived from relaxation were maintained seven months later. *The Relaxation and Stress Reduction Workbook*, 4th Ed. by Davis, Robbins Eshelman, and McKay (1997) is an excellent book from which to learn relaxation methods.

3. **Exercise**
Physical exercise is an excellent way to enhance biological toughness to stress, as well as to improve our physical and mental well-being. Aerobic exercise, which is any exercise that stimulates the cardiovascular system, produces sympathetic nervous system arousal. When the person exercises regularly, adrenaline and noradrenaline are used, depleted, and built up again, between workouts. This cycle has a positive impact on both mind and body.

4. **Fun and Humor**
Clients can benefit from bringing balance to their lives by including entertainment, fun, and humor. It is especially helpful if they find and make time for an activity they thoroughly enjoy.

Lack of Assertiveness

In my experience, many clients' emotional problems result from their not being able to stand up for themselves, not knowing how to set limits, and not being willing to take risks or to seek out challenges. Assertiveness is related to issues about control. Nonassertive people do not exercise the interpersonal control they could have, in which case their sense of lack of control may be displaced or projected onto an entirely different situation, possibly a phobic situation. Nonassertiveness leads to feelings of helplessness which, in turn, can increase anxiety, hopelessness, and/or depression. In contrast, practicing assertiveness can bring about a sense of mastery and self-worth.

Cognitions

The greatest obstacles to acting assertively usually are internal. They come from within the person, much more than from external forces. People stop themselves from being assertive by labeling themselves negatively, catastrophizing about the possible consequences, fearing being seen as too aggressive, and so forth. A more immediate negative effect of nonassertiveness is that a great deal of energy is spent nonproductively. Unfinished business lingers in one's mind. A good measure of whether something was insignificant or needs some follow-through is how much time is spent thinking about it.

Strategies for Becoming Assertive

1. **Taking Care of Oneself and Recognizing the Rights of Others**
Many people think that if they look out for their own needs, they are being selfish. But taking care of oneself does not imply a disregard for the feelings and rights of others. However difficult, a balance can be found. For my women clients who exhibit this problem, I often recommend Pamela Butler's book *Self-Assertion for Women* (1992), which I think is an excellent guide.

2. **The Main Goal of Assertiveness: Expressing Oneself**
   Clients sometimes say that they will not get what they ask for, even if they do stand up for themselves, so *why try?* (This is the maladaptive thought "Giving Up.") Yet the probability of the person getting what is wanted goes much higher when the person speaks up than if he or she stays silent. This does not mean that situations always turn out the way we want them to. However, even if the desired objective is not obtained, there is tremendous value simply in standing up for oneself.

3. **Knowing What You Want, but Not Having to Justify It**
   I emphasize to clients it is important to state very clearly what it is they want. Clarity helps to get their point across. The fewer words used in the assertive message, the less likely that the person will become entangled in a web of justifications and arguments. Often, using the broken record technique can be helpful, i.e., repeating the same request over and over with minor or no modifications.

4. **"I" Versus "You" Statements**
   The more the person uses "I" statements, the more likely that he or she will not be perceived as if attacking the other person. As soon as "you" sentences are used, especially at the beginning of the sentence, the more likely that he or she will seem to be attacking the other person. When feeling attacked, the other person is bound to lash back, and an argument ensues. In contrast, it is difficult to argue with one's expressed feelings and needs (stated in "I" terms).

5. **Making a Request**
   When giving an assertive message, it can be extremely helpful to make a request. At times just saying "no" may be the most appropriate course of action. Often, however, it is helpful not just to set a limit, but to request exactly what is desired. This applies as much to a business transaction (e.g., asking for a refund) as to a personal situation. For instance, besides asking a spouse not to engage in an annoying behavior, the person setting the limit simultaneously lets the spouse know what alternative behavior is desirable.

6. **Teaching Others How You Like to Be Treated**
   As Pamela Butler (1992) states, setting limits is a way of teaching others how you like to be treated. When others infringe on your space, it is not always because they are insensitive. Other people have different values and operate differently. They cannot guess what you want or need. You must let them know. I teach my clients to state clearly what they want and need. The people they interact with cannot be expected to read their minds.

7. **Role Play**
   When your client describes a particularly difficult interaction, you might want to use role play. The event is reenacted with the client playing the other person's role, while you play the client's role. Later, reverse the roles to allow for more profound learning. You can demonstrate all the above techniques through role play.

The Obsession With Control

I have never met a panicker who was not obsessed with control issues. Panickers want to control outside events, e.g., what happens in fearful situations, but even more, they want to control their emotions and physical symptoms. In our culture, unfortunately, people are often permitted to express only a very narrow range of emotions. Many panickers react with disdain and anger when their bodies show any physical signs of anxiety, especially visible signs, such as trembling, shaking, blushing, sweating, etc. They react toward their bodies as if they were the enemy. Likewise, many people, including panickers find crying to be unacceptable, even under very appropriate circumstances.

Cognitions

When panickers are obsessed with control, they pay attention to all the ways they are not in control, e.g., they do not have control over flying the airplane, the elevator breaking down, the traffic being stopped, or their heart rate accelerating. The conclusion they draw is that they do not have control and they react as if they had *no control at all.*

Strategies for Dealing With Control Issues

1. **Distinguishing Between What the Person Can and Cannot Control**
   The first helpful task is to learn to pay attention and recognize what can and cannot be controlled by the individual. Helping your client to make this distinction and to label experiences in terms of this distinction is the first step. You can teach your client to ask himself or herself, "Is this something that I can change directly or at least have influence over or not?" The second step is to accept the reality that many things are not under the individual's control and to apply strategies on how to stop worrying about them.

2. **Concentrating on the Aspects That the Person Can Control**
   Rather than concentrating on situations they do not have control over, clients can learn to concentrate on the many ways in which they can exercise control. This is very helpful in agoraphobic situations but pertains to many other situations, as well.

Perfectionism

Perfectionism is closely related to control issues and expectations. When people hold the view that they must be perfect, they place a very heavy burden on themselves. Since human beings are by their nature imperfect, perfectionists constantly set themselves up for disappointment. When disappointed with themselves, they often experience stress and anxiety.

Cognitions

Situations are viewed in one extreme light or another: either something is one-hundred percent or zero. If it is not perfect, it is unacceptable. At social events, perfectionists think that one faux pas equals a total fiasco. For example, a client had to give one of his many public speeches to a group of peers. His workload had been so heavy that he was unable to prepare well; and he also had little sleep the night before. Consequently, his speech did not go as well as previous ones had. A week later he was still saying to himself, "I should have done better. There is no excuse. I feel badly." Perfectionists also tend to think that they are responsible for others enjoying themselves and for other people's happiness.

Strategies for Dealing With Perfectionism

1. **Thinking in Percentages**

   People can learn to be more reasonable in their expectations of themselves by weighing their resources against the demands in their lives, instead of seeing themselves as operating in a vacuum. A person gives himself or herself more leeway by thinking, "I did this project at 60 percent of my capacity. Given the time constraints I was working under, I did a good job. With more time I could have done better, but that's life."

2. **Practicing Imperfection**

   I often give my perfectionist clients the task of practicing not being perfect. For example, if a woman cannot leave her house with the bed unmade or entertain guests unless her house is in perfect condition, I encourage her to practice leaving the bed unmade, and the house somewhat untidy when guests are expected. Once people learn that they can survive imperfection, it can be extremely liberating. It is not easy, because perfectionists become very anxious when performing at less than their optimum capacity.

Lack of Life Goals

The less people need to be concerned with basic survival, the more issues about the quality of life arise. I have observed that people without goals often feel empty. Sometimes emotional problems develop in this vacuum. When there is a goal, invariably there are problems that come up along the way that must be faced and solved. But these then constitute real problems—not imaginary ones.

Cognitions

Many clients cannot formulate any goals for themselves. Nothing interests them, they do not want to learn anything new, and they do not strive toward anything. Then, imaginary worries are often created in the absence of real ones.

Strategies for Dealing With a Lack of Goals

1. **Setting Goals**

   Obviously, setting a goal or goals is the first step. Goals are particularly helpful to clients if they involve learning or developing skills. Goals can be short-term and long-term. To achieve long-term goals, subgoals may need to be formulated. How can this be accomplished when the person has no intrinsic motivation to look for a goal?

   First, you may try to help your client understand the value and the need for goals. This can be done by exploring feelings of emptiness and the possible lack of meaning in his/her life. Second, work with your client in first seeking very small goals that can be accomplished within a few weeks. You can explore in a later session what effort was put out and how the client felt upon reaching the goal. Third, explore interests and hobbies the client had in the past to see if they can be revived. Fourth, the client can take the very behavioral approach of writing down every day whether an event/experience could be converted into a goal.

2. **Pursuing Goals**

In order to pursue goals, the person needs to create the time and place for them. You can explore with your client how much time and effort will be dedicated to a goal, what difficulties to expect, the cost involved, and how to balance achieving the goal with the responsibilities the client already has. You can attempt to show how pursuing and attaining a particular goal can help to create a sense of competency and mastery.

Meditation

I have placed meditation in a category separate from the relaxation techniques for combating stress, because meditation is truly a different phenomenon. I have been very intrigued by Jon Kabat-Zinn's mindfulness meditation (1990, 1994). There are many forms of meditation, and although their essence is similar, there are variations. Miller, Fletcher, and Kabat-Zinn (1995) describe mindfulness as a way of intentionally paying attention, in a nonjudgmental way, to the present moment, i.e., a nonjudgmental moment-to-moment awareness. This means that mindfulness is brought to breathing, eating, standing, walking, and other routine life activities. Mindfulness has to do with the approach we take to everything we do and being accepting of the moment just the way it is.

Hence mindfulness meditation does not teach a way of living, *but a way of being.* It circumvents diagnosing emotional problems in that they are not addressed directly. Instead, it allows the person to develop a different relationship to the self and the world, and through self-observation and self-regulation to affect the body and mind in positive ways. As Miller et al. (1995) state, the important elements for achieving such a positive impact are the regulation of attention, concentration, relaxation, and insight. By nurturing and cultivating these inner resources, they are then mobilized for healing.

Miller et al. (1995) further state that, like cognitive therapy, mindfulness takes the perspective that thoughts influence emotions. However, unlike cognitive therapy, the aim is not to change one thought for another but to perceive thoughts as the short-lived events they are. Thoughts and emotions come and go and have *no power over us except the power we give to them.* In panic disorder the problem is that people believe their thoughts, reacting to them as if they were indisputable truths.

Mindfulness meditation has been used effectively with people with many physical and emotional problems. Miller et al. (1995) reported clinical improvement in medical patients with anxiety disorders (panic disorder and generalized anxiety disorder). They underwent an eight-week outpatient group training in mindfulness meditation as well as home practice six days a week. Significant positive results on all measures taken had been maintained three years later. Thus mindfulness meditation has been shown to have long-term, beneficial effects on anxiety disorders. It can be used as an alternative to the treatment protocols described in this book, or afterwards as one of the most potent deterrents to relapse.

Summary

Panic attacks do not occur in a vacuum but are connected to other issues in the client's life. Some of the common personality characteristics and life issues to be explored are chronic worry patterns, excessive stress, nonassertiveness, being obsessed with the need for control, being a perfectionist, and lack of goals. Specific cognitions are involved and maintain nonadaptive responses in these areas. You can help your client employ behavioral and cognitive strategies to ameliorate them.

Section 2: Preparing for the Future: Relapse Prevention

During treatment patients with panic disorder frequently ask what the odds are of truly "beating" their condition. They want to know what the likelihood is of their symptoms returning. Will the disorder come back? Is there a cure? I encourage these kinds of questions throughout the course of treatment.

Once a person has had a panic attack and responded fearfully to it, he or she is likely to have one again. Isolated panic attacks are very likely to recur because the client's body and mind know how to get there; the person is primed for having another attack. Hope and recovery lie in overcoming the fear of panicking again. I tell clients that they are ready to leave the group when they say, "I haven't had a panic for a long time. But if I have one again, so what?" This is in marked contrast to the expression, "I haven't had a panic for a long time. I sure hope I won't ever have one again!" The latter view is a set-up. These questions and discussions about relapse provide opportunities during treatment to emphasize again and again that fear is what we are trying to change. When fear subsides, panics usually subside. If the person truly no longer fears panics, the recurrence is likely to remain an isolated event.

Having a panic again does not mean that panic disorder must recur. Unfortunately, having panic disorder *with agoraphobia* complicates the situation. As I have stated previously, agoraphobia is not simply a complication of panic disorder; it takes on a life of its own. It appears that even if the person has overcome his or her fear of panics, the tendency to avoid as a way of coping with anxiety and stress is very pervasive. Therefore, *unless* your client has truly *overcome all avoidance*, agoraphobia is likely to return.

I recommend that during treatment sessions, you bring up relapse prevention issues. I also like to devote parts of the last two sessions to relapse prevention in a more formal manner. In Session 11, I ask clients to list circumstances that may trigger panics again and describe how fear might return. I elaborate on the examples they produce. Some common situations that bring fear back are listed below. Help your clients to find ways of preparing themselves by knowing which circumstances tend to come up again and how to deal with them.

Circumstances That May Trigger a Panic Attack

- *High Stress*
  Some stress is external. However, as seen in Section 1 of this chapter, people frequently create undue stress for themselves, sometimes because they are envisioning how things "should" be rather than how they are. The more clients learn to pay early attention to external and self-imposed stress, the more they can be prepared to deal with it and find ways to soften the impact of the stress.

- *Illness in Self or Loved Ones, or Excessive Fatigue*
  Conditions that weaken defenses or bring about other physiological changes can help bring on panics. This includes the effects of some medications, going through menopause, and aging, etc.

- *When Agoraphobic Fears Were Not Totally Overcome*
  As long as some fear remains, the person is vulnerable to a relapse. For instance, if the person can now drive on freeways but not when it is raining, or not farther than fifty miles, cannot spend the night far from home, or cannot go to very crowded stores, the basic fear is still present, waiting to erupt again.

- *Getting Off Medications*
  You will see in chapter 10 that what your client learns while in a drug state may not transfer to a drug-free state. At times, the person may need to go through a new course of CBT. If your client has done so once, he or she is likely to need a shorter sequence the second time.

Circumstances That Can Bring on Fear With a New Panic

- *The Panic Came When Least Expected*
  Some clients easily accept a return of panic under high stress because it is in some way "expected." They often react differently when the panic is totally unexpected. Such a surprise occurs when they are going through a very calm period in their lives; the last thing they expect is a panic attack. I try to teach my clients to view unexpected panics as a "wake-up call." The client can use the panic to review what is going on in his or her life. There could be stress that he or she is denying or not acknowledging. The person may have unacceptable feelings, not be standing up to others, etc. In other words, rather than obsessing about the panic attack itself, it is very helpful to think about the circumstances under which the panic re-occurred and then look for solutions.

- *Your Client Could Not Stop the Panic*
  Even if your client learned techniques to help curb or stop panics, these do not always succeed. A full-blown panic attack may still occur. Perfectionist tendencies often stand in the way, because the person thinks that if he or she did everything *right*, an attack should not have occurred or should be easily controlled.

- *The Symptoms Were Different or Worse Than Ever, or Occurred at Night*
  If your client has been used to certain symptoms in a panic and not to others, fear can return. Encourage your client to look at the *DSM-IV* (American Psychiatric Association 1994) symptom list to verify which types of symptoms can be expected in panic attacks. This list is available in my book *An End to Panic* (1995). If your client becomes fearful by assuming that stronger anxiety symptoms signify greater danger, he or she needs to work again with Worksheet 4: Challenging Automatic Thoughts. Similarly, when the client starts to have nocturnal panics after having had only diurnal ones, he or she may react with fear.

- *The Panic Occurred in a New Situation*
  If the person never had a panic on the freeway or at the dentist before and now has had one, he or she could start to fear this new situation.

Strengthening Gains Made and Strategies for Coping With Setbacks

Setbacks are an integral part of treatment, but they do not have to mean relapse. Yet since the underprediction of panic is so powerful a factor in prompting a return of fear, the person should be prepared for a future attack (Cox and Swinson 1994). The therapeutic alliance that you build with your client will go a long way in preparing him or her for possible future setbacks. Encourage your client to prepare a list of red flags, or warning signs, as to when panics could occur or how fear may return. Your client can further prepare for a re-occurrence by writing out a list of ways to handle the different difficulties that could arise. People do not return to square one. Seeking additional help is not failure. Even if they have a very difficult time temporarily, if the rapport is there, you can help them to regain lost ground quickly. What has been learned is seldom lost; but it may need to be practiced and repeated again.

- *If Agoraphobic Symptoms Persist at End of Treatment*
  Clients are far more likely to continue with exposures if by the last treatment session they have prepared a *written plan for continued exposures.* This plan should not be as rigorous as during treatment but one that the person can live with easily. You can help your client assess which exposures to do and how often to do them.

- *Having a Coach*
  If a coach helped during the exposure work, a commitment from that person to provide further assistance can be very helpful.

- *Not Resting on One's Laurels*
  The person with agoraphobia cannot afford to rest on his or her laurels. If he or she overcame the fear of crossing bridges, further exposure to bridges is indicated, even if not a part of the person's routine. Any situation that has not been confronted for a long time can surprise the person with a fear reaction.

- *Continuing to Apply the Coping Skills*
  This involves continuing to practice diaphragmatic breathing, challenging negative automatic thoughts, and exposing oneself to fearful activities and situations. These are most likely to be practiced if the client makes a plan to integrate them into his or her life after treatment.

- *Adjuncts to Success*
  This means continuing to work on issues having to do with assertiveness, chronic worry, and limiting stress, as laid out in the first section of this chapter.

- *The First Recurrence of Panic*
  If a panic recurs, ideally it should be viewed as a "wake-up call," as stated earlier. It is also important to return to the place where the panic occurred as soon as possible to prevent it from acquiring phobic properties.

- *Avoidance "Creeping Up"*
  This is one of the most prominent red flags for which to watch. The best way to deal with this is to watch for any tendency to avoid situations or activities that the person had stopped avoiding. Clients often ask how to distinguish between what is a "normal" response and what is not. All of us avoid certain situations on occasion. I may not feel like going to a party, or I might postpone a visit to a friend out of town because of stormy weather, etc. The give-away is a big sigh of relief at not going or a pattern of avoidance visibly emerging. If your client avoids the freeway one day because it is raining, the next day because it is foggy, the next time because he or she is too tired, this is a sign of an emerging pattern. It can happen very subtly, because it is usually easier to justify our actions with logic than to admit fear. The answer is to immediately set up an exposure plan. Tell your clients to remember that it is easier to overcome a fear a second time early in the fear process. Once fear has a stranglehold, it is much harder to change the pattern. Hence, any subtle avoidance or relief equals *a need for further exposures!*

- *Booster Sessions*
  In chapter 9, I describe my monthly Anxiety Support Group for graduates from

any of my anxiety groups. This drop-in group provides an opportunity for clients to return spontaneously for support when they need it. In the past I had periodically scheduled booster sessions, which I later eliminated due to time constraints. Similarly, I urge you to plan some kind of support sessions.

- *Anxiety Support Groups in the Community*
  One of the best deterrents to relapse for your client is to join a support group and attend regularly. Subscribing to anxiety newsletters in another option (see the Resources list in the back of the book).

Repeated panic attacks seem to sensitize the nervous system and mood-congruent fear can be expected to return. Clients fear "its" return. However, as Dr. Robert DuPont put it so well at the keynote address of the 1997 conference of the Anxiety Disorders Association of America, even if a return of panic creates a bad feeling and momentary discomfort, it does not have to mean loss of control over the person's life—if that person is well prepared.

In sum, although uncomfortable, a recurrence of panic attacks can be viewed as an opportunity to learn more about them and how to handle them. The more the person prepares to view setbacks as challenges to be mastered, the less likely the chances are of becoming demoralized by a re-occurrence.

Summary

Successful treatment of panic disorder does not mean that the client will be forever free of panics. Rather, once panic disorder sets in, a panic attack is bound to recur sooner or later. Yet an occasional setback does not have to equal relapse. The best deterrent for the latter is the absence of fear in connection with panic. Clients can be helped to deal with setbacks by recognizing the circumstances that may trigger a new panic attack, how fear can return, and by strengthening the skills they have learned. Being armed with strategies for coping with setbacks takes one a long way toward long-lasting recovery.

8

Treatment Module V: When Agoraphobia Is Present: Mastery (In Vivo) Exposure *(Sessions 1–12)*

Overview of Treatment Module V

My first instruction in panic control treatment was with Drs. David Barlow and Michelle Craske at the conference of the Anxiety Disorders Association of America in the fall of 1987. When I started my first Panic/Phobia Group in early 1988, I immediately instructed my clients to do exposures along with the panic work. I assumed that the phobias needed to be targeted separately and have since found that indeed the panic and agoraphobia treatments can take place simultaneously. They complement each other and have synergistic effects. Although, ideally, the panic control treatment should precede the phobia work, I find it impractical in short-term treatment. My experience has also been that clients with agoraphobia frequently want to work on their phobias more than on their panics. This is also the finding of Başoğlu, et al. (1994b). They speculate that avoidance becomes an entrenched habit separate from the fear of panic attacks. Their clients reported that having the freedom to travel was more important to them than becoming panic-free. In sum, I believe that it saves time to focus on both disorders simultaneously. Since the agoraphobia work will thus occur in parallel with the panic control treatment, it will extend from Sessions 1 through 12.

Session 1

I ask my clients to do homework exposures at the end of the first session. The message is that exposures are important, and that I have the confidence that they can take this initial step. In fact, they seem eager to get started right away. It is amazing how some clients report at the second session that they engaged in an activity they had avoided for years, such as driving, going to the store, walking outside, etc. When this happens, it gives clients an immediate boost to their self-confidence. Some report that their exposure was easier than they expected. It seems that their lack of self-confidence had made the habit of avoidance too hard to break on their own.

In the first session I cover the physiology of fear and panic, as discussed in chapter 4. There is limited time for planning home exposures. Hence my goal with the agoraphobia work in this session is just to plan an initial exposure with the client (or clients in a group). I ask the client to start thinking about goals, i.e., what he or she hopes to achieve in various areas of dysfunction. This will then be pursued in the next two sessions.

Sessions 2 and 3

I provide my clients with the following basic information about phobias. Phobias are common, crippling, and curable. They do not respond to simple reason. They are curable precisely because the symptoms themselves are the problem; to overcome them, it is not necessary to understand what induced them. It is understandable why people begin to avoid: It seems logical not to do something that is frightening. However, while it may feel better at the moment to be able to avoid, a high price is paid. The price is that *agoraphobia reinforces fear*; it does not make fear and anxiety go away. *The more your client avoids the feared situation, object, or activity, the more the fear grows.*

The sections labeled "What is Avoided in Agoraphobia," "Setting Goals," and "Instructions for Exposures" provide the information I cover during Sessions 2 and 3, but some information may be postponed to Session 4, depending on time constraints.

Following Up and Planning Home Assignments

I dedicate about ten minutes of an individual session and twenty to thirty minutes of a group session to the home exposures. (In my two-hour Panic/Phobia Group, I spend thirty to forty minutes on home exposures.) Sessions 2 through 12 start with the agoraphobia work (clients report back on accomplishments and we plan new exposures). Worksheets to list goals and track them and to record home assignments are provided. Thereafter, I move to the agenda of the panic work (including reading and/or worksheet assignments).

Subsequent Sessions (4 through 12)

At the end of each subsequent session I review the previous weeks' accomplishments and collaborate with the client on planning the new exposure assignments. Stumbling blocks are discussed as well as any need to modify goals.

What the Research Says About How Exposure Works

Although in vivo exposure is a powerful treatment for agoraphobia, its mechanism of action is not yet fully understood. The controversies and differing views are outlined briefly, as well as their implications for exposure work.

Behavior Therapy Versus Cognitive Therapy in Agoraphobia

It has been decades since phobias were proved to be best treated by behavioral exposure. In a 1994 study by van den Hout, et al. the authors found that cognitive therapy did not reduce agoraphobia in spite of achieved panic reduction. They speculated that although cognitive therapy addresses fears of bodily sensations and their catastrophic consequences, it does not fully address two areas where agoraphobic people score very high: The fear of being unable to cope with panic and thereby losing control (becoming "hysterical," screaming, etc.), and the fear of social repercussions from anxiety and panic (being laughed at, thought of as weird, and causing embarrassment to self or others). Hence agoraphobia involves a large amount of social catastrophes. Although the authors speculated that cognitive therapy might enhance agoraphobia treatment if it addressed the fears of losing control and social embarrassment, agoraphobia needs treatment in its own right, i.e., in vivo exposure. As Bandura (1977) stated, people find their own behavioral accomplishments more convincing than rational dialogue. Cognitive mechanisms are useful if they help clients appraise their performance successes in a way that maximizes a general sense of mastery (Williams 1988).

Other authors (van Hout, et al. 1994) studied changes in physiological measures, subjectively reported anxiety, and self-statements in agoraphobic clients during in vivo exposure. In vivo exposure had a positive effect on cognitive change. However, neither cognitive change nor habituation fully explained the positive effects of exposure. In fact, heart rate did not habituate across sessions. Subjective anxiety did show a steady decline and was almost absent at the end of treatment. The authors found that those who improved the least continued to employ negative self-talk.

The best overall effect might be achieved by adding cognitive therapy to in vivo exposure. There are also preliminary findings suggesting that interoceptive exposure has a positive effect on in vivo exposure.

Habituation

It has been proposed that exposure reduces fear through *habituation* (Foa and Kozak 1986; Grayson, Foa, and Steketee 1982). Habituation refers to a decrease in heart rate and subjective anxiety that is achieved through prolonged and repeated exposures. Not *every* exposure leads to habituation. Fear is reduced if the information of harmlessness is incorporated into the memory network. One of the conditions for the integration of new information is attentional focus. Thus, focusing on the feared stimulus during the exposure permits more complete emotional processing (defined as a decrease in emotional fear responses) than distraction. Note that *within* an exposure *session*, focusing on the feared stimulus does not seem to produce more habituation than distraction does. However, focusing improves the *between-session* habituation, thus facilitating greater treatment gains.

Empirical findings ultimately must confirm or disconfirm theory. As you will see in this section, the mechanism by which exposure works is much more complex than we would like to believe, and even the habituation theory has been challenged. Exposure to a feared situation (even prolonged, focused exposure), in and of itself does not always lead to lasting therapeutic benefit.

Attentional Focus

As Rodriguez and Craske (1993) have summarized, most theoretical models on exposure state that distraction has a negative impact on fear reduction. Yet the experimental findings have shown inconclusive results. The authors state that it is possible that the impact of attentional focus (focused versus distracted) depends on the individual's coping style. However, at present, too little is known about how to match the attentional focus with a particular individual. More research is needed before the role of distraction can be fully understood. Most prominent clinicians and researchers known to me suggest that clients should do exposures without distractions. Distractions are viewed as a form of "safety behavior."

The Bias to Overpredict Fear

Recently a great deal of attention has been placed on the person's prediction of fear in a phobic encounter. A number of investigators have found that individuals with fears consistently overestimate the amount of fear they will experience when they expose themselves to fear-provoking situations (Cox and Swinson 1994; Schmidt, Jacquin, and Telch 1994; Taylor and Rachman 1994a; Taylor and Rachman 1994b; Telch, Valentiner, and Bolte 1994; van Hout and Emmelkamp 1994). This phenomenon was found when clients were asked to predict the fear they expected to experience in an exposure, using SUDS levels from 0 to 100 to quantify the fear they expected to feel (0 = no fear and 100 = intolerable fear) (Taylor and Rachman 1994b). This was then compared with the level of fear they reported experiencing in the actual situation. Underprediction occurred when the person predicted less fear in the situation than was subsequently experienced, which is what happens with an *unexpected* panic attack (Cox and Swinson 1994). The overprediction of fear in specific feared situations may help to maintain agoraphobia. Agoraphobics also tend to overpredict fear in new and unfamiliar situations (Cox and Swinson 1994).

Schmidt et al. (1994) and van Hout and Emmelkamp (1994) concluded that there is a strong persistence of the bias toward overprediction. They found that with repeated exposures, however, the overprediction bias decreased; but it took many such disconfirmation exposures before the bias actually decreased. They also found that self-efficacy increases after an overprediction of fear. On the other hand, one single underprediction led to a dramatic increase in future predicted fear.

Why is this bias to overpredict so tenacious? One reason may be that it is related to other predictive biases, such as the overprediction of danger, and the underprediction of safety information (controllability, available exits for escape, etc.) (Schmidt et al. 1994; Taylor and Rachman 1994b; Telch et al. 1994). It is speculated that danger information takes precedence over safety information, and when someone's attention is focused on cues of potential danger, fewer attentional resources are available to process safety information. These recent findings seem congruent with Beck and Emery, with Greenberg's (1985) cognitive model of anxiety. In anxiety, the danger mode stands out, i.e., threat and danger are easily evoked. In situations perceived as dangerous, the highly selective cognitive processes that come into play are exclusionary. They produce "tunnel vision," so that information not relevant to the threat is blocked. Thus the anxious person sees only the danger in the situation and none of the safety factors.

The Impact of Underprediction on Fear

As stated earlier, many exposures are needed for disconfirmation of fear, yet one unexpected panic attack (underprediction of fear) can mean the return of fear in full force. Beck and Emery, with Greenberg's (1985) theory could explain the findings regarding the impact of underprediction on fear. They point out that in the face of threat, the person's evaluation of danger and harm is weighed against perceived coping resources, that is, how the person can cope with the threatening situation. If the coping skills seem inadequate vis-à-vis the danger, the person feels vulnerable instead of self-confident. Even with continued behavioral successes, if the person's basic view of himself or herself continues to be that of being vulnerable, one bad experience may shift the focus from being skillful to being weak. This is more likely to occur if the person continues to evaluate his or her behavior by the degree of anxiety experienced, expects perfection, or has an excessive need for control.

How Self-Efficacy Theory Explains Phobic Behavior

As mentioned earlier in this book, Bandura (1988) and Williams (1988) strongly challenge the theory of habituation of fear through stimulus exposure. They believe that self-efficacy theory, not anxiety arousal, explains phobic behavior. The problem is seen as the person's perceived inability behaviorally and cognitively to cope with potentially threatening activities. Low self-efficacy leads to an anticipation of danger and fear and to the complex behavioral pattern of agoraphobia. It is also possible that perceptions of danger influence phobic behavior independent of self-efficacy (Williams 1996). According to this theory, experiencing high anxiety during exposures is not viewed as beneficial, i.e., anxiety is not seen as being therapeutic in itself (Williams 1990), and furthermore there is empirical support which shows that anxiety arousal is not linked to therapeutic behavior change (Bandura 1988; Williams 1988). In a study by Williams, Kinney, and Falbo (1989), self-efficacy predicted outcome in agoraphobia even when perceived danger and anticipated anxiety and panic were held constant.

Bandura (1977) and Williams (1990, 1995) believe that effective treatment for phobias helps clients integrate information that strengthens their perception of being able to cope. Clients need tangible evidence that they possess the necessary skills to master fear-challenging situations. As expected, successful performance (behavioral accomplishments) in phobic situations is the primary vehicle to achieve increased self-efficacy and thereby change. Although less effective than behavioral accomplishments, other sources of information for positively affecting self-efficacy are vicarious experiences (observing others engage in the feared activity), verbal persuasion (verbal-cognitive dialogue), emotional and physiological arousal (perceived autonomic arousal and feeling states interpreted as a sign of ability or inability to cope), and imaginal experiences (systematic desensitization and implosion, i.e., visualizing oneself perform). According to Williams (1995), although the psychological mechanism of change is cognitive, the most powerful psychological procedure for change is behavioral.

Research has brought other findings to light. If self-efficacy is raised in one area of fear, it generalizes to other areas, but not completely, suggesting that dysfunctions in different areas are partly independent (Williams et al. 1989). Kinney and Williams (1988) found that self-efficacy ratings as measured by the Self-Efficacy Scales for Agoraphobia (where clients judge how much they can do in a given phobic situation) are strongly correlated with actual behavioral accomplishments, more so than the Fear Questionnaire and the Mobility Inventory (see chapter 3). However, nothing replaces behavioral tests. The best measure of behavior is actual behavior. Finally, mastery-oriented treatment seems particularly helpful in severe and refractory phobias (Williams et al. 1984).

Implications for Exposure Work

These theories and empirical findings have implications for exposure work. Arntz et al. (1995) speculated that when anxious clients perceive danger, they do not check whether this is a false alarm. Instead of having such persons focus on their subjective anxiety level during exposures, they could be taught to pay attention to objective information about danger and safety. Beck and Emery, with Greenberg (1985) also state that confidence can be retained if the person remains focused on the task rather than on evaluating his or her performance. Further, the person must believe in his or her competence in coping with the feared task.

Combining these positions then, if clients can be taught to pay attention to objective information about the stimulus, and this is coupled with applying cognitive and behavioral coping skills to maximize success in task performance, their self-confidence or self-efficacy can be significantly enhanced. With these techniques, it is hoped that the unexpected panic will be perceived as a challenge, a problem to be solved, rather than as a sign of returning weakness (which would activate the vulnerability mode). Exposure is a powerful behavioral method. The various findings suggest that it works differently for different people, i.e., no single theory explains how or why it works.

Section 1: Exposure Strategies

In Vivo Exposure

In vivo exposure is a powerful method to treat agoraphobia. However, many clients drop out of treatment and others benefit little or moderately. A smaller number overcome their agoraphobia. Why? Exposure is hard work. It requires time, persistence, and the willingness to endure intense discomfort.

Research has provided clues on how in vivo exposure should be conducted. However, as you will see in the subsequent section, guided mastery exposure has yielded more detailed information that can greatly enhance the success of exposure.

Craske and Barlow (1994) and Craske and Rodriguez (1994) reviewed many studies on exposure and drew the following conclusions:

- *Massed versus spaced.* Long, continuous sessions are better than short or interrupted sessions. A very intensive exposure plan would be three to four hours a day, five days a week. However, attempting to make too many changes in a very short time may lead to greater dropout rates and tends to be more stressful for the family. The final choice should be the client's.

- *Graduated or graded versus intense.* Graduated means going from least to most fearful; intense means going to the most fearful situation immediately. Although fewer people accept massed and intense exposure, the results are at least as effective, if not more so, than spaced and graduated exposure.

- *Self-directed versus therapist-directed.* Minimal therapist contact seems as effective as therapist-aided exposure, as long as it is structured and programmed. Those with extreme avoidance may need coaches. Family members can serve as coaches.

- *Focused versus distracted.* Although the use of distraction is a common practice, both with clients and therapists, it is not believed to produce as good, long-lasting results as when the exposure is focused.

- *Controlled escape versus endurance.* Controlled escape refers to returning to the situation as soon as possible after an escape. Maximal fear elicitation is not essential, i.e., good results can be achieved even without endurance of high levels of anxiety.

- *Applying coping skills.* Skills, such as diaphragmatic breathing and coping self-statements, seem to decrease dropout from exposure.

Similarly, Marks (1985, 1987), Michelson and Marchione (1991), and Zarate and Agras (1994) concluded that exposure work needs to emphasize setting clear goals, doing systematic programmed practice, and using relatives as co-therapists, if needed. It is preferable that practices be done daily, even if it means that clients must give up something else in their lives in order to fit in the frequent exposures. It is important to record exposures, with information such as number of attempts, distance and time covered, and anxiety level. It is ideal to stay in the feared situation until the anxiety diminishes and the urge to escape has abated.

Fiegenbaum (1988) conducted an extraordinary study in Germany involving intense and massed exposure. He compared two groups, both receiving massed exposure. The graded group, unlike the intense group, followed a hierarchy from less to more anxiety-producing situations. That is, one group's exposure was massed and intense and the other group's was massed and graded (graduated). The exposure was completed in six to ten consecutive days.

A number of the clients were housebound or otherwise severely limited. Clients traveled to different cities and to another country by car and/or train; were confined in a small, dark room; ate in restaurants; spent nights in a hotel and train; used public transportation; took a lift to the top of a mountain; walked in unfamiliar areas; and flew in a sporting plane, etc. Five years later, at follow-up, almost 78 percent of the intense group considered themselves completely symptom-free. Eighty percent of the intense group were able to complete the behavioral tests (where they exposed themselves to their formerly most fear-provoking situation), compared to 22 percent of the graded group. The author concluded that the two factors most likely responsible for the long-term benefits were performing the exposures with no possibility of obvious or subtle avoidance, and the clients' conviction that they should stay in fearful situations until their anxiety was gone.

Why Clients' Own Exposures Often Do Not Work

According to Craske and Barlow (1994) the reasons that self-directed exposures fail are these: Clients often do exposures only when they have to; they do not do the exposures often or long enough; they use safety signals and safety behaviors; they escape from but do not immediately return to the phobic situation, and they do not give themselves enough credit or reward. This explains why clients often enter a treatment program saying that they have always exposed themselves to feared situations and it has not worked.

Guided Mastery Exposure

The exposure guidelines (including strategies and techniques) in this section derive from the following sources: Williams (1990, 1995), Williams, et al. (1984), and Williams and Zane (1989). Mastery exposures are structured so that they promote performance accomplishments in order to increase a strong sense of self-efficacy. (Lang (1979) also postulated that the best way to eliminate fear is to confront fearful situations while the therapist coaches and reinforces the client's exposures and responses step by step.) I will share these guided mastery exposure guidelines with you, which I have found exceedingly helpful.

Self-Efficacy Ratings

Judgments of coping capabilities can be measured easily. Measurement involves rating how confident the client is that he or she can perform a graded sequence of feared tasks, on a scale from 1 to 100. The ratings help assess progress over time.

The Therapist's Role

The therapist's role during treatment is to promote performance success, which is done by assisting the client as an expert field helper. The therapist accompanies the client into the field, helping the client to enter grocery stores and elevators, and to drive on freeways, etc. Not only do therapists give support, encouragement, and reassurance, they also help with specific techniques structured to assist the client to act with more assurance. The therapist provides behavioral guidance (sometimes by modeling coping strategies) when the client has difficulty making progress and gives all the assistance and reinforcement the client needs to perform well.

Once the client can do a task rather well, although not necessarily free of rituals, the therapist encourages him or her to move to the next step. While the therapist will accept the client's escape if the client really needs it, he or she encourages the client to try and stay in the situation a bit longer. The defensive maneuvers (safety behaviors) used remind the client of his or her incompetence and are eliminated in the course of treatment. In sum, the therapist helps raise self-efficacy by pointing out the client's performance successes and comparing them with previous attempts; however, the therapist is not so close that personal accomplishments cannot be reached. The client's raised self-efficacy becomes the primary mediator of change in overcoming the phobias.

Strategies and Techniques in Guided Mastery Exposure

There are three general strategies aimed at unconditional self-efficacy and mastery of phobic situations. (Williams 1990; Williams, et al. 1984; Williams and Laberge 1994). They are as follow:

1. Using a large repertoire of techniques, including behavioral guidance, to help boost clients' self-efficacy and performance

2. Abandoning defensive maneuvers and varying performance

3. Withdrawing assistance as soon as possible to promote independence

The goal is to help a client master challenges, actively and rapidly. The specific techniques follow.

Verbal Support in Joint Exposure

The client is encouraged to engage in exposures and thus learn behaviorally that he or she can manage. Clients learn that even if very uncomfortable, anxiety is temporary and they gain confidence. The therapist asks direct questions about confidence and anxiety levels, as appropriate. Also, the therapist encourages the client to act normally even if he or she is feeling terrible. When behavior improves, e.g., the client's posture is relaxed and confident, the therapist comments on that. The client is encouraged to tackle the next harder step quickly because the previous step will then seem easy. Note that doing exposures especially on "bad" days is advocated, because the client learns to manage when the circumstances are not ideal.

Mastery of Subtasks/Proximal Goals/Graduated Time

When a task is particularly difficult, it is broken into smaller components and each component is practiced. The more dysfunctional the person and the slower the progress, the more the need to set intermediate goals and to work on subtasks. With difficult tasks, the time is graduated from shorter to longer exposures.

Modeling/Physical Support/Mechanical Aids

Often the therapist models a behavior first. Physical support can consist of holding the therapist's arm when, e.g., approaching a railing with a client who fears heights. Aids can be used, but are to be eliminated as soon as possible.

Eliminating Defensive Maneuvers/Self-Protective Rituals

When the client performs a task in an odd or rigid way, e.g., driving while leaning forward and gripping the steering wheel with white knuckles, the therapist gives suggestions for eliminating those behaviors. Some other safety behaviors that must be eliminated are these: driving slowly in the right-hand lane, having the radio on, clinging to the shopping cart while rushing, sitting near exits (in trains, cinemas), fidgeting (or other displays of nervousness), shopping only during off-peak hours, standing in a frozen posture at a balcony railing, etc. These rituals must be abandoned as soon as possible. Behaviors that the therapist encourages are leaning back, lowering the shoulders, and loosening the grip on the steering wheel, balcony railing, or shopping cart, and walking in a relaxed and natural manner, etc.

Varied Performance

Tasks are done in a variety of ways. This can involve changing lanes, passing slower cars, standing in different places in the elevator, walking along the center and sides in a mall, and so forth.

Successive Withdrawal of Therapist's Aid

- *Supermarket:* Initially, the therapist is close behind the client when a small purchase is made, then a few steps away, then near the store entrance, and then outside. The next day the client goes alone from home to the supermarket to purchase many items. The therapist can stay close to a phone as another step in the transition toward independence (this is true in regards to other exposures, too).

- *Mall:* While the therapist is at the entrance, a second strategic person can be at another location in the shopping mall. The distance between the therapist and the assistant is progressively increased.

- *Freeway:* The therapist rides with the client, perhaps seated in the back seat. Next, the therapist follows immediately behind in another car, then with progressively longer distances. The same tactic can be used driving in the streets, riding, walking, or using other means of transportation.

- *Heights:* The therapist remains close to aid and guide the client on each successive floor until the client feels somewhat more comfortable. Later, the therapist waits on the ground floor.

Teaching Client Self-Coaching

Assistance is withdrawn as soon as possible while maintaining progress. The therapist teaches clients to coach themselves effectively. This is done by giving feedback about performance and mastery principles. For instance, the therapist teaches the client that self-efficacy is particularly enhanced when the client does the exposures when not feeling his or her best. Then, the client learns that he or she can function under difficult circumstances.

Summary

In vivo exposure is the treatment of choice for agoraphobia, but its mechanism of action is still being debated. While some theorists propose habituation, others believe that exposure works by increasing the person's ability to cope. It is possible that not one single theory accounts for the changes made. These theoretical differences have led to distinct exposure strategies, i.e., by in vivo versus guided mastery exposure. The latter uses the therapist's close guidance as a vehicle to achieve the desired outcome.

Section 2: An Individualized Exposure Plan

I have outlined in Section 1 of this chapter Williams' guided mastery therapy guidelines. Here, I will provide further principles and specific suggestions for treating phobic clients. As you plan your own program, you can try the methods and techniques described.

Setting the Stage for Exposure Work

- *Being Willing to Take Risks.* Total security is an illusion. Being alive is risky, and the only certain thing in life is death. In this same vein, anyone can be in the wrong place at the wrong time. However, clients will be working on low-risk situations, whether driving, flying, using an elevator, or crossing the street, etc.

- *Moderating the Desire for Control and Perfectionism.* I start with the premise that every being of every species would like to have control over its life. Your client needs to learn to distinguish between the fact that some things are under his or her control and others are not, and to accept those differences. Hence to be a passenger in a car, bus, or airplane, one must be willing to let someone else control the vehicle. Traffic, lines in stores or at the bank, weather conditions, etc., are not under our control. Likewise, in interactions with others, we cannot always predict what will take place interpersonally, and we cannot be expected to always speak and react in "perfect" ways.

- *Being Willing to Confront the Feared Object or Situation.* Exposure is needed in order to overcome phobias. This means that your client must be willing to accept some anxiety during exposures.

- *Identifying the Goals.* Clients must target situational avoidances, activities, safety signals, and safety behaviors. These are addressed in the exposures.

What Is Avoided In Agoraphobia

1. **Places/Situations Commonly Avoided**
   - Driving and/or being a passenger
   - Walking outside
   - Supermarkets
   - Shopping malls
   - Crowds
   - Public transportation
   - Being far from home
   - Being home alone
   - Movies/Theaters
   - Bridges/Tunnels
   - Waiting in line
   - Meetings
   - Elevators/Escalators

- New places
- Walking across open spaces
- Jury duty
- Flying

2. **Other Feared Experiences/Activities**

   - Exercise
   - Excitement brought on by movies, news on TV, ball games
   - Relaxation and inactivity
   - Optional social events
   - Situations that can lead to disagreement or arguments, that create intense emotions, such as anger and excitement
   - Setting limits with others, when their wishes might cause conflict
   - Changing jobs
   - Caffeinated drinks
   - Eating in front of others

3. **Safety Signals/Safety Behaviors**
   Safety signals are seen as preventing bad things from happening (Craske and Barlow, 1994; Hoffart 1993)

   - Having a "safe" person along
   - Medications or empty pill bottles
   - Small paper bag
   - Water/Sodas
   - Telephone numbers of nearby hospitals
   - Lucky charms (supposed to prevent panics)
   - Focusing on escape plans
   - Holding one's breath
   - Grasping the steering wheel with "white knuckles"
   - Always driving in the slow lane
   - Driving with radio on
   - Leaning on shopping cart
   - Sitting near exits
   - Knowing where bathrooms are
   - Tensing up
   - Using distractions
   - Doing things on sunny versus cloudy days
   - Doing things on "good" versus "bad" days (the day is dictated by how much anxiety is felt, often in the morning, which in turn determines how much the client feels that he or she can handle)

◆ Having a "safe zone" beyond which your client feels incapable of going, especially when driving or walking

◆ Sitting down

◆ Holding onto objects

◆ Making an effort to control one's thoughts

◆ Wearing sunglasses

◆ Any object or behavior that is supposed to "save" the client from panics or disastrous consequences

Typical Fears Behind Agoraphobic Situations

• Having a panic attack with its feared consequences

• Vomiting or fainting

• Loss of urinary or bowel control

• Feeling hot/unable to breathe

• Losing control, making "a fool" of oneself, "standing out" too much

• Showing signs of anxiety

• Collapsing from weakness

Setting Goals

Right from the start, your client should list what the desired goal is for every type of feared situation. Many clinicians have the client list goals in sequence from the easiest to the hardest and begin therapeutic work with the easiest. I prefer a more practical approach. Your client can begin with the easiest goal, the goal he or she most wants to achieve first, the goal that can be worked on most often, or the goal with which your client thinks he or she will succeed best. In other words, I recommend to start anywhere except with very difficult goals or those that cannot easily be broken into small segments (notably, flying or having surgery). It is preferable to first choose goals that can be worked on *at least three times a week*. Clients can work on more than one goal at a time. In fact, ideally, the client should work on some step of each goal, weekly, if that is at all feasible.

Two worksheets are provided for your clients, numbers 9 and 10, with the accompanying Therapist Record forms for you, numbers 9T and 10T, where "T" denotes "therapist." Clients list their goals on Worksheet 9: Goal and the Steps to Achieve It (one copy of the worksheet must be made for each goal). An example is provided. You can copy your client's goal sheets and/or transfer the goals onto Therapist Record 9T: Tracking Goal Progress (designed for an individual client or a group). After each session, you simply check off those goals that were actually worked on during the preceding week. In column 1 you can check the goals worked on since Session 1 (at the time they were planned); you get this information in Session 2. I find that this simple form of record-keeping allows me to keep track of the goals and the client's work on them. Your client does not need to follow the steps rigidly to reach a goal (Worksheet 9). The steps provide opportunities to break down each goal into smaller components and to track progress visually. (Whether the client writes dates in the small circles that hold the client's descriptions of how he or she plans to take a step is optional.) Ultimately, it is your client's responsibility to keep track of the progress made toward each goal.

The client transfers his or her goals onto Worksheet 10: Your Weekly Exposures. The same worksheet is used to record the weekly assignments. The accompanying Therapist Record 10T: Tracking Client's Weekly Exposures is similar. Weekly assignments (Planned Exposures) are recorded: The steps, distance covered (e.g., on the freeway) or amount of time (e.g., riding the elevator), and the number of attempts planned for the week are also recorded. Both you and your client note the relevant information on your respective worksheets during the session. In the following session, the client reports back from his or her worksheet the actual efforts that were made regarding each step, which you then record onto your record sheet. (Afterwards, you check off on 9T which goal was worked on.) Therapist Record 10T can be used for one client in individual therapy for several weeks (you record the date in each new section instead of repeating the client's name), or a group (one or more sheets per week, depending on group size).

Instructions for Exposures

In addition to the guidelines described earlier by several researchers, I will give additional instructions for exposure work that are based on my training and experience. Further, I will describe behavioral and cognitive coping techniques. The latter overlap sometimes. Finally, I will mention additional difficulties and fears.

Therapist-Aided (Guided Mastery) Exposures

At one time I did not accompany my clients on their exposures. This changed during the last few years, in great part as a result of my additional training. I first accompanied my clients at the Kaiser Medical Facility to elevators, a small, dark storage room, and an empty hallway to increase the challenge with interoceptive exposures. Since then I have accompanied them to the cafeteria (when some feared eating in front of others) and to the outside stairs of a five-story parking garage (when some clients feared heights). In a limited way, I have used the approaches developed by Dr. Williams described earlier in this chapter. In my private practice, I accompany individual clients who need to practice driving on major highways and freeways. Those with whom I have worked found it invaluable. Of course, the biggest problem with this excellent way of working with clients is the time and money involved. It is hoped that computer-generated virtual reality will become widespread for therapeutic use in the future. The drawback with virtual reality is that only one client can work with one piece of equipment at a time. In the meantime, I am looking into redesigning my group programs to incorporate more therapist-aided exposure. It may require the aid of one or two additional therapists, which may make therapy logistically more difficult. It is especially important to consider therapist-aided guided mastery exposures for debilitating phobias, although many clients are able to do well with home assignments (Williams and Laberge 1994).

Role Play

Role playing with a group can be helpful, although it is not as effective as doing the exposures in real life situations. I have re-enacted a few scenarios. We arranged chairs in the group room and pretended to board and sit in an airplane, drive on the freeway in a minivan, faint in a department store, run uncontrollably out of a meeting, and act insane. If you as the therapist are willing to play first, for instance, the role of the fainter, clients will follow quickly, even though they may be shy. We increase the intensity of fear exposures with expressions such as, "Wow, you look anxious! Is there something wrong?" Even with

Worksheet 9: **Goal and the Steps to Achieve It**

Reward for Goal Achieved: _____

Goal No. _____

Date Achieved: _____

Currently able to do:

Date starting: _____

(Use all, some, or add circles, as needed)

Example: Goal and the Steps to Achieve It

Worksheet 9: Goal and the Steps to Achieve It

Reward for Goal Achieved: *Go with husband to dinner and theater play.*

Goal No. *1* :
Shop in grocery store alone any time.

Date achieved: *11-7-98*

Go to rather crowded store alone.

Shop alone without husband waiting. Buy 10 items or more. Store not crowded.

Husband waits at home while I shop. He is available by phone.

Buy a few items from different aisles alone. Husband waits in car.

Buy 3 items alone. Husband waits outside.

Go alone into store. Husband is outside and joins me after 15 min.

Currently able to do: Go to grocery store accompanied.

Date starting: *8-2-98*

Start shopping with husband. He leaves me alone for 10 min. and returns.

(Use all, some, or add circles, as needed)

Therapist Record 9T: **Tracking Goal Progress**

Check if Progress Made on Goals

Name	Goals	Treatment Weeks															
		1	2	3	4	5	6	7	8	9	10	11	12	13	14	15	16

Worksheet 10: **Your Weekly Exposures**

Goals: 1. _____   5. _____

2. _____   6. _____

3. _____   7. _____

4. _____   8. _____

Week Starting	Planned Exposures		Actual Effort	
	Steps	Distance/Time No. attempts per week	Steps	Distance/Time No. attempts per week

For every step, record: Distance covered or Time, and Number of attempts per week.

Therapist Record 10T: **Tracking Client's Weekly Exposures**

Week Starting: _____

Name	Planned Exposures		Actual Effort	
	Steps	Distance/Time No. attempts per week	Steps	Distance/Time No. attempts per week

the bad acting we generally do, it does seem to work. When "driving," the client with that specific fear does become very anxious, sweating, and revealing thoughts or behaviors that are illuminating and can be targeted for further work. (These role plays generate a lot of laughter in the group.)

Frequency of Exposures

The more time spent on exposures, the better. In reality, many clients do not set aside or find the time to do as many exposures as they need. Lately, when clients ask at the end of the assessment session if the treatment produces successful results, I ask, in turn, how much time they are willing to set aside for in vivo exposures. Based on their answers, I explain the correlation between time and effort spent on the one hand and expected improvement on the other. I tell them that a minimum of six hours a week, spread over three or four days is required, preferably more. I also remind them that avoiding a number of situations usually takes time away from them or from someone else in the family. If the person is very limited, e.g., he or she never walks or drives alone, then I expect him or her to do exposures every single day, i.e., the more incapacitated, the more important it is to practice daily. In sum, quick, steady progress early on seems greatly advantageous.

Graduated, Prolonged, and Repeated Exposures

Graduated or *graded* means to break the tasks into small steps, starting with easier ones to make the exposures manageable. If no anxiety is felt, it is not a challenge. Some anxiety is unavoidable, but it does not have to be at a high level. *Prolonged* means to stay in a situation until the anxiety and the urge to escape have subsided, which could mean staying in a situation for one and one-half to two hours. Some exposures are very brief by their very nature, e.g., elevator and escalator rides, driving to the next exit on the freeway, and walking around the block. In these cases it is best to *repeat* the exposure three to four times in a row or even more. Other exposures are naturally long-lasting, e.g., buying many items in crowded stores, sitting through a movie, or a long airplane flight. The motto is *repeat, repeat, repeat* exposures. The person can move to the next higher step before the previous one is fully mastered.

Planning Exposures in Advance

Most clients benefit from planning the day and time of the exposures in advance. Usually it does not help to put off the exposure until they feel better, because they may never feel better. Following a schedule often means high anxiety right before embarking on the exposure, but the anticipatory anxiety is prolonged if the exposure is postponed. Planning ahead is the surest way for exposures to actually take place. Occasionally, clients strongly prefer to go out "on the spur of the moment." Whatever the initial approach is, it must be varied later to avoid having it become a ritual or rigid rule that must be followed as a safety behavior. Flexibility is required in real life, and the goal is to prepare the client for real-life situations. One further advantage with planning ahead is that it allows for the possible inclusion of coaches in the early stages.

Using Safety Signals and Safety Behaviors

During the assessment and subsequent sessions, the use of these signals and behaviors should be ascertained. Their use permits only partial exposure because it does not allow for full disconfirmation of the catastrophic fears. The message the client gives to himself or herself when using safety signals and behaviors is, "If I had not done X, something terrible would have happened." If used initially, the client should be aware of it and rid himself or herself of such safety devices as soon as possible.

Self-Reward

It is helpful if the client incorporates self-rewards into his or her plan. These are most effective if they immediately follow the exposure. Rewards should be under the client's control as much as possible. The reward can be something material, pleasurable activities, acknowledgment from someone else, and self-reinforcement.

Coping Techniques During Exposures

These are techniques that my clients have found helpful in their attempts to cope with their fear in agoraphobic situations.

Behavioral Coping Techniques

1. **Diaphragmatic Breathing**
   The slow, diaphragmatic breathing learned early during treatment helps the client manage the physical symptoms of anxiety and panic. Many clients find it very helpful, even if done for only a few minutes. It is the body's *natural relaxant.*

2. **Planning "Exits" at the Beginning of the Mastery Exposure**
   I learned from Alec Pollard at the 1995 conference of the Anxiety Disorders Association of America how to help clients distinguish between and apply "exits" versus "escape." When a client leaves a situation because compelled by anxiety, he or she escapes. When the client leaves a situation according to a preset plan, that is exiting. In agoraphobia the fear of entrapment is predominant. A person can leave many, though not all situations, and it is appropriate for the client to learn to exercise the freedom to leave. This is especially useful in the beginning of treatment and should be planned if the client complains of entrapment. The entrapment is often due to imaginary social constraints. Again, there is nothing like behavioral testing of a belief.

   Excellent situations where this distinction can be exercised are leaving a line, a movie, or a theater (especially when sitting in the middle of a row), the mall, or a store. Likewise, the client can practice leaving meetings or a classroom (when not jeopardizing a job or a test), parties, and restaurants. The plan can involve leaving after five, fifteen, or thirty minutes after arrival, and later in therapy after longer intervals. As a passenger in a bus or streetcar, the person can get off at the next stop, and on the freeway at the next exit. The person can plan to leave the situation in question several times until he or she is absolutely convinced that it is possible to leave. As a comparison, people without phobic fears do not feel trapped because they know they can leave most situations when they want to. Obviously, it is not practical to demand the right to leave an airplane when the doors close, or to stop dental or surgical procedures, or to needlessly stop the car on the shoulder of a freeway or on a bridge because of the danger and/or the cost involved.

   I encourage you to be creative, as I many times have needed to be. For example, one of my clients had a flight coming up and she was feeling quite fearful because of her fear of entrapment. I discovered the precise situation that evoked her worst fear. She was envisioning herself sitting in the middle of a row and everyone having their food trays open and extended in front of their laps. If she needed to go to the bathroom, she felt she would not be able to maneuver past all the passengers and their food trays. I convinced her to test her hypothesis. We went over exactly what it would entail. Everyone between her and the aisle would be greatly inconvenienced, she would probably have to have someone else hold her tray, but it could be done! Afterwards, she reported having flown comfortably and had not needed to test this. Another client feared gagging (he had often had true gag attacks) in a meeting while giving a speech, because he did not have access to a throat lozenge or water. He went to get these and started his meeting fifteen minutes late. He apologized and went on with business. (Later he worked on ridding himself of these safety signals.)

3. **How to Cope With the Urge to Leave or "Escape"**
   If your client feels that he or she cannot cope or is about to have a panic, escape is an option. The ideal practice, however, is for the client to stay in the situation a bit longer before leaving. The client can ask himself or herself, "What would happen if I continue a bit longer?" It is better that the client leave after the anxiety level is lowered. If the person escapes, he or she should return as soon as possible, preferably only a few minutes later, but at the very least by the following day. Otherwise, the fear will grow.

4. **Use a Paradoxical Approach With Feared Sensations**
   Instruct your client to pay attention to all of the sensations. In anxiety and panic, fighting the sensations does not work. A great deal of control can be achieved if the person invites the symptoms, e.g., when driving, the client can alternately tense and relax the body. Similarly, clients can try to induce "disastrous" consequences such as collapsing or going crazy. In these situations, good judgment must be exercised. It would hardly be responsible for a therapist to encourage a client to try collapsing while driving. However, in other situations, such as where there is soft padding to fall onto, the suggestion to collapse is an excellent idea. It then becomes a true disconfirmation that the dreaded event does not take place.

5. **Committing a Faux Pas**
   In regard to social fears, the client can plan committing blunders on purpose, as long as these do not have objectively serious consequences. For example, a woman might introduce herself at a party saying, "I am Mr. X." A man might introduce his wife saying, "I'd like you to meet my wife . . . (and "forgets" her first name)." A person might go into a hardware store and ask, "Do you carry plumbing or hardware supplies?"

6. **Returning to the Scene of the "Crime"**
   Encourage your client to go back to the place where the first or worst panic occurred or to the situation of the worst fear. Otherwise this fear will always be a stumbling block.

Cognitive Coping Techniques

1. **Using Worksheet 4: Challenging Automatic Thoughts**
   Your client can use this worksheet to challenge fearful automatic thoughts or can do the same challenges mentally. The following steps are involved:
   • Identifying the specific situation or sensations triggering the fear

- Identifying the automatic thought (what is feared about the situation or sensations)

- Estimating the probability of the automatic thought being true from 0–100 percent

- Stating the evidence for the fear and describing how this evidence can be refuted

- Stating alternative hypotheses with their probabilities, and

- Facing up to the automatic thought. This includes looking anew at the probability of the automatic thought being true, from 0 to 100 percent.

2. **Being a Participant-Observer and Staying in the Here and Now**
When a person asks "What if . . . happens?," he or she is projecting into the future. No one can handle all the probable events that might happen to us. Learning how to stay in the here and now is very helpful to phobic people. The client can ask "What is the worst that is happening right now, at this very moment?" This question is best combined with an objective view of what is actually happening at the moment. At times, it is useful for the person to describe what is taking place around him or her. This should not be done as a distraction but as a way not to be too self-absorbed.

3. **Perceived Control Versus Lack of Control**
Clients tend to tune into danger signals, which involves scrutinizing their environment for the ways in which they lack control, e.g., "There are too many people here," "I can't see the exit." Instead, the person can learn to see the same situation in terms of all the ways he or she *does* have control, "Even if there are lots of people here, I can still get around. These people are not bothering me. In fact, they seem friendly/neutral." "I know exactly in what direction the exits are, in case of an emergency."

4. **Plan on How to Cope With Anxiety and Panic**
There is an advantage to being prepared for anxiety and panic. The client can ask himself or herself, "If I have a panic while riding in the elevator or on the airplane, how will I handle it?" It is helpful for the client to rehearse exactly what cognitive and behavioral strategies to use. Sometimes, of course, the only recourse is to just ride through the panic. Learning to use humor can also help.

5. **Testing Hypotheses via Behavioral Experiments**
This kind of testing involves cognitive and behavioral techniques. The person can predict what will happen during the exposure (preferably writing the prediction down) and later compare the written note with the actual outcome. In this way, the person gathers tangible evidence to challenge fearful automatic thoughts. Afterwards, the person asks himself or herself "Did it happen? What actually took place? What is my explanation?" *Note that it is not helpful to test feelings of anxiety or panic but rather to test behavioral events.*

Some Specific Difficulties

Specific difficulties some clients have experienced are described below.

"I'm Not Willing to Live With Uncertainty and Risk."

A client who has a basic view that he or she is not willing to take risks can be very difficult to treat. One approach you might try is to use Socratic questioning to show the client that he or she takes risks in many other areas of life. You can also explore the meaning of this view; it may cover up a greater fear, or magical thinking, etc. Ultimately, if the client's goal is absolute certainty, there is no hope. If that goal persists, the client may not be ready for therapy at this time.

"I Can't Do Exposures Today. I'm Having a Bad Day."

As a first step, explore what exactly this feeling is based on. Next, use cognitive techniques to challenge the assumption that a feeling must necessarily be translated to behavior. Use analogies to make this point, e.g., if someone is intensely angry at work, and envisions punching the boss out, that fantasy is rarely acted upon. Another approach is to make an agreement with clients that a "bad" day equals a "need for exposure" and they agree to a more extensive exposure than has been planned for the day. Finally, some clients find exposures too difficult to do on some days. The best response to that situation may be for them to get out of bed immediately and get going with the activities of the day rather than analyze their feelings. This can be combined with thought stopping.

Frequent or Chronic Dizziness

For clients who experience frequent or chronic dizziness, a medical examination is imperative. Assuming there is no organic pathology, Brandt (1996) helps a client to decatastrophize both with cognitive and behavioral means. The client is discouraged from paying attention to the symptoms and is instructed to desensitize by repeatedly exposing himself or herself to the situations that evoke dizziness. Besides naturalistic situations, interoceptive exercises targeting dizziness sensations are appropriate, starting with about fifteen seconds and building up to longer time periods.

Fears of Vomiting, Choking, and Gagging

I have treated clients with fears of vomiting, choking, and gagging (within the context of panic disorder and specific phobias). However, a few of them have actually vomited, and one woman suffered from severe gag attacks. In their cases, panic attacks would occur in conjunction with and often precipitated the vomiting and gagging. I treated them with breathing retraining, cognitive restructuring, interoceptive, and in vivo exposures.

Ball and Otto (1194) studied a few patients with choking phobia. They found that a single incident of choking, even if minimal, produced phobic fear in clients with a previous long-standing fear of death. Barsby (1997) reported that many people with a strong gag reflex (frequently observed in dentistry) often hyperventilate, even before any procedure take place. He found that having patients apply diaphragmatic breathing is a very useful coping strategy, which can be combined with cognitive restructuring.

People with these fears are likely to engage in many safety behaviors besides the possible avoidance of situations and activities. At the 1997 conference of the Anxiety Disorders Association of America, Karen Lynn Cassiday, Ph.D., and Marleen Lorenz, R.N., M.A. recommended some helpful exposures outlined below (some of these are described in the interoceptive section):

- Visual and auditory simulations of gagging and vomiting

- Using drinking fountains

- Pressing the back of the tongue with a tongue depressor or the back of a spoon

- Swallowing fast six times in a row
- Pressure on throat
- Eating quickly
- Eating dry foods, e.g., dry granola or similar cereal
- Watching movies (available on video) about choking and vomiting, e.g., "Stand by Me," "The Exorcist," "Animal House," and Monte Python's "The Meaning of Life"
- Shaking head side-to-side and spinning (for gagging)

Barskby (1997) reported that many people with a strong gag reflex (frequently observed in dentistry) often hyperventilate, even before any procedure takes place. He found that having the patients apply diaphragmatic breathing is a very useful coping strategy, which can be combined with cognitive restructuring.

Experiences and Fears of Shortness of Breath and Diarrhea Attacks

When clients have a medical condition in addition to panic disorder, I provide additional empathic support, because their task is more difficult: they must learn to separate illness-related from anxiety-related fears. Sometimes aids can be used. In this vein, clients with asthma often use a peak flow meter to help make the decision.

The exposures frequently involve smaller steps, at least in the beginning. Those with actual diarrhea attacks (including irritable bowel syndrome) need to accept that bodily functions are normal and therefore the need to have a bathroom nearby is not abnormal. As they take small steps applying coping strategies and become less obsessed with fear, their confidence grows.

Many of these clients reach a new sense of freedom, which is one of the rewards of this type of therapeutic work

Summary

In addition to the guidelines and strategies for exposure outlined in the previous section of this chapter, there are principles and specific instructions that clients need to agree to and follow in order for exposure to be successful.

The client can work with his/her individual exposure plan by recognizing the avoidant behaviors, setting goals accordingly, and breaking the latter into manageable steps. The client has a number of behavioral and cognitive coping techniques that can aid in the arduous exposure tasks. Client and therapist record the in vivo exposure assignments (those planned and the actual accomplishments) from session to session.

9

The Ideal Modality: Group Treatment

I have found group therapy to be an exceptionally powerful format for the treatment of panic disorder and phobias. I treat many clients with these disorders and cannot envision seeing them all individually, where I would have to repeat the same interventions many times. These groups are energizing, lively, and fun to conduct. Since I led my first group in 1988, I have conducted all of my anxiety disorder groups by myself except for the Social Phobia Group. I encourage you to conduct your groups by yourself. Most likely you will feel anxious, initially, as I did, but you may find working alone to be as rewarding as I do. I used to spend a significant amount of time preparing, including the evening before and the morning of the session. However, with every successive group it became easier. I attempt to establish good rapport with my clients and, generally, we work well together. Many clients initially are very skeptical, even resistant, to group treatment. Over the years I have become very good at persuading them to try this format. I explain the cognitive-behavioral treatment components, list the advantages of working in a group, and give them an account of my past work with individuals and groups. At the Kaiser facility where I work, when clients are first evaluated by other staff members they are a little less likely to accept group treatment than if I am their first contact. The therapist's belief in and comfort with groups is clearly conveyed to the client.

It is very rare that I now treat an adult client individually, unless there is a very unusual circumstance involved. I treat adult clients who exhibit animal phobias individually, and children. Even children would be treated in groups if the numbers were greater. The size of my groups has ranged from two to eleven; the usual size falling somewhere between six and ten. I have a definite preference for larger groups (seven to ten), which I find to be more dynamic and inspiring. Once clients are in the group, they also seem to prefer a not too small size. Even the most skeptical clients become comfortable in the group very quickly. The only exceptions have been clients with social phobias. Those with social phobia tend to have the hardest time in groups; they need a great deal of motivation to come to and stay in treatment. Generally, they are better treated in social anxiety/social phobia groups, where their apprehensions about being in the group can be worked on more extensively. However, I have had a number of clients with panic disorder and social phobia who have done well. A few of them proceeded to social phobia groups to target their social fears more directly.

Section 1: The Efficacy of Group Therapy

Group Treatment: What the Research Indicates

Group psychotherapy has gained increasing endorsement as a viable treatment modality. Group formats have been used in cognitive, interpersonal, and psychodynamic treatments. However, group treatment, whether cognitive-behavioral or psychodynamic, requires that the therapist be appropriately trained.

Group Therapy Versus Individual Therapy

Toseland and Siporin (1986) reviewed thirty-two studies in which clients were randomly assigned to individual or group treatment. The same theoretical background and techniques were utilized in both treatment formats. They found equivalent results in 75 percent of the studies, but the group format was more effective in 25 percent of the studies. In no case did the authors find that individual treatment was more effective than group treatment. They also reported that group treatment was more efficient and cost-effective, which are major considerations in this era of cost-containment in the mental health field. In agencies it is an efficient use of staff. The authors reported that in spite of the efficacy of group treatment, a significant portion of patients declined group when given a choice.

Another study compared time-limited individual and group psychotherapy and found an equivalent outcome (Budman, Demby, Redondo, et al. 1988). However, they reported that when asked directly, patients claimed to benefit more from individual than from group therapy. Some of the preference may come from clients' perception that less individual time equals less benefit, i.e., although they benefited extensively, they still liked group less.

Groups for Panic Disorder and Agoraphobia

In a meta-analysis Trull, et al. (1988) found exposure therapy to have significant effect on agoraphobia. They also found a more beneficial outcome when treatment was delivered by doctoral-level versus nondoctoral-level therapists. Group treatment was generally more beneficial than individual treatment.

Telch, Lucas, Schmidt, et al. (1993) treated panic disorder in groups of four to five clients. The groups were one and one-half hours long, and there were twelve sessions in eight weeks. Clients were assessed at baseline, posttreatment, and six-month follow-up. A number of outcome measures were used. Resolution of panic attacks was achieved by 85 percent of the clients, significantly more than in the untreated controls. Full recovery was seen in 63 to 80 percent of clients. Essentially, the same results were obtained at the six-month follow-up. Although more than half (61 percent) were on medications, they kept the dose constant, and their results were the same as those of the other clients.

Evans, et al. (1991) also provided group cognitive-behavior therapy for clients with agoraphobia and panic attacks. There was a brief, intensive, two-day group format, delivered in the form of a workshop. They provided information and taught stress management and other techniques to gain mastery, including in vivo exposure and flooding. Further, they asked clients to set goals and encouraged independence. Based on outcome measures (on the average, at one-year posttreatment) 48.6 percent were totally free of symptoms, 36.5 percent were improved enough to allow them to function normally, and 14.9 percent showed no change or deteriorated. The unimproved clients exhibited a significant amount of negative self-statements. This intervention was effective for 85 percent of the clients.

Belfer, Munoz, Schachter, et al. (1995) treated clients with agoraphobia and panic disorder (with emphasis on the agoraphobia), using cognitive-behavioral methods. Although the authors do not have comparison groups and outcome data, they prefer the group modality for treating these disorders. A brief description of their group therapy protocol follows.

There are four to nine members per group, with one or two leaders. The groups are twelve to sixteen-weeks long or open-ended, and each session lasts two hours. Sessions are divided into three segments. The first one is for introduction of new material, review of homework, and plans for subsequent exposures. Next, about half of the sessions are used for actual in vivo exposure, conducted alone, in small groups, or with a group leader. Exposures involve walking, driving, using public transportation, and going to stores, etc. Afterwards, the group reconvenes, constituting the third segment, to process the exposure work and contract for further homework. Exposures are graduated from the least to the most fearful. If they panic, clients are instructed to stay in feared situations to allow their anxiety to diminish before leaving the situation. The therapist's role during in vivo work is to be a technical expert and coach for the cognitive and behavioral techniques that are applied.

The Clinical Practice Guidelines for the Treatment of Panic Disorder in Psychiatry of the Kaiser Permanente Northern California Region (Peters, Gonzales, Harris, et al. 1995) recommended CBT, and specifically, group treatment, whenever possible.

Since the earlier-mentioned studies comparing group and individual therapy, group treatment has become much more common. Client acceptance has increased considerably, as we have observed at Kaiser. In my private practice, the majority of clients prefer to work with a group after I describe the treatment and benefits of this modality. Clients with panic and phobias easily feel set apart from others and welcome an opportunity to be with fellow clients who have the same fears.

How Yalom's Curative Factors Apply to Panic and Phobia Groups

Yalom (1970) has identified a number categories of curative factors in group therapy. In the sections below, I will try to show how his ten categories apply to groups, sometimes citing specific examples from my practice.

Imparting of Information

People with anxiety disorders are hungry for information about the myriad manifestations of anxiety and fear, as well as for learning how to cope. There is a great deal of education involved in the cognitive-behavioral treatment of panic disorder and agoraphobia. It is much more cumbersome to impart this amount of information to an individual compared to teaching a group. However, as in all groups, the therapist is not the only source of valuable information. Members share their different perspectives and information, as well.

For example, today, a client who fears a heart attack asked in my New Panickers Group (directing the question at me), "I have never asked anyone this, but does an electrocardiogram give information about the state of your heart just the day it is done—or in general?" In my usual style of trying to involve the other members, I looked around to see if anyone would take the bait. Several members gave the right answer (in this case, that the test is a good indicator of the general health of the heart), among them were two nurses. The client who asked the question then said that the group's answers made her feel much more confident.

Instillation of Hope

Yalom includes in this category hope in therapy and faith in the treatment mode. A major reason for my strong preference for ongoing groups is that newcomers overlap with "graduating" clients. As much as you, the therapist, may try to instill hope, your words can never be as powerful as witnessing someone else's recovery. This is especially noticeable in my New Panickers and Senior Anxiety groups, where people often leave feeling confident and symptom-free. They offer testimonials to what they learned in group and tell how they overcame their fears, but they also describe how anxious they were when they started. This helps newcomers to understand that the confident, advanced members who are leaving the group were once as frightened as they are now.

The following case, though somewhat unusual, illustrates the power of the group. A client, a flight attendant, who had his first three panic attacks was quickly evaluated and joined the New Panickers Group. He feared suffocation and losing control, and suddenly the fears were transferred to flying, i.e., his job. He was very vocal in the first group session. Since he had a long flight coming up, we spent some time on his fears. By the second session, he said that he no longer needed treatment because he had overcome his fear; the first group session had provided him with a unique eye-opener. He understood that the symptoms are all anxiety-related and did not signify a true threat. The group's experiences and input seemed more valid than anything I could have said in a single individual session. On occasion, such a quick reframing of the meaning of the symptoms is possible, bringing about a shift in the emerging fear structure.

Universality

Clients feel isolated with their problems. Those with anxiety disorders feel potentially even more alone when family and friends say, "You have nothing to fear. Snap out of it." Being with others who have the same strange sensations and thoughts allows for a normalizing experience. Clients in my groups invariably say that they felt good meeting others with the same problems.

One of my Senior Anxiety Group members feared writing in public. (She actually had social phobia, and this is a group for clients with mixed anxiety disorders.) It had handicapped her socially for fifteen years, because she had avoided many situations that presented even the remote possibility of having to write something. She did home assignments and wrote in group, but I observed that she was not totally committed to treatment. She said several times "My problem is so weird!" In spite of the group's support, her attendance became erratic. Fortunately for her, two more clients with the exact same fears suddenly joined the group. From then on she was committed to attending group.

Altruism

This category refers to the benefit derived from helping other members. People with panic and phobias often feel demoralized. Those with a long history of agoraphobia feel "weak," dependent, and a burden to others. As Yalom says, people want to feel needed. After having felt demoralized and defeated by the disorder, they can now guide others. Members share their fears, coping strategies and successes, and are quick to celebrate the successes of other members. (We often clap and cheer when someone has taken a difficult step or has achieved a long sought-after goal.) Many members are touchingly supportive of each other. Helping others seems to add to their self-esteem. I am frequently touched by the great sensitivity clients convey toward more fragile members. They often say, "I have been there."

The clients' insights can be very refreshing. Today a client in my New Panickers Group said to another member in a soft, very caring tone, "You worry about your heart, about having a heart attack. Then you said that you fear continued panics could make you unable to care for your young son, and that would break your heart. You also said that you love him with all your heart. Then you told us that you are having severe heartburn. All these expressions contain the word "heart." I can truly understand why you are so focused on your heart.

The Corrective Recapitulation of the Primary Family Group

Group therapy resembles the client's first group experience—the family. In the original family, experiences of maladaptive relationships become frozen in a growth-inhibiting manner. In contrast, the psychotherapy group provides opportunities to challenge the experiences that took place in the family of origin and to work through unfinished business. This phenomenon occurs less in these panic/phobia groups, but it does occur. My Panic/Phobia Group is more highly structured than my other groups. Yet even here, where we do not explore many other issues, a few clients have taken the opportunity to resolve a major internal conflict. For instance, a man worked through the sudden loss of a sibling early in his life, which had slightly dampened many joyful experiences for two decades.

Development of Socializing Techniques

According to Yalom, in all therapy groups, clients learn some basic social skills. The skills learned vary from explicit skills that are taught to the feedback obtained from other members in regard to maladaptive behaviors. In my groups, this learning occurs directly through the brief assertiveness training, which is partly practiced by role play. This is the component where it is most likely that interpersonal and self-esteem issues arise.

For example, last week a woman in my Panic/Phobia Group discussed a current conflict with her in-laws. She described how when she and her husband dined at her in-laws' home, she would nudge her husband not to take second helpings (he was overweight). Her mother-in-law would observe this and defiantly refill her son's plate. My client became angry but never said anything. In the group she learned that she was also acting as her husband's mother and setting herself up to compete with her mother-in-law. Both women were treating the husband as if he were a boy unable to make his own decisions. Discussing this issue provided the client with information about social roles and behaviors, which in her case were closely linked to her desire for control.

Imitative Behavior

Yalom states that imitation is an effective therapeutic force. I agree. I have found that modeling is indeed a powerful component in these groups. For instance, in the process of learning how to overcome feared sensations in the interoceptive exercises, observing how others cope can be extremely helpful. Although there is room to explore other issues in the New Panickers and Senior Anxiety groups, clients find it difficult to make the switch from a structured agenda to more traditional psychotherapy. Yet when some people in the group divulge their innermost fears, the others learn that it is safe to do so and are enabled to take risks themselves. This willingness to open up and take risks leads to Yalom's next curative category, interpersonal learning.

Interpersonal Learning

Interpersonal growth involves the client learning about the impression he or she makes on others, as well as learning how to get along and resolve conflicts. In the structured cognitive-behavioral groups for anxiety, there is more positive than negative affect expressed. Since more can be learned from dealing with "negative" affect among members, this limits the potential for learning compared to more dynamic groups.

In spite of the limitations stated above, panic and phobia groups provide unique opportunities to address automatic thoughts, assumptions, and core beliefs pertaining to interpersonal fears. Social fears and insecurities constitute a large component of agoraphobia and, if comorbid with social phobia, even more so. Many clients catastrophize about the social consequences of their anxiety, and, in this respect at least, reveal deep insecurities and the perception of others as being harsh, judgmental, and ridiculing. They are overly sensitive to feeling embarrassed. Challenging these issues provides a good opportunity to hear and absorb the reactions of others. For instance, many clients think that they would be extremely embarrassed if they fainted. Yet when asked how they have reacted or are likely to react if someone else fainted in their vicinity, invariably they say that they would feel concern and want to help. It does not occur to them that the person who fainted should feel embarrassed. Sometimes, this is enacted in role play, where we have the person pretend to faint, with other members playing various roles. The members provide feedback and this behavioral test is often more powerful than just verbal reassurance. In sum, reconciling their reactions with those of others in the group and learning to be less critical of themselves provides excellent social learning while raising self-confidence.

Group Cohesiveness and the Sense of Belonging

This is a complex construct pertaining to the attractiveness of the group and to the forces holding it together. When members feel accepted, their commitment to the group increases. Because of the homogeneity of these anxiety groups, the initial adjustment is relatively quick.

In my anxiety groups, some members drop out very early, and others attend erratically before they drop out. Most members do make a commitment and seem to value the group highly. Those who stay feel the commonality between themselves and the other members, to a large extent because of the similarity of shared problems. When members are more eager to report their exposure experiences to the entire group rather than to me specifically, I know that they feel a true sense of belonging to the group. They receive guidance and suggestions from other members. Sometimes, when confronting a particularly challenging task, they report having felt the entire group behind them; and that they did not want to let the group down.

There is a tradition in some clinics, which I believe greatly undermines the group and the task it is intended to do. In the name of efficiency, group leaders allow psychiatrists to see clients for brief medication visits during the group time. One client leaves the group to meet with the psychiatrist, then returns, then another client does the same, etc. In addition to the annoying interruption, the group work may then be viewed as less important because clients are permitted to come and go. The equivalent dynamic would be if the therapist went to the psychiatrist's office to remove the client from the medication visit for a psychotherapy session, and then returned the client to the psychiatrist. What is viewed as important? I do think that having medication visits immediately before or after group can save time and effort, which is very different from having the group interrupted.

Catharsis

Catharsis has to do with the expression of positive and negative feelings in the group, often involving other group members. This category operates to a lesser degree in the cognitive-behavioral groups. However, when working on core beliefs, which touches on innermost beliefs, clients are able to explore deeper self-worth issues. Some members discover they have core beliefs contrary to those they thought they had. Often this is a very emotional stage in the treatment.

Other Curative Factors: Group Pressure and Support for Change

The group provides an opportunity to learn new beliefs and behaviors and thereby fosters change. This occurs, in part, through pressure and support for change. As mentioned earlier, members are accountable to the group, not just to the therapist. The group's expectations help clients to follow through with their interoceptive and in vivo home assignments. Also, other members' struggles and successes spur the client on. In this manner, the group mediates curative change. I have found in individual therapy that the client is much more likely to come for office visits and report not having done the exposure. (Note here that guided mastery exposure can help clients overcome hurdles in their exposures, which is likely to increase their compliance with home assignments.)

One client in my Panic/Phobia Group feared walking to the beach, which was about a half an hour's walk from her home. Over a few weeks, she worked on approaching the beach more and more. On one of her outings, with tears in her eyes, she froze midway from fear. The other members followed her progress with great empathy. One day she arrived with a small box and apologized sheepishly that she was not bringing cookies. She opened the box and said, "I wanted to show you that I went to the beach." She had brought everyone tiny packages of sand wrapped neatly in cellophane and tied on the top with taffeta bows. Her pride was immense as group members clapped. She had brought a true gift to share, a tangible token of her work. I keep mine in my office. It symbolizes the rewards of this work.

While generally supportive, clients are not easily misled by their peers and are willing to confront issues usually avoided, such as medication use. For example, one client, Doris, was so frightened by her panic attacks that she had been prescribed a benzodiazepine before I saw her for my initial evaluation. Within two weeks she was in my New Panickers Group. She told the members in her first group session that she was convinced that she would suffocate to death. Even drinking water had become panicogenic (provoking a panic) for her. She said unabashedly, "I'll *never* get off the clonazepam!" As she struggled to overcome her fear of being unable to breathe, especially in hot and closed rooms, group members periodically confronted her about her medication use. We all wanted to see her discontinue the medication, if at all possible, before terminating the group. Finally, she yielded and with the consent of her psychiatrist, she tapered off. She did exceptionally well, even without medication. The group's influence was more powerful than anything the psychiatrist or I alone could have accomplished. She terminated the group with a renewed sense of self-confidence.

Advantages of Group Treatment for Panic and Phobia Disorders

Groups provide unique opportunities through role play. The cognitive challenging, modeled by the therapist, can on occasion be more convincing if done by peers. Groups are not only a potent treatment format, but are cost-effective. Furthermore, in our current era of cost-cutting, where many agencies find it difficult to treat individual clients on a weekly basis, a group offers the opportunity to provide intensive, weekly treatment.

Opportunity for Role Play or Live Simulations

Live simulations can provide an excellent adjunct to the treatment. Dr. Michelle Craske was the first person to encourage me to do role play enactments when confronting clients' fears, e.g., if a client fears fainting, the group can practice fainting. The group enacts the specific, feared scenario, e.g., fainting in a store. Members and therapist play the roles of store clerk and other shoppers. The scene can be played out with the most feared consequences, whether these involve everyone huddling around the person who fainted, staring and whispering, or people running away upon seeing the person on the floor. (In such enactments it is extremely helpful if the therapist role plays the fainter first. It helps clients let go of their inhibitions.) Dr. Craske also suggested that the entire group should practice fainting, which I have done on several occasions. Although none of my clients nor I are good at acting, these simple role plays can be very powerful. A number of clients become as anxious as if it were a real situation, which provides an excellent opportunity to learn to cope. This also occurs when we set up chairs in the room to simulate driving in a minivan or flying in an airplane.

Cognitive Work in Group

Cognitive restructuring also lends itself well to practice in group. One person takes on the role of the fearful individual while the other challenges his or her catastrophic automatic thoughts and vice versa. This is particularly helpful when a fear is tenacious, e.g., when a client confuses an unhelpful (even dangerous) behavioral *solution* (using brakes for no reason on the freeway) with the actual automatic thought ("If I don't slow down, I will crash"). By challenging each other's fears, as opposed to only the therapist doing it, they gain added learning opportunities.

Summary

There are some studies indicating that group psychotherapy is at least as effective as individual treatment. There are few randomized studies on the efficacy of panic and phobia groups, but the results thus far are promising. Yalom's curative factors apply to these cognitive-behavioral groups, which, in addition, provide unique opportunities of their own as agents of change.

Section 2: Group Formats for Panic and Phobia

There are a number of group formats for panic disorder. My Panic/Phobia Group was originally a twelve-session closed group. This no longer seems feasible because of the long waiting period it means for some clients. Also, for a busy therapist, it was very labor-intensive. I had to keep track of the waiting-list clients and worry about dropouts. It was also a problem when a few clients dropped out after starting and the remaining group was diminished in size. Furthermore, while dropouts in closed groups are essentially "failures," the stay of members in ongoing groups varies, and the therapist praises the accomplishments made.

The format of my current fourteen-session Panic/Phobia Group and the format of other groups I conduct are described below. In addition, a brief summary follows of two additional groups run by colleagues at other Kaiser facilities. All my groups except for the Anxiety Support Group meet weekly. In private practice you may be able to conduct only one group, while in larger agencies, such as Kaiser, several groups can be run, further targeting specific client needs.

In my Panic/Phobia groups, I have clients with panic disorder without agoraphobia, chronic; panic disorder with agoraphobia; agoraphobia without history of panic disorder; and specific phobias. Those with specific phobias fear driving on the freeway, heights, blood-injection-injury (the latter have had additional phobias and/or panic), and enclosed places. What many laypeople call claustrophobia is actually agoraphobia. They are misled by the experience, which is described as *feeling* closed in, unable to get out, and unable to breathe, but occurring in many open places, not only in small enclosures. Even those with specific phobias benefit from the panic work, especially since, as described in chapter 1, they often have interoceptive fears, i.e., they fear their anxiety reactions. This is very pronounced in claustrophobia where the person fears literally small enclosures (usually the fear is of suffocating or of not being able to get out).

My fourteen-session Panic/Phobia Group, which runs for two hours per session, is the group I conduct in my private practice. At Kaiser I am currently conducting a sixteen-session Panic/Phobia Group, of one and-one-half hours per session. I prefer the two-hour sessions because of the amount of material involved. In that group, I begin every session (except the first one) with the phobia assignments, i.e., I follow up on what clients worked on the preceding week and we set up exposures for the following week. This takes about half an hour. The subsequent one-and-a-half hours are devoted to panic-related (and in later sessions to chronic worry and assertiveness-related) work. The fourteen-session private practice group is also designed for new panickers without phobias. Only the sixteen-session Panic/Phobia Group at Kaiser is open to family members, but few attend. My private practice clients have not wished partners to attend. In my other groups, a significant amount of psychotherapy occurs, rendering them inappropriate for family members.

Home Assignments

Because I have clients use my self-help book *An End to Panic,* I will list the assignments that are given in that book. If you do not use this book, you may nonetheless choose to follow the general format described. I go over most of the material that will be assigned. On a rotating basis, a member is asked to prepare a very brief summary for the following session, mostly highlighting what applies to him/her or is especially helpful or hard to understand. This approach greatly increases the likelihood of clients complying with the reading assignments.

As mentioned earlier, I begin the sessions by having each group member give an account of the exposure homework done and we plan new exposures. When reporting on their agoraphobia assignments, clients often begin to elaborate on the difficulties they encountered, and so forth. I sometimes cut these descriptions short and, needless to say, this can be difficult. I remind them to be brief so that we can accomplish the tasks planned for the session. Next I ask for a quick report on the previous reading. This provides an opportunity to briefly review the material covered in the previous session and to answer questions. Then, we go over any worksheets that were given as assignments. Finally, I introduce the new topic for the session. Although I encourage interaction among members, we stay focused on the task.

Panic/Phobia Group

The group consists of four modules. Members can start in the first session of any module. Occasionally, some members do not need all four modules.

1. **Module I**
   (learning about anxiety, the physiology of fear and panic, and diaphragmatic breathing), four sessions.

2. **Module II**
   (challenging and altering catastrophic and unhelpful thoughts and beliefs about panic and phobias), four sessions.

3. **Module III**
   (overcoming fear of the physical sensations in panic), four sessions. (Although this is the least ideal module to begin with, it usually works.)

4. **Module IV**
   (standing up for oneself and setting limits with others, dealing with chronic worry, preparing for the future i.e., relapse prevention), two or four sessions. (If the group is fourteen-weeks long, with two-hour sessions, there are two sessions in this module, in which case some of the topics are introduced at the end of Module III. If sixteen-weeks long, with one-and-one-half hour sessions, there are four sessions in this module.)

Fourteen-Week Panic/Phobia Group, Two Hours per Session

Module I—Session 1

FOR CLIENTS WHO START HERE	*Before* the first group session: Read Part I (Chapters 1 through 6). How to fill out Worksheet 1: Panic Frequency and Intensity.
Introductions	Setting the stage, Expectations of treatment.
Report from Clients	Chapters 1–6. Examples of Worksheet 1.
Motivation and Self-Reward (Chapter 5)	Brief discussion of motivation and what may get in the way. Rewarding oneself, especially for in vivo exposures. How to fill out Worksheet 2: My Personal Coping Affirmations.
Anxiety and Panic (Chapter 3)	About Anxiety. Diagnosis of panic disorder and agoraphobia. Substance abuse in panic disorder.
Fear and Panic Physiology (Chapter 7)	Physiology of fear: How the fight/flight response affects the body, mind, and behavior. The connection between fear and panic, how they are the same and how they differ. Nocturnal panics and fainting. The three-response system model of anxiety. How to fill out Worksheet 3: The Components of a Panic Attack.
Home Assignments	Chapter 7. Worksheets 1–3. With each member: Plan agoraphobia exposures.

Module I—Session 2

Home Assignments	With each member: Review agoraphobia assignments accomplished and plan new exposures. This will be recorded on Worksheet 10 *weekly* and read from at subsequent sessions. Chapters 8 and 11. Worksheet 9.
Report from Clients	Chapter 7. Examples of Worksheets 1–3.
Breathing Retraining (Chapter 8)	Overbreathing test *after* going over the Exceptions. Breathing physiology. Acute and chronic hyperventilation. The four ways to stop hyperventilation. Breathing test (taking a deep breath). Teaching diaphragmatic breathing.
Uncertainty and Control (Chapter 4)	Learning to accept uncertainty. Not having control over outside events.
Preparing for Phobia Work (Chapter 11)	Types of avoidances, including safety signals and safety behaviors. In vivo exposure versus mastery exposure.
Setting Goals (Chapter 12)	How to fill out Worksheet 9: Goal and the Steps to Achieve It.

Module I—Session 3

Home Assignments	With each member: Review agoraphobia assignments accomplished and plan new exposures. Chapter 12.
Report from Clients	Chapters 8 and 11. Examples of Worksheet 9.
Phobias (Chapter 12 cont.)	Causes, Risk, Control, Perfectionism. Planning exposures: Frequency, Time, Planned Exits versus Escape. Mastery Exposure.

Module I—Session 4

Home Assignments	With each member: Review agoraphobia assignments accomplished and plan new exposures. Review entire Part I. Review Chapters 7 and 8 of Part II. Review Chapters 11 and 12 of Part III. Worksheet 4, 1st Step.
Report from Clients	Chapter 12.
Cognitive Restructuring (Chapter 9)	How to fill out Worksheet 4: Challenging Automatic Thoughts, 1st Step.

Module II—Session 1

| FOR CLIENTS WHO START HERE | *Before* the first group session: Read Part I (Chapters 1 through 6). How to fill out Worksheet 1: Panic Frequency and Intensity. Diaphragmatic breathing instructions in Chapter 8 with home practice. |

Home Assignments — With each member: Review agoraphobia assignments accomplished and plan new exposures. Chapter 9, Sections 1 and 2, up to Focal Fears. Worksheet 4.

Report from Clients — Questions on anything in the reviewed chapters (briefly). Examples of Worksheet 4, 1st Step (briefly).

Cognitive Restructuring (Chapter 9) — Definitions: Cognitive, cognitions, automatic thoughts. Feelings versus thoughts. Irrational thoughts or cognitive distortions:
1. Exaggerating or Overestimating Risk
2. Catastrophizing
3. Control at All Costs
4. Perfectionism or All-or-Nothing Thinking
5. Emotions as Evidence

Unhelpful or maladaptive thoughts:
1. Disaster Expectation
2. Giving Up
3. The Unanswerable Question: Why? Why? Why?

How to fill out entire Worksheet 4: Challenging Automatic Thoughts.

Module II— Session 2

Home Assignments — With each member: Review agoraphobia assignments accomplished and plan new exposures. Chapter 9, Focal Fears, pages relevant to each person. Worksheet 4 pertaining to Focal Fears.

Report from Clients — Chapter 9, Sections 1 and 2, up to Focal Fears. Examples of Worksheet 4.

Cognitive Restructuring (Chapter 9, cont.) — Focal Fears.

Module II—Session 3

Home Assignments — With each member: Review agoraphobia assignments accomplished and plan new exposures. Chapter 9, Section 3. Worksheets 4 and 5.

Report from Clients	Examples of Worksheet 4.
Cognitive Restructuring (Chapter 9, cont.)	Underlying or Core Beliefs. How to fill out Worksheet 5: Unfolding the Belief.

Module II—Session 4

Home Assignments	With each member: Review agoraphobia assignments accomplished and plan new exposures. Review entire Chapter 9. Worksheets 4, 5, and 6.
Report from Clients	Chapter 9, Section 3. Examples of Worksheets 4 and 5.
Cognitive Restructuring (Chapter 9, cont.)	Work on Evidence Continuum. How to fill out Worksheet 6: Core Belief Log.

Module III—Session 1

FOR CLIENTS WHO START HERE	*Before* the first group session: Read Part I (Chapters 1 through 6). How to fill out Worksheet 1: Panic Frequency and Intensity. Diaphragmatic breathing instructions in Chapter 8 with home practice.
Home Assignments	With each member: Review agoraphobia assignments accomplished and plan new exposures. Chapter 10.
Report from Clients	Questions on anything in the reviewed chapters (briefly).
Interoceptive Exposure (Chapter 10)	Conditioning aspect of panic fear. Combining cognitive restructuring with behavioral experiments. Exclusions. Go over all exercises on list using Worksheet 7: Interoceptive Exposure Record. (These stay with the therapist until next session.)

Module III—Session 2

Home Assignments	With each member: Review agoraphobia assignments accomplished and plan new exposures. Ask each client to do his or her feared interoceptives at home using Worksheet 8.
Report from Clients	Chapter 10 (briefly).

Interoceptive Exposure (Chapter 10, cont.)	Pair up clients to work on the feared interoceptives using Worksheet 8: Repeating Interoceptive Exercises. Interoceptives to be done at home.

Module III—Session 3

Home Assignments	With each member: Review agoraphobia assignments accomplished and plan new exposures. Ask each client to do his or her feared interoceptives at home and outside using Worksheet 8. Chapter 13.
Report from Clients	Interoceptives worked on and recorded on Worksheet 8.
Interoceptive Exposure	Pair up clients and continue to work on interoceptives. Naturalistic interoceptives.
Accepting Feelings and Assertiveness (Chapter 13)	In what context did the panic disorder develop. Not exercising control in interpersonal situations.

Module III—Session 4

Home Assignments	With each member: Review agoraphobia assignments accomplished and plan new exposures. Continue to work through feared interoceptives using Worksheet 8. Chapter 14.
Report from Clients	Interoceptives worked on and recorded on Worksheet 8. Chapter 13.
Coping with Stress and Chronic Worry (Chapter 14)	Knowing one's limits and limiting stress level. Panic as a wake-up call. Coping with worry. Relaxation and fun, goals. Biological toughening up.

Module IV—Session 1

FOR CLIENTS WHO START HERE	*Before* the first group session: Read Part I (Chapters 1 through 6). How to fill out Worksheet 1: Panic Frequency and Intensity. Diaphragmatic breathing instructions in Chapter 8 with home practice.
Home Assignments	With each member: Review agoraphobia assignments accomplished and plan new exposures. Chapters 15 and 16.
Report from Clients	Interoceptives worked on and recorded on Worksheet 8, very briefly. Chapter 14.

Setbacks (Chapter 15)	Best mindset: Being prepared for the next one. How fear can return.
Here and Now (Chapter 16)	Living in the here and now. Learning to let thoughts pass.
Termination	Preparing for termination.

Module IV—Session 2

Report from Clients	With each member: Review agoraphobia assignments accomplished. Chapters 15 and 16.
Planning ahead	With each member: Goals and plans for continued exposures.
Termination Good-byes	

New Panickers Group

After I grew comfortable with my Panic/Phobia Group, which started in 1988, I pondered increasingly on what to do with new panickers. I knew that they would not fit into my existing group, in part because of the chronicity of the disorder in many clients and the presence of phobias. In addition, two factors described in the literature seemed significant: Onset of panics is often preceded by significant stress; and some outcome studies suggest that improvement in overall end-state functioning is not as good as elimination of panics. When planning to create a group for new panickers, I believed that these two issues had to be addressed. Thus I developed a group that includes crisis work to look at the stresses that led up to the attacks and the exploration of chronic worry. The latter included issues pertaining to anxiety sensitivity. My New Panickers Group started in 1990. Other facilities in the Northern California Kaiser Region subsequently implemented similar groups.

The New Panickers group is an ongoing group for clients with recent onset or recent recurrence of panics (without prior history of agoraphobia) and essentially no avoidances. I say "essentially" no avoidances, because there are a few clients who have just begun to avoid but can expose themselves to the feared situations simply upon urging. They are then candidates for this group. This is justified as there are very few clients who truly have *no* avoidance, either of a situation or an activity.

Clients have ready access; they can join at any time after the evaluation, and they are asked to give a two-week notice to terminate. Most clients stay from six to fifteen sessions; some stay for twenty. Having attended the New Panickers Group, clients do not ever return to that group. In part this is because the group maintains a very hopeful tone. If a relapsed client returned to this group, new panickers might find it harder to be optimistic about their potential for full recovery. If there is a relapse, clients who attended the New Panickers group are eligible for the Panic/Phobia Group (which is designed for clients showing more chronicity, even in the absence of agoraphobia).

The group consists of two parts:

1. The cognitive-behavioral components for the treatment of panic disorder: Psychoeducation, breathing retraining, cognitive restructuring, and interoceptive exposure. In each cycle of ten to twelve sessions, assertiveness, chronic worry, and relapse prevention are included.

2. Crisis-oriented psychotherapy.

Thus clients work on the panics, fear of panics, and current stresses and they often learn to confront and change long-standing patterns of worry, nonassertiveness, and perfectionism. About one hour of each session is devoted to the panic work and about half an hour to more general psychotherapy. Clients can enter the group at any week. To help socialize newcomers, older members review briefly previous material. Under the influence of Padesky with Greenberger (1995), I ask experienced members to also explain succinctly the principles of CBT. This group truly allows for individualized treatment and preliminary outcome measures suggest high end-state functioning.

Senior Anxiety Group

Mature and elderly clients can be in any of the groups described above. However, I have quite a few clients who either because of age and/or physical ailments essentially cannot do interoceptive exposures, or their motivation or cognitive abilities are such that they would not fit into the more rigorous groups described. Since 1994, I have been conducting this ongoing group for clients with any anxiety disorder (except for those with severe obsessive-compulsive disorder), including panic disorder and agoraphobia. The ages range between fifty-six (hardly a "senior") and people in their eighties. Some older clients have too many cognitive limitations even for this group. I conduct it in a less rigorous way than the other groups. I have found this to be another delightful group.

The group meets weekly for one-and-one-half hours. Clients start at any time and give a two-week notice to terminate. Members stay anywhere between six and twenty sessions. The components of the panic and phobia work are: psychoeducation, diaphragmatic breathing, cognitive restructuring, and exposure work. The only exposures I have conducted in vivo are going into a small storage room and using elevators. Although the cognitive restructuring is simplified compared to the other groups, clients respond exceedingly well to it. In addition, we work on chronic worry, obsessions and compulsions, social fears, assertiveness, and relapse prevention.

Anxiety Support Group

I designed my first Panic/Phobia Group with booster sessions at one, three, and six months posttreatment. The advantage of these sessions was that clients had set goals and attempted to reach them by the next booster session. Here, I saw many clients who continued to improve during the interim, and several with long-standing agoraphobia who had become symptom-free. After a few years, however, this plan no longer seemed feasible. I had to call each client a couple of weeks prior to the sessions and send reminder letters, a very laborious task. Invariably, some clients would drop out. I also had clients from my other anxiety groups to whom I wanted to provide support. I implemented the Anxiety Support Group in 1992 in lieu of the former booster sessions.

This group meets the first Thursday of every month and is strictly a drop-in group. Anyone having completed any of my anxiety groups receives a letter with information about this support group and a number to call to ensure that I am not absent that day. I accommodate this group to whatever needs the attending members wish to address. They have either had a setback or a trying time. On occasion, a member comes to celebrate his or her success. Clients can attend this group indefinitely as long as there are available sessions (usually twenty a year). If a client has a more serious relapse or requests it, the Panic/Phobia Group can be repeated.

I have also conducted a Teen Anxiety Group for clients with a mix of anxiety disorders, and a time-limited Social Phobia Group for adults.

Although some group treatments I am familiar with are only eight-weeks long, many range from twelve to sixteen or twenty weeks' duration. I find that less than twelve sessions is usually insufficient, especially for clients with agoraphobia. There are exceptions. For instance, clients in my New Panickers Group (without agoraphobia) sometimes stay for five or six sessions. The ideal is to have the flexibility for clients to stay a shorter or longer time, depending on the need. Most of my clients have not needed more than twenty sessions.

Other Group Formats

Based on the descriptions of the various groups above, you have undoubtedly noticed that there is no one single ideal group format. Each group has its advantages and disadvantages. I have described my groups (which are always evolving) as a guide. Descriptions of two groups that were developed by colleagues are provided below as additional guides. You can design your own group based on the setting in which you work and the number and type of clients seeking your services.

Panic Disorder With Agoraphobia Group
by John T. Peters, Ph.D., Redwood City Kaiser

This group is for clients diagnosed with panic disorder without agoraphobia, panic disorder with agoraphobia, and some specific phobias. It has two modules, a Coping Basics Module and an Exposure Module. Both groups meet weekly. Spouses or partners are strongly encouraged to participate unless contraindicated. The group uses Barlow and Craske's *Mastery of Your Anxiety and Panic II* (1994).

Coping Basics Module

The Coping Basics Module is four-weeks long, and each session lasts one-and-one-half hours. This module covers basic concepts about panic and anxiety, the physiology of panic and hyperventilation, breathing retraining, and cognitive restructuring (specifically probability overestimation and catastrophizing). Clients who miss more than one session must repeat this module before proceeding to the next one.

Exposure Module

After completing the Coping Basics Module, clients join the Exposure Module, which meets for one-and-one-half hours, on the same weekday, starting half an hour after the Coping Basics Module ends. This module is ongoing and clients stay for the length of time needed within their Kaiser benefit limit. In alternating months, either interoceptive exposure or in vivo exposure is emphasized in the group meetings. Meanwhile, clients continue working on designated exposure tasks. As clients improve, they can taper the frequency of sessions and can return for booster sessions. Tapering is agreed upon between therapist and client.

Advantages

- Rather rapid access (once a month).
- Inclusion of significant others.

- Duration of treatment is customized up to benefit limit (usually twenty sessions).

- Visit intensity is tapered, as needed.

- Provides opportunity for booster sessions.

- Newer members in the Exposure Module receive encouragement and modeling from more advanced members.

- The in vivo exposure includes some guided mastery. Dr. Peters uses facility elevators, small, enclosed rooms, heated rooms, and some driving (in a minivan if a client with that fear has one).

Disadvantages

- If a client is primarily working on in vivo exposure, attending the interoceptive treatment month does not fully address his or her needs.

- Because the membership in the Exposure Module is revolving, it diminishes group cohesion. Also tracking clients is more difficult because of logistics.

Panic Recovery Group
by Jim Boyers, Ph.D. and Steven Marcus, Ph.D., Santa Clara Kaiser

This group is primarily for clients with panic disorder and agoraphobia. (They are encouraged to first attend the Anxiety Orientation Meeting.) The Panic Recovery Group is a four-week, intensive program (meeting weekly) to teach clients the basic tools for panic recovery. Each of the four sessions is three-hours long. Because this is an intensive treatment program, there is a strong emphasis for clients to do a large amount of work between sessions. The work involves reading assignments and in vivo exposure. Clients who need more treatment can repeat Phase 1. The therapists are planning to implement a Phase 2 component with greater emphasis on exposure. Clients are strongly recommended to read my book *An End to Panic*. A brief description of each session follows. Each session includes a review of the material from previous sessions.

Session I: Relaxation and Breathing Retraining

The main task of this session is to teach clients to decrease their anxiety symptoms physiologically, and specifically to learn a relaxed breathing pattern.

Session II: Cognitive Restructuring

The focus of this session is to identify and eliminate anxiety-producing thought patterns and replace them with positive coping thoughts.

Session III: Interoceptive Exposure

The focus is to desensitize anxiety-provoking physical sensations.

Session IV: In Vivo Exposure

Clients are taught to plan how to challenge and master fearful places and situations. In vivo work is encouraged from Session I.

Advantages

- Rather rapid access (once a month).
- Intense treatment.
- Short treatment duration (four sessions), resulting in very low dropout rate.
- Clients can repeat the sequence.

Disadvantages

- Many clients do not comply with all of the homework.
- Even though most clients are sufficiently recovered at the end of Phase 1, there are a few clients needing further work and for them Phase 2 has been planned.

Summary

A number of group treatment formats have been designed; a few of which are described here. All of them have some disadvantages, including mine. When you design your own group, consider following the guidelines below:

- Access to the group should be relatively quick. Most facilities in the Northern California Kaiser Region have found one month as the acceptable upper limit.
- Major treatment components should be included.
- Include, if possible, a guided mastery approach, i.e., accompany your clients to the in vivo exposures, possibly using the format of Belfer et al. (1995).
- Include, if possible, significant others.
- Make provisions for the client to repeat the treatment, if needed.
- Provide booster sessions.

10

Treatment With Medications

Section 1: Guide for the Physician
Randall L. Solomon, M.D.*

General Information

Ever since Klein and Fink's 1962 landmark study demonstrating the effectiveness of imipramine for preventing panic attacks, psychiatrists have been searching for more and better ways to manage this often debilitating condition. Although most patients have received some form of treatment, one study revealed that only 15 percent of the patients had received adequate treatment (Agras 1993). The search is on for the most effective treatment plan. In this section, I will attempt to delineate the various medical options available. It is important to keep in mind that the specific choice of medical treatment will be affected by the availability of a therapist competent in cognitive-behavior therapy and the specific characteristics of the patient's presentation.

First, some general statements regarding pharmacotherapy and panic disorder should be made. Until very recently, imipramine (Tofranil™) and later alprazolam (Xanax™) were seen as the first-line treatments. Consequently, most studies have focused on these two medications, and imipramine has been the gold standard for comparisons. In 1992, for example, the Cross-National Collaborative Panic Study, Second Phase Investigators published results comparing imipramine, alprazolam, and placebo. The alprazolam-treated patients showed improvement in the first two weeks and the imipramine-treated patients by week four. By week eight, both drugs were equally effective. In another study, patients remained stable for six months of maintenance on either imipramine or alprazolam without requiring an increased dosage (Schweizer, Rickels, Weiss, et al. 1993). In an article written for primary care physicians in the *Annual Review of Medicine,* Agras (1993) recommends a combination of psychotherapy and medication beginning with a tricyclic antidepressant and followed, if necessary, by a high-potency benzodiazepine.

In a recent discussion of treatment options for panic disorder, John Marshall, M.D. (1997) emphasizes the chronic nature of panic disorder and points out the potential need for

---

* Dr. Solomon graduated from the University of Chicago School of Medicine and did his psychiatric residency at the University of California, San Diego. He currently practices in Alameda County.

life-long treatment. Mark Pollack, M.D. (1997) cautions that medications must be made manageable for patients, as they may need them indefinitely. He predicts an increase in the use of these drugs. In contrast, Michael Otto, Ph.D. (1997) emphasizes the advantages of cognitive-behavior therapy. "'We don't really have to discontinue treatment. We just give away the therapy to the patients and have them continue doing it as part of new habits.' Thus, exposure therapy continues for the rest of the patient's life." In actual practice, though, therapists will use those treatments they are most comfortable and familiar with, and those that are consistent with their ideology (Cox, et al. 1991a).

Part of the difficulty in coming to terms with these disparate viewpoints lies in the assumptions made by practitioners of what treatment is actually supposed to do or accomplish. Patients, emergency room physicians, and primary care physicians seek the rapid elimination of panic attacks, but Dr. Mavissakalian (1993) wisely reminds us that this is not really treatment for the condition so long as the patient remains afraid of panic attacks and continues to avoid fearful situations. It is important to keep this in mind while evaluating efficacy statements in research articles.

Panic disorder patients are highly suggestible. I have had a great number of patients improve almost magically with just support, reassurance, and a frank discussion of the medical component of the illness. Agras (1993) found that almost one third of his patients recovered completely with a placebo. Yet placebos can be counterproductive. In a double-blind, placebo-controlled study, a woman suffered gastrointestinal pains so severe that she required transfer to a hospital where she underwent extensive testing. Only later was it discovered that she had been receiving a placebo (Hoffart, Due-Madsen, Lande, et al. 1993). Because of this "negative placebo effect," you must be cautious when discussing a medication's side effects and explain to patients that they will rapidly become much less sensitive to any side effects they may experience from the medications. It is a good idea to be readily available to patients at this time (Roy-Byrne, Wingerson, Cowley, et al. 1993). Some physicians suggest that the patient take the first dose of medication in the office and that the physician remain with the patient providing reassurance until the patient feels safe (Ballenger, Pecknold, Rickels, et al. 1993).

When medication is discontinued, different outcomes may be observed. The ideal is when there is no change, at which time it is concluded that treatment was successful. Often, however, there is relapse, rebound, or withdrawal, or any combination of these.

Pecknold (1993) defines these terms as follow:

- *Relapse* is the "recurrence of the original condition from which the patient suffered."

- *Rebound* is "relapse characterized by greater symptom intensity than that present before treatment."

- *Withdrawal* is a "discontinuation-emergent symptom . . . not found before treatment, or, . . . a symptom [not found in] panic-related disorders." Further, according to Lader (1983), it is "the emergence of a well-defined syndrome with predictable onset, duration and offset of action containing psychological and bodily symptoms not previously complained of by patients. It can be suppressed by the reinstitution of the discontinued medication."

Certain substances can increase or even cause anxiety, and although patients should not feel that they must avoid them, there are some general precautions to be observed. Foods with caffeine such as coffee, black teas, sodas, and chocolate should be taken in moderation. One cup of coffee or tea, or one caffeinated soda a day is a reasonable guideline. Pseudoephedrine (found in many over-the-counter medications) should not be avoided if needed, but patients should be informed that it might increase anxiety. Marijuana, cocaine, amphetamines (including diet pills), or any other stimulants, however, should not be used at all.

There are particular problems with alcohol. Alcohol can cause its own anxiety disorder, and although one or two glasses of wine per week is reasonable (for someone who is not an alcoholic), further use may result in rebound anxiety. Alcohol abuse and misuse is increasingly common and is also very difficult to spot. You must always keep substance abuse in mind, especially for patients who do not seem to be responding as they should or are using alcohol or other substances to medicate their anxiety condition (Alexander 1992; Tesar and Rosenbaum 1993; Agras 1993). I would proceed very cautiously with patients who are seeking medication to manage stress, anxiety, or panic caused by difficult life situations, particularly when they claim to be too busy for therapy and just need "something" to help them get through. In this kind of situation, medications may be a set-up for disaster (Roy-Byrne et al. 1993).

Antidepressant Therapy

There are three basic categories of antidepressants useful in the treatment of panic disorder. I will begin with the current first-line treatment and progress to the least commonly used of these medications.

Selective Serotonin Reuptake Inhibitors (SSRIs)

The pharmacologic treatment of panic disorder has changed dramatically since the appearance of the SSRIs. All of them appear to be effective agents for treating panic. Currently, each SSRI has either been approved by the FDA for this purpose or is in the process of obtaining FDA approval. SSRIs have almost completely replaced tricyclic antidepressants as first-line drugs for panic disorder due to their safety and the fact that they are better tolerated. The SSRIs have the advantage of once-a-day dosing, good treatment success, and very few side effects, especially when compared with the tricyclic antidepressants. They generally do not result in adverse reactions when taken with other medications, including most over-the-counter formulations, and they are much safer in overdose situations (Rosenbaum, et al. 1995; Hoehn-Saric, McLeod, and Hipsley 1993; Peselow 1996). Dr. Peselow asserts that after an SSRI blocks the panic attacks, the patients' avoidance behavior decreases. Although this may be true on occasion, it is wise to remember here Dr. Mavissakalian's (1993) concern that if a patient is still showing agoraphobic avoidance, he or she is not fully treated.

The SSRIs have several common side effects, many of which abate within a few days after initial dosage. These include mild headache, sedation or agitation, and queasiness or nausea. A number of clients experience continuing sedation, insomnia, or sexual dysfunction, and, as a result, some discontinue treatment. To minimize the initial discomfort of side effects, it is recommended to begin with half the usual dose and increase as slowly as is comfortable for the patient. Recommended initial dosages are 5 to 10 mg of fluoxetine (Prozac™) and paroxetine (Paxil™), and 25 to 50 mg of sertraline (Zoloft™). Optimal dosing is generally 20 to 40 mg of Prozac and Paxil, and 50 to 100 mg of Zoloft. Aspirin or Tylenol may be taken safely, as needed, for headache. Patients should be cautioned that they may not begin to notice the drug's effects until four to six weeks after starting. At the end of this time, should there still be no response, the dosage can be raised to the higher dose (e.g., from 20 to 40 mg of Prozac or Paxil, and from 50 to 100 mg of Zoloft.)

If treatment with SSRIs alone fails, tricyclic antidepressants are sometimes added. But this must be done cautiously. SSRIs inhibit the hepatic cytochrome P-450 2D (as well as the 3A4 and the 1A2) system. These are the liver enzymes that metabolize the tricyclic antidepressants, and their inhibition can lead to an unanticipated increase in the blood levels of other drugs metabolized by these enzymes and taken concurrently with the SSRIs. If patients are taking tricyclic antidepressants along with SSRIs, alarmingly high blood levels of the tricyclic may be reached that could lead to anticholinergic toxicity. These patients should have EKGs, serial blood tricyclic levels, and more frequent visits (Peselow 1996). *SSRIs should not be used in conjunction with MAOIs;* in combination they can cause a *fatal* serotoninergic syndrome. It is recommended to allow a five-week interval after discontinuing SSRIs before beginning treatment with MAOIs (Brown, et al. 1991). The shorter acting SSRIs, paroxetine and fluvoxamine (Luvox™) have been known to cause a "discontinuation syndrome" characterized by dizziness, headache, lethargy, paresthesias, nausea, vivid dreams, irritability, and unsteadiness of gait (Coupland, Bell, and Potokar 1996). The syndrome typically lasts about a week, but may continue for up to three weeks and can be treated or prevented by a more gradual tapering off of the medication, or by switching to Prozac or Zoloft, which have longer half-lives.

Tricyclic Antidepressants

The tricyclic antidepressants have been extensively studied in this regard since Klein and Fink (1962) recognized that imipramine treatment can block panic attacks, but it is only minimally effective on phobic avoidance or on anticipatory anxiety. In addition to being the most studied class of medication for the treatment of panic disorder, tricyclic antidepressants are usually available in cost-effective generic form. Their once-a-day dosing schedule helps patients comply with prescription regimes (Ballenger et al. 1993).

Tricyclic Antidepressant Side Effects

The side effects associated with the tricyclic antidepressants limit their usefulness. As with the SSRIs, tricyclic antidepressants do not begin to show any effect for up to four to six weeks, but in addition, they are generally sedating and can also cause a 20- to 30-pound weight gain. They are anticholinergic, which causes the side effects of dry mouth (an almost universal complaint commonly relieved with sugarless gum), constipation, blurred vision, and, occasionally, memory difficulties. Although sedative effects are common, as many as 20 percent of all patients may experience an activation syndrome. This is manifested as jitteriness and tenseness that can mimic a panic attack and may increase the patient's fears and anxiety (Klerman 1992). On the other hand, and entirely independent of their antipanic and antidepressant effects, tricyclic antidepressants have been shown to have excellent anti-anxiety properties. An early double-blind, placebo-controlled study compared the effects of imipramine and chlordiazepoxide (Librium™) for relieving anxiety symptoms. By the second week of the study, imipramine demonstrated superiority to chlordiazepoxide for the treatment of anxiety (Kahn, McNair, Lipman, et al. 1986). These findings were replicated in 1993 and the authors noted that the more specific symptoms of worry and apprehension were also better treated with imipramine than with diazepam (Valium™) (Rickels, Downing, Schweizer, et al. 1993a).

Side effects frequently cause patients to discontinue their medications, and in one long-term study, half of the patients stopped their medication due to side effects, most often because of weight gain (Noyes, Garvey, and Cook 1989). Some side effects are themselves dangerous. These include the cardiac toxicity associated with overdose, tachycardia (abnormal rapidity of heart beat) and orthostatic (postural) hypotension. This last side effect is a frequent cause of falls and can be especially dangerous in bathrooms. Tricyclic overdose is very often fatal, and one must remember that up to 20 percent of panic disorder patients have a history of suicide attempts (Alexander 1992). An ingestion of 3000 mg (3 gms) is generally considered a lethal dose, and this is only a one-month supply of medication for patients taking 100 mg per day. Two specific cardiac conditions require mention. Heart block, a condition where the electrical impulses that control the contractions of the heart are incompletely transmitted to the heart muscle, is a *contraindication* to tricyclic use. Mitral valve prolapse, which is frequently seen with panic disorder patients, is not a contraindication (Brown et al. 1991). A baseline electrocardiogram with occasional monitoring is recommended for all panic patients who are using tricyclic antidepressants.

The length of time patients should optimally remain on medications has been studied, most often with imipramine as the medication used. A minimum of six months is considered standard with no loss of efficacy in the prevention of panic observed (Agras 1993). During this time, patients develop a tolerance to the side effects of the imipramine except for the anticholinergic side effect of dry mouth (Schweizer et al. 1993). After six months of active imipramine therapy, Mavissakalian and Perel (1992) observed a successful maintenance of the treatment gains for an additional twelve months by reducing the dose 50 percent. Side effects were significantly reduced at the lower dose, and the attrition rate also decreased. Seventy-five percent of patients experienced a relapse of their panic disorder the first six months after discontinuing medications. This was completely avoided during the half-dose maintenance phase. However, the relapse rate rose once medication was completely stopped (Mavissakalian and Perel 1992). In another study, seven of twelve patients were unable to stop taking the medication (imipramine) due to the increased anxiety experienced during medication discontinuation (Nagy, Krystal, Charney, et al. 1993).

Dosages

Opinions about tricyclic antidepressant dosage have varied through the years. Pollack (1997) recommends using the highest dose the patient can tolerate—up to 300 mg/day. Other studies, however, have revealed a more complex dose/response reaction. In a three-dosage study (high, medium, low), low-dose patients did not respond significantly differently from the placebo controls, and the high-dose and medium-dose groups were very much alike in their response to treatment with the exception that more subjects in the high-dose group dropped out because of side effects (Agras 1993). The author recommends a mid-range dosage, 100–150 mg, as tolerated.

Mavissakalian and Perel (1995) studied symptom response at various blood levels. Panic symptoms showed continued improvement with tricyclic antidepressants up to a blood level of about 140 ng/ml with no further gains at higher doses. Phobic symptoms responded best in a therapeutic window of 110–140 ng/ml, and the therapeutic effect was noted to diminish when the dose was increased. These effects were replicated when imipramine and its N-desmethylimipramine metabolite (desipramine) were considered separately. While at first glance this may seem to be an unsurprising finding, the two compounds imipramine and desipramine work through different neurotransmitter systems. Imipramine binds strongly to serotonin receptor sites and is considered essentially serotonergic, while desipramine is strongly noradrenergic, binding to norepinephrine receptors. It is impossible to extrapolate from the tricyclic data hypotheses regarding the SSRIs' mode of action, however, Pollack (1997) recommends: an intermediate dose of about 2.25 mg/kg per day to treat both panic and phobic symptoms. This corresponds to a daily dose of about 100 to 150 mg per day. Occasional testing of tricyclic antidepressant blood levels is the best method to ensure appropriate dosage.

Monoamine Oxidase Inhibitors (MAOIs)

The MAOI class of antidepressants has shown good antipanic and antiphobic effects (Klerman 1992). Some authors believe that they are the most powerful medications for treating panic (Bakish, Saxena, Bowen, et al. 1993), but they can be difficult to take. Patients must adhere to a low tyramine diet to prevent a potentially fatal hypertensive crisis. Tyramine is found in aged cheeses, red wines, yeast, liver, bananas, chocolate, and yogurt, among other foods. The hypertension seen with a combination of tyramine and MAOIs *may be fatal* and can lead to an intracranial hemorrhage. With a well-motivated patient, MAOIs remain a realistic option. However, due to the difficulties involved, including severe drug-drug interactions, patients' worries about catastrophic medical calamities, and the increased anxiety caused by the potential difficulties, these agents are rarely used (Alexander 1991; Taylor, et al. 1989).

Two new selective and reversible monoamine oxidase-A inhibitors (moclobemide and brofaromine) have been successfully used in treating panic and social phobia. They have fewer side effects and, most importantly, do not require a low tyramine diet because of their reversibility and their specificity for MAO-A (Rosenbaum et al. 1995; Bakish et al. 1993). Currently they are being used in Europe and are unavailable in the U.S.

Benzodiazepines

When patients are in the midst of a panic attack, they want immediate relief and they often want benzodiazepines. Any sort of long-term treatment, including learning medication-free coping skills, is not on their immediate agenda. The benzodiazepines provide quick relief (Sanderson and Wetzler 1993). To compromise, patients are often placed on a combination therapy of a benzodiazepine and an antidepressant. The hope is to wean the patient off the benzodiazepines, but this is not always possible. In fact, there may be inherent differences between those patients able to come off the benzodiazepines and those who cannot. For instance, benzodiazepine users tend to have less confidence about their test performance than nonusers (Wardle, Hayward, Higgitt, et al. 1994). It is possible that those who present to us for treatment already taking benzodiazepines (prescribed from another source) have less effective coping skills. Finally, it appears that panic disorder patients are less sensitive to diazepam (Valium) than comparison subjects. This effect seems to be a consequence of anxiety in general, rather than because of any specific anxiety disorder. It may be that the GABA-benzodiazepine receptor complex is functionally sensitive to the phenomenon of anxiety (Ray-Byrne, Wingerson, Radant, et al. 1996).

The hazards of benzodiazepine use and abuse are well-known. The American Psychiatric Association even has a Task Force on Benzodiazepine Dependence, Toxicity and Abuse to address these concerns. But there are advantages to the use of benzodiazepines. They have a rapid onset of action in treating anxiety and relatively little toxicity. They have far fewer side effects than tricyclic antidepressants or MAOIs and are much better tolerated by patients. They do not induce hepatic metabolism so that patients do not need progressively higher doses, nor does tolerance develop to the anti-anxiety and antipanic effects. Patients tend not to escalate their original doses, and there is no evidence that the use of therapeutic doses leads to recreational use (Salzman 1993; Roy-Byrne et al. 1993; Ballenger et al. 1993). Benzodiazepines are frequently used in combination with an antidepressant in the early weeks of treatment to provide some symptom relief while waiting for the antidepressant to begin to work. Low doses in the range of 0.25 to 0.50 mg of clonazepam or alprazolam two or three times daily are generally used for the purpose of treating the anticipatory anxiety. Higher doses, i.e., 4–6 mg/day of clonazepam or alprazolam are effective for treating the panic itself (Peselow 1996). Patients may remain at this dose for long periods, and will occasionally reduce the dose themselves (Agras 1993). Clearly the benzodiazepines are helpful, and, depending on the patient, may be the only treatment that will be both tolerable and successful.

Benzodiazepines are the most widely prescribed class of central nervous system depressants and they depress all its functions (Schuckit 1995). Up to 10 percent of benzodiazepine users suffer from a depression directly caused by the chronic use of the medication (Rosen-baum et al. 1995). The treatment for this depression is to stop the benzodiazepine. This figure is much lower for alprazolam and though not an antidepressent, it has been marketed as such in addition to being an anxiolytic.

In addition to depressing mood, benzodiazepines depress memory. There is an acute "anterograde amnesia," or memory loss, that begins after the drug is taken. (A "retrograde amnesia" means memory loss just prior to the trauma, or whatever caused the amnesia.) Anterograde amnesia is precisely the outcome desired by surgeons, who prescribe this medi-cation pre-operatively. The benzodiazepine, usually Valium, is given about an hour prior to surgery. There is also a "gradual reduction of recall" that occurs with long-term chronic use of benzodiazepines. This effect is dose dependent (Salzman 1993) and is perhaps of greatest importance with elderly people who are often prescribed benzodiazepines for anxiety and sleep. Numerous physiological changes occur in our bodies as we age that result in a higher blood level of benzodiazepines than might be expected. Additionally, older people are ex-quisitely sensitive to anything that may impair memory or thinking.

Two studies reported surreptitious use of benzodiazepines in a small number of sub-jects (Schweizer et al. 1993; Curran, Bond, O'Sullivan, et al. 1994). Although it is encouraging that the numbers are small, this merely underscores our inability to control for this highly desired, frequently abused, and widely available substance. Along the same lines, it has been noted that patients tend to take their medication when they want it, on an as-needed basis instead of the regular dosage schedule that is more often prescribed (Romach, Busto, Somer, et al. 1995). This can be helpful, should it result in a dosage decrease. But, if this is a pattern, the patient then becomes even more dependent on the medication as he or she uses it to treat symptoms as they arise. This is counter to the basic premise of CBT and greatly undermines its efficacy.

Benzodiazepines depress the capability to learn from exposure. In animal studies, the effect of in vivo exposure is lessened with the presence of benzodiazepines, and this appears to apply to some extent with humans, as well (van Balkom, de Beurs, Koele, et al. 1996). Chronic use of any of the central nervous system depressants including alcohol leads to an increase in anxiety, which is best treated by discontinuing the substance (Cohen 1995). It may also be that the benzodiazepines decrease an individual's tolerance to anxiety and discomfort, or put another way, they increase anxiety sensitivity. "Such increase in anxiety sensitivity would hinder lasting relief from panic upon drug discontinuation and would provide an explanation for the striking differences in long-term outcome between behavioral and pharmacological therapies in panic disorder. We should not be blind to the possibility that benzodiazepines may increase chronicity in panic disorder . . ." (Fava and Bruce 1996).

Withdrawal, Rebound, and Relapse

Alexander (1992) feels that a relapse experienced after discontinuation of benzodiazepi-nes is evidence of the chronic nature of the disorder. Benzodiazepine therapy, while effective in the short term, seems to have served to postpone more definitive treatment. At any rate, benzodiazepine discontinuation can be highly uncomfortable, can sometimes lead to sei-zures, and should be treated medically. A gradual tapering off and/or a substitution of a longer-acting benzodiazepine for a shorter-acting one helps alleviate symptoms. Salzman (1993) also asserts that occasionally a non-benzodiazepine such as propranolol, a barbiturate, clonidine, or an anticonvulsant can be substituted. However, you must remember that these substitutions create much more complicated treatments and expose the patient to increased risk. They should be left to those with expertise in detoxification procedures. There is always the problem of convincing patients to give up their valued benzodiazepine. Cohen (1995) advises informing the patients of the dangers of benzodiazepines, and that their chronic use actually increases anxiety. He supports their efforts to come off the drugs and assures them that after a few weeks of discomfort, they will feel better than they have in a long time. Of course, this requires solid rapport with the patient.

Many patients and their families fear that the patient may become addicted and dependent on the drug. In this instance, the two terms are used interchangeably (Ballenger et al. 1993). Roy-Byrne et al. (1993) state that the "risk of benzodiazepines has been alternately ignored and blown way out of proportion." With the exception of patients with a history of benzodiazepine abuse, or substance abuse, benzodiazepine treatment for panic disorder, even at high doses, has not been shown to lead to abuse or addiction. Patients in long-term treatment tend to take lower, rather than higher doses (Salzman 1993; Roy-Byrne 1992; Roy-Byrne et al. 1993). "Physical dependence" refers to the real neuroadaptive changes that occur in response to a continual presence of benzodiazepines and is the cause of withdrawal reactions upon discontinuation of the medication (Ballenger et al. 1993). "Addiction" and "drug dependence," on the other hand, are conditions that have core behavioral features of the progressive increase of the dose over time, a functional impairment secondary to the addiction, and an overwhelming preoccupation with obtaining and using the drug of choice (Ballenger et al. 1993; Romach et al. 1995). It must be remembered that the physical dependence that occurs with benzodiazepines also occurs with many other classes of drugs including anti-epileptics and cardiovascular medications (Ballenger et al. 1993).

Alprazolam (Xanax)

Alprazolam was the first benzodiazepine to demonstrate effectiveness with treating panic. In fact, it was the first medication to receive FDA approval for the treatment of panic disorder. It is a high potency benzodiazepine with a short half-life. It begins to work in twenty to thirty minutes, and so has been widely used in breaking a panic attack. (However, it should be noted that most panic attacks naturally subside within thirty minutes.) Alprazolam has the side effects of sedation, irritability, impaired memory, weight loss, and ataxia. As treatment continues, the side effects lessen, but can still be troublesome (O'Sullivan, Noshirvani, Başoğlu, et al. 1994). Amnesia, as measured by impaired word recall, has been shown to remain significant even five to eight weeks after stopping the drug (Curran et al. 1994). Despite all of these difficulties, alprazolam has continued to have strong patient acceptance (Schweizer et al. 1993; O'Sullivan et al. 1994). The frequency, but not the severity, of major panic attacks before starting treatment can be used to judge dosage (Schweizer et al. 1993), which ranges anywhere from a low of 0.25 mg three to four times a day to greater than 2 mg four times a day. Patients are then taking anywhere from a low of 1 mg to a high of 6–10 mg per day.

Nagy et al. (1993) studied patients for three years in a naturalistic study. That is, the patients were followed without having a formal protocol imposed on the treatment. They found little evidence to support an increase of difficulties discontinuing alprazolam versus imipramine. They speculated that the differences they did observe between the two groups could be explained by differences in the population receiving alprazolam, who often were patients who had failed to improve with previous treatment. Most other authors do not seem to be of the same opinion and cite significant withdrawal, rebound, and relapse difficulties with alprazolam.

Alprazolam has a potentially severe withdrawal reaction characterized by confusion, clouded sensorium, heightened sensory perception, dystonia, paresthesias, muscle cramps, muscle twitch, blurred vision, diarrhea, decreased appetite, and weight loss (Pecknold 1993). On rare occasions I have also observed frank psychosis characterized by auditory hallucinations and paranoid delusions. It would be helpful to have some way to predict a severe withdrawal reaction. So far, the indicators to predict withdrawal severity are only that the patient is male and had a large number of panic attacks prior to treatment (Rickels, Schweizer, Weiss, et al. 1993b).

Because of alprazolam's short half-life, dosing must be either three times a day or, more often, four times a day. Patients are exquisitely aware of just when their last dose is wearing off and when they can take their next dose. This interdose rebound makes them more conscious of their need for each pill (Rosenbaum et al. 1995), and forces them to carry their medicine with them at all times (Salzman 1993). These patients are keenly aware of what time it is throughout the day and when they can take their next dose. For instance, patients will begin to become anxious at three P.M. because they know they need to wait a full hour until they can take their next dose at four P.M. This phenomenon is called "clock-watching" and many patients remain "on the drug to treat the drug's own discontinuation symptoms" (Rosenbaum 1990). Of course, this works against any cognitive treatment that might free the patient of symptoms.

Tapering off of alprazolam is particularly difficult. Some patients use the drug surreptitiously, some restart it shortly after successfully getting off, and some just refuse to come off the medication at all. This can be seen in up to a third of all patients treated with alprazolam. Of 41 percent of the patients who remained on medication in one study, 82 percent of them were on alprazolam and were either unwilling or unable to discontinue it (Rickels et al. 1993b). Pecknold (1993) noted in a study that patients who had been taking benzodiazepines prior to entering his study were the ones who had the most difficulty weaning themselves. He recommends a prolonged tapering-off period after a minimum of six months of treatment.

In one study, 70 percent of patients had some discontinuation symptoms when tapering off (Peselow 1996), and in the Cross-National Collaborative Panic Study, Second Phase Investigators (1992), 51 percent of the patients relapsed and 35 percent had rebound panics. Because of this, Pecknold (1993) noted that many patients were unable to taper off alprazolam, and some just flatly refused. Some patients, as we have already noted, take benzodiazepines surreptitiously no matter what the treatment plan. It is the recurrence of anxiety upon drug taper, and not of panic or phobia, that leads to relapse when the alprazolam is stopped. According to Pecknold (1993) this anxiety also occurs with gradual taper and is more significant with alprazolam than with diazepam.

It should not be surprising then that a rapid onset of action combined with increased anxiety and other panic symptoms, both interdose and during taper, keeps patients anxious if not desperate to remain on the drug, and experienced physicians are loath to subject their already anxious patients to the additional distress of the self-reinforcing clock-watching syndrome. Rickels et al. (1993b) state, "one final sobering fact: over the long term patients originally treated with imipramine or placebo did as well at follow-up as patients treated with alprazolam, without the problems of physical dependence and discontinuation that any long-term alprazolam therapy entails."

Clonazepam (Klonopin ™)

Clonazepam is also a high-potency benzodiazepine that had been used almost exclusively as an anticonvulsant medication. Until recently it was felt that, except for the high potency, short-acting alprazolam (Xanax), benzodiazepines were effective only for *anticipatory* anxiety. However, studies began to show that clonazepam (Klonopin) was also effective in panic disorder, and it has been approved by the FDA. Its onset of action is one to two weeks, and its effectiveness does not diminish over time (Pollack 1997). Clonazepam is twice as potent as alprazolam, so patients require only about half the dose and average 1–5 mg per day (Cox et al. 1991a) with a mean dose of 2.5 mg/day (Tesar, Rosenbaum, Pollack, et al. 1991). Commonly reported side effects are drowsiness and ataxia, especially during the first week of treatment. As a side note, drowsiness was also the most frequently reported side effect of the placebo group in this study (Tesar et al. 1991). Clock watching and interdose rebound are not seen with clonazepam, and there is little problem with abuse. Due to its long half-life, clonazepam can be given in twice-a-day dosing. It does, however, pose a greater risk of treatment-emergent depression than alprazolam (Peselow 1996).

Patients can be successfully switched form alprazolam to clonazepam to taper (Herman, Rosenbaum, and Brotman 1987). In their study of those who succeeded, 82 percent rated clonazepam "better" than alprazolam due to its longer half-life, less frequent dosing, and lack of clock watching, and interdose rebound. Understandably, some patients are afraid to let go of their alprazolam, but I have found patients eager to come off it if they know that they can be placed on something equally effective. The procedure is not very difficult and takes about two weeks.

Rosenbaum (1990) recommends starting clonazepam at one-quarter of the alprazolam dose given twice a day, in the morning and at bedtime. During the first week, patients are instructed to continue taking their alprazolam on an as-needed basis, up to their full amount, and to keep their alprazolam with them at all times for anxiety or rebound panic. On day eight, patients stop all alprazolam and are to use extra clonazepam if needed. Once a satisfactory clonazepam dose is reached, patients are instructed to take the clonazepam only twice a day, by the clock. Extra as-needed doses are then not often needed. I have not found it difficult to taper patients from clonazepam because there is no interdose rebound. You must go slower, though, for patients who have been on alprazolam for a long time. The taper can generally be completed in about two weeks, but, on occasion, I have slowed it down to two months. In any case, a schedule must be established that the patient can tolerate.

Other Medications

Beta-adrenergic blocking agents, commonly referred to as beta-blockers, have been used most often for the occasional relief of social phobia, e.g., stage fright. They work peripherally and only minimally cross the blood-brain barrier, and so reduce many of the somatic symptoms of anxiety, such as tachycardia, trembling, and sweating (Michelson and Marchione 1991). They have not been found effective in panic disorder and they do nothing for the cognitive fear of panic. To the extent that beta-blockers *are* able to cross the blood-brain barrier, they can cause a depression indistinguishable from major depression. Propranolol is most often the culprit here, as atenolol is almost completely kept out of the central nervous system.

The antidepressants maprotiline, amoxapine, trazodone, and bupropion (Wellbutrin™) have not been found helpful in treating panic (Klerman 1992; Roy-Byrne et al. 1993). Buspirone (Buspar™), a non-benzodiazepine anxiolytic without addictive qualities, is likewise ineffective for panic (Alexander 1992). Clonidine is an alpha-2 receptor agonist used for hypertension. It decreases locus ceruleus firing and has been shown to have some effect on panic initially, but it wears off after about a month. Patients taking it complain of drowsiness, sedation, fatigue, weakness, and dizziness. There has been some suggestion that the non-benzodiazepine anticonvulsant valproic acid (Valproate™), now being widely used in the treatment of manic-depressive disorder, might have some efficacy in panic. Calcium channel blockers have also been studied, but their use is limited due to their cardiac side effects and requires pulse and blood pressure monitoring (Rosenbaum et al. 1995; Peselow 1996).

Maintenance Issues

Klerman (1992) in his review found that anywhere between 20 and 80 percent of patients with panic disorder relapse if antidepressant medications are discontinued after a few weeks and up to one year. Relapse rates, according to Roy-Byrne (1992) tend to be higher with benzodiazepines than with antidepressants. Consequently, medication treatment for panic disorder can be a lengthy process. Some clinicians liken it to taking medication for asthma or diabetes—it can become a lifetime necessity (Klerman 1992). Patients who have not responded to cognitive-behavior therapy or who have refused to come off medications will require extended treatment (Alexander 1991). Those on alprazolam are either more likely to require lengthier medication treatment, and/or are more willing to continue to remain in treatment (Schweizer et al. 1993). Although the medications have been shown to be safe if taken long-term without loss of effectiveness (Peselow 1996; Alexander 1991), we should try to minimize its risks by using the smallest dose necessary to maintain treatment gains.

Complicating Factors

There is not a consistent set of variables used to define treatment success. Merely reducing the number and severity of panic attacks does not address the fear and avoidance components that make up the heart of the debilitation. Rickels et al. (1993b) found that patients likely to require long-term medication were those who had come to treatment already on medication, or were initially more severely impaired by phobias. Their study involved several different treatments. They found that patients who completed the study, no matter which treatment group they were in, were more likely to be free of panic than those who dropped out before completing the study. They speculated that some unintentional cognitive changes were obtained merely by *participating* in treatment regardless of the type of treatment. Poor outcome is also associated with older age, male gender, history of depression, and longer duration of illness (Başoğlu, Marks, Swinson, et al. 1994c). Patients treated with alprazolam suffered from more anxiety, both long-term and short-term. It is difficult to isolate causal factors. Perhaps as suggested above, these patients had more severe illness, were the treatment-refractory patients, or had increased anxiety from the alprazolam treatment itself (Nagy et al. 1993). At any rate, it is important to reevaluate those treatment-refractory patients for other situational or medical causes that may have been previously overlooked. Caffeine, poor sleep (possibly secondary to working swing shift or "graveyard" shift), and comorbid psychiatric disorders are common contributing factors (Roy-Byrne et al. 1993).

Summary

The psychopharmacological treatment for panic disorder began in the 1960s with the use of imipramine. Many medications have been used since, but treatment has centered on the antidepressants. The SSRIs are currently considered the first-line pharmacological treatment for preventing panic attacks. Other classes of antidepressants as well as a few atypical drugs have been used as well. The latter are limited due to their negative side effect profile. The benzodiazepines are often prescribed in emergency departments and have been used for anticipatory anxiety. The high potency benzodiazepines alprazolam and clonazepam, often prescribed on a long-term basis, are able to block the panic attacks themselves. On the whole, the benzodiazepines are best used short-term as long-term use increases the risks of withdrawal and rebound. In all cases, it must be remembered to coordinate cognitive-behavior therapy with pharmacotherapy.

Section 2: Combining Cognitive-Behavior Therapy and Pharmacotherapy
Elke Zuercher-White, Ph.D. and Randall L. Solomon, M.D.

According to the Cross-National Collaborative Panic Study, Second Phase Investigators (1992), the question of combining psychotherapy and pharmacotherapy is still unresolved. Most drug studies have not included a drug-free follow-up phase (Başoğlu 1992; Marks, Greist, Başoğlu, et al. 1992), making the efficacy of medication treatment difficult to assess. In reanalyzing their data from the Cross-National Study, Marks et al. (1992) reported that exposure is superior to alprazolam, and moreover, the study overemphasized the benefits of alprazolam over exposure treatment while minimizing its disadvantages. In order to more fully understand the efficacy of each, cognitive-behavior therapy and pharmacotherapy, and of their combination, we need long-term studies comparing the outcomes of patients continuously on medication versus patients in continued psychotherapy. It would be even more helpful to study the long-term outcomes of a large group of patients who had discontinued *all* forms of treatment.

Pharmacological interventions can be effective in blocking anxiety and panic symptoms, but they do not necessarily affect psychosocial changes, particularly cognitive change at a deeper level. Should these changes not take place, patients are more likely to relapse upon discontinuation of the medication, especially when they must confront intolerable physical sensations again. This is more likely to occur if the client has learned to believe that the only way to decrease the intensity and frequency of panics is to take medication. A lingering, untreated fear of symptoms may be manifested in avoidance of caffeine use or vigorous exercise (Otto, Gould, and Pollack. 1994). If anxiety symptoms then reemerge, fear may return in full force with the accompanying anxious apprehension, vigilance, and catastrophic interpretation of the symptoms, setting off a new cycle of panic attacks (Otto, Pollack, Meltzer-Brody, et al. 1992; Otto et al. 1994).

Pharmacotherapy and Cognitive-Behavior Therapy: How They Interact

Pharmacotherapy and cognitive-behavior therapy are frequently used concurrently, but not always by the same clinician. It is important for us to have some understanding of any interactions the two treatments might have on one another, and whether they work synergistically or antagonistically.

Does Cognitive-Behavior Therapy Increase the Efficacy of Medication Treatment?

In vivo exposure has been a confounding variable in many medication studies. Mavissakalian (1993) reported several studies which showed that in vivo exposure enhances the effects of imipramine on agoraphobia, and also that imipramine enhanced the effects of exposure. He proposed that combining the two treatments would maximize initial response and minimize relapse upon drug discontinuation. In addition, cognitive-behavior therapy may result in reduced amounts of medication on those occasions when it is necessary to use the two forms of treatment together rather than if medications are used alone (Tesar and Rosenbaum 1993). In two long-term naturalistic studies, patients received a comprehensive four-month-long behavior group therapy (actually cognitive-behavior) along with alprazo-lam or imipramine treatments (Nagy, Krystal, Woods, et al. 1989; Nagy, et al. 1993). When patients were reinterviewed from one to five years later, half of the imipramine group, but only a third of the alprazolam group, were medication-free.

More recent studies compared alprazolam alone versus alprazolam and cognitive-be-havior therapy (Bruce, et al. 1995). The patients had already been on medication for an average of 20.5 months prior to the study. Cognitive-behavior therapy was used to taper off medications. At the end of the study, 90 percent of the cognitive-behavior therapy group were off medications, while only 40 percent of the alprazolam group were able to discon-tinue. The combined treatment group was significantly less anxious and depressed, had less anticipatory anxiety and catastrophic thinking, and overall was less disabled. Otto, Pollack, Sachs, et al. (1993) found in their study that with cognitive-behavior therapy three times as many patients were able to discontinue benzodiazepines compared to just a slow taper without cognitive-behavior therapy. Pollack and Smoller (1995) concluded that cognitive-be-havioral techniques offer some protection against relapse upon medication discontinuation, particularly if aimed at dealing with the distress associated with withdrawal symptoms.

Do Medications Add to Cognitive-Behavior Therapy?

It has been suggested that benzodiazepines may be detrimental to in vivo exposure (Başoğlu 1992; Marks et al. 1992; Marks, et al. 1993; van Balkom et al. 1996; Wardle et al. 1994). In their study, Charney and Woods (1989) speculated that the treatment gains appar-ently derived from benzodiazepines could have resulted from the concurrent group psycho-therapy. Wardle et al. (1994) found no detrimental effect on agoraphobic symptoms from low-dose benzodiazepam (diazepam) use. The authors concluded furthermore that there was no evidence to support the addition of benzodiazepines to the behavioral treatment of agoraphobia. Other authors report that the presence of benzodiazepines decreases the effects of psychological intervention and treatment (van Balkom et al. 1996; Sanderson and Wetzler 1993). Another study found that imipramine did not increase the benefits of exposure at follow-up (Marks, et al. 1983).

Otto's (1997) position is that despite the gains afforded by initiating treatment with pharmacotherapy, it may reduce the long-term benefits available through cognitive-behavior therapy alone. Taking benzodiazepines on an as-needed basis in particular reinforces psy-chological dependence.

Pharmacological treatment may impede the effectiveness of behavioral therapy via the suppression of anxiety sensations. For example, with benzodiazepines a person is less likely to learn to cope with higher levels of anxiety and panic. As mentioned earlier, anxiety sensitivity seems an important construct, and changes in this appear to be associated with resistance to relapse. Fava, Grandi, Belluardo, et al. (1994) found improvement in anxiety and anxiety sensitivity in a group of patients with panic disorder and agoraphobia, who had successfully completed behavioral treatment. Although they had been on benzodiazepines for two years or more prior to the behavioral treatment, they were subsequently able to withdraw from medications.

Craske and Rodriguez (1994) reported that the studies they reviewed show mixed results when combining medications and cognitive-behavior therapy. Gould et al. (1995) and Otto, et al. (1994) concluded from their reviews that cognitive-behavior therapy alone showed better results than when combining it with medications. Craske (1996) determined from her review of the literature that there seems to be some evidence that the combination is slightly superior to either treatment alone in the short-term but not necessarily in the long-term (i.e., combined treatments may be less effective than cognitive-behavior therapy alone).

How Drugs May Interfere With Cognitive-Behavior Therapy

There have been several explanations proposed to explain the interference observed when medications are combined with cognitive-behavior therapy, however, more research is needed to substantiate these claims (Başoğlu 1992; Başoğlu, Marks, Kiliç, et al. 1994a; Brown and Barlow 1995; Clark 1986; Clum 1989; Craske 1991b, 1996; Craske and Rodriguez 1994; Curran et al. 1994; Gould et al. 1995; Otto et al. 1994; Sanderson and Wetzler 1993; Sholom-skas and Woods 1992; Swinson, Cox, Shulman, et al. 1992a; Telch, Tearnan, and Taylor 1983). We will try to summarize their conclusions. (Although they are listed separately for clarity, they partially overlap.)

1. **State-dependent or context-specific learning.**
   Gains are made under drug sedation and may not transfer well to a drug-free state. For example, exposure in a drug-induced state may result in fear reduction specific to the drug state. Similarly, if exposure occurs only in the presence of a therapist, it may fail to generalize to other states. One reason may be that while fear acquisition often generalizes across contexts, fear elimination is more context-specific.

2. **Self-efficacy.**
   Improvement is attributed to medications vis-à-vis one's own efforts. Attribution is linked to beliefs and expectations of one's own responsibility and contribution to and control over the situation. In other words, does the treatment promote a sense of self-confidence or does the person primarily trust the drug? Patients who rely on medications to help them tend to have more withdrawal symptoms and more relapse. Some patients rely so strongly on medications that they report almost instantaneous relief after taking a tablet. Several authors report that patients who conclude their success is due to an outside agent (drug, therapist, or other safety signals and safety behaviors) will have less confidence in their own efforts and ability to cope. Hence, attribution affects the expectation about one's future ability to cope; this might play a role in the long-term effects of cognitive-behavior therapy.

3. **Interference with habituation and extinction in exposure.**
   A number of authors (but not all) emphasize that high levels of anxiety are necessary to achieve maximum benefit of exposure therapy, i.e., increased habituation and extinction of the fear response. Medications, especially benzodiazepines, interfere with experiencing anxiety.

4. **Reinforcement of fear via safety signals.**
   Patients who take medications on an as-needed basis, as opposed to a regular schedule, may be reinforcing their fear of anxiety sensations. The medication becomes a safety signal, i.e., a negative coping strategy. Unless weaned from the medication, it can help mask the pathology. For instance, it has often been observed that avoidance behavior without medication is more extensive than with medication.

5. **Decreased tolerance to symptoms of anxiety.**
   It is essential for patients to learn to tolerate bodily arousal, i.e., anxiety sensations, without provoking a full panic response. Medications suppress these bodily fluctuations; consequently, patients are unable to get the full effect of their cognitive restructuring and interoceptive deconditioning work.

6. **Interference with short-term memory and recall.**
   Interference with memory and recall as observed with benzodiazepines may

interfere with therapies that involve learning, so that these drugs may be counterproductive. Long-term use may increase this effect. See Section 1 of this chapter for a discussion of alprazolam and memory.

7. **Influence of higher medication relapse rates.**
   Because relapse rates for medications are higher than for cognitive-behavior therapy, combining the two treatments can produce higher relapse rates than for cognitive-behavior therapy alone. This makes cognitive-behavior therapy appear to be less successful than it actually is.

8. **Loss of motivation.**
   If the medication succeeds in fully suppressing symptoms, the client may lose motivation to learn coping skills.

Why Start Treatment With Cognitive-Behavior Therapy Only

So, what should be the first-line treatment—cognitive-behavior therapy or pharmacotherapy? Some authors favor medications in order to reduce or eliminate most symptoms prior to any psychological therapy (Klerman 1992). Many of those adhering to a strict biological causality liken panic disorder to chronic physical illnesses requiring long-term treatment. In addition, the chronicity of panic disorder has been taken as proof of the necessity for long-term drug maintenance treatment. However, it is possible that drugs may foster dependence and iatrogenic morbidity. At least in some patients long-term medication treatment is needed primarily to prevent discontinuation symptoms (Antonuccio, Danton, and DeNelsky 1995; Eisenberg 1992; Pollack and Smoller 1995; Rosenbaum et al. 1995). Another way of saying this is that panic disorder is chronic primarily when it is treated with medications (Otto and Pollack 1994).

In this context, cognitive-behavior therapy has distinct advantages. It is free of drug-induced side effects and does not interact with other medications, it is effective, and it works directly on the anticipatory anxiety and phobic behaviors that are the most disabling aspects of panic disorder. Cognitive-behavior therapy does not minimize the symptoms the patient experiences, but rather provides tools to free the patient from being at the mercy of his or her emotions or somatic sensations.

A number of clinicians and researchers have proposed that cognitive-behavior therapy be the first line of intervention (Agras 1993; Craske et al. 1995; Michelson and Marchione 1991; Otto and Whittal 1995; Rosenbaum et al. 1995; Sanderson and Wetzler 1993; Tesar and Rosenbaum 1993). Clum (1989) unequivocally recommends behavior therapy for the treatment of panic. Likewise, Jacobson and Hollon (1996) draw the same conclusion based on evidence that cognitive-behavior therapy shows remarkable success at preventing relapse. Gould et al. (1995) state that it is a particularly promising intervention in the treatment of panic disorder in terms of cost and tolerance.

Advantages of Integrating Cognitive-Behavior Therapy and Pharmacotherapy

In her excellent review of the integration of cognitive-behavior therapy and pharmacotherapy, Craske (1996) set forth the problems with each. As successful as cognitive-behavior therapy is, there are some sobering facts. Twenty-five percent of clients reject behavior therapy, 10 to 20 percent drop out, with a higher rate when agoraphobia is present. Positive effects are usually not reached for four to six weeks, and it is not effective with 15 to 20 percent of clients. A high percentage (about 75 percent) of those seeking help, at least in a medical clinic, believe that the cause of their panic disorder is both psychological and biological and they prefer combined treatments; it is speculated that their beliefs may affect treatment outcome.

In regard to medications, Dr. Craske continues, many clients do not accept them, and others do not tolerate the side effects, with dropout rates of 15 to 28 percent. Attrition from combined behavior therapy and imipramine is also high, about a third of clients. Neither tricyclic antidepressants nor benzodiazepines are effective with 35 to 40 percent of clients, and withdrawal and relapse pose formidable problems. Many clients cannot discontinue medications. (There is much less research data available on the SSRIs at this time.) According to Otto et al. (1993), from 40 to 80 percent of clients remain symptomatic after long-term medication use.

Whatever the medication treatment, the less anxiety is felt, the less successful the discontinuation tends to be. Without cognitive-behavior therapy, patients are unprepared for managing the anxiety and the bodily sensations inherent in medication discontinuation (Otto et al. 1993). It is important to remember that even a slow taper, which minimizes rebound and withdrawal symptoms, still does not address the fears.

Treatment with benzodiazepines and cognitive-behavior therapy possesses a certain symmetry. The first provides quick results and is easy to use, but is hard to discontinue. The second requires substantial work and commitment on the part of the patient initially, but becomes second nature with practice.

How to Best Integrate the Treatments

Some patients are unable or unwilling to participate in treatment until symptom reduction has been achieved through medication (Tesar and Rosenbaum 1993). Along these lines, Mavissakalian (1993) favors achieving maximal response at the beginning for the practical reason that it might keep patients in treatment. This can be done rapidly only with pharmacotherapy, and with benzodiazepines in particular as tricyclic antidepressants and SSRIs take too long. He would then combine cognitive-behavior therapy and medication to allow discontinuation of the medication.

In contrast, Craske (1996) suggests that when cognitive-behavior therapy and medication treatment are integrated, to start both simultaneously. That way, improvement will not be as easily attributed to medications, and medications will less likely be used as safety signals. Dr. Craske further asserts that comorbidities argue for combining cognitive-behavior therapy and medications as first-line intervention, and many clients presenting to clinics have comorbidities. The same applies to those clients who want medications.

The clinicians providing treatment should present a comprehensive conceptualization of panic disorder, i.e., the cause of the disorder lies in biological and psychological factors (Craske 1996; Otto et al. 1994). Along these lines, the clinician points out that there are differences in anxiety proneness and emotional reactivity, as well as in past emotional anxiety-related experiences. Also, anxiety and panic can be perpetuated by fear of the symptoms. This is in contrast with a strict biological view, which states that panic disorder results from a chemical imbalance. Prospective clients must also know that the findings to date show that biological and psychological treatments are efficacious regardless of etiology (Craske 1991b; Gorman et al. 1989). Further, discussion should focus on the pitfalls of using medications as safety signals with their detrimental effect on self-efficacy, and the finding that subsequent dependence on medications is greater the more the person attributes gains to them. The clinician should emphasize the need to comply with the planned medication regimen to maximize a positive outcome, and the need for exposure practices. Patients should be put on a routine dose of medication and instructed to take it by the clock rather than by how they feel (Otto 1997).

To conclude, it is important for all treating clinicians to present a comprehensive view rather than sabotage each other's treatments by presenting a very one-sided viewpoint.

Cognitive-Behavior Therapy and Medication Discontinuation

One major issue is weaning the client off medications while he or she is undergoing cognitive-behavioral treatment. When cognitive-behavior therapy is added to help withdraw the patient from medications, the aim is to both decrease the conditioned fears of somatic sensations and the catastrophic misinterpretation of those sensations, as well as to help develop coping skills to minimize discontinuation symptoms.

Sanderson and Wetzler (1993) state that the ideal would be to slowly wean the patient off medications during the beginning of the cognitive restructuring and interoceptive exposure components of cognitive-behavior therapy. Taper should be completed as soon as possible, preferably before cognitive-behavior therapy ends. The cognitive-behavior therapy should be modified slightly at medication discontinuation time. The focus should return again to fears and cognitions around bodily sensations. Patients are informed what they can expect to feel and are provided interoceptive exposure to similar sensations (Otto et al. 1993). According to Craske (1996), after the basic cognitive-behavioral treatment, biweekly or monthly booster sessions for several months are needed for the patient to become truly independent and for maximum self-efficacy. As also stated by the previous authors, both interoceptive and in vivo exposures should take place without medications.

Otto, Pollack, and Barlow (1995) have developed a manual for benzodiazepine discontinuation called *Stopping Anxiety Medication.* The workbook is to be used by a therapist to help the client taper off medications. It closely integrates every aspect of drug monitoring with psychological work, i.e., learning new strategies every step of the way. It includes various taper schedules for alprazolam and clonazepam.

Otto et al. (1993) found no significant difference when their patients discontinued from alprazolam and clonazepam. In spite of this finding, one of us (RLS) has almost always found it difficult to taper off of alprazolam and recommends switching over to clonazepam as detailed earlier in this chapter. Tapering from clonazepam can be accomplished in as short a time as two weeks; this can be increased, however, based on the particular needs of the patient. The longer the patient has been on medication, the longer the taper will need to be extended. You can probably reduce medications by 0.5 mg at a time until reaching 1 mg. At that point slowing to 0.25 mg reductions works well.

Although all of the recommendations above on the integration of treatments are helpful, they are often difficult to put into practice. In busy clinics and agencies, particularly when clients have a limited number of sessions available, it may be difficult to follow the guidelines. One of us (EZW) has been able to provide booster sessions via the Anxiety Support Group. Clients can also repeat the Panic/Phobia Group at a later time, particularly if they are having difficulty with medication discontinuation.

A final point is presented very well by Rosenbaum (1997). When a client's symptoms persist and no improvement is otherwise seen, rather than adding layer upon layer of another treatment (whether medications or cognitive-behavioral techniques aimed at symptom reduction), the clinician should explore what stands in the way. Has the client received an adequate dose of medications, or are there comorbidities, or are psychosocial stresses maintaining the persistent symptomatology? From a cognitive perspective, we may need to move to an ideographic formulation to understand the underlying core beliefs, as mentioned in the Introduction of this book.

Summary

The combination of cognitive-behavior therapy and pharmacotherapy can be complex. It has been found that cognitive-behavior therapy often enhances the effects of medications and facilitates discontinuation. The effects of medications on cognitive-behavior therapy are less clear, possibly leading to poorer outcome than that of cognitive-behavior therapy alone in the long-term.

Cognitive-behavior therapy as a first-line intervention offers certain advantages, though it requires persistence and hard work. In many instances, a combination is preferred, particularly if the client is in great distress, has comorbidities, or requests medications. In those cases, cognitive-behavior therapy should be provided during the discontinuation phase as well. Finally, cognitive-behavior therapy can be used during discontinuation when the client has previously had successful medication treatment.

11

Panic Disorder in Medical Settings: Recognition and Intervention

The Prevalence of Panic Disorder in the Medical Setting

In several studies, panic disorder patients have been shown to be the highest utilizers of medical services, including other anxiety disorders and major depression (Katon, von Korff, and Lin 1992; Michelson et al. 1990). A recent study by Katerndahl and Realini (1995) showed that although 26 percent of those with panic attacks sought care in mental health settings, as many as 49 percent sought care from medical practitioners. Medical services are overutilized when symptoms remain unexplained: patients keep seeking consultation. In those instances where no organic cause is found, the physician should strongly consider panic disorder (Katon 1996). The high cost of panic disorder in primary care is reflected in the fact that these patients seek health care services three times more often than the average person, comprising up to 8 percent of primary care patients (Katon 1996; Katon et al. 1992).

Panic patients present with cardiac (irregular heart beat, atypical chest pain, tachycardia), pulmonary (breathlessness, suffocation), neurologic (dizziness, headaches, vertigo, syncope, paresthesias), and gastrointestinal (epigastric distress, irritable bowel syndrome) symptoms. Other common symptoms are labile hypertension, peptic ulcer disease, and choking sensations (Katon et al. 1992). If the problem is not correctly diagnosed, these patients continue to search for medical specialists and to undergo costly and unnecessary tests. For instance, 70 percent of the patients studied by Sheehan, Ballenger, and Jacobsen (1980) had sought relief for their symptoms from nonpsychiatric physicians more than ten times.

The most common sites frequented are the offices of general or family physicians and emergency rooms in hospitals. According to Katon (1996), further economic consequences of misdiagnosis result from the fact that these patients receive more diagnostic tests and hospital admissions than control subjects. For instance, up to 43 percent of patients with chest pain who have angiogram testing with negative results have panic disorder (Katon et al. 1992). Furthermore, they receive significantly more psychotropic and nonpsychotropic medications.

Often primary care and emergency room physicians see these patients with their first panic attacks. As much as this could provide a unique opportunity to identify the disorder early and avoid the chronicity and the concomitant high medical utilization (Katon 1989;

Swinson, Cox, and Woszczyna 1992b), there is a significant underrecognition of panic disorder in emergency rooms and primary care (Yingling, Wulsin, Mussion Arnold, et al. 1993).

Understandably, physicians are more confident assessing and treating physical rather than emotional problems. Emotional problems are still viewed in many cases as stigmatic by both patients and physicians. Patients seek a physical explanation for their distress, and health care workers collude in the construct of mind-body dualism by considering only physical symptoms. Emotional distress is then overlooked. Olfson, Gilbert, Weissman, et al. (1995) concluded that some physicians make a conscious decision not to ask about emotional factors, because they would not know what to do. Extensive or repeated testing may give the impression that the physician is uncertain of his or her diagnosis and reinforces the idea that something is seriously wrong. Sometimes the patient is told that the tests are normal, and there is nothing to worry about (Bass 1991). I have seen a number of panickers who complained bitterly that they were told they were merely under stress and were then sent home. These patients felt they had not been understood or treated properly, and, often, more time elapsed before they received appropriate treatment.

Depression, which also leads to high medical utilization rates, is recognized more readily than anxiety disorders. Part of the difficulty in recognizing anxiety disorders seems to be that anxiety is often seen as a symptom, not a syndrome, i.e., symptoms of anxiety are seen as expected adjustment reactions to stressful life events (Katon, Vitaliano, Russo, et al. 1986). Furthermore, many patients present with subthreshold panic symptoms. Even though they do not meet all the criteria for a panic disorder diagnosis, they are still significantly impaired (Olfson, Broadhead, Weissman, et al. 1996).

Panic disorder patients often self-medicate with alcohol, tranquilizers, and other drugs. They avoid many activities for fear of aggravating the physical symptoms, and they avoid situations and places, becoming agoraphobic. The distress caused by the disorder can lead to significant impairment in social and vocational functioning. If untreated, many panic patients become unemployed, receiving disability payments and seeing themselves as sick for extended periods (Bass 1991). Bass concludes that early detection leads to fewer iatrogenic complications (complications inadvertently caused by the treatment) in addition to fewer medical tests, less distress, and less functional disability.

Diagnosis of Panic Disorder

Briefly, to make the diagnosis of panic disorder, there must be a report of a sudden rush of intense fear or anxiety peaking within ten minutes that is accompanied by at least four of the following thirteen symptoms: Palpitations/pounding heart; sweating; trembling/shaking; shortness of breath/smothering; choking sensations; chest pain or discomfort; nausea/abdominal distress; dizziness/light-headedness/faint feelings; numbness/tingling; cold or hot flushes; feelings of unreality; fear of dying; and fear of going crazy or losing control. The diagnosis further requires that some panic attacks must occur unexpectedly. The symptoms are often accompanied by fear of the possible consequences and behavioral repercussions (e.g., visits to the emergency room or avoidance). The panic attacks usually last from five to thirty minutes and are often followed by high anxiety. For more information on the diagnosis, see chapter 1.

Panic attacks themselves are not emergencies and should not be responded to as such, according to the National Institutes of Health Consensus Statement (Treatment of Panic Disorder 1991). Therefore, if the patient claims an inability to function, the true urgency of that claim must be assessed. In this context, functional impairment would consist of imminent loss of job or primary relationship and/or rapid generalization of avoidance.

Nonfearful Panic Disorder

When patients describe panic attacks exclusively in terms of physical and/or behavioral manifestations and without the accompanying fear, this is called nonfearful panic disorder (Kushner and Beitman 1990). Such patients present to nonpsychiatric physicians with unexplained physical symptoms and not with anxiety. In the medical setting, they comprise 20 to 40 percent of those with panic disorder. The authors postulate that an extreme lack of awareness of their emotions could be one reason for the absence of verbally expressed fear. Patients with primarily somatic complaints can be difficult to engage in psychological treatment, but their disorder does respond to medications just as in panic disorder with concomitant fear (Bass 1991; Kushner and Beitman 1990). Although these patients are more likely to be seen in medical departments, their disorder may remain unrecognized, especially if the treating physician does not consider the anxiety diagnosis when fear has not been reported (Kushner and Beitman 1990).

Several approaches may help identify these patients in medical settings and can be utilized by mental health professionals to engage the nonfearful panicker in treatment. One is to look for and emphasize the behavioral repercussions of symptoms, e.g., if the patient denies fear of suffocation when encountering breathing anomalies and yet repeatedly visits the emergency room, such behavior is often an indication of fear. Another approach is to invite the client to engage in a few interoceptive exercises with you. (Note that if you are not the client's physician, you need to inquire about medical conditions that may exclude the client from some interoceptive exercises, as laid out in chapter 6). Particularly helpful here are hyperventilation (from one-and-one-half to three minutes), spinning (for one minute), and breathing through a cocktail straw (for two minutes). If clients show any apprehension, you can ask them why they do not wish to do this exercise. Similarly, if anxiety is felt during and after the exercise, it can open the door to the exploration of a hidden fear component. Finally, one can inquire about any avoidances, whether obvious (driving, elevators, crowds), or subtle (sitting down, tensing up, etc.). That is, does the client engage in any behavior that is somehow meant to deter a catastrophe?

In my treatment, the New Panickers Group allows these clients to gain insight at their own pace. They are often very quiet at the beginning of treatment, but they listen closely while others describe similar sensations, which are accompanied by fear and behavioral repercussions, such as seeking assurance, or resorting to subtle avoidances, as mentioned above.

Differential Diagnosis

In patients with a medical illness, physicians often focus on the illness and overlook a psychiatric disorder. Yet the physical illness may exacerbate a preexisting anxiety condition, and illness may give rise to worries about physical disability and mortality (Valente 1996). When panic disorder coexists, the autonomic nervous system arousal associated with it may have a deleterious impact on the course of the medical illness, with a subsequent increase in medical utilization. Often the medical illness escalates until the panic disorder is adequately treated. Furthermore, the treatment of panic disorder is usually successful whether or not there is a comorbid medical condition (Zaubler and Katon 1996). In sum, if the primary care physician recognizes the panic disorder and refers the patient for appropriate treatment, there is a great savings in cost.

Many physicians recommend diagnosing anxiety disorders by first excluding other medical illnesses. This can be accomplished with the use of laboratory tests, diagnostic procedures, and consultation with specialists. In this vein, Goldberg (1988) and Raj and

Sheehan (1987) test for a complete blood count, urinalysis, renal and hepatic abnormalities, serum calcium and phosphorus levels, and take an electrocardiogram to rule out a medical condition. On the other hand, Katon (1989) suggests a thorough biopsychosocial history and physical examination. He deems this sufficient especially when the patient is young and reports classic panic attack symptoms, avoidance behavior, and depressive symptoms. If the physical symptoms predominate and stressors are minimized, a brief laboratory screen (complete blood count, blood chemistry panel, and thyroid function tests) suffices. As Katon suggests, if you suspect panic disorder, it is advisable to tell your patient that you believe his or her symptoms are due to an autonomic nervous system arousal, but that tests will help to rule out a medical condition. Because at times both are present, that is, an anxiety disorder as well as a medical condition, you need to be flexible. The more patients you see with panic disorder, the more easily you will recognize common patterns, and the better able you will be to identify aberrations, which may then prompt you to do additional medical testing.

Hypochondriasis, Somatization, Illness Phobia

Several studies have reported an association between panic disorder, hypochondriasis, and somatization disorder (Katon 1990; Pollard and Lewis 1989). Some somatizing and hypochondriacal patients panic and interpret their symptoms as further evidence of catastrophic illness (Pollard and Lewis 1989). Barsky, Barnett, and Cleary (1994) report 25 percent of panic disorder patients have hypochondriasis as a comorbidity. In the *DSM-IV* (American Psychiatric Association 1994) definition of hypochondriasis, the person has the conviction that he or she has a serious disease, and the preoccupation persists in spite of medical reassurance. Although both panickers and hypochondriacs are preoccupied with their bodies, the hypochondriac believes that the illness is already present in the body, while the panicker fears that the *panic attack itself will cause* imminent catastrophic illness (heart attack, stroke, insanity). Patients with illness phobia fear a specific illness, seek reassurance, and recognize that their fear is unreasonable. They seem to fear future illness rather than being convinced that they have a serious disease at the present (Noyes, Wesner, and Fisher 1992). They are more concerned with their fearful thoughts than with somatic symptoms. In somatization, according to the *DSM-IV*, typically, there are many complaints in the course of the disorder, including pain, gastrointestinal, sexual, and pseudoneurological symptoms.

To summarize, there is an overlap between panic disorder, hypochondriasis, illness phobia, and somatization. To differentiate between them, the panicker's fears are focused on one (possibly two or three) consequence of the panic attack itself. Once the panic has passed, and the dreaded event has not occurred, the person is reassured, but only until the next attack.

Asthma

Panic disorder afflicts anywhere from six to 30 percent of asthmatics, but it often goes unrecognized (Carr, Lehrer, Rausch, et al. 1994; Smoller, et al. 1996). In patients with asthma and chronic obstructive pulmonary disease, panic disorder is the most frequent psychiatric diagnosis (Van Peski-Oosterbaan, Spinhoven, Van der Does, et al. 1996). The latter authors found little difference in the prevalence of panic disorder in asthmatic and nonasthmatic patients. They concluded that the high rates of panic disorder they found are not specific for asthma or pulmonary disease. Zaubler and Katon (1996) summarized studies showing the following: patients with asthma who develop panic disorder are not necessarily those with a more serious illness, but they are more fearful of bodily sensations, i.e., they have high anxiety sensitivity.

Symptoms experienced in panic disorder and asthma are dyspnea, or shortness of breath, smothering sensations, and choking. Although asthma attacks and panic attacks have such similarities, Schmaling and Bell (1997) found differences as well. The symptoms that discriminate best between the two are: wheezing, coughing, and mucous production, all characteristic of asthma attacks. These authors recommend that panic disorder be considered in cases where the asthma is not controlled by the treatment regimen as expected (based on objective measures such as peak flows or the results of pulmonary function or methacholine challenge tests), there is excess fear or panic, and/or the patient overuses medications. In cases where patients suffer from both conditions, differentiation can be improved via the use of objective measures of airflow obstruction, such as peak flow meters and the presence of the above-named discriminating symptoms of asthma. Panic attacks, on the other hand, have a more sudden onset, peak within ten minutes, and a shorter total duration.

In one study, subjects with panic disorder displayed less airway impedance than those without panic disorder, suggesting a greater respiratory preparedness for stress, i.e., greater ventilation abilities in fight/flight situations (Carr, Lehrer, Hochron, et al. 1996). While this may promote hyperventilation, the authors speculated that it may be beneficial to patients with asthma. In contrast, Smoller et al. (1996) found that, in some cases, panic and hyperventilation can exacerbate an asthma condition. Although the panic fear does not seem related to the severity of the pulmonary disease, the distress can be significant.

Cognitive, conditioning, and biological theories have been proposed to explain the association between panic disorder and respiratory illness (Zaubler and Katon 1996). There may be a subclinical lung abnormality, such as a minimal obstruction of lung airways, regulated by the autonomic nervous system. Such dysregulation may explain not only the association between panic disorder and asthma, but also between panic disorder and allergies. Patients with panic disorder may have a conditioned hypersensitivity to carbon dioxide mediated through the locus ceruleus. A person who had respiratory illness early in life may have become conditioned to respond with anxiety to respiratory dysfunction. These theories are not mutually exclusive and may explain the comorbidity between the respiratory illness and panic disorder.

When it comes to treating these comorbidities, Smoller at al. (1996) recommend a combination of medication, cognitive-behavior therapy, and coping mechanisms. They, as well as Schmaling and Bell (1997) urge physicians to exercise caution in the use of benzodiazepines, as these can produce respiratory depression and worsen existing hypercapnia, in part by blunting carbon dioxide sensitivity. If prescribed for patients with asthma and panic disorder, the dose should be smaller than usual and be carefully monitored. Smoller at al. (1996) further recommend that benzodiazepines be avoided by those with sleep apnea. Tricyclic antidepressants and even more selective serotonin reuptake inhibitors (SSRIs) can be considered. Monoamine oxidase inhibitors (MAOIs) are to be avoided because of a possible hypertensive reaction to beta-agonists used in treating exacerbations of the pulmonary illness. The authors recommend cognitive-behavior therapy because of its safety compared to pharmacotherapy. Therapists should consult the patient's primary care physician to distinguish between cognitive distortions and realistic restrictions and fears. Other nonpharmacologic approaches also can be helpful, such as relaxation, breathing retraining, and psychosocial support.

Audiovestibular Dysfunctions

Dizziness and disequilibrium are very common and may be caused by either peripheral or central vestibular abnormalities. Such abnormalities may lead to vertigo and balance disorders (Shumway-Cook and Horak 1989). Dizziness and subjective balance disturbance are characteristics of phobic postural vertigo, which manifests in episodes of unsteadiness and anxiety (Brandt 1996). Triggers can be perceptual and/or social stimuli leading to phobic avoidance of bridges, staircases, streets, large stores, and restaurants and theaters. Some people become so preoccupied with their balance regulation that they check it continuously and thereby detect minute sensorimotor discrepancies ignored by most. Some patients go on to develop panic disorder and agoraphobia. Shumway-Cook and Horak (1989) recommend treatment with vestibular habituation exercises, balance retraining, and aerobics. These may produce better outcomes in the long-term than the medications prescribed by many physicians.

Cardiac Symptoms

According to a report by Katon (1990), over 80 percent of patients who complain of chest pain in primary care have no organic etiology. Studies have found that between 17.5 and 25 percent of patients going to the emergency room for chest pain had panic disorder (Yingling, et al. 1993; Fleet, Dupuis, Marchand, et al. 1996). When clients present to a cardiac unit and cardiac disease has been excluded, panic disorder is one of the first to be considered in the etiology of the symptoms (Carter, Maddock, Amsterdam, et al. 1992). Those with a psychiatric diagnosis as opposed to coronary artery disease tend to be female and younger (Yingling et al. 1993). The physician should inquire not only about chest pain and palpitations but also about breathlessness, dizziness, light-headedness, paresthesias, and fatigue. The presence of these latter symptoms means that a noncardiac etiology is more likely. In contrast, patients with panic disorder seldom complain of the crushing chest pain associated with acute ischemic cardiac syndromes (Pollard and Lewis 1989).

Noncardiac chest pain has been variously labeled: Da Costa's Syndrome, irritable heart, effort syndrome, neurocirculatory asthenia, and cardiac phobia (Serlie, Erdman, Passchier, et al. 1995). The authors define cardiac phobia essentially as a condition where a client repeatedly complains of chest pain, palpitations, and other somatic sensations, which are interpreted as leading to heart attack and death. I have also observed that a few of these patients significantly curtail their activities for fear of precipitating some imagined catastrophic event. In their review of the literature, the authors concluded that emotional problems are more frequently exhibited in patients with normal coronary arteries than in patients with diseased coronary arteries.

In controlled experiments, panic disorder patients exhibit greater cardiac awareness than controls; they pay close attention to their heartbeats (Ehlers and Breuer 1992; Ehlers, Breuer, Dohn, et al. 1995). This awareness appears to be a stable characteristic and not one resulting from high anxiety. Such awareness may contribute to the maintenance of panic disorder. It has been observed that patients with noncardiac chest pain misinterpret and amplify the physical sensations they perceive (Taylor, Davig, and Schauss 1993). More specifically, because of their fears of having a heart attack they anticipate chest-localized sensations and pains, pay attention to them, and catastrophize, labeling them impending heart attacks (Bass 1991; Serlie et al. 1995). Hyperventilation often can bring on and/or maintain the symptoms.

Other causes of noncardiac chest pain in addition to hyperventilation are esophageal reflux, esophageal spasm, pain from the thoracic spine, chronic obstructive airways disease, costochondritis, intercostal muscle spasm, and Prinzmetal's angina (Bass 1991; Katon 1990). Fleet et al. (1996) found in their study that 44 percent of patients with panic disorder had prior histories of coronary artery disease. The authors concluded that anxiety increases the risk of cardiovascular complications, especially in men. Most patients in the same study were referred for mental health evaluation and treatment by their physicians, but the physicians did not recognize the condition as panic disorder.

Neither panic disorder nor cardiac phobia preclude the possibility of cardiovascular disease (Yingling et al. 1993). One study demonstrated a comorbidity of 21 percent between cardiovascular disease and panic disorder (Gerdes, Yates, and Clancy 1995). In instances of heart-related problems, it is easy for the physician to focus on the medical illness while overlooking the panic disorder. Panic disorder may worsen coronary artery disease, and cardiac ischemia, for instance, can exacerbate panic symptoms, so that a vicious cycle develops where both reinforce each other (Zaubler and Katon 1996). One of my colleagues conducts a group for cardiac (mostly bypass surgery) patients, where many suffer from panic disorder. It is sometimes more difficult to treat panic disorder in this context, since client fears are not merely imaginary.

Other Medical Conditions

Gerdes et al. (1995) found irritable bowel syndrome in 18 percent of panic disorder patients. Other comorbid medical diagnoses are mitral valve prolapse, hypertension, neurological, endocrine, gynecological, and pulmonary disorders. In their review of studies, Zaubler and Katon (1996) drew the following conclusions:

Irritable Bowel Syndrome

Patients with comorbid irritable bowel syndrome and panic disorder are overly sensitive to stimuli in a number of organ systems. There are indications that this is mediated by dysregulation in the autonomic nervous system and the locus ceruleus.

Mitral Valve Prolapse

Panic disorder is not more common in those with mitral valve prolapse than the general population. Yet panic disorder is found more commonly in those patients seeking cardiology consultation, whether or not they have mitral valve prolapse. It is important to consider panic disorder in patients with mitral valve prolapse and to give them the standard treatment for panic disorder.

Hypertension

There can be an increased incidence of hypertension as well as of labile hypertension among patients with panic disorder. The latter often returns to normal when the panic disorder is treated with psychoactive medications. Although the association between hypertension and panic disorder has not been explained with certitude, there are theories of hyperventilation being the physiological link between the two, as well as increased adrenergic activity, centrally and peripherally.

Partial Complex Seizures

Patients with atypical panic attacks, i.e., those associated with focal paresthesias or sensory distortions, should be referred to a physician. An electroencephalogram (EEG) showing focal paroxysmal changes during panic attacks may indicate partial complex seizures.

General Guidelines for the Initial Interview

Katon (1996) identifies who may be at increased risk for panic disorder or other anxiety disorders when no organic etiology has been found for persistent unexplained physical symptoms. These patients often exhibit the following:

- Complaints of anxiety and tension

- Recent onset of hypochondriacal concerns

- Complaints of cardiac, neurologic, or gastrointestinal symptoms

- Presence of migraine headaches and peptic ulcer disease

The general recommendation is this: Listen to the patient without interruption for at least several minutes, and pay close attention to clues for pertinent psychological and social variables. Inquire about life circumstances and stressors as well as about the use of alcohol and other substances. Often patients will not volunteer such information. Legitimize your patient's concerns, which includes recognizing that the symptoms are real. Show empathy and ask open-ended questions. When these guidelines are observed, patients are much more likely to follow your recommendations. Once the diagnosis has been made, it is appropriate to tell the patient that this is a psychiatric condition (Menninger 1995). Then discuss the appropriate psychological and medication treatment options.

Wichowski and Benishek (1996) have developed a questionnaire entitled *Anxiety Inventory* for use in primary care. It takes about fifteen minutes to administer. Based on my review of the literature (Apfeldorf, Shear, Leon, et al. 1994; Katon 1996; Katon et al. 1986; Kushner and Beitman 1990; Noyes et al. 1992; Rifkin 1990), I suggest using the questions below to aid your diagnosis.

Further questions could be about a family history of anxiety and mood disorders; and about depression (feelings of sadness and hopelessness, loss of regular interests and activities, feelings of guilt, disturbed sleep patterns, loss of appetite, and suicidal ideation).

Questions to Help Diagnose Panic Disorder

If there is time for only one question, use this general query:

Do you feel pretty much convinced that something is medically wrong with you in spite of reassurance by a physician? What do *you* think may be wrong?

If you can, ask more specific questions, such as those below:

1. Do you experience sudden episodes of intense, unexpected fear or anxiety?

2. Do you experience any symptoms with these sudden, intense episodes?

3. Do you fear that these episodes could lead to a medical problem, even death, or to your losing control or embarrassing yourself?

4. Do you feel uneasy or avoid places or activities that most people do not fear? (If needed, list examples, such as being in crowds, driving, using public transportation, experiencing heat, riding in elevators, going out alone, and exercising).

5. Have you been under a lot of stress lately or have you felt unable to resolve a difficult dilemma, maybe one of an interpersonal nature?

It is helpful to inquire about the patient's health beliefs. Does the patient know others with the same condition? Does he or she worry about something serious? How the patient perceives his or her general health gives clues to the underlying distress. Those whose perceptions are that they have poor health are higher utilizers of medical services than those who perceive their health in a more positive light (Olfson et al. 1995). Their catastrophic cognitions may reveal fear of heart disease and death despite reassurance that they are healthy (Bass 1991).

Interventions

Once panic disorder has been diagnosed in the medical setting, the physician or other provider has a unique opportunity to intervene. A growing percentage of patients with anxiety are treated in primary care settings (Valente 1996). Brief psychological interventions and medications can be provided. When the condition needs more targeted treatment, the client can be referred to a trained mental health provider.

Why Physicians May Need to Intervene

We are now in the era of managed care, which in many cases severely curtails access to mental health services, and limits the range of treatment options (Olfson et al. 1995). Although patients may be referred to group therapy or to self-help groups, or for up to ten sessions of individual psychotherapy (often provided by master's-level therapists), according to Menninger (1995) the result of such policies is that psychiatric treatment is now limited essentially to the prescription of medications. In fact, primary care physicians, the first point of contact for many patients with panic disorder, often initiate or refer for medication treatment, usually long before referral to a cognitive-behavior therapist is made (Otto et al. 1994; Otto and Whittal 1995). Gerdes et al. (1995) note that from 1980 to 1990, there was a significant increase in pharmacological interventions for patients with panic disorder by psychiatric consultants. Although many outpatients in 1990 were encouraged to seek psychotherapy, 100 percent were advised to take psychotropic medication.

In contrast to the above reality, Deans and Skinner (1992) found in their interviews with general practitioners and trainees that most thought that counseling would be as effective as benzodiazepines. It was widely recognized that employing counselors and clinical psychologists to deal with anxiety problems encountered in primary care is very helpful. Pollard and Lewis (1989) concluded that acute pharmacologic intervention is often less crucial than psychological intervention, even for patients coming to the emergency room with panic attacks. Furthermore, a number of panic management techniques can be taught to the patient even in an emergency situation.

Implications for Primary Care Physicians

When patients visit their doctors for general physical exams, tests, and procedures, and follow-up visits for medical conditions, they often mention their anxiety symptoms only as an afterthought. Many patients with panic disorder will report the same or similar symptoms on several visits. Often, physicians do not have the time to elicit more information or to record these symptoms in the patient's chart (Kroenke 1992). Nonetheless, primary care physicians need to recognize panic disorder and other anxiety disorder symptoms. Traditionally, primary care physicians prescribe sedative hypnotics for anxiety symptoms, but these are ineffective in panic disorder and may even worsen a concurrent depression.

Those primary care physicians who have a more complete understanding of panic and anxiety provide more appropriate treatment and far fewer extraneous tests to these patients. Generally, an ongoing relationship with the patient provides more opportunity for collaborative care. Shear and Schulberg (1995) recommend assessing anxiety and depressive symptomatology at each primary care visit. These visits can cover general counseling and medication management. Sorby, Reavley, and Huber (1991) developed a booklet on anxiety management, *Anxiety: An Explanation and Self-Help Manual*, which they give to their clients in primary care and they spend about ten minutes explaining it. They found that clients who used the booklet benefited in about two weeks, showing a reduction in generalized anxiety and panic.

Health Education departments have become commonplace, especially in HMOs, and they may be particularly helpful if they offer materials and relevant classes on how to deal with anxiety and panic problems. Other patients may require a referral to a mental health professional, particularly if their fear of panics is extreme, if they have seen a provider for the same problems previously, if they are under significant stress, or if agoraphobia has set in. The physician's challenge is to identify those who would benefit from information/guidance/psychoeducational classes on the one hand, and those who need psychiatric/psychological intervention on the other. The two are not mutually exclusive, but can complement and build on each other.

Implications for Emergency Room Physicians

In many cases, panic patients who go to the emergency room are just beginning to experience panic attacks, thus providing a unique opportunity to prevent a more chronic course of the panic disorder (Swinson, Soulios, Cox, et al. 1992c).

In their review of a number of studies, Pollard and Lewis (1989) found that although many patients go to the emergency room with anxiety and panic attacks, they are less likely to be referred for psychiatric consultation and treatment than are patients with depression and schizophrenia. The "out of the blue" panic attack prompts many patients to visit the emergency room, but by the time they get there, the peak has often subsided. The physician reports negative test results and alludes to "stress" or a "nervous condition," and the patients often leave more apprehensive and discouraged than before their arrival. Also, they are often given tranquilizers. Without a diagnosis of a physical illness, these individuals become even more concerned that there is something really wrong with them. This is often followed by more health care visits and unnecessary medical tests.

Pollard and Lewis (1989) make the following recommendations:

1. Take a careful history and pay close attention to the symptoms to determine which laboratory tests are indicated.

2. Question the patient to determine the presence of panic disorder:
   - Is the patient afraid of losing control or of dying during an attack?
   - Is there a family history of anxiety disorders?
   - Is there avoidance of places or activities due to fear?
   - Does the patient feel safer in the emergency room or with significant others?
   - Has the patient experienced recent stressful life events? Because of the "spontaneity" of the attacks, patients often do not, on their own, associate the attacks with stress.

The first goal of the intervention should be to assist the patient to reduce his or her acute anxiety. Swinson et al. (1992c) in their study provided a brief intervention either before the patient left the emergency room or within two days after the emergency room visit. They compared a brief intervention of reassurance versus exposure instructions. Patients in the exposure group were told that a particularly effective way of coping with their fear was to return to the place of their first attack. They were encouraged to return as soon as possible and to stay in the situation until the anxiety decreased. Although each person was given only a one-hour individual session, on follow-up assessments three and six months later, the exposure group did much better than the reassurance group.

As mentioned earlier, acute pharmacologic intervention is not always necessary but psychological intervention can be crucial. If severe anxiety persists in spite of brief psychological intervention, a medication such as a benzodiazepine can be prescribed. Pollard and Lewis recommend one or two oral doses of diazepam (5 to 10 mg), lorazepam (0.5 to 2 mg), or alprazolam (0.25 to 1.0 mg). They further recommend a maximum three-day supply of benzodiazepines. Educational materials are helpful, as well as a referral to a mental health provider, preferably someone who specializes in anxiety disorders.

Brief Psychological Intervention

Psychological interventions should include education about panic attacks and some basic cognitive and behavioral techniques (Pollard and Lewis 1989). Patients with panic attacks benefit enormously from receiving timely, relevant information on what panics are; they do not benefit from vague references to "a stress condition." Hyperventilation can be explained and basic diaphragmatic breathing can be taught. Furthermore, the client can be helped to distinguish between sensations and catastrophic thoughts, i.e., feared consequences. Short-term counseling can be provided by physician assistants, nurses, and social workers, functioning as physician aides (Olfson et al. 1995; Shear and Schulberg 1995).

1. **Hyperventilation Test and Breathing Retraining**
   Some of the patients complaining of chest pain, shortness of breath, smothering sensations, light-headedness, dizziness, feelings of unreality, blurred vision, and tingling sensations in the extremities, may be chronically or acutely hyperventilating. The signs to look for are short breaths from the upper chest, sighs and gasping, deep respirations, chest wall tenderness, and frequent throat clearing (Bass 1991; Katon 1989; Tavel 1990). Hyperventilation is a common and treatable condition.
   The steps involved in the assessment and amelioration of hyperventilation are as follow:
   - Explain that you suspect there might be an overbreathing condition causing some of the symptoms. You are not certain, however, and a simple test will help clarify this. (I do not label this hyperventilation at this time, so as not to unduly alarm the client because of the connotations of the word). Counterindications for hyperventilation are discussed in chapter 4.

   - Do an overbreathing test from one-and-one-half to three minutes. Have your patient breathe deeply through the mouth, as if panting, but a little slower. Have him or her make the breath audible. Stand and join your patient in taking a few breaths. Then, once you have corrected your patient's breathing, tell him or her that you will begin timing and that you will also do the breathing for a short while. Ask him or her to pay full attention to the sensations reported. If the patient seems to be slowing down, encourage them to continue for the time indicated.

• When the time is up, tell the patient to stop, and question him or her about the sensations. Then, point to any similarities and differences from the panic sensations reported.

• Next, teach diaphragmatic breathing (see page 65).

• Advise the patient to practice diaphragmatic breathing daily. You may add that although not all the symptoms will disappear, it may help his or her condition somewhat. Propose a follow-up appointment within two weeks to assess progress.

• At the next session, check on the patient's breathing. If the person is doing it correctly and has derived any benefit, encourage him or her to extend the practices to daily life as described on page 67.

2. **Catastrophic Automatic Thoughts Need to Be Recognized and Distinguished from Uncomfortable but Harmless Sensations.**
Some people fear extreme consequences. However, light-headedness and dizziness in panic rarely lead to fainting; palpitations do not lead to heart attacks; trembling or tingling extremities do not lead to loss of control of the limbs; racing thoughts do not lead to insanity, and so forth.

3. **Exposure Is Crucial.**
An effective way to master fear is to return as soon as possible to the place of the first or worst attack, and to stay there until the anxiety has diminished. Likewise, if there is a tendency to avoid places, situations, or activities, patients need to purposefully and frequently expose themselves to such situations. Confrontation with the feared object or situation brings mastery and raises self-confidence.

4. **For More Extensive Interventions, Consult the Rest of This Book or Consider a Referral to a Mental Health Professional Specializing in Anxiety Disorders.**
For a full description and recommendation regarding medications, see chapter 10. Katon's *Panic Disorder in the Medical Setting* (1989) is another source for medication information.

Summary

Unrecognized panic disorder in the medical setting often results in repeated utilization of medical services. Nonetheless, panic disorder is challenging to diagnose, because it presents with symptoms that are identical or similar to those of a number of medical and other psychological conditions. Frequently, the end result is that the condition becomes more chronic and costly.

A few targeted questions can help determine the presence of panic disorder and aid in differentiating it from medical illnesses. There are some psychological interventions that can be applied and some medications that can be prescribed. Finally, referral to a mental health professional specializing in anxiety disorders may be indicated.

Appendix A: Worksheets

Worksheet 1: **Panic Frequency and Intensity**

Name: _____   Month & Year: _____

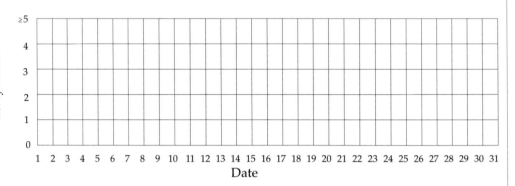

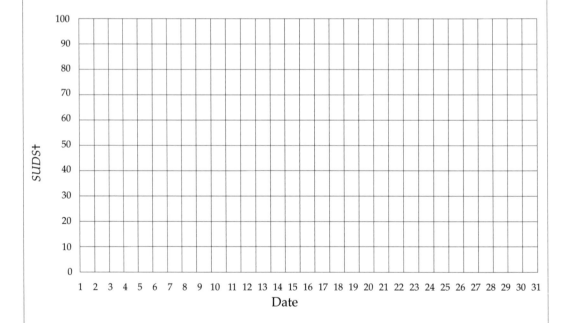

*   Panic is defined here as a very sudden, intense surge of fear.

†   If one or more panics, rate highest SUDS. SUDS: Subjective Units of Anxiety-Distress Scale. 0 = Totally calm,

no anxiety or fear. 50 = Moderate level of anxiety/fear. 100 = Intolerable level of anxiety/fear.

Worksheet 2: **My Personal Coping Affirmations**

1. _____

2. _____

3. _____

4. _____

5. _____

6. _____

7. _____

8. _____

9. _____

10. _____

Worksheet 3: **The Components of a Panic Attack**

Event/Situation: _____ Date: _____ Put each component of the specific panic attack or fearful event on a separate line.	State if P, C, B: Physiological, Cognitive, or Behavioral
1. _____	
2. _____	
3. _____	
4. _____	
5. _____	
6. _____	
7. _____	

Event/Situation: _____ Date: _____ Put each component of the specific panic attack or fearful event on a separate line.	State if P, C, B: Physiological, Cognitive, or Behavioral
1. _____	
2. _____	
3. _____	
4. _____	
5. _____	
6. _____	
7. _____	

Worksheet 4: Challenging Automatic Thoughts, 1st Step

1. Date.

2. Specific Trigger: **Situation and/or physical symptom.**

3. Automatic Thought (Negative Thought). **The *exact* bad thing that will happen if you feel or do** (write #2 here): _____
   is:

   How strongly do you believe your Automatic Thought will happen, 0–100%? _____

Worksheet 4: Challenging Automatic Thoughts, 1st Step

1. Date.

2. Specific Trigger: **Situation and/or physical symptom.**

3. Automatic Thought (Negative Thought). **The *exact* bad thing that will happen if you feel or do** (write #2 here): _____
   is:

   How strongly do you believe your Automatic Thought will happen, 0–100%? _____

Worksheet 4: **Challenging Automatic Thoughts**

---

1. Date.

---

2. Specific Trigger: **Situation and/or physical symptom.**

---

3. Automatic Thought (Negative Thought). **The *exact* bad thing that will happen if you feel or do** (write #2 here): _____
   is:

   How strongly do you believe your Automatic Thought will happen, 0–100%? _____

---

4. My Evidence. **Why do you think #3, your Automatic Thought, will happen?**

   Then Refute!

---

5. Alternative Thought(s) (Positive Thought). **Can the trigger** (#2 above) **have an explanation/lead to something** (other than #3) **with a harmless result?** List 1–3 with the probability of each, from 0–100%.

---

6. Face Up to Automatic Thought (#3). **"Just because _____ does not mean _____"** or **"So what if _____!"**

   How strongly do you believe in your Automatic Thought (#3) NOW, 0–100%? _____

Worksheet 5: Unfolding the Belief

Automatic Thought

**Unfolding the Belief
(top down)**

Worksheet 6: **Core Belief Log**

1. Old Core Belief.

2. Why I want to change my old Core Belief.

3. New Core Belief (State a core belief that is more user-friendly).

4. List Current and Future Experiences (however small) that Support the New Core
   Belief.

   Date   **Experiences**

This list is to be continued for a number of months to really affect change.

Worksheet 7: Interoceptive Exposure Record

Name: _____ Date _____

SUDS: Subjective Units of Anxiety-
Distress Scale

0 = Totally calm, no anxiety/fear
50 = Moderate level of anxiety/fear
100 = Intolerable level of anxiety/fear

Exercise	Describe Any Sensations Felt	SUDS	Check if SUDS≥20
Shake head, 30 sec.			
Head down, 1.5 min.			
Run in place, 1 min.			
Body tension, 1 min.			
Hold breath, 30 sec.			
Spin, 1 min.			
Straw breathing, 2 min.			
Hyperventilation, 1.5 min.			
Throat pressure, 1 min.			
Stare at spot, 2 min.			
Quick swallowing, 4 times			
Sensation in imagery, 2 min.			

Worksheet 8: **Repeating Interoceptive Exercises**

Name of person doing the exercises: _____

Use this column first

Date	Exercise being worked on	SUDS

Then use this column

Date	Exercise being worked on	SUDS

COACH: Guide the person doing the exercises.

Before exercise:
- Allow yourself to feel the sensations fully; pay attention to them.

After exercise:
- What was your SUDS level?
- What was going on in your mind, your thoughts/images?
Challenge any negative Automatic Thoughts/Images!
- What is your evidence that _____ would happen?
- What are alternative thoughts (positive thoughts)?
If lower SUDS than previously:
- What do you think you are learning?

Repeat exercise till SUDS is less than 20. Stop any given exercise after three trials. Repeat exercise on other days, in other places.

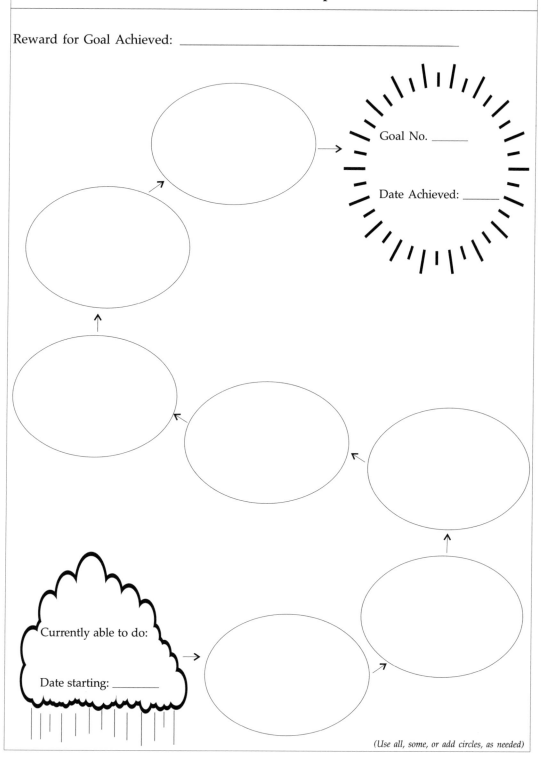

Worksheet 9: **Goal and the Steps to Achieve It**

Reward for Goal Achieved: _____

Goal No. _____

Date Achieved: _____

Currently able to do:

Date starting: _____

(Use all, some, or add circles, as needed)

Therapist Record 9T: **Tracking Goal Progress**

Check if Progress Made on Goals

Name	Goals	Treatment Weeks															
		1	2	3	4	5	6	7	8	9	10	11	12	13	14	15	16

Worksheet 10: **Your Weekly Exposures**

Goals:
1. _____
2. _____
3. _____
4. _____
5. _____
6. _____
7. _____
8. _____

Week Starting	Planned Exposures		Actual Effort	
	Steps	Distance/Time No. attempts per week	Steps	Distance/Time No. attempts per week

For every step, record: Distance covered or Time, and Number of attempts per week.

Therapist Record 10T: **Tracking Client's Weekly Exposures**

Week Starting: _____

Name	Planned Exposures		Actual Effort	
	Steps	Distance/Time No. attempts per week	Steps	Distance/Time No. attempts per week

Appendix B: Assessment Form

There are specific questions that must be answered in order to assess panic disorder. I have found the *Anxiety Disorders Interview Schedule for DSM-IV* (*ADIS-IV*, DiNardo, Brown, and Barlow 1994) particularly useful for designing the questions for my initial interview. I have used this assessment form in my interviews for a decade and am providing you with the latest version. However, it should not be confused with the *ADIS-IV*, in that it is not an instrument that has been researched and shown to have a certain level of reliability and validity.

The questions in this form are to be used by *the therapist* for assessing panic disorder. They should not be given to the client to fill out. As you gain more experience with this highly specific mode of interviewing, you will soon detect when there is confusion with a question and how to clarify it.

The idea to elicit belief ratings of central (focal) fears during the assessment (see question 8b) for later comparison comes from Cox (1996). The scores you get can later be nicely compared with belief ratings obtained during the cognitive restructuring work (see chapter 5, Belief Ratings—IV).

Panic/Phobia Assessment*

NAME: _____ DATE: _____

DoB: _____ AGE: _____ ADDRESS: _____

PHONE: Home ( ) _____ Work ( ) _____

Please tell me *in just a few words* what brings you to see me. _____

_____

_____

Now I would like to ask you some very specific questions, and I'll ask you more details about the above.

PANIC DISORDER

Panic Attacks

   1a. Have you *ever* had an anxiety episode that was very intense and came on suddenly, like a sudden, intense rush?

   b. How long does it take from the beginning of the symptoms until they reach a peak? (Must be within 10 minutes)

   2. During these sudden attacks, have you experienced any of the following symptoms? (These questions don't pertain to other states of high anxiety, when you might feel similar symptoms)

Symptom	No	Mild	Moderate	Severe
Shortness of breath/smothering	___	___	___	___
Choking sensations	___	___	___	___
Chest pain or discomfort	___	___	___	___
Palpitations/pounding heart	___	___	___	___
Dizziness/light-headedness/faint feelings	___	___	___	___
Hot or cold flushes	___	___	___	___
Sweating	___	___	___	___
Trembling or shaking	___	___	___	___
Numbness or tingling	___	___	___	___
Nausea/abdominal distress (lavatory use?)	___	___	___	___
Feelings of unreality/depersonalization	___	___	___	___
Fear of dying	___	___	___	___
Fear of going crazy or losing control	___	___	___	___
Other _____	___	___	___	___

---

* Adapted from *Anxiety Disorders Interview Schedule for DSM-IV* (*ADIS-IV*, DiNardo, Brown, and Barlow 1994). Copyright ©1987 by Graywind Publications, Inc. Reproduced by permission of publisher, The Psychological Corporation. All rights reserved.

Name: _____

First Panic

3a. When did you have your *very first* panic attack, the first one in your life, and what happened?

  b. Were you going through any unusual stress just prior to that event?

Panic Disorder

4. In what situations have you had these sudden, intense panic attacks?

5. Have they ever come unexpectedly, totally out of the blue?
   If Yes: How often have they occurred unexpectedly?

   Have you ever awakened in panic from sleep, other than from a nightmare?

6. Have you gone to an Emergency Room or sought other medical help because of these attacks? _____ If Yes: What did the physician tell you?

7. Are the panics worse now or were they worse in the past?

   At their worst, how frequent are/were the attacks?

Fear Cognitions, Safety Signals/Behaviors

8a. Do you fear these attacks a lot?

    What is your worst fear during these attacks? (Usually one, sometimes two or three are given)

  b. On a scale from 0 to 100% (0% = You don't believe at all it will happen, 100% = You believe absolutely it will happen, and any number in between), how strongly do you believe _____ will happen?
   Fear _____% Fear _____% Fear _____%

  c. This fear (*repeat the above-stated fear*, e.g., "of heart attack"), what leads you to believe it will happen?

9a. What do you do then to help yourself? (For example, do you sit, stand, walk, talk in a certain way?)

  b. Do you carry with you things that can save you, or do you bring another person along? (Medications, water?)

  c. Do these things work, i.e., do they stop the worst in a panic from happening?

Name: _____

PHOBIAS

10a. Do you have *any* phobias? That is, are there situations you *avoid* because of fear or do you do them anyway, *with fear*? (E.g., driving, being a passenger in a car or bus, going to grocery stores or malls, crowds, airplanes, elevators, being at home alone, movies, tunnels, bridges, restaurants, parties) Check also for social and specific phobias.

  b. Which was your very first phobia, and when did it start?

11. Do you worry *a great deal* about saying or doing something embarrassing or humiliating, or that others may think badly of you?

Fear Cognitions, Safety Signals/Behaviors in Phobic Situations

12. What are you afraid will happen in (list a few of the phobic situations mentioned)?

Situation	Fear
_____	_____
_____	_____
_____	_____

13. How do you attempt to cope? (What actions do you engage in to help you deal with the fearful situation/activity?)

OCD & GAD

15. Do you have any rituals in thought or behavior that you tend to repeat/that feel intrusive? (Recurrent, intrusive thoughts, doing things over and over, e.g. counting, checking, washing repeatedly)

16a. Aside from panic and phobias, do you worry *excessively* about things?
    If Yes: About what?

    Do you worry too much about really *small* things?

  b. Do you feel tense and stressed for *no* apparent reason?

  c. Do you have symptoms with your general anxiety? (Tenseness, restlessness, irritability, easily fatigued, difficulty concentrating)

  d. Do you consider the tendency to worry and your general nervousness to be a significant problem?
    If Yes: Since when? (See if it coincides with first panic)

Name: _____

DEPRESSION

17a. Have there been any changes in your appetite or weight *recently*?

How is your sleep?

b. Do you feel currently depressed, sad, hopeless, or have you lost interest in many of your usual activities?

c. Do you feel that your thinking has slowed down or it is hard to make decisions?

d. Do you blame yourself a lot or feel guilty?

e. Are you down on yourself or feel like a failure?

18. Do you have thoughts and plans to harm yourself? No _____ Yes _____

Anyone else? No _____ Yes _____

19. What do you think is the reason for feeling so low? (Secondary to panics?)

PHYSICAL HEALTH

20a. When did you have your last physical exam?
Do you have any health problems now that you are aware of?

b. What medications and how much do you take now?

21. How often do you drink alcohol/take drugs?

Excessive use of alcohol or drugs in the past?

Coffee with caffeine?   Other caffeinated drinks daily?   Smoke?

TREATMENTS

22a. Have you had any treatment for your panic/phobias before, including medications?

b. Have you had any other psychotherapy or counseling?

23. Has anyone in your family (blood relatives) suffered form anxiety, depression, alcohol or drug abuse, or other emotional problems? (Treatments/hospitalizations)

Name: _____

ADDITIONAL INFORMATION

24. Living conditions (Family life/Job)

25. Are you struggling with any particular stresses now?

26. Do you tend to be assertive? (Stand up for yourself, say "no" to people when you need to)

27. Do you have a support system?

    Do you exercise regularly?

28. Are there events from your childhood or adult life relevant to your fears and worries?

MSE:

Diagnosis:

Plan:

Meds by Dr: Interviewer:

References

Note: Öst is listed under the letter o; although in the Swedish alphabet it is listed after Z.

Acierno, R.E., Hersen, M., and Van Hasselt, V.B. 1993. "Interventions for Panic Disorder: A Critical Review of the Literature." *Clinical Psychology Review* 13:561–578.

Agras, W.S. 1993. "The Diagnosis and Treatment of Panic Disorder." *Annual Review of Medicine* 44:39–51.

Alexander, P.E. 1991. "Management of Panic Disorders." *Journal of Psychoactive Drugs* 23(4):329–333.

Alexander, P.E. 1992. "Treatment of Panic Disorder." *Rhode Island Medicine* 75:253–257.

American Psychiatric Association. 1980. *Diagnostic and Statistical Manual of Mental Disorders, Third Edition.* Washington, D.C.: American Psychiatric Association.

American Psychiatric Association. 1987. *Diagnostic and Statistical Manual of Mental Disorders, Third Edition, Revised.* Washington, D.C.: American Psychiatric Association.

American Psychiatric Association. 1994. *Diagnostic and Statistical Manual of Mental Disorders, Fourth Edition.* Washington, D.C.: American Psychiatric Association.

Antonuccio, D.O., Danton, W.G., and DeNelsky, G.Y. 1995. "Psychotherapy Versus Medication for Depression: Challenging the Conventional Wisdom with Data." *Professional Psychology: Research and Practice* 26(6):574–585.

Apfeldorf, W.J., Shear, M.K., Leon, A.C., and Portera, L. 1994. "A Brief Screen for Panic Disorder." *Journal of Anxiety Disorders* 8(1):71–78.

Argyle, N. 1988. "The Nature of Cognitions in Panic Disorder." *Behaviour Research and Therapy* 26(3):261–264.

Arntz, A., Rauner, M., and van den Hout, M. 1995. "'If I Feel Anxious, There Must Be Danger': Ex-Consequentia Reasoning in Inferring Danger in Anxiety Disorders." *Behaviour Research and Therapy* 33(8):917–925.

Asmundson, G.J.G., Norton, G.R., Wilson, K.G., and Sandler, L.S. 1994. "Subjective Symptoms and Cardiac Reactivity to Brief Hyperventilation in Individuals with High Anxiety Sensitivity." *Behaviour Research and Therapy* 32(2):237–241.

Asmundson, G.J.G. and Stein, M.B. 1994. "A Preliminary Analysis of Pulmonary Function in Panic Disorder: Implications for the Dyspnea-Fear Theory." *Journal of Anxiety Disorders* 8(1):63–69.

Bach, M., Nutzinger, D.O., and Hartl, L. 1996. "Comorbidity of Anxiety Disorders and Hypochondriasis Considering Different Diagnostic Systems." *Comprehensive Psychiatry* 37(1):62–67.

Bakish, D., Saxena, B.M., Bowen, R., and D'Souza J. 1993. "Reversible Monoamine Oxidase-A Inhibitors in Panic Disorder." *Clinical Neuropharmacology* 16(Suppl. 2):S77–S82.

Ball, S.G., and Otto, M.W. 1994. "Cognitive-Behavioral Treatment of Choking Phobia: 3 Case Studies." *Psychotherapy Psychosomatics* 62:207–211

Ballenger, J.C. and Fyer, A.J. 1993. "Examining Criteria for Panic Disorder." *Hospital and Community Psychiatry* 44(3):226–228.

Ballenger, J.C., Pecknold, J., Rickels, K., and Sellers, E.M. 1993. "Medication Discontinuation in Panic Disorder." *Journal of Clinical Psychiatry* 54(10, Suppl.):15–21.

Bandura, A. 1977. "Self-Efficacy: Toward a Unifying Theory of Behavioral Change." *Psychological Review* 84(2):191–215.

Bandura, A. 1988. "Self-Efficacy Conception of Anxiety." *Anxiety Research* 1:77–98.

Barlow, D.H. 1986. "Behavioral Conception and Treatment of Panic." *Psychopharmacology Bulletin* 22(3):802–806.

Barlow, D.H. 1988. *Anxiety and Its Disorders: The Nature and Treatment of Anxiety and Panic.* New York: The Guilford Press.

Barlow, D.H. 1990. "Long-Term Outcome for Patients with Panic Disorder Treated with Cognitive-Behavioral Therapy." *Journal of Clinical Psychiatry* 51(12, Suppl. A):17–23.

Barlow, D.H. 1996. "Health Care Policy, Psychotherapy Research, and the Future of Psychotherapy." *American Psychologist* 51(10):1050–1058.

Barlow, D.H. 1997. "Cognitive-Behavioral Therapy for Panic Disorder: Current Status," and "Discussion: Cognitive-Behavioral Therapy." *Journal of Clinical Psychiatry* 58(Suppl. 2):32–37.

Barlow, D.H. and Craske, M.G. 1994. *Mastery of Your Anxiety and Panic II.* San Antonio, TX: Graywind Publications/The Psychological Corporation.

Barlow, D.H., Craske, M.G., Cerny, J.A., and Klosko, J.S. 1989. "Behavioral Treatment of Panic Disorder." *Behavior Therapy* 20:261–282.

Barlow, D.H., Vermilyea, J., Blanchard, E.B., Vermilyea, B.B., DiNardo, P.A., and Cerny, J.A. 1985. "The Phenomenon of Panic." *Journal of Abnormal Psychology* 94:320–328.

Barsby, M.J. 1997. "The Control of Hyperventilation in the Management of 'Gagging.'" *British Dental Journal* 182(3):109–111.

Barsky, A.J., Barnett, M.C., and Cleary, P.D. 1994. "Hypochondriasis and Panic Disorder. Boundary and Overlap." *Archives of General Psychiatry* 51(11):918–925.

Başoğlu, M. 1992. "Pharmacological and Behavioural Treatment of Panic Disorder." *Psychotherapy Psychosomatics* 58:57–59.

Başoğlu, M., Marks, I.M., Kiliç, C., Brewin, C.R., and Swinson, R.P. 1994a. "Alprazolam and Exposure for Panic Disorder With Agoraphobia: Attribution of Improvement to Medication Predicts Subsequent Relapse." *British Journal of Psychiatry* 164:652–659.

Başoğlu, M., Marks, I.M., Kiliç, C., Swinson, R.P., Noshirvani, H., Kuch, K., and O'Sullivan, G. 1994b. "Relationship of Panic, Anticipatory Anxiety, Agoraphobia and Global Improvement in Panic Disorder With Agoraphobia Treated with Alprazolam and Exposure." *British Journal of Psychiatry* 164:647–652.

Başoğlu, M., Marks, I.M., and Şengün, S. 1992. "A Prospective Study of Panic and Anxiety in Agoraphobia With Panic Disorder." *British Journal of Psychiatry* 160:57–64.

Başoğlu, M., Marks, I.M., Swinson, R.P., Noshirvani, H., O'Sullivan, G., and Kuch, K. 1994c. "Pre-Treatment Predictors of Treatment Outcome in Panic Disorder and Agoraphobia Treated with Alprazolam and Exposure." *Journal of Affective Disorders* 30:123–132.

Bass, C. 1991. "Unexplained Chest Pain and Breathlessness." *Medical Clinics of North America* 75(5):1157–1173.

Baxter, L.R., Schwartz, J.M., Bergman, K.S., Szuba, M.P., Guze, B.H., Mazziotta, J.C., Alazraki, A., Selin, C.E., Ferng, H.-K., Munford, P., and Phelps, M.E. 1992. "Caudate Glucose Metabolic Rate Changes with Both Drug and Behavior Therapy for Obsessive-Compulsive Disorder." *Archives of General Psychiatry* 49:681–689.

Beck, A.T. and Emery, G., with Greenberg, R.L. 1985. *Anxiety Disorders and Phobias: A Cognitive Perspective*. New York: Basic Books.

Beck, A.T., Epstein, N., Brown, G., and Steer, R.A. 1988. "An Inventory for Measuring Clinical Anxiety: Psychometric Properties." *Journal of Consulting and Clinical Psychology* 56(6):893–897.

Beck, A.T., Sokol, L., Clark, D.A., Berchick, R., and Wright, F. 1992. "A Crossover Study of Focused Cognitive Therapy for Panic Disorder." *American Journal of Psychiatry* 149(6):778–783.

Beck, A.T., Ward, C.H., Mendelson, M., Mock, J., and Erbaugh, J. 1961. "An Inventory for Measuring Depression." *Archives of General Psychiatry* 4:561–571.

Beck, J.S. 1995. *Cognitive Therapy: Basics and Beyond*. New York: The Guilford Press.

Belfer, P.L., Munoz, L.S., Schachter, J., and Levendusky, P.G. 1995. "Cognitive-Behavioral Group Psychotherapy for Agoraphobia and Panic Disorder." *International Journal of Group Psychotherapy* 45(2):185–206.

Borkovec, T.D., Grayson, J.B., and Cooper, K.M. 1978. "Treatment of General Tension: Subjective and Physiological Effects of Progressive Relaxation." *Journal of Consulting and Clinical Psychology* 46(3):518–528.

Brandt, T. 1996. "Phobic Postural Vertigo." *Neurology* 46:1515–1519.

Brown, C.S., Rakel, R.E., Wells, B.G., Downs, J.M., and Akiskal, H.S. 1991. "A Practical Update on Anxiety Disorders and Their Pharmacologic Treatment." *Archives of Internal Medicine* 151:873–884.

Brown, T.A. and Barlow, D.H. 1992. "Comorbidity Among Anxiety Disorders: Implications for Treatment and DSM-IV." *Journal of Consulting and Clinical Psychology* 60(6):835–844.

Brown, T.A. and Barlow, D.H. 1995. "Long-Term Outcome in Cognitive-Behavioral Treatment of Panic Disorder: Clinical Predictors and Alternative Strategies for Assessment." *Journal of Consulting and Clinical Psychology* 63(5):754–765.

Bruce, T.J., Spiegel, D.A., Gregg, S.F., and Nuzzarello, A. 1995. "Predictors of Alprazolam Discontinuation With and Without Cognitive Behavior Therapy in Panic Disorder." *American Journal of Psychiatry* 152(8):1156–1160.

Budman, S.H., Demby, A., Redondo, J.P., Hannan, M., Feldstein, M., Ring, J., and Springer, T. 1988. "Comparative Outcome in Time-Limited Individual and Group Psychotherapy." *International Journal of Group Psychotherapy* 38(1):63–86.

Burns, D.D. 1989. *The Feeling Good Handbook*. New York: William Morrow & Co.

Burns, D.D. 1997. *Therapist's Toolkit: State-of-the-Art Assessment Tools for the Mental Health Professional*. Dr. Burns, 11987 Murietta Lane, Los Altos Hills, CA 94022.

Butler, P.E. 1981. *Self-Assertion for Women*. San Francisco: Harper & Row Publishers.

Carr, R.E., Lehrer, P.M., and Hochron, S.M. 1995. "Predictors of Panic-Fear in Asthma." *Health Psychology* 14(5):421–426.

Carr, R.E., Lehrer, P.M., Hochron, S.M., and Jackson, A. 1996. "Effect of Psychological Stress on Airway Impedance in Individuals with Asthma and Panic Disorder." *Journal of Abnormal Psychology* 105(1):137–141.

Carr, R.E., Lehrer, P.M., Rausch, L.L., and Hochron, S.M. 1994. "Anxiety Sensitivity and Panic Attacks in an Asthmatic Population." *Behaviour Research and Therapy* 32(4):411–418.

Carter, C., Maddock, R., Amsterdam, E., McCormick, S., Waters, C., and Billett, J. 1992. "Panic Disorder and Chest Pain in the Coronary Care Unit." *Psychosomatics* 33(3):302–309.

Carter, M.M., Hollon, S.D., Carson, R., and Shelton, R.C. 1995. "Effects of a Safe Person on Induced Distress Following a Biological Challenge in Panic Disorder With Agoraphobia." *Journal of Abnormal Psychology* 104(1):156–163.

Chambless, D.L., Caputo, G.C., Jasin, S.E., Gracely, E.J., and Williams, C. 1985. "The Mobility Inventory for Agoraphobia." *Behaviour Research and Therapy* 23(1):35–44.

Chambless, D.L. and Gillis, M.M. 1993. "Cognitive Therapy of Anxiety Disorders." *Journal of Consulting and Clinical Psychology* 61(2):248–260.

Charney, D.S. and Woods, S.W. 1989. "Benzodiazepine Treatment of Panic Disorder: A Comparison of Alprazolam and Lorazepam." *Journal of Clinical Psychiatry* 50(11):418–423.

Clark, D.B., Hirsch, B.E., Smith, M.G., Furman, J.M.R., and Jacob, R.G. 1994. "Panic in Otolaryngology Patients Presenting with Dizziness and Hearing Loss." *American Journal of Psychiatry* 151(8):1223–1225.

Clark, D.M. 1986. "A Cognitive Approach to Panic." *Behaviour Research and Therapy* 24(4):461–470.

Clark, D.M. 1989. "Anxiety States: Panic and Generalized Anxiety." In: *Cognitive Behaviour Therapy for Psychiatric Problems: A Practical Guide*. Eds. K. Hawton, P.M. Salkovskis, J. Kirk, and D.M. Clark. New York: Oxford University Press.

Clark, D.M. 1993. "Cognitive Mediation of Panic Attacks Induced by Biological Challenge Tests." *Advances in Behavior Research and Therapy* 15:75–84.

Clark, D.M. and Ehlers, A. 1993. "An Overview of the Cognitive Theory and Treatment of Panic Disorder." *Applied and Preventive Psychology* 2:131–139.

Clark, D.M., Salkovskis, P.M., Hackmann, A., Middleton, H., Anastasiades, P., and Gelder, M. 1994. "A Comparison of Cognitive Therapy, Applied Relaxation and Imipramine in the Treatment of Panic Disorder." *British Journal of Psychiatry* 164:759–769.

Clum, G.A. 1989. "Psychological Interventions vs. Drugs in the Treatment of Panic." *Behavior Therapy* 20:429–457.

Clum, G.A. and Knowles, S.L. 1991. "Why Do Some People with Panic Disorders Become Avoidant?: A Review." *Clinical Psychology Review* 11:295–313.

Cohen, S.I. 1995. "Alcohol and Benzodiazepines Generate Anxiety, Panic and Phobias." *Journal of the Royal Society of Medicine* 88:73–77.

Coupland, N.J., Bell, C.J., and Potokar, J.P. 1996. "Serotonin Reuptake Inhibitor Withdrawal." *Journal of Clinical Psychopharmacology* 16:356–362.

Cowley, D.S. 1992. "Alcohol Abuse, Substance Abuse, and Panic Disorder." *American Journal of Medicine* 92(Suppl. 1A):41–48.

Cox, B.J. 1996. "The Nature and Assessment of Catastrophic Thoughts in Panic Disorder." *Behaviour Research and Therapy* 34(4):363–374.

Cox, B.J., Endler, N.S., and Swinson, R.P. 1995. "An Examination of Levels of Agoraphobic Severity in Panic Disorder." *Behaviour Research and Therapy* 33(1):57–62.

Cox, B.J. and Swinson, R.P. 1994. "Overprediction of Fear in Panic Disorder With Agoraphobia." *Behaviour Research and Therapy* 32(7):735–739.

Cox, B.J., Swinson, R.P., and Endler, N.S. 1991a. "A Review of the Psychopharmacology of Panic Disorder: Individual Differences and Non-Specific Factors." *Canadian Journal of Psychiatry* 36:130–138.

Cox, B.J., Swinson, R.P., Endler, N.S., and Norton, G.R. 1994. "The Symptom Structure of Panic Attacks." *Comprehensive Psychiatry* 35(5):349–353.

Cox, B.J., Swinson, R.P., Kuch, K., and Reichman, J.T. 1993a. "Dimensions of Agoraphobia Assessed by the Mobility Inventory." *Behaviour Research and Therapy* 31(4)427–431.

Cox, B.J., Swinson, R.P., and Shaw, B.F. 1991b. "Value of the Fear Questionnaire in Differentiating Agoraphobia and Social Phobia." *British Journal of Psychiatry* 159:842–845.

Cox, B.J., Swinson, R.P., Shulman, I.D., Kuch, K., and Reichman, J.T. 1993b. "Gender Effects and Alcohol Use in Panic Disorder With Agoraphobia." *Behaviour Research and Therapy* 31(4):413–416.

Craske, M.G. 1991a. "Phobic Fear and Panic Attacks: The Same Emotional States Triggered by Different Cues?" *Clinical Psychology Review* 11:599–620.

Craske, M.G. 1991b. "Models and Treatment of Panic: Behavioral Therapy of Panic." *Journal of Cognitive Psychotherapy: An International Quarterly* 5(3):199–214.

Craske, M.G. 1996. "An Integrated Treatment Approach to Panic Disorder." *Bulletin of the Menninger Clinic* 60(2, Suppl. A):A87–A104.

Craske, M.G. and Barlow, D.H. 1988. "A Review of the Relationship Between Panic and Avoidance." *Clinical Psychology Review* 8:667–685.

Craske, M.G. and Barlow, D.H. 1990. "Nocturnal Panic: Response to Hyperventilation and Carbon Dioxide Challenges." *Journal of Abnormal Psychology* 99(3):302–307.

Craske, M.G. and Barlow, D.H. 1993. "Panic Disorder and Agoraphobia." In: *Clinical Handbook of Psychological Disorders: A Step by Step Treatment Manual,* Second Edition. Ed. D.H. Barlow. New York: Guilford Press.

Craske, M.G. and Barlow, D.H. 1994. *Agoraphobia Supplement to the Mastery of Your Anxiety and Panic II (MAP II Program).* San Antonio, TX: Graywind Publications/The Psychological Corporation.

Craske, M.G., Brown, T.A., and Barlow, D.H. 1991. "Behavioral Treatment of Panic Disorder: A Two-Year Follow-Up." *Behavior Therapy* 22:289–304.

Craske, M.G. and Freed, S. 1995. "Expectations About Arousal and Noctural Panic." *Journal of Abnormal Psychology* 104(4):567–575.

Craske, M.G., Maidenberg, E., and Bystritsky, A. 1995. "Brief Cognitive-Behavioral Versus Nondirective Therapy for Panic Disorder." *Journal of Behavior Therapy and Experimental Psychiatry* 26(2):113–120.

Craske, M.G., Meadows, E., and Barlow, D.H. 1994. *Therapist's Guide for the Mastery of Your Anxiety and Panic II & Agoraphobia Supplement.* San Antonio, TX: Graywind Publications/The Psychological Corporation.

Craske, M.G. and Rodriguez, B.I. 1994. "Behavioral Treatment of Panic Disorders and Agoraphobia." *Progress in Behavior Modification* 29:1–26.

Cross-National Collaborative Panic Study, Second Phase Investigators. 1992. "Drug Treatment of Panic Disorder: Comparative Efficacy of Alprazolam, Imipramine, and Placebo." *British Journal of Psychiatry* 160:191–202.

Curran, H.V., Bond, A., O'Sullivan, G., Bruce, M., Marks, I., Lelliot, P., Shine, P., and Lader, M. 1994. "Memory Functions, Alprazolam and Exposure Therapy: A Controlled Longitudinal Study of Agoraphobia With Panic Disorder." *Psychological Medicine* 24:969–976.

Davis, M., Robbins-Eshelman, E., and McKay, M. 1995. *The Relaxation & Stress Reduction Workbook,* 4th Ed. Oakland: New Harbinger Publications.

Deans, H.G. and Skinner, P. 1992. "Doctors' Views on Anxiety Management in General Practice." *Journal of the Royal Society of Medicine* 85(2):83–86.

de Beurs, E., Garssen, B., Buikhuisen, M., Lange, A., van Balkom, A., and Van Dyck, R. 1994. "Continuous Monitoring of Panic." *Acta Psychiatrica Scandinavica* 90:38–45.

Dienstbier, R.A. 1989. "Arousal and Physiological Toughness: Implications for Mental and Physical Health." *Psychological Review* 96(1):84–100.

Dienstbier, R.A. 1991. "Acquiring Physiological Stress Resistance: The Toughness Model." Presented as an invited address to the International Congress on Stress, Anxiety, and Emotional Disorders at the Universidade do Minho in Braga, Portugal.

Dijkman-Caes, C.I.M., Kraan, H.F., and deVries, M.W. 1993. "Research on Panic Disorder and Agoraphobia in Daily Life: A Review of Current Studies." *Journal of Anxiety Disorders* 7:235–247.

DiNardo, P.A., Brown, T.A., and Barlow, D.H. 1994. *Anxiety Disorders Interview Schedule for DSM-IV (ADIS-IV).* San Antonio, TX: Graywind Publications/The Psychological Corporation.

Edelman, R.E. and Chambless, D.L. 1993. "Compliance During Sessions and Homework in Exposure-Based Treatment of Agoraphobia." *Behaviour Research and Therapy* 31(8):767–773.

Ehlers, A. 1993. "Interoception and Panic Disorder." *Advances in Behavior Research and Therapy* 15:3–21.

Ehlers, A. and Breuer, P. 1992. "Increased Cardiac Awareness in Panic Disorder." *Journal of Abnormal Psychology* 101(3):371–382.

Ehlers, A. and Breuer, P. 1996. "How Good are Patients with Panic Disorder at Perceiving Their Heartbeats?" *Biological Psychology* 42(1-2):165–182.

Ehlers, A., Breuer, P., Dohn, D., and Fiegenbaum, W. 1995. "Heartbeat Perception and Panic Disorder: Possible Explanations for Discrepant Findings." *Behaviour Research and Therapy* 33(1):69–76.

Ehlers, A., Margraf, J., Roth, W.T., Taylor, C.B., and Birbaumer, N. 1988. "Anxiety Induced by False Heart Rate Feedback in Patients with Panic Disorder." *Behaviour Research and Therapy* 26(1):1–11.

Eisenberg, L. 1992. "Treating Depression and Anxiety in Primary Care: Closing the Gap Between Knowledge and Practice." *New England Journal of Medicine* 326(16):1080–1084.

Epstein, S. 1994. "Integration of the Cognitive and the Psychodynamic Unconscious." *American Psychologist* 49(8):709–724.

Evans, L., Holt, C., and Oei, T.P.S. 1991. "Long Term Follow-Up of Agoraphobics Treated by Brief Intensive Group Cognitive Behavioural Therapy." *Australian and New Zealand Journal of Psychiatry* 25:343–349.

Faravelli, C., Pallanti, S., Biondi, F., Paterniti, S., and Scarpato, M.A. 1992. "Onset of Panic Disorder." *American Journal of Psychiatry* 149(6):827–828.

Fava, G.A. and Bruce, T.J. 1996. "Anxiety Sensitivity (letter)." *American Journal of Psychiatry* 153:1109–1110.

Fava, G.A., Grandi, S., Belluardo, P., Savron, G., Raffi, A.R., Conti, S., and Saviotti, F.M. 1994. "Benzodiazepines and Anxiety Sensitivity in Panic Disorder." *Progress in Neuro-Psychopharmacology and Biological Psychiatry* 18:1163–1168.

Fava, G.A., Grandi, S., Rafanelli, C., and Canestrari, R. 1992. "Prodromal Symptoms in Panic Disorder With Agoraphobia: A Replication Study." *Journal of Affective Disorders* 85:85–88.

Fava, G.A., Zielezny, M., Savron, G., and Grandi, S. 1995. "Long-Term Effects of Behavioural Treatment for Panic Disorder With Agoraphobia." *British Journal of Psychiatry* 166:87–92.

Fennell, M.J.V. 1989. "Depression." In: *Cognitive Behaviour Therapy for Psychiatric Problems: A Practical Guide.* Eds. K. Hawton, P.M. Salkovskis, J. Kirk, and D.M. Clark. New York: Oxford University Press.

Fiegenbaum, W. 1988. "Long-Term Efficacy of Ungraded Versus Graded Massed Exposure in Agoraphobics." In: *Panic and Phobias 2: Treatments and Variables Affecting Course and Outcome.* Eds. I. Hand and H.-U. Wittchen. New York: Springer-Verlag.

First, M., Gibbon, M., Spitzer, R.L., and Williams, J.B. 1996. *Structured Clinical Interview for DSM-IV, Axis I Disorders, Clinical Version.* Washington, D.C.: American Psychiatric Press.

Fleet, R.P., Dupuis, G., Marchand, A., Burelle, D., Arsenault, A., and Beitman, D.B. 1996. "Panic Disorder in Emergency Department Chest Pain Patients: Prevalence, Comorbidity, Suicidal Ideation, and Physician Recognition." *American Journal of Medicine* 101(4):371–380.

Foa, E.B. and Kozak, M.J. 1986. "Emotional Processing of Fear: Exposure to Corrective Information." *Psychological Bulletin* 99(1):20–35.

Fyer, A.J., Mannuzza, S., and Coplan, J.D. 1995. "Anxiety Disorders." In: *Comprehensive Textbook of Psychiatry/VI.* Eds. H.I. Kaplan and B.J. Sadock. Baltimore: Williams and Wilkins.

Garssen, B., de Ruiter, C., and van Dyck, R. 1992. "Breathing Retraining: A Rational Placebo?" *Clinical Psychology Review* 12:141–153.

Gerdes, T., Yates, W.R., and Clancy, G. 1995. "Increasing Identification and Referral of Panic Disorder Over the Past Decade." *Psychosomatics* 36(5):480–486.

Goisman, R.M., Warshaw, M.G., Peterson, L.G., Rogers, M.P., Cuneo, P., Hunt, M.F., Tomlin-Albanese, J.M., Kazim, A., Gollan, J.K., Epstein-Kaye, T., Reich, J.H., and Keller, M.B. 1994. "Panic, Agoraphobia, and Panic Disorder With Agoraphobia: Data From a Multicenter Anxiety Disorders Study." *Journal of Nervous and Mental Disease* 182(2):72–79.

Goisman, R.M., Warshaw, M.G., Steketee, G.S., Fierman, E.J., Rogers, M.P., Goldenberg, I., Weinshenker, N.J., Vasile, R.G., and Keller, M.B. 1995. "DSM-IV and the Disappearance of Agoraphobia Without a History of Panic Disorder: New Data on a Controversial Diagnosis." *American Journal of Psychiatry* 152(10):1438–1443.

Goldberg, R.J. 1988. "Clinical Presentations of Panic-Related Disorders." *Journal of Anxiety Disorders* 2:61–75.

Goldfried, M.R. and Wolfe, B.E. 1996. "Psychotherapy Practice and Research: Repairing a Strained Alliance." *American Psychologist* 51(10):1007–1016.

Goldstein, D.S. 1987. "Stress-Induced Activation of the Sympathetic Nervous System." *Bailliere's Clinical Endocrinology and Metabolism* 1(2):253–278.

Gorman, J.M., Liebowitz, M.R., Fyer, A.J., and Stein, J. 1989. "A Neuroanatomical Hypothesis for Panic Disorder." *American Journal of Psychiatry* 146(2):148–161.

Gould, R.A., Otto, M.W., and Pollack, M.H. 1995. "A Meta-Analysis of Treatment Outcome for Panic Disorder." *Clinical Psychology Review* 15(8):819–844.

Grayson, J.B., Foa, E.B., and Steketee, G. 1982. "Habituation During Exposure Treatment: Distraction vs Attention-Focusing." *Behaviour Research and Therapy* 20:323–328.

Greenberger, D. and Padesky, C.A. 1995. *Mind Over Mood: A Cognitive Therapy Treatment Manual for Clients.* New York: The Guilford Press.

Guyton, A.C. 1991. *Textbook of Medical Physiology.* Philadelphia: W.B. Saunders Co.

Hassan, R. and Pollard, C.A. 1994. "Late-Life-Onset Panic Disorder: Clinical and Demographic Characteristics of a Patient Sample." *Journal of Geriatric Psychiatry and Neurology* 7:84–88.

Hazen, A.L., Walker, J.R., and Eldridge, G.D. 1996. "Anxiety Sensitivity and Treatment Outcome in Panic Disorder." *Anxiety* 2:34–39.

Hecker, J.E. and Thorpe, G.L. 1992. *Agoraphobia and Panic: A Guide to Psychological Treatment.* Boston: Allyn and Bacon.

Herman, J.B., Rosenbaum, J.F., and Brotman, A.W. 1987. "The Alprazolam to Clonazepam Switch for the Treatment of Panic Disorder." *Journal of Clinical Psychopharmacology* 7:175–178.

Hoehn-Saric, R., McLeod, D.R., and Hipsley, P.A. 1993. "Effect of Fluvoxamine on Panic Disorder." *Journal of Clinical Psychopharamcology* 13(5):321–326.

Hoffart, A. 1993. "Cognitive Treatments of Agoraphobia: A Critical Evaluation of Theoretical Basis and Outcome Evidence." *Journal of Anxiety Disorders* 7:75–91.

Hoffart, A. 1995. "Cognitive Mediators of Situational Fear in Agoraphobia." *Journal of Behaviour Research and Experimental Psychiatry* 26(4):313–320.

Hoffart, A., Due-Madsen, J., Lande, B., Gude, T., Bille, H., and Torgersen, S. 1993. "Clomipramine in the Treatment of Agoraphobic Inpatients Resistant to Behavioral Therapy." *Journal of Clinical Psychiatry* 54(12):481–487.

Hoffart, A., Thornes, K., Hedley, L.M., and Strand, J. 1994. "DSM-III-R Axis I and II Disorders in Agoraphobic Patients With and Without Panic Disorder." *Acta Psychiatrica Scandinavica* 89:186–191.

Hoffman, D.L., O'Leary, D.P., and Munjack, D.J. 1994. "Autorotation Test Abnormalities of the Horizontal and Vertical Vestibulo-Ocular Reflexes in Panic Disorder." *Otolaryngology-Head and Neck Surgery* 110(3):259–269.

Hornsveld, H., Garssen, B., and van Spiegel, P. 1995. "Voluntary Hyperventilation: The Influence of Duration and Depth on the Development of Symptoms." *Biological Psychology* 40:299–312.

Horwath, E., Lish, J.D., Johnson, J., Hornig, C.D., and Weissman, M.M. 1993. "Agoraphobia Without Panic: Clinical Reappraisal of an Epidemiologic Finding." *American Journal of Psychiatry* 150(10):1496–1501.

Howard, K.I., Moras, K, Brill, P.L., Martinovich, Z., and Lutz, W. 1996. "Evaluation of Psychotherapy: Efficacy, Effectiveness, and Patient Progress." *American Psychologist* 51(10):1059–1064.

Ingram, R.E. and Kendall, P.C. 1987. "The Cognitive Side of Anxiety." *Cognitive Therapy and Research* 11(5):523–536.

Ito, L.M., Noshirvani, H., Başoğlu, M., and Marks, I.M. 1996. "Does Exposure to Internal Cues Enhance Exposure to External Cues in Agoraphobia With Panic?" *Psychotherapy Psychosomatics* 65:24–28.

Jacob, R.G., Furman, J.M., Durrant, J.D., and Turner, S.M. 1996. "Panic, Agoraphobia, and Vestibular Dysfunction." *American Journal of Psychiatry* 153(4):503–512.

Jacobson, N.S., and Hollon, S.D. 1996. "Cognitive-Behavior Therapy Versus Pharmacotherapy: Now That the Jury's Returned Its Verdict, It's Time to Present the Rest of the Evidence." *Journal of Consulting and Clinical Psychology* 64(1):74–80.

Judd, F.K. and Burrows, G.D. 1986. "Panic and Phobic Disorders—Are Psychological or Pharamcological Treatments Effective?" *Australian and New Zealand Journal of Psychiatry* 20:342–348.

Kabat-Zinn, J. 1990. *Full Catastrophe Living: Using the Wisdom of Your Body and Mind to Face Stress, Pain, and Illness.* New York: Dell Publishing.

Kabat-Zinn, J. 1994. *Wherever You Go, There You Are: Mindfulness Meditation in Everyday Life.* New York: Hyperion.

Kagan, J. 1996. "Three Pleasing Ideas." *American Psychologist* 51(9):901–908.

Kahn, R.J., McNair, D.M., Lipman, R.S., Covi, L., Rickels, K., Downing, R., Fisher, S., and Frankenthaler, L.M. 1986. "Imipramine and Chlordiazepoxide in Depressive and Anxiety Disorders. II. Efficacy in Anxious Outpatients." *Archives of General Psychiatry* 43:79–85.

Katerndahl, D.A., and Realini, J.P. 1995. "Where do Panic Attack Sufferers Seek Care?" *Journal of Family Practice* 40(3):237–243.

Katon, W. 1989. *Panic Disorder in the Medical Setting*. National Institute of Mental Health, DHHS Pub. No.(ADM)89–1629. Washington, D.C.: Supt. of Docs., U.S. Govt. Print Off.

Katon, W.J. 1990. "Chest Pain, Cardiac Disease, and Panic Disorder." *Journal of Clinical Psychiatry* 51(5, Suppl.):27–30.

Katon, W. 1996. "Panic Disorder: Relationship to High Medical Utilization, Unexplained Physical Symptoms, and Medical Costs." *Journal of Clinical Psychiatry* 57(Suppl. 10):11–18.

Katon, W., Hollifield, M., Chapman, T., Mannuzza, S., Ballenger, J., and Fyer, A. 1995. "Infrequent Panic Attacks: Comorbidity, Personality Characteristics and Functional Disability." *Journal of Psychiatric Research* 29(2):121–131.

Katon, W., Vitaliano, P.P., Russo, J., Cormier, L., Anderson, K., and Jones, M. 1986. "Panic Disorder: Epidemiology in Primary Care." *Journal of Family Practice* 23(3):233–239.

Katon, W.J., von Korff, M., and Lin, E. 1992. "Panic Disorder: Relationship to High Medical Utilization." *American Journal of Medicine* 92(Suppl. 1A):7S–11S.

Katschnig, H., Amering, M., Stolk, J.M., and Ballenger, J.C. 1996. "Predictors of Quality of Life in a Long-Term Followup Study in Panic Disorder Patients After a Clinical Drug Trial." *Psychopharmacology Bulletin* 32(1):149–155.

Kenardy, J., Evans, L., and Oei, T.P.S. 1992. "The Latent Structure of Anxiety Symptoms in Anxiety Disorders." *American Journal of Psychiatry* 149(8):1058–1061.

Kessler, R.C., McGonagle, K.A., Zhao, S., Nelson, C.B., Hughes, M., Eshleman, S., Wittchen, H.-U., and Kendler, K.S. 1994. "Lifetime and 12-Month Prevalence of DSM-III-R Psychiatric Disorders in the United States: Results From the National Comorbidity Survey." *Archives of General Psychiatry* 51:8–19.

Keyl, P.M. and Eaton, W.W. 1990. "Risk Factors for the Onset of Panic Disorder and Other Panic Attacks in a Prospective, Population-Based Study." *American Journal of Epidemiology* 131(2):301–311.

Kinney, P.J. and Williams, S.L. 1988. "Accuracy of Fear Inventories and Self-Efficacy Scales in Predicting Agoraphobic Behavior." *Behaviour Research and Therapy* 26(6):513–518.

Klein, D.F. 1993. "False Suffocation Alarms, Spontaneous Panics, and Related Conditions: An Integrative Hypothesis." *Archives of General Psychiatry* 50:306–317.

Klein, D.F. and Fink, M. 1962. "Psychiatric Reaction Patterns to Imipramine." *American Journal of Psychiatry* 119:432–438.

Klerman, G.L. 1992. "Treatments for Panic Disorder." *Journal of Clinical Psychiatry* 53(3, Suppl.):14–19.

Klosko, J.S., Barlow, D.H., Tassinari, R., and Cerny, J.A. 1990. "A Comparison of Alprazolam and Behavior Therapy in Treatment of Panic Disorder." *Journal of Consulting and Clinical Psychology* 58(1):77–84.

Kroenke, K. 1992. "Symptoms in Medical Patients: An Untended Field." *American Journal of Medicine* 92(Suppl. 1A):3S–6S.

Krystal, J.H., Niehoff Deutsch, D., and Charney, D.S. 1996. "The Biological Basis of Panic Disorder." *Journal of Clinical Psychiatry* 57(Suppl. 10):23–31.

Kushner, M.G. and Beitman, B.D. 1990. "Panic Attacks Without Fear: An Overview." *Behaviour Research and Therapy* 28(6):469–479.

Kushner, M.G., Mackenzie, T.B., Fiszdon, J., Valentiner, D.P., Foa, E., Anderson, N., and Wangensteen D. 1996. "The Effects of Alcohol Consumption on Laboratory-Induced Panic and State Anxiety." *Archives of General Psychiatry* 53:264–270.

Laberge, B., Gauthier, J. Cote, G., Plamondon, J., and Cormier, H.J. 1992. "The Treatment of Coexisting Panic and Depression: A Review of the Literature." *Journal of Anxiety Disorders* 6:169–180.

Lader, M. (1983) Quoted by: Pecknold, J.C. 1993. "Discontinuation Reactions to Alprazolam in Panic Disorder." *Journal of Psychiatric Research* 27(Suppl. 1):155–170.

Lang, P.J. 1979. "A Bio-Informational Theory of Emotional Imagery." *Psychophysiology* 16(6):495–512.

Lelliott, P. and Bass, C. 1990. "Symptom Specificity in Patients with Panic." *British Journal of Psychiatry* 157:593–597.

Lelliott, P., Marks, I., McNamee, G., and Tobeña, A. 1989. "Onset of Panic Disorder With Agoraphobia: Toward an Integrated Model." *Archives of General Psychiatry* 46:1000–1004.

Ley, R. 1985. "Blood, Breath, and Fears: A Hyperventilation Theory of Panic Attacks and Agoraphobia." *Clinical Psychology Review* 5:271–285.

Ley, R. 1988. "Panic Attacks During Sleep: A Hyperventilation-Probability Model." *Journal of Behavior Therapy and Experimental Psychiatry* 19(3):181–192.

Ley, R. 1989. "Dyspneic-Fear and Catastrophic Cognitions in Hyperventilatory Panic Attacks." *Behaviour Research and Therapy* 27(5):549–554.

Lidren, D.M., Watkins, P.L., Gould, R.A., Clum, G.A., Asterino, M., and Tulloch, H.L. 1994. "A Comparison of Bibliotherapy and Group Therapy in the Treatment of Panic Disorder." *Journal of Consulting and Clinical Psychology* 63(4):865–869.

Lum, L.C. 1987. "Hyperventilation Syndromes in *Medicine* and Psychiatry: A Review." *Journal of the Royal Society of Medicine* 80:299–231.

Magarian, G.J. 1982. "Hyperventilation Syndromes: Infrequently Recognized Common Expressions of Anxiety and Stress." *Medicine* 61(4):219–236.

Magee, W.J., Eaton, W.W., Wittchen, H.-U., McGonagle, K.A., and Kessler, R.C. 1996. "Agoraphobia, Simple Phobia, and Social Phobia in the National Comorbidity Survey." *Archives of General Psychiatry* 53(2):159–168.

Maier, S.F., Watkins, L.R., and Fleshner, M. 1994. "Psychoneuroimmunology." *American Psychologist* 49(12):1004–1017.

Marchione, K.E., Michelson, L., Greenwald, M., and Dancu, C. 1987. "Cognitive Behavioral Treatment of Agoraphobia." *Behaviour Research and Therapy* 25(5):319–328.

Margraf, J., Barlow, D.H., Clark, D.M., and Telch, M.J. 1993. "Psychological Treatment of Panic: Work in Progress on Outcome, Active Ingredients, and Follow-Up." *Behaviour Research and Therapy* 31(1):1–8.

Margraf, J., Ehlers, A., and Roth, W.T. 1986. "Biological Models of Panic Disorder and Agoraphobia—A Review." *Behaviour Research and Therapy* 24(5):553–567.

Marks, I. 1985. "Behavioral Psychotherapy for Anxiety Disorders." *Psychiatric Clinics of North America* 8(1):25–35.

Marks, I.M. 1987. "Behavioral Aspects of Panic Disorder." *American Journal of Psychiatry* 144(9):1160–1165.

Marks, I.M., Gray, S., Cohen, D., Hill, R., Mawson, D., Ramm, E., and Stern, R.S. 1983. "Imipramine and Brief Therapist-Aided Exposure in Agoraphobics Having Self-Exposure Homework." *Archives of General Psychiatry* 40:153–162.

Marks, I., Greist, J., Başoğlu, M., Noshirvani, H., and O'Sullivan, G. 1992. "Comment on the Second Phase of the Cross-National Collaborative Panic Study." *British Journal of Psychiatry* 160:202–205.

Marks, I.M. and Mathews, A.M. 1979. "Brief Standard Self–Rating for Phobic Patients." *Behaviour Research and Therapy* 17:263–267.

Marks, I.M., Swinson, R.P., Başoğlu, M., Kuch, K., Noshirvani, H., O'Sullivan, G., Lelliott, P.T., Kirby, M., McNamee, G., Şengün, S., and Wickwire, K. 1993. "Alprazolam and Exposure Alone and Combined in Panic Disorder With Agoraphobia: A Controlled Study in London and Toronto." *British Journal of Psychiatry* 162:776–787.

Marshall, J.R. 1997. "The Course and Impact of Panic Disorders. pp. 36–38 In: Panic Disorder: A Treatment Update." *Journal of Clinical Psychiatry* 58:36–42.

Mavissakalian, M. 1990. "The Relationship Between Panic Disorder/Agoraphobia and Personality Disorders." *Psychiatric Clinics of North America* 13(4):661–684.

Mavissakalian, M. 1993. "Combined Behavioral Therapy and Pharmacotherapy of Agoraphobia." *Journal of Psychiatric Research* 27(1):179–191.

Mavissakalian, M. and Perel, J.M. 1992. "Clinical Experiments in Maintenance and Discontinuation of Imipramine Therapy in Panic Disorder With Agoraphobia." *Archives of General Psychiatry* 49:318–323.

Mavissakalian, M.R. and Perel, J.M. 1995. "Imipramine Treatment of Panic Disorder With Agoraphobia: Dose Ranging and Plasma Level-Response Relationships." *American Journal of Psychiatry* 152:673–682.

McCaffrey, R.J., Rapee, R.M., Gansler, D.A., and Barlow, D.H. 1990. "Interaction of Neuropsychological and Psychological Factors in Two Cases of 'Space Phobia'." *Journal of Behavior Therapy and Experimental Psychiatry* 21(2):113–120.

McNally, R.J. 1990. "Psychological Approaches to Panic Disorder: A Review." *Psychological Bulletin* 108(3):403–419.

McNally, R.J. 1994. *Panic Disorder: A Critical Analysis.* New York: The Guilford Press.

McNally, R.J., Hornig, C.D., and Donnell, C.D. 1995. "Clinical Versus Nonclinical Panic: A Test of Suffocation False Alarm Theory." *Behaviour Research and Therapy* 33(2):127–131.

McNally, R.J. and Lorenz, M. 1987. "Anxiety Sensitivity in Agoraphobics." *Journal of Behavior Therapy and Experimental Psychiatry* 18(1):3–11.

Mellman, T.A. and Uhde, T.W. 1990. "Patients with Frequent Sleep Panic: Clinical Findings and Response to Medication Treatment." *Journal of Clinical Psychiatry* 51(12):513–516.

Menninger, W.W. 1995. "Challenges to Providing Integrated Treatment of Anxiety Disorders." *Bulletin of the Menninger Clinic* 59(2, Suppl. A):A86–A93.

Merikangas, K.R., Angst, J., Eaton, W., Canino, G., Rubio-Stipec, M., Wacker, H., Wittchen, H.-U., Andrade, L., Essau C., Whitaker, A., Kraemer, H. Robins, L.N., and Kupfer, D.J. 1996. "Comorbidity and Boundaries of Affective Disorders with Anxiety Disorders and Substance Misuse: Results of an International Task Force." *British Journal of Psychiatry*(Suppl. 30):58–67.

Michelson, L. 1984. "The Role of Individual Differences, Response Profiles, and Treatment Consonance in Anxiety Disorders." *Journal of Behavioral Assessment* 6(4):349–367.

Michelson, L.K. and Marchione, K. 1991. "Behavioral, Cognitive, and Pharmacological Treatments of Panic Disorder With Agoraphobia: Critique and Synthesis." *Journal of Consulting and Clinical Psychology* 59(1):100–114.

Michelson, L., Marchione, K., Greenwald, M., Glanz, L., Testa, S., and Marchione, N. 1990. "Panic Disorder: Cognitive-Behavioral Treatment." *Behaviour Research and Therapy* 28(2):141–151.

Miller, J.J., Fletcher, K., and Kabat-Zinn, J. 1995. "Three-Year Follow-up and Clinical Implications of a Mindfulness Meditation-Based Stress Reduction Intervention in the Treatment of Anxiety Disorders." *General Hospital Psychiatry* 17:192–200.

Milrod, B. and Shear, M.K. 1991. "Dynamic Treatment of Panic Disorder: A Review." *Journal of Nervous and Mental Disease* 179(12):741–743.

Mizes, J.S. and Crawford, J. 1986. "Normative Values on the Marks and Mathews Fear Questionnaire: A Comparison as a Function of Age and Sex." *Journal of Psychopathology and Behavioral Assessment* 8(3):253–262.

Moisan, D. and Engels, M.-L. 1995. "Childhood Trauma and Personality Disorder in 43 Women with Panic Disorder." *Psychological Reports* 76:1133–1134.

Munjack, D.J., Brown, R.A., and McDowell, D.E. 1993. "Existence of Hyperventilation in Panic Disorder With and Without Agoraphobia, GAD, and Normals: Implications for the Cognitive Theory of Panic. *Journal of Anxiety Disorders* 7:37–48.

Nagy, L.M., Krystal, J.H., Charney, D.S., Merikangas, K.R., and Woods, S.W. 1993. "Long-Term Outcome of Panic Disorder After Short-Term Imipramine and Behavioral Group Treatment: 2.9-Year Naturalistic Follow-Up Study." *Journal of Clinical Psychopharmacology* 13(1):16–24.

Nagy, L.M., Krystal, J.H., Woods, S.W., and Charney, D.S. 1989. "Clinical and Medication Outcome After Short-Term Alprazolam and Behavioral Group Treatment in Panic Disorder: 2.5-Year Naturalistic Follow-Up Study." *Archives of General Psychiatry* 46:993–999.

Norton, G.R., Harrison, B., Hauch, J., and Rhodes, L. 1985. "Characteristics of People With Infrequent Panic Attacks." Journal of Abnormal Psychology 94(2):216–221.

Noyes, R., Garvey, M., and Cook, B. 1989. "Follow-Up Study of Patients With Panic Attacks Treated With Tricyclic Antidepressants." *Journal of Affective Disorders* 16:247–257

Noyes, R., Wesner, R.B., and Fisher, M.M. 1992. "A Comparison of Patients with Illness Phobia and Panic Disorder." *Psychosomatics* 33(1):92–99.

Olfson, M., Broadhead, W.E., Weissman, M.M., Leon, A.C., Farber, L., Hoven, C., and Kathol, R. 1996. "Subthreshold Psychiatric Symptoms in a Primary Care Group Practice." *Archives of General Psychiatry* 53(10):880–886.

Olfson, M., Gilbert, T., Weissman, M., Blacklow, R.S., and Broadhead, W.E. 1995. "Recognition of Emotional Distress in Physically Healthy Primary Care Patients Who Perceive Poor Physical Health." *General Hospital Psychiatry* 17:173–180.

Öst, L.-G. 1987. "Applied Relaxation: Description of a Coping Technique and Review of Controlled Studies." *Behaviour Research and Therapy* 25(5):397–409.

Öst, L.-G. 1988. "Applied Relaxation vs. Progressive Relaxation in the Treatment of Panic Disorder." *Behaviour Research and Therapy* 26(1):13–22.

Öst, L.-G., Westling, B.E., and Hellström, K. 1993. "Applied Relaxation, Exposure In Vivo and Cognitive Methods in the Treatment of Panic Disorder With Agoraphobia." *Behaviour Research and Therapy* 31(4):383–394.

O'Sullivan, G.H., Noshirvani, H., Başoğlu, M., Marks, I.M., Swinson, R., Kuch, K., and Kirby, M. 1994. "Safety and Side-Effects of Alprazolam: Controlled Study in Agoraphobia With Panic Disorder." *British Journal of Psychiatry* 165:79–86.

Otto, M.W. 1997. "Integrated Treatment of Panic Disorder. pp. 40–42 In: Panic Disorder: A Treatment Update." *Journal of Clinical Psychiatry* 58:36–42.

Otto, M.W., Gould, R.A., and Pollack, M.H. 1994. "Cognitive-Behavioral Treatment of Panic Disorder: Considerations for the Treatment of Patients Over the Long Term." *Psychiatric Annals* 24(6):307–315.

Otto, M.W. and Pollack, M.H. 1994. "Treatment Strategies for Panic Disorder: A Debate." *Harvard Review of Psychiatry* 2:166–170.

Otto, M.W., Pollack, M.H., and Barlow, D.H. 1995. *Stopping Anxiety Medication: A Workbook for Patients Wanting to Discontinue Benzodiazepine Treatment for Panic Disorder.* San Antonio, TX: Graywind Publications/The Psychological Corporation.

Otto, M.W., Pollack, M.H., Meltzer-Brody, S., and Rosenbaum, J.F. 1992. "Cognitive-Behavioral Therapy for Benzodiazepine Discontinuation in Panic Disorder Patients." *Psychopharmacology Bulletin* 28(2):123–130.

Otto, M.W., Pollack, M.H., Sachs, G.S., Reiter, S.R., Meltzer-Brody, S., and Rosenbaum, J.F. 1993. "Discontinuation of Benzodiazepine Treatment: Efficacy of Cognitive Behavioral Therapy for Problems with Panic Disorder." *American Journal of Psychiatry* 150:1485–1490.

Otto, M.W. and Whittal, M.L. 1995. "Cognitive-Behavior Therapy and the Longitudinal Course of Panic Disorder." *Psychiatric Clinics of North America* 18(4):803–820.

Padesky, C.A. 1994. "Schema Change Processes in Cognitive Therapy." *Clinical Psychology and Psychotherapy* 1(5):267–278.

Padesky, C.A. with Greenberger, D. 1995. *Clinician's Guide to Mind Over Mood.* New York: Guilford Press.

Papp, L.A., Klein, D.F., and Gorman, J.M. 1993. "Carbon Dioxide Hypersensitivity, Hyperventilation, and Panic Disorder." *American Journal of Psychiatry* 150(8):1149–1157.

Papp, L.A., Martinez, J.M., Klein, D.F., Coplan, J.D., and Gorman, J.M. 1995a. "Rebreathing Tests in Panic Disorder." *Biological Psychiatry* 38:240–245.

Papp, L.A., Welkowitz, L.A., Martinez, J.M., Klein, D.F., Browne, S., and Gorman, J.M. 1995b. "Instructional Set Does Not Alter Outcome of Respiratory Challenges in Panic Disorder." *Biological Psychiatry* 38:826–830.

Pecknold, J.C. 1993. "Discontinuation Reactions to Alprazolam in Panic Disorder." *Journal of Psychiatric Research* 27(Suppl. 1):155–170.

Persons, J.B. 1989. *Cognitive Therapy in Practice: A Case Formulation Approach.* New York: W.W. Norton and Company.

Peselow, E.D. 1996. "Psychopharmacology of Panic Disorder." *Mental Health Institute.* August.

Peters, J., Gonzales, P., Harris, L., Richman, D., Schreiber, G., Sisova, N., Spence, R., and Zuercher-White, E. 1995. *Clinical Practice Guidelines for the Treatment of Panic Disorder in Psychiatry.* Kaiser Permanente Northern California Region.

Pollack, M.H. 1997. "Psychopharmacology Update." pp 38–40. In: Panic Disorder: A Treatment Update. *Journal of Clinical Psychiatry* 58:36–42.

Pollack, M.H., Otto, M.W., Rosenbaum, J.F., and Sachs, G.S. 1992. "Personality Disorders in Patients with Panic Disorder: Association with Childhood Anxiety Disorders, Early Trauma, Comorbidity, and Chronicity." *Comprehensive Psychiatry* 33(2):78–83.

Pollack, M.H., Otto, M.W., Rosenbaum, J.F., Sachs, G.S., O'Neil, C., Asher, R., and Meltzer-Brody, S. 1990. "Longitudinal Course of Panic Disorder: Findings from the Massachusetts General Hospital Naturalistic Study." *Journal of Clinical Psychiatry* 51(12, Suppl. A):12–16.

Pollack, M.H. and Smoller, J.W. 1995. "The Longitudinal Course and Outcome of Panic Disorder." *Psychiatric Clinics of North America* 18(4):785–801.

Pollard, C.A. and Lewis, L.M. 1989. "Managing Panic Attacks in Emergency Patients." *Journal of Emergency Medicine* 7:547–552.

Pollard, C.A., Obermeier, H.J., and Cox, G.L. 1987. "Inpatient Treatment of Complicated Agoraphobia and Panic Disorder." *Hospital and Community Psychiatry* 38(9):951–958.

Pollard, C.A., Tait, R.C., Meldrum, D., Dubinsky, I.H., and Gall, J.S. 1996. "Agoraphobia Without Panic: Case Illustrations of an Overlooked Syndrome." *Journal of Nervous and Mental Disease* 184(1):61–62.

Poulton, R.G. and Andrews, G. 1996. "Change in Danger Cognitions in Agoraphobia and Social Phobia During Treatment." *Behaviour Research and Therapy* 34(5/6):413–421.

Rachman, S. 1993. "A Critique of Cognitive Therapy for Anxiety Disorders." *Journal of Behavior Therapy and Experimental Psychiatry* 24(4):279–288.

Raj, A. and Sheehan, D.V. 1987. "Medical Evaluation of Panic Attacks." *Journal of Clinical Psychiatry* 48(8):309–313.

Rapee, R.M. 1991. "Panic Disorder." *International Review of Psychiatry* 3:141–149.

Rapee, R.M. 1993. "Psychological Factors in Panic Disorder." Advances in *Behavior Research and Therapy* 15:85–102.

Rapee, R.M. and Barlow, D.H. 1988. "Cognitive-Behavioral Treatment." *Psychiatric Annals* 18(8):473–477.

Reiss, S. 1987. "Theoretical Perspectives on the Fear of Anxiety." *Clinical Psychology Review* 7:585–596.

Reiss, S., Peterson, R.A., Gursky, D.M., and McNally, R.J. 1986. "Anxiety Sensitivity, Anxiety Frequency and the Prediction of Fearfulness." *Behaviour Research and Therapy* 24(1):1–8.

Rickels, K., Downing, R., Schweizer, E., and Hausman, H. 1993a. "Antidepressants for the Treatment of Generalized Anxiety Disorder: A Placebo-Controlled Comparison of Imipramine, Trazodone, and Diazepam." *Archives of General Psychiatry* 50:884–895.

Rickels, K., Schweizer, E., Weiss, S., and Zavodnick, S. 1993b. "Maintenance Drug Treatment for Panic Disorder: II. Short- and Long-Term Outcome After Drug Taper." *Archives of General Psychiatry* 50:61–68.

Rifkin, A. 1990. "Solving Panic Disorder Problems." Postgraduate *Medicine* 88(6):133–138.

Rodriguez, B.I. and Craske, M.G. 1993. "The Effects of Distraction During Exposure to Phobic Stimuli." *Behaviour Research and Therapy* 31(6):549–558.

Romach, M., Busto, U., Somer, G., Kaplan, H.L., and Sellers, E. 1995. "Clinical Aspects of Chronic Use of Alprazolam and Lorazepam." *American Journal of Psychiatry* 152:1161–1167.

Rosenbaum, J.F. 1990. "Switching Patients From Alprazolam to Clonazepam." *Hospital and Community Psychiatry* 41(12):1302 and 1305.

Rosenbaum, J.F. 1992. "Evaluation and Management of the Treatment-Resistant Anxiety Disorder Patient." *Bulletin of the Menninger Clinic* 56(2, Suppl. A):A50–A60.

Rosenbaum, J.F. 1997. "Treatment-Resistant Panic Disorder." *Journal of Clinical Psychiatry* 58(Suppl. 2):61–64.

Rosenbaum, J.F., Pollock, R.A., Otto, M.W., and Pollack, M.H. 1995. "Integrated Treatment of Panic Disorder." *Bulletin of the Menninger Clinic* 59(2, Suppl. A):A4–A26.

Rothbaum, B.O., Hodges, L.F., Kooper, R., Opdyke, D., Williford, J.S., and North, M. 1995. "Effectiveness of Computer-Generated (Virtual Reality) Graded Exposure in the Treatment of Acrophobia." *American Journal of Psychiatry* 152(4):626–628.

Roy-Byrne, P R. 1992. "Integrated Treatment of Panic Disorder." *American Journal of Medicine* 92(Suppl. 1A):49S–54S.

Roy-Byrne, P., Wingerson, D., Cowley, D., and Dager, S. 1993. "Psychopharmacologic Treatment of Panic, Generalized Anxiety Disorder, and Social Phobia." *Psychiatric Clinics of North America* 16(4): 719–735.

Roy-Byrne, P.R., Wingerson, D.K., Radant, A., Greenblatt, D.J., and Cowley, D.S. 1996. "Reduced Benzodiazepine Sensitivity in Patients With Panic Disorder: Comparison with Patients With Obsessive-Compulsive Disorder and Normal Subjects." *American Journal of Psychiatry* 153:1444–1449.

Salkovskis, P.M. and Clark, D.M. 1990. "Affective Responses to Hyperventilation: A Test of the Cognitive Model of Panic." *Behaviour Research and Therapy* 28(1):51–61.

Salkovskis, P.M. and Clark, D.M. 1991. "Cognitive Therapy for Panic Attacks." *Journal of Cognitive Psychotherapy: An International Quarterly* 5(3):215–226.

Salkovskis, P.M., Clark, D.M., and Hackmann, A. 1991. "Treatment of Panic Attacks Using Cognitive Therapy Without Exposure or Breathing Retraining." *Behaviour Research and Therapy* 29(2):161–166.

Salzman, C. 1993. "Benzodiazepine Treatment of Panic and Agoraphobic Symptoms: Use, Dependence, Toxicity, Abuse." *Journal of Psychiatric Research* 27(Suppl. 1):97–110.

Sanderson, W.C., Rapee, R.M., and Barlow, D.H. 1989. "The Influence of an Illusion of Control on Panic Attacks Induced Via Inhalation of 5.5% Carbon Dioxide-Enriched Air." *Archives of General Psychiatry* 46:157–162.

Sanderson, W.C. and Wetzler, S. 1993. "Observations on the Cognitive Behavioral Treatment of Panic Disorder: Impact of Benzodiazepines." *Psychotherapy* 30(1):125–132.

Sartory, G., Rachman, S., and Grey, S. 1977. "An Investigation of the Relation Between Reported Fear and Heart Rate." *Behaviour Research and Therapy* 15:435–438.

Schmaling, K.B. and Bell, J. 1997. "Asthma and Panic Disorder." *Archives of Family Medicine* 6:20–23.

Schmidt, N.B., Jacquin, K., and Telch, M.J. 1994. "The Overprediction of Fear and Panic in Panic Disorder." *Behaviour Research and Therapy* 32(7):701–707.

Schmidt, N.B., Lerew, D.R., and Jackson, R.J. (1997.) "The Role of Anxiety Sensitivity in the Pathogenesis of Panic: Prospective Evaluation of Spontaneous Panic Attacks During Acute Stress." *Journal of Abnormal Psychology.* 106(3):355–364

Schoene, R.B. and Pierson, D.J. 1992. "Clinical Approach to Disorders of Ventilatory Control." In *Foundations of Respiratory Care*, ed. D.J. Pierson, and R.M. Kacmarek. New York: Churchill Livingstone.

Schuckit, M.A., 1995. *Drug and Alcohol Abuse: A Clinical Guide to Diagnosis and Treatment,* Fourth Edition. New York, pp. 28–29.

Schwartz, J.M., Stoessel, P.W., Baxter, L.R., Martin, K.M., and Phelps, M.E. 1996. "Systematic Changes in Cerebral Glucose Metabolic Rate After Successful Behavior Modification Treatment of Obsessive-Compulsive Disorder." *Archives of General Psychiatry* 53:109–113.

Schweizer, E., Rickels, K, Weiss, S., and Zavodnick, S. 1993. "Maintenance Drug Treatment of Panic Disorder: I. Results of a Prospective, Placebo-Controlled Comparison of Alprazolam and Imipramine." *Archives of General Psychiatry* 50:51–60.

Seligman, M.E.P. 1990. *Learned Optimism.* New York: Pocket Books.

Selye, H. 1976. *Stress in Health and Disease.* Boston: Butterworths.

Serlie, A.W., Erdman, R.A.M., Passchier, J., Trijsburg, R.W., and ten Cate, F.J. 1995. "Psychological Aspects of Non-Cardiac Chest Pain." *Psychotherapy Psychosomatics*(64):62–73.

Shear, M.K., Ball, G., Fitzpatrick, M, Josephson, S., Klosko, J., and Frances, A. 1991. "Cognitive-Behavioral Therapy for Panic: An Open Study." *Journal of Nervous and Mental Disease* 179(8):468–472.

Shear, M.K., Cooper, A.M., Klerman, G.L., Busch, F.N., and Shapiro, T. 1993. "A Psychodynamic Model of Panic Disorder." *American Journal of Psychiatry* 150(6):859–866.

Shear, M.K. and Maser, J.D. 1994. "Standardized Assessment for Panic Disorder Research." *Archives of General Psychiatry* 51:346–354.

Shear, M.K., Pilkonis, P.A., Cloitre, M., and Leon, A.C. 1994. "Cognitive Behavioral Treatment Compared with Nonprescriptive Treatment of Panic Disorder." *Archives of General Psychiatry* 51:395–401.

Shear, M.K. and Schulberg, H.C. 1995. "Anxiety Disorders in Primary Care" *Bulletin of the Menninger Clinic* 59(2, Suppl. A):A72–A85.

Sheehan, D.V., Ballenger, J., and Jacobsen, G. 1980. "Treatment of Endogenous Anxiety With Phobic, Hysterical, and Hypochondriacal Symptoms." *Archives of General Psychiatry* 37:51–59.

Sheikh, J.I. 1992. "Anxiety Disorders and Their Treatment." *Clinics in Geriatric Medicine* 8(2):411–426.

Sherbourne, C.D., Wells, K.B., and Judd, L.L. 1996. "Functioning and Well-Being of Patients with Panic Disorder." *American Journal of Psychiatry* 153(2):213–218.

Sholomskas, D.E. and Woods, S.W. 1992. "Anxiety Disorders: Structured Psychotherapy." *New Directions for Mental Health Services* 55:85–99.

Shulman, I.D., Cox, B.J., Swinson, R.P., Kuch, K., and Reichman, J.T. 1994. "Precipitating Events, Locations and Reactions Associated With Initial Unexpected Panic Attacks." *Behaviour Research and Therapy* 32(1):17–20.

Shumway-Cook, A. and Horak, F.B. 1989. "Vestibular Rehabilitation: An Exercise Approach to Managing Symptoms of Vestibular Dysfunction." *Seminars in Hearing* 10:196–209.

Siegel, L., Jones, W.C., and Wilson, J.O. 1990. "Economic and Life Consequences Experienced by a Group of Individuals With Panic Disorder." *Journal of Anxiety Disorders* 4:201–211.

Silove, D., Manicavasagar, V., Curtis, J., and Blaszczynski, A. 1996. "Is Early Separation Anxiety a Risk Factor for Adult Panic Disorder?: A Critical Review." *Comprehensive Psychiatry* 37(3):167–179.

Silove, D., Manicavasagar, V., O'Connell, D., and Blaszczynski, A. 1993. "Reported Early Separation Anxiety Symptoms in Patients with Panic and Generalised Anxiety Disorders." *Australian and New Zealand Journal of Psychiatry* 27:489–494.

Silove, D., Manicavasagar, V., O'Connell, D., and Morris-Yates, A. 1995. "Genetic Factors in Early Separation Anxiety: Implications for the Genesis of Adult Anxiety Disorders." *Acta Psychiatrica Scandinavica* 92:17–24.

Smoller, J.W., Pollack, M.H., Otto, M.W., Rosenbaum, J.F., and Kradin, R.L. 1996. "Panic Anxiety, Dyspnea, and Respiratory Disease: Theoretical and Clinical Considerations." *American Journal of Respiratory and Critical Care Medicine* 154:6–17.

Sobel, D.S. and Ornstein, R. 1996. *The Healthy Mind, Healthy Body Handbook.* Los Altos, CA: DRX.

Sokol, L., Beck, A.T., Greenberg, R.L., Wright, F.D., and Berchick, R.J. 1989. "Cognitive Therapy of Panic Disorder: A Nonpharmacological Alternative." *Journal of Nervous and Mental Disease* 177(12):711–716.

Sorby, N.G.D., Reavley, W., and Huber, J.W. 1991. "Self Help Programme for Anxiety in General Practice: Controlled Trial of an Anxiety Management Booklet." *British Journal of General Practice* 41:417–420.

Stahl, S.M. and Soefje, S. 1995. "Panic Attacks and Panic Disorder: The Great Neurologic Imposters." *Seminars in Neurology* 15(2):126–132.

Stanley, M.A., Beck, J.G., Averill, P.M., Baldwin, L.E., Deagle, E.A., and Stadler, J.G. 1996. "Patterns of Change During Cognitive Behavioral Treatment for Panic Disorder." *Journal of Nervous and Mental Disease* 184(9):567–572.

Starcevic, V., Kellner, R., Uhlenhuth, E.H., and Pathak, D. 1993a. "The Phenomenology of Panic Attacks in Panic Disorder With and Without Agoraphobia." *Comprehensive Psychiatry* 34(1):36–41.

Starcevic, V., Uhlenhuth, E.H., Kellner, R., and Pathak, D. 1993b. "Comparison of Primary and Secondary Panic Disorder: A Preliminary Report." *Journal of Affective Disorders* 27:81–86.

Swinson, R.P., Cox, B.J., Shulman, I.D., Kuch, K, and Woszczyna, C.B. 1992a. "Medication Use and the Assessment of Agoraphobic Avoidance." *Behaviour Research and Therapy* 30(6):563–568.

Swinson, R.P., Cox, B.J., and Woszczyna, C.B. 1992b. "Use of Medical Services and Treatment for Panic Disorder With Agoraphobia and for Social Phobia." *Canadian Medical Association Journal* 147(6):878–883.

Swinson, R.P., Fergus, K.D., Cox, B.J., and Wickwire, K. 1995. "Efficacy of Telephone-Administered Behavioral Therapy for Panic Disorder With Agoraphobia." *Behaviour Research and Therapy* 33(4):465–469.

Swinson, R.P., Soulios, C., Cox, B.J., and Kuch, K. 1992c. "Brief Treatment of Emergency Room Patients with Panic Attacks." *American Journal of Psychiatry* 149(7):944–946.

Tavel, M.E. 1990. "Hyperventalation Syndrome—Hiding Behind Pseudonyms?" *Chest* 97(6):1285–1288

Taylor, C.B., King, R., Margraf, J., Ehlers, A., Telch, M., Roth, W.T., and Agras, W.S. 1989. "Use of Medication and In Vivo Exposure in Volunteers for Panic Disorder Research." *American Journal of Psychiatry* 146(11):1423–1426.

Taylor, L. and Gorman, J. 1992. "Theoretical and Therapeutic Considerations for the Anxiety Disorders." *Psychiatric Quarterly* 63(4):319–342.

Taylor, M.L., Davig, J.P., and Schauss, S.L. 1993. "A Cognitive Behavioral Treatment Approach to Noncardiac Chest Pain: The Mayo Clinic Experience." Poster presented at the ADAA 13th National Conference, Charleston: SC.

Taylor, S. and Rachman, S. 1994a. "Role of Selective Recall in the Overprediction of Fear." *Behaviour Research and Therapy* 32(7):741–746.

Taylor, S. and Rachman, S.J. 1994b. "Stimulus Estimation and the Overprediction of Fear." *British Journal of Clinical Psychology* 33:173–181.

Telch, M.J., Lucas, J.A., Schmidt, N.B., Hanna, H.H., Jaimez, T.L., and Lucas, R.A. 1993. "Group Cognitive-Behavioral Treatment of Panic Disorder" *Behaviour Research and Therapy* 31(3):279–287.

Telch, M.J., Schmidt, N.B., Jaimez, T.L., Jacquin, K.M., and Harrington, P.J. 1995. "Impact of Cognitive-Behavioral Treatment on Quality of Life in Panic Disorder Patients." *Journal of Consulting and Clinical Psychology* 63(5):823–830.

Telch, M.J., Tearnan, B.H., and Taylor, C.B. 1983. "Antidepressant Medication in the Treatment of Agoraphobia: A Critical Review." *Behaviour Research and Therapy* 21(5):505–517.

Telch, M.J., Valentiner, D., and Bolte, M. 1994. "Proximity to Safety and its Effects on Fear Prediction Bias." *Behaviour Research and Therapy* 32(7):747–751.

Tesar, G.E. and Rosenbaum, J.F. 1993. "Recognition and Management of Panic Disorder." *Advances in Internal Medicine* 38:123–149.

Tesar, G.E., Rosenbaum, J.F., Pollack, M.H., Otto, M.W., Sachs, G.S., Herman, J.B., Cohen, L.S., and Spier, S.A. 1991. "Double-Blind, Placebo-Controlled Comparison of Clonazepam and Alprazolam for Panic Disorder." *Journal of Clinical Psychiatry* 52(2):69–76.

Thorpe, S.J. and Salkovskis, P.M. 1995. "Phobic Beliefs: Do Cognitive Factors Play a Role in Specific Phobias?" *Behaviour Research and Therapy* 33(7):805–816.

Torgersen, S. 1983. "Genetic Factors in Anxiety Disorders." *Archives of General Psychiatry* 40:1085–1089.

Toseland, R.W. and Siporin, M. 1986. "When to Recommend Group Treatment: A Review of the Clinical and the Research Literature." *International Journal of Group Psychotherapy* 36(2):171–201.

Treatment of Panic Disorder. 1991. *NIH Consensus Development Conference, Consensus Statement* Sept. 25–27, 9(2).

Trull, T.J., Nietzel, M.T., and Main, A. 1988. "The Use of Meta-Analysis to Assess the Clinical Significance of Behavior Therapy for Agoraphobia." *Behavior Therapy* 19:527–538.

Valente, S.M. 1996. "Diagnosis and Treatment of Panic Disorder and Generalized Anxiety in Primary Care." *Nurse Practitioner* 21(8):26–45.

van Balkom, A.J.L.M., de Beurs, E., Koele, P., Lange, A., and van Dyck, R. 1996. "Long-Term Benzodiazepine Use Is Associated With Smaller Treatment Gain in Panic Disorder With Agoraphobia" *Journal of Nervous and Mental Disease* 184(2):133–135.

van den Hout, M., Arntz, A., and Hoekstra, R. 1994. "Exposure Reduced Agoraphobia but Not Panic, and Cognitive Therapy Reduced Panic but Not Agoraphobia." *Behaviour Research and Therapy* 32(4):447–451.

van Hout, W.J.P.J. and Emmelkamp, P.M.G. 1994. "Overprediction of Fear in Panic Disorder Patients with Agoraphobia: Does the(Mis)Match Model Generalize to Exposure In Vivo Therapy?" *Behaviour Research and Therapy* 32(7):723–734.

van Hout, W.J.P.J., Emmelkamp, P.M.G., and Scholing, A. 1994. "The Role of Negative Self-Statements During Exposure in Vivo: A Process Study of Eight Panic Disorder Patients With Agoraphobia." *Behavior Modification* 18(4):389–410.

Van Peski-Oosterbaan, A.S., Spinhoven, P., Van der Does, A.J.W., Willems, L.N.A., and Sterk, P.J. 1996. *Behaviour Research and Therapy* 34(4):333–340.

Waddell, M.T., Barlow, D.H., and O'Brien, G.T. 1984. "A Preliminary Investigation of Cognitive and Relaxation Treatment of Panic Disorder: Effects on Intense Anxiety vs. 'Background' Anxiety." *Behaviour Research and Therapy* 22(4):393–402.

Wardle, J., Hayward, P., Higgitt, A., Stabl, M., Blizard, R., and Gray, J. 1994. "Effects of Concurrent Diazepam Treatment on the Outcome of Exposure Therapy in Agoraphobia." *Behaviour Research and Therapy* 32(2):203–215.

Welkowitz, L.A., Papp, L.A., Cloitre, M., Liebowitz, M.R., Martin, L.Y., and Gorman, J.M. 1991. "Cognitive-Behavior Therapy for Panic Disorder Delivered by Psychopharmacologically Oriented Clinicians." *Journal of Nervous and Mental Disease* 179(8):473–477.

Wichowski, H.C. and Benishek, D. 1996. "An Assessment Tool to Identify Panic Disorder." *Nurse Practitioner* 21(8):48–59.

Williams, S.L. 1987. "On Anxiety and Phobia." *Journal of Anxiety Disorders* 1:161–180.

Williams, S.L. 1988. "Addressing Misconceptions About Phobia, Anxiety, and Self-Efficacy: A Reply to Marks." *Journal of Anxiety Disorders* 2:277–289.

Williams, S.L. 1990. "Guided Mastery Treatment of Agoraphobia: Beyond Stimulus Exposure." *Progress in Behavior Modification* 26:89–121.

Williams, S.L. 1992. "Perceived Self-Efficacy and Phobic Disability." In: *Self-Efficacy: Thought Control of Action.* Ed. R. Schwarzer. Washington, DC: Hemisphere.

Williams, S.L. 1995. "Self-Efficacy, Anxiety, and Phobic Disorders." In: *Self-Efficacy, Adaptation, and Adjustment: Theory, Research, and Application.* Ed. J.E. Maddux. New York: Plenum Press.

Williams, S.L. 1996. "Therapeutic Changes in Phobic Behavior Are Mediated by Changes in Perceived Self-Efficacy." In: *Current Controversies in the Anxiety Disorders.* Ed. R.M. Rapee. New York: Guilford Press

Williams, S.L., Dooseman, G., and Kleifield, E. 1984. "Comparative Effectiveness of Guided Mastery and Exposure Treatments for Intractable Phobias." *Journal of Consulting and Clinical Psychology* 52(4):505–518.

Williams, S.L., Kinney, P.J., and Falbo, J. 1989. "Generalization of Therapeutic Changes in Agoraphobia: The Role of Perceived Self-Efficacy." *Journal of Consulting and Clinical Psychology* 57(3):436–442.

Williams, S.L. and Laberge, B. 1994. "Panic Disorder With Agoraphobia." In: *Adult Behavior Therapy Casebook*. Eds. C.G. Last and M. Hersen. New York: Plenum Press.

Williams, S. L., and Zane, G. 1989. "Guided Mastery and Stimulus Exposure Treatments for Severe Performance Anxiety in Agoraphobics." *Behaviour Research and Therapy* 27(3):237–245.

Wittchen, H.-U. and Essau, C.A. 1993. "Epidemiology of Panic Disorder: Progress and Unresolved Issues." *Journal of Psychiatric Research* 27(Suppl. 1):47–68.

Yalom, I.D. 1970. *The Theory and Practice of Group Psychotherapy*. New York:Basic Books, Inc., Publishers.

Yardley, L., Britton, J., Lear, S., Bird, J., and Luxon, L.M. 1995. "Relationship Between Balance System Function and Agoraphobic Avoidance." *Behaviour Research and Therapy* 33(4):435–439.

Yingling, K.W., Wulsin, L.R., Mussio Arnold, L., and Rouan, G.W. 1993. "Estimated Prevalences of Panic Disorder and Depression Among Consecutive Patients Seen in an Emergency Department With Acute Chest Pain." *Journal of General Internal Medicine* 8(5):231–235.

Zarate, R. and Agras, W.S. 1994. "Psychosocial Treatment of Phobia and Panic Disorders." *Psychiatry* 57:133–141.

Zaubler, T.S. and Katon, W. 1996. "Panic Disorder and Medical Comorbidity: A Review of the Medical and Psychiatric Literature." *Bulletin of the Menninger Clinic* 60(2, Suppl. A):A13–A38.

Zoellner, L.A., Craske, M.G., and Rapee, R.M. 1996. "Stability of Catastrophic Cognitions in Panic Disorder." *Behaviour Research and Therapy* 34(5/6):399–402.

Zuercher-White, E. 1995. *An End to Panic: Breakthrough Techniques for Overcoming Panic Disorder*. Oakland: New Harbinger Publications.

Resources

Agoraphobics Building Independent Lives (ABIL)
    Shirley Green
    1418 Lorraine Avenue
    Richmond, VA 23227
    (804) 266-9409

Agoraphobics in Motion (AIM)
    1729 Crooks Street
    Royal Oak, MI 48067
    (313) 547-0400

American Counseling Association
    5999 Stevenson Avenue
    Alexandria, VA 22304-3300
    (703) 823-9800

American Psychiatric Association (APA)
    1400 K Street, NW
    Washington, DC 20005
    (202) 682-6000

American Psychological Association (APA)
    750 First Street, NE
    Washington, DC 20002
    (202) 336-5500

Anxiety Disorders Association of America (ADAA)
    6000 Executive Blvd., Suite 513
    Rockville, MD 20852-3801
    (301) 231-9350

Anxiety Disorders Behavioral Program
    Michelle G. Craske, Ph.D.
    Department of Psychology
    University of California, Los Angeles
    405 Hilgard Avenue
    Los Angeles, CA 90024-1563
    (310) 206-9191

Anxiety Disorders Center
    C. Alec Pollard, Ph.D.
    St. Louis University Health Sciences Center
    1221 S. Grand Blvd.
    St. Louis, MO 63104-1094
    (314) 577-8718

Association for the Advancement of Behavior Therapy (AABT)
    15 West 36th Street
    New York, NY 10018
    (212) 279-7970

Center for Anxiety and Related Disorders
    David H. Barlow, Ph.D.
    Boston University
    648 Beacon Street, 6th Floor
    Boston, MA 02215-2015

Freedom From Fear
    308 Seaview Avenue
    Staten Island, NY 10305
    (718) 351-1717

Lehigh University
    Lloyd Williams
    Department of Psychology
    Chandler-Ullman Hall
    17 Memorial Drive East
    Bethlehem, PA 18015-3068

National Alliance for the Mentally Ill
    2101 Wilson Blvd., Suite 302
    Arlington, VA 22201
    (800) 950-NAMI

National Anxiety Foundation
    3135 Custer Drive
    Lexington, KY 40517

National Institute of Mental Health (NIMH)
    Information Resources and Inquiry Branch, Room 15C-05
    5600 Fishers Lane
    Rockville, MD 20857
    (301) 443-4513
    (800) 64-PANIC

National Mental Health Association
    1021 Prince Street
    Alexandria, VA 22314-2971
    (703) 684-7722

National Panic/Anxiety Disorder Newsletter (NPAD)
    Cyma J. Siegel, R.N.
    1718 Burgundy Place, Suite B
    Santa Rosa, CA 95403
    (707)-527-5738

Phobics Anonymous
   P.O. Box 1180
   Palm Springs, CA 92263
   (619) 322-COPE

University of Oxford
   David M. Clark, D.Phil.
   Department of Psychiatry
   Warneford Hospital
   Oxford, OX3 7JX
   United Kingdom

Index

Elke Zuercher-White, Ph.D. received her degree from the University of Louisville, Kentucky and has been specializing in anxiety disorders for over fifteen years. She is certified in the psychosocial treatment of panic disorder by Psychosocial Therapeutic Systems and in group psychotherapy by the National Registry of Certified Group Psychotherapists (affiliated with the American Group Psychotherapy Association). She is a pioneer in the use of group therapy to treat panic disorder and has given numerous addresses and training workshops on anxiety disorders throughout North and South America. Dr. Zuercher-White has been on the staff of the Kaiser Permanente Medical Group since 1981 and maintains a private practice in the San Francisco Bay Area. She is the author of *An End to Panic: Breakthrough Techniques for Overcoming Panic Disorder.*

Also Available from New Harbinger

Client Workbooks

AN END TO PANIC
Breakthrough Techniques for Overcoming Panic Disorder
Helps clients overcome the feared physical sensations of panic, target catastrophic thinking, cope with avoidance of phobic situations, deal with stress and conflict, and avoid relapse. By Elke Zuercher-White, Ph.D.
 Item END Paperback, $17.95

THE ANXIETY & PHOBIA WORKBOOK
Second Edition
This is the single most popular anxiety reference among therapists and the book most often recommended to clients. By Edmund J. Bourne, Ph.D.
 Item PHO2 Paperback, $17.95

More Professional Reading

SHORTER TERM TREATMENTS FOR BORDERLINE PERSONALITY DISORDERS
This much-needed guide offers treatment approaches aimed toward realistic short-term goals: helping clients stabilize emotions, decrease vulnerability, and work toward more adaptive day-to-day functioning. By John D. Preston, Psy.D.
 Item BOPA Hardcover, $39.95

HANDBOOK OF CLINICAL PSYCHOPHARMACOLOGY FOR THERAPISTS
Second Edition
This newly revised classic helps nonmedical mental health professionals recognize diagnostic signs, understand how medications work, and monitor treatment response. By John D. Preston, Psy.D., John H. O'Neal, M.D., and Mary C. Talaga, R.Ph., M.A.
 Item PHA2 Hardcover, $39.95

TREATING DEPRESSED CHILDREN
A full twelve-session course of treatment incorporates cartoons, stories, games, and role playing to make concepts used to treat depression in adults understandable to children. By Charma D. Dudley, Ph.D.
 Item TDC Hardcover, $39.95

DIAGNOSIS AND TREATMENT OF SOCIOPATHS AND CLIENTS WITH SOCIOPATHIC TRAITS
Offers the most effective treatment for sociopathy yet to emerge, based on a psychodynamic approach that helps clincians avoid common countertransference traps. By Debra H. Benveniste, M.S.W.
 Item SOPA Hardcover, $44.95

ON THE CLIENT'S PATH
Provides step-by-step instructions for using the "solution-focused" model of brief therapy. By A. J. Chevalier, Ph.D.
 Item PATH Hardcover, $39.95

Call toll-free 1-800-748-6273 to order. Have your Visa or Mastercard number ready. Or send a check for the titles you want to New Harbinger Publications, 5674 Shattuck Avenue, Oakland, CA 94609. Include $3.80 for the first book and 75¢ for each additional book to cover shipping and handling. (California residents please include appropriate sales tax.) Allow four to six weeks for delivery.

Prices subject to change without notice.

Some Other New Harbinger Self-Help Titles

Scarred Soul, $13.95
The Angry Heart, $13.95
Don't Take It Personally, $12.95
Becoming a Wise Parent For Your Grown Child, $12.95
Clear Your Past, Change Your Future, $12.95
Preparing for Surgery, $17.95
Coming Out Everyday, $13.95
Ten Things Every Parent Needs to Know, $12.95
The Power of Two, $12.95
It's Not OK Anymore, $13.95
The Daily Relaxer, $12.95
The Body Image Workbook, $17.95
Living with ADD, $17.95
Taking the Anxiety Out of Taking Tests, $12.95
The Taking Charge of Menopause Workbook, $17.95
Living with Angina, $12.95
PMS: Women Tell Women How to Control Premenstrual Syndrome, $13.95
Five Weeks to Healing Stress: The Wellness Option, $17.95
Choosing to Live: How to Defeat Suicide Through Cognitive Therapy, $12.95
Why Children Misbehave and What to Do About It, $14.95
Illuminating the Heart, $13.95
When Anger Hurts Your Kids, $12.95
The Addiction Workbook, $17.95
The Mother's Survival Guide to Recovery, $12.95
The Chronic Pain Control Workbook, Second Edition, $17.95
Fibromyalgia & Chronic Myofascial Pain Syndrome, $19.95
Diagnosis and Treatment of Sociopaths, $44.95
Flying Without Fear, $12.95
Kid Cooperation: How to Stop Yelling, Nagging & Pleading and Get Kids to Cooperate, $12.95
The Stop Smoking Workbook: Your Guide to Healthy Quitting, $17.95
Conquering Carpal Tunnel Syndrome and Other Repetitive Strain Injuries, $17.95
The Tao of Conversation, $12.95
Wellness at Work: Building Resilience for Job Stress, $17.95
What Your Doctor Can't Tell You About Cosmetic Surgery, $13.95
An End to Panic: Breakthrough Techniques for Overcoming Panic Disorder, $17.95
Living Without Procrastination: How to Stop Postponing Your Life, $12.95
Goodbye Mother, Hello Woman: Reweaving the Daughter Mother Relationship, $14.95
Letting Go of Anger: The 10 Most Common Anger Styles and What to Do About Them, $12.95
Messages: The Communication Skills Workbook, Second Edition, $13.95
Coping With Chronic Fatigue Syndrome: Nine Things You Can Do, $12.95
The Anxiety & Phobia Workbook, Second Edition, $17.95
Thueson's Guide to Over-the-Counter Drugs, $13.95
Natural Women's Health: A Guide to Healthy Living for Women of Any Age, $13.95
I'd Rather Be Married: Finding Your Future Spouse, $13.95
The Relaxation & Stress Reduction Workbook, Fourth Edition, $17.95
Living Without Depression & Manic Depression: A Workbook for Maintaining Mood Stability, $17.95
Coping With Schizophrenia: A Guide For Families, $13.95
Visualization for Change, Second Edition, $13.95
Postpartum Survival Guide, $13.95
Angry All the Time: An Emergency Guide to Anger Control, $12.95
Couple Skills: Making Your Relationship Work, $13.95
Stepfamily Realities: How to Overcome Difficulties and Have a Happy Family, $13.95
The Chemotherapy Survival Guide, $11.95
The Deadly Diet, Second Edition: Recovering from Anorexia & Bulimia, $13.95
Last Touch: Preparing for a Parent's Death, $11.95
Self-Esteem, Second Edition, $13.95
I Can't Get Over It, A Handbook for Trauma Survivors, Second Edition, $15.95
Dying of Embarrassment: Help for Social Anxiety and Social Phobia, $12.95
The Depression Workbook: Living With Depression and Manic Depression, $17.95
Prisoners of Belief: Exposing & Changing Beliefs that Control Your Life, $12.95
Men & Grief: A Guide for Men Surviving the Death of a Loved One, $13.95
When the Bough Breaks: A Helping Guide for Parents of Sexually Abused Children, $11.95
When Once Is Not Enough: Help for Obsessive Compulsives, $13.95
The Three Minute Meditator, Third Edition, $12.95
Beyond Grief: A Guide for Recovering from the Death of a Loved One, $13.95
Leader's Guide to the Relaxation & Stress Reduction Workbook, Fourth Edition, $19.95
The Divorce Book, $13.95
Hypnosis for Change: A Manual of Proven Techniques, Third Edition, $13.95
When Anger Hurts, $13.95
Lifetime Weight Control, $12.95

Call **toll free, 1-800-748-6273,** to order. Have your Visa or Mastercard number ready. Or send a check for the titles you want to New Harbinger Publications, Inc., 5674 Shattuck Ave., Oakland, CA 94609. Include $3.80 for the first book and 75¢ for each additional book, to cover shipping and handling. (California residents please include appropriate sales tax.) Allow four to six weeks for delivery.

Prices subject to change without notice.